TRUTH, RATIONALITY, AND PRAGMATISM

Truth, Rationality, and Pragmatism

Themes from Peirce

CHRISTOPHER HOOKWAY

CLARENDON PRESS · OXFORD

OXFORD

UNIVERSITY PRESS

Great Clarendon Street, Oxford OX2 6DP

Oxford University Press is a department of the University of Oxford.
It furthers the University's objective of excellence in research, scholarship,
and education by publishing worldwide in

Oxford New York

Athens Auckland Bangkok Bogotá Buenos Aires Calcutta
Cape Town Chennai Dar es Salaam Delhi Florence Hong Kong Istanbul
Karachi Kuala Lumpur Madrid Melbourne Mexico City Mumbai
Nairobi Paris São Paulo Singapore Taipei Tokyo Toronto Warsaw

with associated companies in Berlin Ibadan

Oxford is a registered trade mark of Oxford University Press
in the UK and in certain other countries

Published in the United States
by Oxford University Press Inc., New York

British Library Cataloguing in Publication Data

Data available

Library of Congress Cataloging in Publication Data

Hookway, Christopher.
Truth, rationality, and pragmatism: themes from Peirce/Christopher Hookway.
Includes bibliographical references and index.
1. Peirce, Charles S. (Charles Sanders), 1839–1914. I. Title.
B945.P44 H67 2000   191—dc21   99–089742

ISBN 0-19-823836-3

1 3 5 7 9 10 8 6 4 2

Typeset in Minion by
Cambrian Typesetters, Frimley, Surrey

Printed in Great Britain
on acid-free paper by
Biddles Ltd
Guildford and King's Lynn

PREFACE

This book results from my research on issues arising out of Peirce's philosophy since I completed *Peirce*, a general study of his work which appeared in the Arguments of the Philosophers series in 1985. As explained in the Introduction, it is unified by a concern with topics that are central to Peirce's view of rational self-control: his account of truth and reference; his development of a system of scientific metaphysics; his use of ideas drawn from the common-sense tradition; and his claims about the different demands of theory and practice. Seven of the chapters have been published before, although I have made some changes, adding cross-references, correcting some errors, clarifying obscure passages, and making the structure of the argument clearer. Of the material that has not been previously published, Chapters 2 to 4 contain the most recent work, an extended treatment of Peirce's views about truth and reference. Chapter 8 returns to the topic of an earlier paper 'Critical Common-sensism and Rational Self-control' (1990), reformulating and extending the views defended there. The other unpublished piece is the final chapter, a discussion of Peirce's search for a proof of his pragmatism.

Unlike the earlier book, this does not pretend to be a general introduction to Peirce's philosophy. Instead it deals with a range of important and central issues in more detail than was possible in that volume. The introduction sets out these issues and places them in the wider context of Peirce's philosophical ideas. It also contains a sketch of the main elements of Peirce's thought. As well as explaining the relations between the topics discussed, this will, I hope, help to make the book reasonably self-contained.

Since the writing of this material was spread over a dozen years, I have been helped by more people than I can now remember or acknowledge. Two chapters were given as papers to meetings of the Charles S. Peirce Society (Chapters 1 and 12), and others were given to conferences on Peirce at the University of Toronto (Chapter 9) and Aarhus University (Chapter 6), to the Charles S. Peirce Sesquicentennial Congress at Harvard (Chapter 7) and to a conference on the origins of analytical philosophy in Munich (Chapter 5). I also profited from some excellent discussions when I gave talks on Peirce at Penn State University. Material from Chapters 2 to

4 was used for series of seminars at University College London, Aarhus University, and for a talk at the University of York. I am very grateful for the help I received from discussions on all these occasions as well as from my colleagues in Birmingham and Sheffield. Detailed comments on the new material from David Bell, Peter Carruthers, Carl Hausman, Richard Holton, David Owens, Timothy Sprigge, Bob Stern, and Leif Wenar have led to many improvements to Chapters 2 to 4. Conversations with Stephen Makin and Jennifer Saul have also helped me to clarify my views. And I must also express my thanks for Peter Momtchiloff's valuable advice on my plans for the book, and for Sarah Dancy's supportive copy-editing which has produced many improvements. Finally, I am grateful to Cheryl Misak whose comments on the manuscript as a whole, but especially on the material on truth, have been extremely helpful. As with my earlier books, my wife Jo has had a lot to put up with as I struggled to complete the book, and has provided a remarkable degree of support and forebearance.

I am grateful to the editors and publishers for permission to include the chapters based upon previously published papers. Details of first publication are as follows: 'Belief, Confidence and the Method of Science', *Transactions of the Charles S. Peirce Society* XXIX, 1993: 1–32. 'Vagueness, Logic and Interpretation', in D. Bell and N. Cooper (eds), *The Analytic Tradition: Reflections on Meaning, Thought and Knowledge*, Oxford: Blackwell, 1990: 61–82. 'Design and Chance: the Evolution of Peirce's Evolutionary Cosmology', *Transactions of the Charles S. Peirce Society* XXXIII, 1997: 1–34. 'Metaphysics, Science, and Self-Control', published as 'Metaphysics, Science and Self-Control: A Response to Apel', in K. Ketner (ed.), *Peirce and Contemporary Thought*, New York: Fordham University Press, 1995: 398–415. 'Sentiment and Self-Control', in J. Brunning and P. Forster (eds), *The Rule of Reason: The Philosophy of Charles Sanders Peirce*, Toronto, University of Toronto Press, 1997: 199–220. 'Doubt: Affective States and the Regulation of Inquiry', *Canadian Journal of Philosophy*, Supplementary Volume 24, 1998: 203–26. 'On Reading God's Great Poem', *Semiotica* 87, 1991: 147–66.

C.H.

CONTENTS

LIST OF ABBREVIATIONS

References to Peirce's writings use the standard forms of citation indicated in the list below. Where possible, the authoritative but currently incomplete *Writings of Charles S. Peirce* is used.

CP   *Collected Papers of Charles Sanders Peirce*, eight volumes, eds C. Hartshorne, P. Weiss, and A. Burks (Cambridge: Harvard University Press, 1931–60) (vol./paragraph).

EP   *The Essential Peirce: Selected Philosophical Writings*, vol. I (1867–93), ed. N. Houser and C. Kloesel; vol. II (1893–1913), ed. the Peirce Edition Project (Indiana: Indiana University Press, 1992, 1998) (vol./page). This extremely valuable collection contains most of the works discussed in this volume.

MS   *The Charles S. Peirce Papers, microfilm edition* (Cambridge: Harvard University Photographic Service, 1966). Reference numbers are those used by Richard Robin, *Annotated Catalogue of the Papers of Charles S. Peirce* (Amherst: University of Massachusetts Press, 1967).

NEM   *The New Elements of Mathematics by Charles S. Peirce*, four volumes in five, ed. Carolyn Eisele (The Hague: Mouton, 1976). (vol./page).

RLT   *Reasoning and the Logic of Things*, ed. K. Ketner (Cambridge: Harvard University Press, 1992).

SS   *Semiotic and Significs: The Correspondence between Charles S. Peirce and Victoria Lady Welby*, ed. C. Hardwick (Bloomington: Indiana University Press, 1977).

W   *Writings of Charles S. Peirce: A Chronological Edition*, five volumes published before 1999, eds M. Fisch, E. Moore, C. Kloesel, N. Houser *et al.* (Bloomington: Indiana University Press, 1982–93) (vol./page).

INTRODUCTION

Pragmatism and the Materials of Rational Self-Control

1. Introduction

Charles Sanders Peirce (1839–1913) was a philosopher with a very great range. He is best known to the wider philosophical community for his writings about the nature of truth and for the papers in which he formulated and defended his 'pragmatist principle'. He also wrote on probability and the foundations of statistical reasoning and constructed a complex account of meaning and representation which he called 'semiotic' or 'semeiotic'. Mindful of the Kantian roots of his thought, he relied upon an original theory of categories, a theory which, from the late 1890s, was grounded in a kind of phenomenological investigation. He also worked on ethics and aesthetics, on the foundations of mathematics, on the nature of mind, and on the construction of an ambitious system of evolutionary metaphysics. This list merely samples his philosophical interests and does not touch on his mathematical and scientific work.

The best way of finding unity in this wide range of philosophical activities is to respect Peirce's own favoured self-description: he was a 'logician'. His contributions to formal logic were extensive and seminal, their importance only now being fully appreciated (See Houser, Roberts, and Van Evra 1997). However, in Peirce's usage, 'logic' also encompasses much of what contemporary philosophers would include in epistemology and the philosophy of language. He had a deep interest in the normative standards, rules and methods, that guide us when we carry out inquiries, when we try to solve problems and arrive at settled beliefs. These standards enable us to exercise rational or 'logical' self-control, to inquire in a responsible and effective manner. Some of them will be derived from the formal character of thought and representation, and others reflect the abstract structure of deductive and inductive arguments. Still more may offer methodological advice on how to plan inquiries and assess our progress.

A major focus for Peirce's work was to describe the normative standards we follow and to explain how our use of them is rational, to show that inquiring well and responsibly will take us to the truth. Studies in logic show what logical self-control consists in and explain how it is possible. Even those of his writings which did not deal directly with issues of this kind were concerned with how we can be confident that these normative standards are objectively 'correct'; how we can be warranted in relying upon them. Thus his work on 'logic', properly so-called, was embedded in a subtle and complex philosophical system with a carefully worked-out structure. The semiotic theory, for example, was actually part of logic; but the phenomenological study of categories and his investigations of ethical and aesthetic normative standards form part of the wider context in which questions about truth, correctness, and objectivity can be addressed. As is explained in Chapter 7, Peirce's attempt to develop a system of scientific metaphysics and his ambitious evolutionary cosmology were seen as required for the legitimation of these norms of rational inquiry. Hence, if we are to understand Peirce's logical views, it will not be enough to take account of his detailed discussions of issues about representation, deductive and inductive reasoning, and methodology. We must also understand how these discussions are embedded in this more extensive 'system', and the architectonic structure that he imposed upon it.

My previous book on Peirce (1985) was primarily about this overall architectonic structure and with placing his more detailed views within the perspective that it provides. I was concerned with the ways in which his architectonic reflected his reading of Kant's philosophy and with such issues as: Why did he take mathematics to be a discipline which needs no foundations but can provide foundations for philosophy? Why did he believe that his work in logic required a system of categories, and why did he seek to ground his categories through a phenomenological investigation? Why did he then think that the study of logical norms should depend upon work in the other normative sciences: ethics and aesthetics? Finally why, having developed his logical ideas, did he find it necessary to work on a system of scientific metaphysics? Why are all these resources needed in order to explain how objective standards of inquiry—including the principle of pragmatism itself—are possible. I was concerned with the overall picture; how was it all meant to hang together? Why did it take the form that it did?

I still stand by the general structure of the interpretation offered in that book.[1] The present volume explores a range of issues in greater depth than

---

[1]   A more recent presentation of my view of the overall character of Peirce's thought is contained in Hookway (1998).

was possible then and examines at length topics that were passed over in little more than a few sentences in the first one. This means that there is more focus on themes in Peirce which are relevant to contemporary work on epistemic norms, for example, an extended discussion of Peirce's views on truth. Although his own writings contain rather little on that topic, these have had a large impact on non-scholarly discussion of Peirce's views. The chapters that follow are concerned with a related set of three broad issues: Peirce's views about truth and the progress of inquiry; his views about the materials that contribute to our ability to exercise rational self-control in carrying out inquiries; and his initially puzzling but important views about the different requirements of theory and practice, and the role of sentiments and emotions in rational self-control. There is one other focus. The present book contains detailed discussions of some issues in the *development* of Peirce's thought, how his ideas changed and what stimulated him to add new ingredients to the mix. I have been particularly interested in the unresolved problems he faced in the 1870s, at the time that he published his most famous papers, 'The Fixation of Belief' and 'How to Make our Ideas Clear'; and in the developments in the early 1880s which enabled him to respond to those very real problems.

The first chapter, 'Belief, Confidence, and the Method of Science', introduces many of the issues that are addressed in more detail in subsequent chapters. It argues that there were important tensions in Peirce's thought when he produced his most famous writings in the 1870s, thus preparing us to appreciate the role of ideas that became prominent in the following decade. It also raises the questions about theory and practice—and the practice of science—which will be discussed in section 4.

The rest of this introduction attempts to sketch in some background. Section 2 introduces the issues that are central to the book and provides a preliminary overview of the subsequent chapters. This is followed by a brief sketch of some of Peirce's most characteristic philosophical commitments, introducing ideas and doctrines that are referred to frequently in the remainder of the book. I hope that this will help to make it accessible to those who are not closely acquainted with Peirce's thought. The final two sections discuss two issues which surface in a number of later papers: first, Peirce's views about theory and practice and some similarities between his thought and that of William James; and second, some questions about how we should think about the development of Peirce's thought.

2. Truth and the Elements of Logical Self-Control

Pragmatism is a form of empiricism that employs a much richer under-standing of *experience* than is familiar from the work of Hume and from twentieth-century logical empiricists. We can see this clearly in William James's 'radical empiricism'. Having declared that 'the only things that shall be debatable among philosophers shall be things definable in terms drawn from experience', he insisted that the parts of experience are 'held together from next to next by relations that are themselves parts of experience' (James 1909 (1975, 6–7), and also James 1912 (1976, passim)). He was thus able to conclude that the 'directly apprehended universe . . . possesses in its own right a concatenated or continuous structure'. As we shall see in section 3 below, Peirce's theory of categories supports a similar view. In the work of both Peirce and James, pragmatism encourages us to clarify hypotheses by examining what difference their truth would make to the future run of experience and to dismiss as cognitively empty any claims whose truth would make no such difference. Peirce's pragmatism, and his developing ideas about how to argue for it, are explored in the final chapter.

Central to the philosophy of both Peirce and James was a philosophical account of truth, one that explained the 'practical' or experiential differ-ence it would make if something were true. James notoriously identified the true with what it is good or satisfactory to believe, or with what is 'expedient in the way of belief'. However he also appreciated the force of an idea which was central to Peirce's own work on truth: it is a mark of a proposition's being true that those who investigate the matter come to agree in believing it, at least in the long run. Peirce thus defined truth in terms of a long-run fated or destined convergence in opinion. Although he repeated this view of truth on a number of occasions, and although it is very important for the overall structure of his thought, his treatments of the topic generally have a throwaway character: nowhere did he provide an extended and detailed presentation and defence of his position. Questions are thus raised about the precise nature of the proposed link between truth and long-run convergence in opinion, and about just how plausible his claims are. Given that there are some truths which are forever lost to us— what Peirce once memorably called 'buried secrets'—it is natural to conclude that the theory is fatally flawed.

Such difficulties aside, it is unclear how distinctive the pragmatist account of truth is. Some commentators, for example, interpret Peirce's position as a kind of coherence theory of truth. Others are struck by how ready he is to adopt the rhetoric of correspondence with reality. Chapter 2 is an attempt to describe the content of Peirce's theory of truth. It is argued that he was largely untroubled by the difficulties posed by 'buried secrets'; and that he may be justified in this once we take note of the special features possessed by pragmatist clarifications of concepts and hypotheses. The pragmatists opposed something that they sometimes described as the 'copy theory of truth' and it is thus unsurprising that they rejected classical versions of the correspondence theory of truth. However, Peirce, and also James, were anxious to retain the rhetoric of correspondence to fact or agreement with reality, and Peirce argued (after 1885) that true propositions provide reliable *iconic* representations of reality. Propositions and theories give us diagrams or maps of our surroundings, and would lack cognitive value if they did not do this. Chapter 3 takes up the relations between pragmatist theories of truth and the 'correspondence intuition' in some detail, discussing in passing some of the relations between pragmatism and realism. During his last two decades, Peirce came to insist that it was essential to his theory of truth that, when we put something forward as true, we commit ourselves only to its *approximate* truth: when I present something as true, I anticipate that some permissible refinement or qualification of it will prove to be defensible in the long run. The issues raised by this claim are discussed in the second chapter and are raised again elsewhere in the book. Chapter 4, an exploration of some of Peirce's views about reference and false belief, discusses how we can refer to individuals and kinds of whose character our understanding is flawed, and Chapter 5 surveys some of his claims about the importance of vagueness and approximate truth.

One set of issues raised by Peirce's theory of truth concerns how this fated convergence on the truth occurs. The scientific method will supposedly take us, eventually, to the truth, but how does it do this? Some critics have supposed that Peirce was committed to a fixed canon of scientific methods whose consistent application could not fail to take any responsible inquirer to the same fated answer to the question under investigation. The model for Peirce's understanding of science was statistical sampling. Just as repeated fair sampling of a population will lead to a settled view about the proportion of its members which possesses some specified property, and would lead anyone to the same view, so steady sampling of the available evidence would take anyone to the same view about the truth value of some specified proposition. However, Peirce was aware of the contingent obstacles that could distort statistical sampling, and he understood the disanalogies between statistical sampling and other kinds of scientific testing. The scientific method is not a simple algorithm for measuring the force of evidence, and we can see how bad luck could hold up progress for a long time. Use of the scientific method is supposed to enable us to be responsible in our inquiries, to exercise rational self-control over the development of our opinions. Several chapters discuss themes in Peirce's thought which are relevant to this.[2]

Some of these themes involve strategies which reflect Peirce's modifications of his Kantian heritage. In 'The Fixation of Belief', Peirce asked how we can identify and defend the most fundamental and important logical norms (W3: 246). We raise the question: what methods ought we to employ when we try to replace doubt or uncertainty by settled belief in some proposition? Peirce refers to this as the 'logical question'. The fundamental norms are those that are 'absolutely essential as guiding principles', and he proposes an apparently Kantian strategy for identifying them. A variety of facts are 'already assumed when the logical question is first asked': these facts serve as presuppositions of inquiry. Then, 'those rules of reasoning which are deduced from the very idea of the process are the ones that are most essential.' We identify the most fundamental norms by showing that they are implicitly assumed when we ask what standards of inquiry we ought to follow. Moreover, reliance on such rules is legitimate: it will not lead from true premises to false conclusions; and the importance of what can be deduced in this way 'turns out to be greater than might be supposed'. This description suggests that he is engaged in constructing what is now often called a 'transcendental argument'.

In fact, Peirce soon came to question the value of transcendental arguments (see Chapters 4, 7, and 12). The fact that something is a presupposition of inquiry or of experience or of thought may provide a good practical reason for *hoping* that it is true; and it may make it rational for us to plan our inquiries on the basis of this hope. But the fact that we should adopt such assumptions as regulative ideas, as hopes, provides no basis for *believing* them to be true. However, even accepting such propositions as hopes imposes some rational obligations upon the development of our philosophical views. We should not accept any scientific or metaphysical views which are inconsistent with the truth of those hopes. If participation in inquiry must proceed against the background of the hope that our sense of plausibility is attuned to the character of reality, or that there are real

---

[2] The current volume does not pretend to be a complete treatment of these issues. It does not explore Peirce's writings on induction, perception, and mathematics in detail. Discussions of those topics can be found in Hookway (1985).

laws and 'would-be's, then Peirce's philosophical system must explain how this is possible. He takes this to require the construction of a system of scientific metaphysics which explains how what we hope can actually be the case. Chapters 6 and 7 explore the development of Peirce's search for a scientific metaphysics after 1880, emphasizing how these views emerge from the need to make sense of regulative ideas, hopes, and assumptions that we bring to our practice of inquiry.

The strategy we have just described takes what Kant called constitutive principles and transforms them into regulative ideas which require further legitimation from subsequent empirical (scientific or metaphysical) inquiry. In Peirce's writings, this co-exists with another strategy, one that draws on the philosophical tradition of common sense. He claims that we possess a range of common-sense certainties. These are propositions that provide a framework for our thought and inquiry, both scientific and practical. Although certain, they are vague, and this leaves room for judgement about how they should be applied in particular cases. Moreover, although their application in connection with primitive concerns of life is secure, their use in novel situations and in the far reaches of theoretical science is much more controversial. Peirce's *critical* common-sensism enjoins us to trust these natural beliefs, but to reflect upon them, trying to question them, particularly when they are applied to new situations. Chapter 8 explores Pierce's use of common-sense ideas, concentrating upon their role in his philosophy and upon how his adoption of 'critical' common sensism reflected his Kantian heritage. This is followed by a general discussion of the role of sentiments and emotions in his account of our use of epistemic and logical norms. The discussion of *doubt* in Chapter 10 provides a more concrete illustration of how these ideas work: doubt is seen as embodying an affective evaluation of our cognitive position, one that motivates us to carry out inquiries. And Chapter 11 then develops that idea, examining his argument for the reality of God and suggesting that he thought that scientific observation was itself a kind of religious experience.

3. Peirce's Philosophical 'Picture'

Since this book is not intended as a general introduction to Peirce's thought as a whole, I shall now sketch the main elements in his overall philosophical picture or system. This will involve explaining some important doctrines that are referred to, but perhaps not explained in detail, in later chapters.

We have already encountered the two most familiar elements of Peirce's philosophical picture: his pragmatism and his account of truth. The former was introduced as a rule for clarifying the contents of concepts and hypotheses, one that many have seen as a forerunner of the logical positivists' verification principle. He held that once we are clear about the differences that the truth of a proposition would make to future experience, we have achieved total clarity about its content. Since Peirce thought of his pragmatism as a 'laboratory philosophy', he tended to express this by saying that we achieve full clarity about a concept, proposition, or hypothesis by explaining what difference our actions would make to future experience if the concept were correctly applied to something or the proposition, or hypothesis were true. If my car is in the garage, then, if I open the garage door, I shall see it; if the powder in the dish is soluble, then, if I stir it in unsaturated water, it will dissolve; and so on. He was committed to showing that science employed no standards or techniques which required an understanding of hypotheses which would not be clarified through this process. And he claimed that any hypothesis that resisted this kind of clarification was empty or devoid of content. 'Ontological metaphysics'—by which he meant a priori or non-scientific metaphysics—could be dismissed; as could the ideas of reality which were employed in formulating familiar philosophical sceptical arguments. If the hypothesis that I am the victim of an evil demon who ensures that my beliefs do not correspond to reality cannot be tested through its experiential consequences, then it is empty. This explanation of why the idea of a 'thing in itself' was incoherent was present in his work from the 1860s, although the principle of pragmatism itself was not formulated until the following decade. The first elements of the picture are thus a pair of ideas: concepts and hypotheses that do not relate to possible experience can be dismissed as incoherent; and it can contribute to good scientific practice to try to clarify our hypotheses by investigating what experiential consequences they would have.

The theory of truth is an application of this idea, and it emerged from a search for a conception of reality which did not carry with it the possibility that there might be 'things-in-themselves' that were in principle unknowable. True propositions are those that we are fated or destined to agree upon if only we inquire diligently enough; they are the propositions that would be the objects of long-run convergence among inquirers (see Chapter 2). If the whole content of a proposition can be unpacked in terms of possible experiences, then anyone who assiduously seeks relevant experiences would eventually reach the truth. And if I think that some proposition is true, then I expect that such a convergence of opinion would be experienced if only everyone inquired into the matter. This idea is present in papers and lectures from the late 1860s; it was explicitly formulated as a pragmatist clarification of truth in 1877; and continued to be endorsed by Peirce throughout his career.

A third element of the picture is the idea that the method of science, properly applied, is sure to take us to this truth. It emerges in an important early paper, 'Grounds of Validity of the Laws of Logic' (W2: 242–72). Peirce consistently attacked psychologism in logic: the goodness of an argument (or a method) was an objective matter, a matter of whether it took us from true premises or inputs to true conclusions. The validity of induction was then explained by showing that continued use of inductive arguments—such as techniques of statistical sampling—would eventually eliminate error and take us to the truth. Although Peirce's understanding of the scientific method developed, and although he came to recognize many assumptions that must be made before we can be confident that we will reach the truth through its use, this general picture of how we are able to improve our fallible opinions and make progress towards the truth was a constant feature of his work.

Early papers written during the late 1860s made much of a fourth element of the picture, Peirce's semiotic, his account of reference and understanding. I shall not attempt to explain this in detail, but will sketch some main ideas.[3] It is natural to think of meaning and representation as involving a dyadic relationship between a sign (a thought or utterance, for example) and some object or state of affairs which it represents. The name 'Rome' stands for a particular city in Italy; the predicate expression '. . . is red' stands for redness; the thought that *Caesar crossed the Rubicon* stands for the state of affairs of Caesar crossing the Rubicon. Peirce insisted that this dyadic picture was too simple: the expression or thought has the content that it does only because it is (or can be) understood or interpreted in that way. Its meaning is determined by how it can affect subsequent thought; signs are always 'directed to' subsequent thoughts which count as their 'interpretants'. An account of meaning and reference must be, fundamentally, an account of how signs are understood or 'interpreted'. The fundamental semiotic relation is triadic: sign *s* denotes object *o* according to interpretant *i*. 'Rome', for example, refers to that Italian city in virtue of its being interpreted as so doing.

---

[3] Further explanations of key notions are found in Chapters 3, 4, and 5. A useful general introduction which explains much of Peirce's complex technical terminology is Liszka (1996).

'Interpretation' need not involve forming a conscious thought about what a sign means, about what it has as an object. My interpretation of a sign can be manifested in the ways in which I use it as a premise in inference, form expectations about the future run of experience, show surprise when experience clashes with it, and so on. The meaning of a sign is fixed by its inferential role, and by the ways in which I am able to track its object through future inquiry. Peirce's later work classified the kinds of interpretants which signs can receive, the variety of objects that each possesses, and about the ways in which the objects of signs are determined and identified. Some of Peirce's most famous classifications of signs—such as that between icon, index, and symbol—emerge from these discussions. Chapter 4 discusses Peirce's reasons for thinking that our fundamental ways of referring to external things must involve *indexical* representation; and Chapter 3 explores his claim that systems of concepts, and languages, which are adequate for thought and inquiry must make use of *iconic* representations.

The next element of the Peircean picture that I shall introduce here is his theory of categories. When we consider the predicates or general terms we use to describe our surroundings, we note that we use relational expressions with different numbers of terms or subjects; in Peirce's phrase, they have different numbers of 'unsaturated bonds' (*CP* 3.421, 3.469). An expression such as '—hits—' expresses a dyadic relation, a relation holding between two objects; and '—gives—to—' expresses a triadic relation, it has three unsaturated bonds. A simple predicate such as '—is red' is monadic, taking only one 'subject'. General terms can be classified according to their number of bonds or subjects; and properties or qualities can be classified in an analogous manner. This provides the basis of an abstract system for classifying phenomena: some involve monadic characters; others involve dyadic relations; yet others involve triadic relations. Peirce claimed that there were irreducible properties of all these kinds: monadic, dyadic, and triadic. He also argued that there were no irreducible properties or phenomena with more than three terms. This observation provided the basis of a classification of the primitive terms of an adequate language, of the kinds of properties and states of affairs found in reality, and of the contents of experiences. Phenomena were described as forms of firstness, secondness, or thirdness according to whether they manifested monadic, dyadic, or triadic characteristics. Thus he often described the underlying insights of his semiotic, that signs have objects only because they can be understood as having them, by claiming that semantic and semiotic properties were forms of thirdness: the representation relation is irreducibly triadic. Indeed the claim that there were irreducible triadic relations was one which, he thought, distinguished his philosophy from that of his more nominalist forebears. Semiotic and mental phenomena were all triadic, as were elements of reality such as laws and natural kinds. The resulting theory of categories is used extensively throughout Peirce's work, not least in his complex systems for classifying signs and representations.

It may be useful to present one illustration of this. When we interpret signs, identifying their objects, we make use of information about the sign, the object, and the relations between them. If *s* is a *symbol* of *o*, then our grounds for identifying it as such are that there exists a practice of using and interpreting *s* as a sign of *o* which the utterance of the sign is exploiting. Interpretation exploits information about triadic relations in which *s* and *o* have previously stood: the ground of interpretation is a form of thirdness. Understanding an *indexical* sign exploits information about a dyadic relation between the sign and object: a 'real existential relation' between the pointing finger and the object it points at, or between the utterance of 'I' or 'That' and the contextually salient object that it denotes. Of course, as Peirce acknowledged, such signs generally depend upon conventions and thus also have a symbolic character. But these conventions do not fix the objects of the signs unaided. Rather, they determine how the signs should be interpreted in context, how we should make use of dyadic relations between signs and objects in order to determine what the sign refers to. *Iconic* signs (Peirce's examples include predicates in natural languages and systems of mathematical notation as well as maps and pictures) exploit similarities between signs and their objects, features which each could have even had the other not existed. The shared abstract similarities on which iconic representation depends are thus forms of firstness. Once again, we appeal to conventions to establish which sorts of similarities are relevant to the interpretation of particular kinds of iconic sign. The classification of signs employs the theory of categories to distinguish the different sorts of relation in which signs can stand to their objects.

The final element in the Peircean picture is much more difficult to introduce. From the beginning to the end, Peirce described himself as a 'realist'.[4] Around 1870, he was confident that his philosophical picture undermined such anti-realist doctrines as nominalism and Berkeleyan idealism. And after 1900, he insisted that pragmatism could only be taken

---

[4] Carl Hausman (1993: ch. 4) has defended an interpretation of Peirce which emphasizes the realist dimensions of his thought.

seriously by someone who shared this commitment to realism. A number of themes are involved in this 'realism'. First, he claimed that many treatments of realism and nominalism, many discussions of universals, rest on the mistaken assumption that if general characters such as redness or solidity are real, they must be special kinds of particulars. Instead, Peirce insisted, the issue is one of *objectivity* (*CP* 8.14). If it is objectively the case that a book is red, or that the ice is solid, then general characters form part of reality. If propositions involving predicates and relational descriptions provide objectively true descriptions of the world, then nominalism about universals has been defeated. Second, from the 1870s, he urged that there are real things 'whose characters are entirely independent of our opinions about them' (W3: 254), and, soon after that, he argued that we could directly perceive this mind-independent external world. Finally, we should note a passage in which he called himself a 'realist of a somewhat extreme stripe' (*CP* 5.470).

Here, more than anywhere else, there is controversy about how much continuity his views displayed. During the 1870s, Peirce described his position as 'the realism of Kant', and his accounts of reality largely involved explaining how objectivity and truth were possible and identifying the real as the object of a true representation. In later years, Kant was criticized for his closet nominalism and Peirce came to believe that realism required a substantial metaphysical grounding. We would normally describe something as real, he may have thought, when it would be a matter of agreement among competent inquirers; but there are further questions, he came to feel, about what the 'mode of being' of these 'reals' consists in. This later realism becomes steadily more robust: Peirce felt obliged to show that thirdness was really operative in nature, and to show that we are aware of triadic phenomena such as law, necessity, and continuity in experience. However, although his views about the further commitments that were carried by a serious acceptance of realism appear to have changed and developed, there can be no doubt that, from the late 1860s, he placed himself on the realist side of most debates which can be formulated in terms of that notion.

There are other themes we could have discussed here, all of which are examined in the chapters that follow. For example, Peirce displayed a continuous sympathy for the common-sense doctrines which dominated Harvard philosophy in the early part of the century. He mistrusted the role of theory in vital and theological matters, and disdained the philosophical practice of taking seriously sceptical doubts that were supported by philosophical speculation but which we did not feel 'in our hearts'. After 1905 he recommended his critical common-sensism as the position that 'Kantism' should lead to when freed of egregious errors. Furthermore, he was always out of sympathy with individualist approaches to philosophy: we investigate the world as members of a community of investigators, sharing information and engaging in critical discussion, and sensitive to the responses of others as a control on our own reasoning and inquiry. Another theme is that he was always a religious believer. His mistrust for theology ensured that he wrote little on the philosophy of religion until late in his career, but he shared the aspiration of other pragmatists to forge a view of mind, knowledge, and reality which could bring religious belief and serious scientific activity into harmony.

4. Theory, Practice, and Sentiments: Peirce and the Will to Believe

A recurrent theme of this book concerns how we should read one of Peirce's most famous papers, 'The Fixation of Belief'. Superficially it is one of the most accessible of his writings. On careful re-reading it reveals some intriguing and often illuminating unclarities—see Chapter 1 for a discussion of this. Peirce's conclusion appears to be that the only respectable method for settling belief, for coming up with answers to theoretical questions, is the method of science. This involves testing beliefs against experience, and results from the rejection of the a priori method of inquiry. The latter requires confidence in our natural inclinations to believe, and urges us to accept what is 'agreeable to reason'. It is rejected because it makes belief a matter of taste; 'but taste, unfortunately, is always more or less a matter of fashion' (*CP* 5.383, and see 2.20). Peirce concludes that we want our beliefs to be fixed by nothing 'extraneous to the facts'. It would be natural to expect Peirce to endorse W. K. Clifford's famous injunction that it is always wrong to believe anything on the basis of insufficient evidence. And in that case he would line up against fellow pragmatist William James's insistence that it is often obligatory to believe 'in advance of the evidence' and on the basis of 'passional considerations'. Indeed, the arguments of the latter's 'The Will to Believe' are often used to mark the great philosophical gulf between the two pragmatists.

When James urges us to believe 'in advance of the evidence', he has several different kinds of case in mind. One concerns beliefs that are self-fulfilling: if I believe that someone likes me, or if I believe that I can jump the wide chasm that stands in from of me, then this will affect my behaviour in ways that make it more likely that the person will indeed like me, or make it more likely that I will possess the confidence required to get across the chasm. A second kind of case emerges when we note that what we experience can be influenced by what we believe and what we expect. James is particularly concerned about the possibility that there may indeed be evidence that supports God's existence, but this evidence may only be available to those who have already formed that belief on non-evidential grounds. The evidence may be salient or significant only to those who are already drawn to the proposition for which it is evidence. Accepting the belief that seems natural, that appeals to our passions and sentiments, is defensible particularly in the face of cases which are of vital importance. These are cases where an urgent resolution of the question is required and the costs of agnosticism may be high. Indeed James thinks that 'the passions' shape all our beliefs: the decision to accept Clifford's injunction and remain agnostic when very strong evidence does not support a candidate for belief is itself a passional choice. In all our cognitive activities, at some point we must *trust* our passional standards or our natural inclinations to believe.

As is discussed in Chapter 1, Peirce gave some lectures in Cambridge, Massachusetts in 1898 in which he defended views that fit poorly with the most natural reading of 'The Fixation of Belief'. First he claimed that belief had no place in science, that it was always irrational to *believe* results arrived at on the basis of the method of science. And second, he argued that it was wrong to trust theory or scientific reflection in connection with 'vitally important matters'. Vital matters should be settled with the aid of instinct, sentiment; we should trust our common-sense standards in making major decisions. Rather than wait for 'evidence', we must go by what is agreeable according to standards that are manifested in our sentimental or 'passional' responses. Although he had always questioned the relevance of theoretical reflection to matters of religious belief, by the time he wrote his 1908 paper 'A Neglected Argument for the Reality of God', he took a step further towards James, urging that a natural religious belief was required before we can obtain the evidence that can fuel a 'scientific' argument for God's reality. It is harder to find traces of James's insistence that belief in advance of sufficient evidence can be supportable because the belief is self-fulfilling. However, Peirce did hold that confidence in our natural sense of plausibility, in our ability to guess which theories are most promising, was required for us to be effective and successful inquirers. Indeed this raises some interesting issues about the interplay between the two strategies described in section 2: cognitive success may often depend upon our possessing confident common-sense *belief* in propositions that we are only really warranted in *hoping* are true.

Chapters 1 and 11 explore some of Peirce's views about how we should resolve vital questions, while taking seriously the thought that participation in science is itself usually the result of a vital decision, the adoption of a particular way of life. Chapters 9 and 10 take up a related set of issues about the role of 'sentiments' within the method of science itself. From the 1860s, Peirce had insisted that science depended upon a distinctive set of altruistic moral views; and in a sequel to 'The Fixation of Belief' he claimed that these took the form of sentiments. Chapter 9 discusses how sentiments can serve this role within science, and Chapter 10 explores some particular examples in connection with Peirce's anti-Cartesian view of *doubt*.

5. The Development of Peirce's Thought

The topically organized eight-volume Harvard *Collected Papers* disguised the fact that Peirce's ideas and concerns changed and developed from the 1860s until his death nearly fifty years later. The issues that dominated his writings in the 1880s seem very different from those that concerned him around 1870; and if we look at his published papers and manuscripts from the 1890s or from ten years later, we find yet further differences of focus and formulation. The importance of taking these changes seriously was first emphasized by Murray Murphey in his seminal work *The Development of Peirce's Philosophy* (1961). Under Murphey's influence, scholars are now sensitive to these developmental questions, and their work has been aided by the new *Chronological Edition* of Peirce's work and by the two-volume *Essential Peirce*, a by-product of work on that edition. Since a number of the papers in this volume are concerned with the pressures that led to these developments, I should say something about how they should be understood.[5]

How much continuity is there in the development of Peirce's thought? Murphey approached this question by asking whether Peirce defended one philosophical system or several. He concluded that there is a succession of different systems, arguing that each in turn succumbed to problems that it could not solve, to be replaced by a new system which was grounded in new ideas in formal logic. Apparent similarities between earlier and later

---

[5] The issues to be discussed here are examined in much more detail in my review of the 1993 re-issue of Murphey's book (Hookway 1994c).

views are thus superficial, concealing underlying differences of substantial importance. A contrasting view might see much more continuity, in its most extreme form holding that Peirce's ideas developed through accumulation, later work filling gaps and extending the range of applications of familiar ideas, but with early ideas surviving in large part.

We probably do best to resist the question when it is put, by asking: how many different philosophical systems did Peirce adopt during his career? Our criteria for counting philosophical systems are very unclear, and there may be no fact of the matter whether some change is sufficient to lead us to say that there has been a change from one 'system' to another. Some of Peirce's own ideas about how scientific ideas develop may help us to adopt an alternative approach. Discussing the history of the kinetical theory of gases, he commented that it began with 'a number of spheres almost infinitesimally small occasionally colliding'. As the theory developed, it was allowed that the forces between the particles included attractive ones as well as those that result from collisions, that molecules were not infinitesimal spheres but were, rather, systems, and that there are considerable limits to the freedom of movement of these molecules. Through this historical development, people's beliefs about the constituents of gases changed a good deal: much that was believed at the beginning was later rejected. But Peirce claimed that these changes involved 'no new hypothetical element' (*CP* 7.216). We might express this by saying that the theory was based upon a general vague 'picture' of how gases worked, and it was allowed from the beginning that this picture might be refined and developed in ways other than those first employed. Changes in our view of matter and in our view of how gases work can be seen as moves within this general picture, as refinements and modifications in the light of problems that arose in the course of applying and developing the theory. Perhaps we should think of the continuities in Peirce's thought in a similar way: from the beginning to the end, there is a general 'philosophical picture' which is common to his evolving body of ideas. But as he attempted to work out this picture in detail, problems became pressing which, a decade earlier, he would not have foreseen. And this can lead to refinements and reformulations of familiar parts of the picture whose necessity could not previously have been anticipated.[6] It can even lead to changes in the structure of his thought and the ways he argues for his positions.

---

[6] A full study of the development of Peirce's ideas would probably reach an intermediate position, finding some changes that merit Murphey's style of description, others that are best understood in the way described here. My objection to the former strategy is directed at its excessive or too ready employment.

If it is accepted that this is how we should look at the development of Peirce's thought, then a strategy for understanding it is suggested which reflects his own ideas about inquiry. A settled body of views can be disturbed by surprising experience or by uncovering other difficulties when we try to work out its implications or apply it. This gives rise to a doubt, to a problem that must be addressed before we can recover our confidence in our body of views. Inquiry, whether philosophical or within the special sciences, attempts to solve these problems, to eliminate these doubts. As the example of the kinetical theory of gases makes clear, this can often involve refining and developing familiar conceptions, recognizing that what seemed simple is complex, that earlier views represent a partial grasp of a more complex reality. In that case, our best way of approaching Peirce's work is to focus on the problems, the doubts, that preoccupied him at any particular time. We must then ask how those doubts were resolved, how those problems were solved, by the new doctrines, or by the refinements of old doctrines, that enter his work at that time. The history of Peirce's thought is the history of the new doubts that emerged and the new ideas that were employed to settle them. At any stage we should expect Peirce to be preoccupied with problems that emerged from his earlier ideas, but which he is struggling to see how to settle.

During the later 1860s, Peirce published a series of papers which introduced his philosophical picture: many of the elements of his thought are there in germ. We encounter the idea that truth can be understood in terms of the long-run agreement of inquirers. We also read that the idea of something *incognizable*, something that can never be known, is nonsensical. We learn that the validity of induction rests on the fact that repeated inductions will inevitably eventually take us to the truth. Much emphasis is laid on the claim that all thought is in signs which are interpreted in inference, and there are hints of the central distinctions of Peirce's semiotic. Finally an early form of Peirce's theory of categories is presented. We make sense of our experience by forming propositions about it in which we ascribe *qualities* to things. We can do this only because we can make relational judgements: qualities are things in virtue of which we can conclude that one thing is *similar* to another. Unless we could judge that *a is similar to b* we could not judge that *a is F*. And we can make these judgements of similarity only because *we* can *understand a as a representation of b*: thought depends upon mastery of the triadic relation of representation (W2: 49–59; and see Hookway 1985: 90–7).

Already in the 1870s, these ideas were undergoing refinement: the theory of categories is formulated more abstractly as the claim that logic requires there to be irreducible dyadic and triadic relations as well as simple monadic characters of things. Much of Peirce's philosophical energy during that decade was devoted to an unsuccessful attempt to write a systematic logic text. All that appeared was a series of papers in the *Popular Science Monthly*, 'The Illustrations of the Logic of Science', which included the papers we have mentioned above: 'The Fixation of Belief' and 'How to Make our Ideas Clear'. One reason these papers are so readable is that some of the most important elements of the picture—Peirce's theory of signs and his system of categories—are entirely absent. However, their importance for his thought is reasserted during the early 1880s. From 1879, Peirce was launched on a series of metaphysical investigations which led by the end of that decade to a system of evolutionary cosmology, a system of 'scientific metaphysics' central to which is the extensive development of his ideas about his categories. And by 1885 Peirce was developing his theory of signs, emphasizing the importance of indexical and iconic representations in language that would be adequate for scientific purposes. So we face two questions: why was there nothing about signs and categories in the papers in the *Popular Science Monthly*? Why did Peirce develop these ideas about indexical and iconic signs and begin to work on a scientific cosmology after 1880?

These issues are addressed by several chapters in this volume. I argue that when Peirce attempted to work out the details of his philosophical picture for his logic text in the early 1870s, he was forced to confront some problems which he could not answer. He was confident that they could be solved within the framework of views provided by the picture, but could not then see how this should be done. The *Popular Science Monthly* papers do much to refine the picture and make it precise, but they do not engage with the problems that we see Peirce confronting in the manuscripts that were intended for his *Logic* text. His writings in the 1880s engage with those problems directly: once his theory of signs enabled him to acknowledge the importance of indexical reference to external things, he could see the way forward. And other problems led him to believe that a fuller working out of his picture required him to embed his theory of categories in a system of scientific metaphysics, in an evolutionary cosmology. We can understand these developments only by identifying the problems or doubts that led Peirce to consider them.

It is against this background that my first chapter, 'Belief, Confidence, and the Method of Science' considers the interpretation of 'The Fixation of Belief'. It is natural, or at least common, to read that paper as arguing that the 'method of science' is indeed an effective method for 'fixing belief' and that it is the only truly effective one. The paper examines the lectures in which Peirce appeared to retract that claim: it is wrong, he suggests, to trust the scientific method when we confront issues of vital practical importance; and, he says, the method of science does not actually *fix* belief at all—'belief has no place in science'. As we saw in the last section, the claims about practice, about 'vital questions' suggest that there may be more continuity between Peirce's views and the position defended by William James in 'The Will to Believe' than is commonly supposed. Moreover (see Chapters 1 and 10), the views supporting these claims about practice and the method of science were already present in writings from the 1860s and 1870s. 'Belief, Confidence, and the Method of Science' uses these puzzles to identify some problems that Peirce struggled with when he was writing 'The Fixation of Belief'. Many of these problems have already been mentioned: they concern Peirce's changing attitudes towards the transcendental philosophy and his changing use of ideas from the common-sense tradition. Two more issues should be noticed here.

Chapter 4, a discussion of Peirce's reaction to the central argument of Royce's 1885 book *The Religious Aspect of Philosophy*, turns directly to the difficulties that Peirce seems to have faced in formulating his ideas about truth in the 1870s. According to Peirce, Royce's criticisms of the theory of truth that Peirce had presented in the 1870s, and his argument that the need for an adequate account of false belief required us to accept a version of absolute idealism, rested upon a flawed philosophical understanding of reference. So long as we suppose that reference to external things is always mediated through general descriptions of them, that we refer to them as whatever fits some description, the criticisms were hard to answer. By 1885, new developments in Peirce's logic and his semiotic theories enabled him to claim that indexical or demonstrative reference had a fundamental role in anchoring our beliefs to the world; it explains how we can have beliefs about things about whose properties we have many false beliefs. The chapter explores the importance of this development for dealing with the problems that appeared to hold up Peirce's attempt to write a logic text in the early 1870s.

Another source of these difficulties may have been a different issue about realism. Peirce came to see that his pragmatism and his theory of truth both called for a non-Humean view about causation. He needed to be a realist about classification, about causal interactions, about laws, and about subjunctive idioms generally. Although he had always claimed to be a 'realist', he did not begin to explain the metaphysical backing of this realism until 1879–80. Chapter 6 explores Peirce's reasons for claiming that the Universe contains elements of absolute chance and considers how far this development in his views enabled him to confront problems that he wrestled with through the 1870s.

Many of the issues raised in Peirce's papers are of continuing philosophical importance. Thinking about his views on truth and normativity, and about the nature of rational reflection and self-control, can offer new perspectives on current issues and new ways of formulating important issues. Most of the chapters that follow have an ostensibly historical focus, being attempts to understand and evaluate Peirce's often difficult texts. The main exception is Chapter 10 which is explicitly borrowing some ideas from Peirce in discussing contemporary issues. However, I think that nearly all treat issues where Peirce can make valuable contributions to current debates, and the issues I have discussed about truth and rational self-control reflect my own interest in those topics.

Belief, Confidence, and the Method of Science

1. Science and Belief: Introduction

During the 1890s, Peirce sometimes insisted that it was unscientific and, indeed, improper for investigators to believe current scientific results. In an 1898 lecture he went further, saying: 'I hold that what is properly and usually called belief . . . has no place in science at all'.[1]

Full belief is willingness to act upon the proposition in vital crises, opinion is will-ingness to act upon it in relatively insignificant affairs. But pure science has noth-ing at all to do with action. The propositions it accepts, it merely writes in the list of premises it proposes to use. (*CP* 1.635; *RLT*: 112)[2]

These remarks occur in the course of an argument for a sharp separation of theory and practice. Peirce has already insisted that we should attach no value to reason or scientific reflection when we attempt to settle practical or vital questions: we should, instead, rely upon instinct, common sense and sentiment. Hence, he accompanies these remarks with the assertion that 'nothing is vital for science; nothing can be' (*CP* 1.635; *RLT*: 112). Although many scientific results 'are almost immediately applicable to human life', the 'true scientific investigator completely loses sight of the utility of what he is about' and, if he were not to do so, 'it would spoil him as a scientific man' (*CP* 1.619; *RLT*: 107). A true scientist 'is not in the least

---

[1] This lecture was the first of the 'Cambridge Conferences', delivered on 10 February 1898. This series of talks has now been published as *Reasoning and the Logic of Things* (*RLT* 1992), with a useful introduction by the editor, Kenneth Ketner. Volume 1 of Peirce's *Collected Papers* contains an edited version of this lecture (*CP* 1.616–48) and part of an alternative draft (*CP* 1.649–77). I have given references to this edition and, where possible, to the corresponding passages in *RLT*.

[2] In another lecture from 1898, Peirce characterized belief as 'a willingness to risk a great deal upon a proposition' and continued: 'But this belief is no concern of science, which has nothing at stake on any temporal venture but is in pursuit of eternal verities (not semblances of truth)' (*CP* 5.589). In a manuscript of 1903, we read that 'pure science has nothing to do with *belief* (*CP* 7.606; see also *CP* 1.239 fn.).

wedded to his conclusions'; since nothing is risked on them, 'he stands ready to abandon one or all as soon as experience opposes them' (*CP* 1.635; *RLT*:112).

Some of them, I grant, he is in the habit of calling established truths but that merely means propositions to which no competent man today demurs. It seems probable that any given proposition of that sort will remain for a long time upon the list of propositions to be admitted. Still it may be refuted tomorrow; and if so, the scientific man will be glad to have got rid of an error. There is thus no proposition at all in science which answers to the conception of belief. (*CP* 1.635; *RLT*: 112)[3]

Such statements appear to conflict with some distinctively 'Peircean', doctrines from the 1860s and 1870s.[4] Consider the model of inquiry found in the first of the *Illustrations of the Logic of Science*, 'The Fixation of Belief'. Belief is a settled state, a stable disposition to act; so long as we are confident of a currently accepted belief, we see no need to doubt it or to inquire further into the grounds of its truth. Inquiry is always motivated by surprise, usually perceptual surprise, which disrupts our harmonious system of beliefs, converting stable belief into living doubt. Doubt is an unsettled state prompting inquiry directed at its elimination; the goal of

---

[3] Inferences which are 'scientific . . . have no true probability and are not matters for belief. We call them in science established truths, that is, they are propositions into which the economy of endeavour prescribes that, for the time being, further inquiry shall cease' (*CP* 5.589).

[4] Indeed, anyone unfamiliar with the writings referred to above might suppose that denying this dualism was one of the marks of 'pragmatism'. If one ignores these passages, it would be hard to question Ursula Niklas's comment that a 'particular strength of Peirce's account of the nature of meaning, given in the maxim of the pragmatic account of intellectual or scientific concepts, lies in the fact that it overcomes the traditional distinction between theory and practice' (1988: 31). As is stressed below, Peirce views science as a kind of practice, and his pragmatist maxim reflects this. Our problem is to see how this can be reconciled with the above cited claims.

The fact that there is a conflict between Peirce's apparent sharp distinction between theory and practice and his insistence that science is a 'mode of life' (*CP* 7.55) is noted by Maryann Ayim (1981: 46). She adds, plausibly: 'All the underlying tenets of Peirce's philosophy cry out against the type of rigid distinction he tried to draw between theory and practice' (p. 51). Ayim proposes that Peirce can use a third kind of science ('the sciences of review') to mediate between theoretical and practical science. This reflects her readiness to interpret Peirce's claims about 'practice' as claims about 'practical science'—which may be supported by passages such as *CP* 1.239. However *CP* 1.234 suggests a certain disdain for practical science: 'I must confess to being utterly bewildered by its motley crowd, but fortunately the natural classification of this branch will not concern us in logic.' In the light of passages cited in the text, it is natural to feel that, for Peirce, 'practical science' is not 'science properly so-called'.

the inquiry is, simply, replacement of doubt by settled belief in the truth or falsity of the disputed proposition. Hence, anything we currently believe is taken as prima facie acceptable; it has a presumption in its favour. It is clear that this picture is intended to apply to scientific inquiries as well as to common-sense ones. But if application of the scientific method cannot (or should not) produce *belief* at all, it is hard to see how we can view the method of science as a method for the fixation of *belief*. Hence one apparent tension between Peirce's 1898 remarks about theory and practice and his philosophical position twenty years earlier.[5]

This sense of tension is heightened when we note Peirce's anti-Cartesian rhetoric: 'let us not pretend to doubt what we do not doubt in our hearts' (W2: 212). Isn't that just what the passages from the 1890s are requiring scientists to do? If 'ought' implies 'can', then Peirce's remarks suggest that scientists can disengage their hearts from scientific propositions, but official Peircean doctrine (and common sense) may lead us to doubt that it is possible for them to do this.

The claim that scientists hold no scientific beliefs is not frequently made in Peirce's writings: it occurs in writings between 1898 and 1903; but soon after this, we find references to 'scientific belief' and comparisons of the logical and semantic properties of 'practical' and 'theoretical' belief.[6] So perhaps the 'no belief thesis' was a temporary lapse from philosophical good sense. Indeed, the context of some of the cited remarks might discourage us from assigning them much weight. They come from the first of the Cambridge Conferences lectures in which Peirce was berating his hosts for doubting that his proposed discussion of the foundations of logic was appropriate for his audience, and for calling instead for 'detached ideas on vitally important topics'.[7] His scepticism that philosophy had much to contribute to what is now called 'applied ethics' led to his claim that 'all sensible talk about vitally important topics must be commonplace,

---

[5] For the subsequent development of my argument, it is important to note that the discussion in 'The Fixation of Belief' locates the concept of belief in two ways: beliefs are dispositions to act, states which operate in concert with desires in order to determine actions; and beliefs have a distinctive functional role in the progress of inquiry—they are settled states of assent which prompt no further inquiry into the proposition assented to. The tensions I am concerned with begin to emerge when it is asked whether these two characteristics identify the *same* states.

[6] See, for example, *CP* 5.539 ff (1903), and, for discussion of Peirce's attempts to draw this distinction, Thompson (1953: 253 ff). And, for contrast, note: 'the scientific spirit requires a man to be ready at all times to dump his whole cartload of *beliefs*, the moment experience is against them' (*CP* 1.55, my italics).

[7] It is also reasonable to suppose that Peirce had William James's recently published *The Will to Believe* in mind. See Skagestad (1981: 208 ff) and Apel (1981: 158 ff).

all reasoning about them unsound, and all study of them narrow and sordid' (*CP* 1.677). He was probably anxious to distance himself from William James's promise that pragmatism might serve as a vehicle for the improvement of human welfare: he was certainly determined to dissociate himself from those who anticipated vital benefit from the study of metaphysics and to urge that a true scientific spirit should govern work in that discipline. Peirce may simply have over-stretched himself in lending rhetorical weight to his conservative distaste for allowing any role for rational reflection in practical or political matters: 'In everyday business, reasoning is tolerably successful, but I am inclined to think that it is done as well without the aid of theory as with it' (*CP* 1.623; *RLT*: 109).

Men many times fancy that they act from reason when, in point of fact, the reasons they attribute to themselves are nothing but excuses which unconscious instinct invents to satisfy the teasing 'whys' of the ego. The extent of this self delusion is such as to render philosophical rationalism a farce. (*CP* 1.631; *RLT*: 111)[8]

But there is more to it than that—indeed, a hint that this is so is provided by the writings of Popper, where a similar political and ethical anti-rationalistic conservatism, together with a view of science which resembles Peirce's in some respects, lead again to the view that scientific propositions should not be believed.[9]

References to scientific belief and theoretical belief need not conflict with Peirce's 'no-belief' doctrine, for scientific belief may be intended to contrast with 'what is properly and usually called belief'. The passage from *CP* 1.635 contrasts scientific assent both with 'belief' and with full belief. If the contrast with full belief can be sustained, it may be a minor verbal matter whether we describe 'what scientists are in the habit of calling established truths' as a kind of belief: what is important is that this state is distinguished from full belief.[10] The context of the 1898 lecture may have

---

[8] Compare: 'If you ever happen to be thrown in with an unprofessional thief, the only really bad kind of thief, you will find that two things characterize him: first, an even more immense conceit in his own reasoning powers than is common, and second, a disposition to reason about the basis of morals' (*CP* 1.666).

[9] See Popper (1972). A rather different form of the thesis that scientific assent is not a form of belief is fundamental to the 'constructive empiricism' of Bas van Fraassen. He holds that rather than presenting theoretical claims as true, the scientists displays them and ascribes to them such 'virtues' as empirical adequacy (1980: 10).

[10] The reference to 'full belief' in these passages may suggest to the reader that Peirce is simply denying that we should be *certain* of scientific results, a lesser degree of belief ('opinion') being permissible. I hope, in the course of this chapter, to make clear that this would be a mistake.

dictated the formulation the point received without leading to a distortion of Peirce's true position. The underlying issue concerns his reasons for distinguishing two kinds of 'assent': it may be relatively unimportant that he was not always consistent about whether he wished to refer to both as forms of belief. There are several reasons for investigating these issues. First, they raise important questions about the nature of what (for the sake of neutrality) I shall call 'scientific assent' ('assent' for short). There are general problems about whether a resolute fallibilism is compatible with the possibility of our believing current scientific opinions, and Peirce's struggle with these may, I hope, illuminate the problems. In this chapter we focus primarily upon a negative claim: scientific assent does not involve the sort of *belief* that is involved in the explanation action. Chapter 2 takes the issue further, exploring some Peircean views about what is distinctive about *scientific* assertion and assent in more detail. In accepting a scientific claim, he claimed, we do not firmly commit ourselves to its truth. Our commitment is often only to the fact that it provides a one-sided approximate formulation of some truths that will be better grasped and formulated through further inquiry.

Second, the investigation forces us to re-examine the structure of 'The Fixation of Belief': we obtain a better focus on some features of that argument which, from Peirce's own point of view, should have been profoundly unsatisfactory.[11] Third, we can hope for insight into Peirce's views about the sources of our confidence in our practical assurances. He was clearly contemptuous of those who expect reason to solve practical problems. But he was no irrationalist; accepting the guidance of instinct and sentiment is a mark of wisdom, a guide to acting well. But the fourth, and most important reason for examining this issue relates to the development of Peirce's thought. Identifying some of the tensions in the arguments of 'The Fixation of Belief' will enable us to place in a proper perspective some of the emphases in Peirce's thought after 1900.

These later writings introduce a variety of themes in order to provide foundations for logic and science: in 1903, he emphasized his phenomenological defence of the categories and proposed that we ground logic in ethics and aesthetics; a few years later, these doctrines were less prominent and Peirce was stressing his critical common-sensism; and by 1908, the

---

[11] This relates to an issue mentioned in note 3 above. The discussion will also, I hope, help to clarify the argumentative structure of this paper—and of the series to which it belongs. It seems to me that commentators have paid insufficient attention to Peirce's explicit claims about what is going on in these papers and have misunderstood them. Related points were made in Hookway (1985: 43 ff).

role of religious belief in grounding science was receiving more attention. Examining the issues surrounding Peirce' s 'no-belief' thesis will clarify the tensions in his thought leading to these developments.[12]

In section 2, an attempt is made to formulate the 'no-belief' thesis and to see how it was supported. This leads (in section 3) to a more detailed discussion of the strategy of 'The Fixation of Belief', and an attempt to show that in 1877 Peirce lacked the resources to formulate issues about theory and practice that ought to have been (and indeed were) of concern to him. We then examine in more detail the conception of scientific assent which emerges in some of his later writings (section 4). Finally (section 5), an issue about theory, practice, and the practice of science is raised which, I shall suggest, forms the background for some of the later developments in Peirce's thinking.

2. Belief: Causes and Reasons

The position Peirce defended in 1898 suggested a distinction between 'full belief' which is linked to action and the 'vital' concerns of life, and 'scientific belief' (or 'assent'), which is not. We could approach the distinction in two ways: by examining Peirce's views about practice, and identifying what is distinctive about our cognitive response to vital questions; or by examining the special features of scientific assent. It would be a mistake to treat either route as fundamental: Peirce has distinctive views about both theory and practice and they independently contribute to his responses to these issues. His understanding of judgements of practice informs his philosophy of science; and his view of scientific rationality informs his philosophical account of practice.[13] In particular, we should resist the conclusion that Peirce's 'sentimentalist' view of practical decision was forced on him by his account of scientific reasoning; his moral conservatism was there from the beginning.[14]

How should we formulate the 'no-belief' thesis? Consider an agent A

---

[12] This chapter is largely devoted to describing the tension I have referred to and to focusing on some issues underlying the 'no-belief' thesis. The role that Peirce assigns to sentiment and instinct in rationality is discussed more fully in Chapters 10 and 11.

[13] For further discussion, see Skagestad (1981: 46–7).

[14] This is most evident in his discussions of religious belief—which answers to a vital question. For example, in 'Critique of Positivism', written before 1870, we read that 'those beliefs which come to all men alike before reflection are generally true', and this is because 'the reasons which produce fallacies depend upon a conscious process of reasoning' (W2: 127–8). More passages of the same sort are presented and discussed in Chapter 11.

who carries out scientific investigations. She proposes the hypothesis *H*, and tests it rigorously, eventually deciding that no further testing is required: the hypothesis is 'established truth'. The strongest version of the thesis holds:

(I) It is wrong for *A* to believe *H*.

We noted passages which appear to deny that *A* should make *H* the object of a 'full belief' (*CP* 1.635). Perhaps this means that it is merely wrong for her to be *certain* of it: in a fallibilist spirit, she can hold it to be probable even if it is not certain. Scientific propositions, Peirce said once, are 'but opinions at most' (ibid.), which suggests, in the light of the other quotation from *CP* 1.635 above, that we may act on them in insignificant matters but not in connection with vital matters. However, as is clear from *CP* 1.689, he denied that the scientific method could even attach probabilities to conclusions: it is as unscientific to regard a conclusion as *probable* as it is to judge it certain. Hence we could reformulate (I) as:

(Ia) It is wrong for *A* to take *H* to be certain or probable.

And a corollary of this appears to be:

(II) It is wrong to use *H* as a guide in answering practical or vital questions.

This is hard to accept. Why is it wrong to act on current scientific assurances? The suggestion that such assurances are but 'opinions at most' may indicate that it is permissible to act on them in relatively insignificant affairs:[15] why, then, should we ignore apparently relevant scientific information when confronting 'vital crises'? One answer is that if we employ scientific opinions in 'vital crises' we acquire an interest in their truth: the discovery that they are false might then be a source of dismay rather than glee at having pushed the human quest for truth one step further. In that case, drawing the distinction in terms of the relative 'significance' of the affairs on which we act would be misleading. Suppose that relying upon a scientific belief offered my best chance of escaping from a serious life-threatening danger. Since such a crisis is momentary, I retain no interest in

---

[15] But recall my comment above that Peirce seems to have thought that the scientific method does not even make conclusions probable.

the proposition's truth once I have reached safety and I could still welcome its refutation. Peirce's perception of the threat posed by live belief in scientific propositions focuses, it seems, upon the way in which my possessing an interest in the truth of a proposition would prevent my subjecting it to proper scientific scrutiny; and exercising a belief to resolve a one-off vital crisis need not affect that. A better example of using a scientific belief in connection with vital purposes would be the case of a micro-biologist who sinks his life savings in the commercial exploitation of his discoveries. We must avoid projects which are pursued alongside our scientific activities and which rest upon the approximate truth of scientific theories currently endorsed within the scientific tradition in which we work.

If that is all that is involved, then Peirce's anxieties seem excessive. If the theories are refuted, then the commercial projects will fail whatever the scientist's view of the matter; if they do not fail, then they do not depend strictly upon the theory in question. Moreover, since, as Peirce insists, science is a co-operative activity, there need be no risk to scientific progress in the fact that I have a commercial interest in a recent discovery so long as I have not persuaded all of my fellow inquirers to invest in my project. It is not obvious that the scientist's commercial venture will block the road of inquiry. Furthermore, Peirce often remarks that in certain circumstances it is rational to act on the basis of propositions that we do not believe but which we *hope* to be true.[16] The prohibition on *belief* in scientific conclusions does not prohibit acting on the *hope* that they are true. In that case, (II) is not obviously a corollary of (I): but if (I) can be accepted while (II) is denied, the rationale for (I) (the 'no-belief' thesis) is very unclear.[17]

A weaker thesis would hold that Peircean scientists should not carry out scientific investigations *for the sake of* their applications. But even if we ought not to undertake investigations out of practical motives, it does not follow that we cannot believe their results. All that follows is that we should not adopt projects of various kinds: perhaps the 'man of science'

---

[16]   See, for example, *CP* 2.113. This possibility seems relevant to the kinds of case that we have considered so far. Although Peirce invoked this possibility in order to argue that fundamental laws of logic are all hopes, (see, for example, *NEM*3: 371), the examples he uses to illustrate his point make clear that it has wider application. Of course, there may be limits to what can be achieved by *hopes*: it is doubtful, for example, that a Christian life could be sustained by the *hope* that Christ is the son of God.

[17]   When Peirce writes that 'the investigator who does not stand aloof from all intent to make practical applications will not only obstruct the advance of pure science, but, what is infinitely worse, he will endanger his own integrity and that of his readers' (*CP* 1.619), the strong impression is given that he is opposed to (II) as well as to (I).

should not make his scientific ventures subordinate to other fundamental projects; but so long as a scientist does not have mixed motives, there seems no obstacle to his believing his results.

Peirce's thesis leads to some implausible claims about applied or 'useful' science (like engineering and surgery). Such inquiry is useful, he tells us, 'only in an insignificant degree' and 'it still has a divine spark in which its petty practicality must be forgotten and forgiven':

But as soon as a proposition becomes vitally important—then in the first place it is sunk to the condition of a mere utensil; and in the second place, it ceases altogether to be scientific, because concerning matters of vital importance reasoning is at once an impertinence towards its subject-matter and a treason against itself. (*CP* 1.671)

Amid the exaggerated rhetoric, Peirce is pointing to an unresolved tension in the intellectual life of an applied scientist. Such inquirers must address questions of two distinct (but confusingly similar) kinds. First: has a particular proposal survived rigorous test sufficiently well that we may exempt it from further test for the time being and use it in theory construction and experimental design? Second: has the proposal been tested sufficiently that we may take it as 'established', applying it in our engineering or surgical practice? Peirce ought to hold that only the first of these is a properly scientific question; once we address the second, we enter the realm where reason is rationalization and instinct and sentiment rule. Logical self-control can be our guide in the first but not in the second. An affirmative answer to the first makes the proposition available for scientific purposes; an affirmative answer to the second makes it more generally available. If these two questions are not kept apart, one's logical integrity is compromised.

There is a useful discussion at *CP* 5.589 where Peirce is contrasting the attitudes towards facts that are appropriate for science and for practice. For the time being science can be content with theories which, it is aware, contain much that is arbitrary or subjective, while 'practice requires something to go upon, and it will be no consolation to it to know that it is on the path to objective truth'. And this is because, 'the actual truth it must have, or when it cannot attain certainty must at least have high probability, that is, must know that, though a few of its ventures may fail, the bulk of them will succeed'.

When an hypothesis has survived rigorous examination, we may reflect: 'this ground has held a long time without showing signs of yielding. I may hope that it will continue to hold for a great while longer.' According to

Peirce, this judgement is 'extra-scientific': it has no role in purely scientific endeavour. But it gives practice a basis for believing the hypothesis: 'I can safely presume that so it will be with the bulk of the cases in which I shall go upon the theory.' This step towards belief has no scientific importance:

Thus those retroductions which at length acquire such high degrees of certainty, so far as they are so probable, are not pure retroductions and do not belong to science, as such; while, so far as they are scientific and are pure retroductions, have no true probability and are not matters for belief . . . they are propositions into which the economy of endeavour prescribes that, for the time being, further inquiry shall cease. (*CP* 5.589)

We shall see below that Peirce's logic, his account of inquiry and self-control, entails that reason (rational self-control) can never produce full belief. Belief (in the proper and usual sense) will always have causes over and above any reasons we may have for holding it. If we fully believe a proposition, it enters into a causal nexus other than that of rational self-control: instinct and sentiment intrude to govern its formation. Since 'I would not allow sentiment or instinct any weight whatsoever in theoretical matters, not the slightest',[18] a theoretical proposition which is believed is to be treated with mistrust. For, in such a case, my acceptance of the proposition has causes other than those of which I am aware. It is under the sway of sentiment and instinct, and so I cannot feel confident of my ability to control my use of it and my acceptance of it. So what is wrong with full belief, from a scientific point of view, is that it is not subject to my control.

Peirce's arguments here depend upon the claim that, with respect to practical matters, sentiment and instinct rule: practical reflection is mere rationalization; the belief that we have reasons for acting as we do is 'self-delusion'. Wisdom allows reflection to be tempered by instinct and sentiment.

Sentimentalism implies Conservatism; and it is of the essence of conservatism to refuse to push any practical principle to its extreme limits—including the principle of conservatism itself. We do not say that sentiment is never to be influenced by reason, nor that under no circumstances would we advocate radical reforms. We only say that the man who would allow his religious life to be wounded by any

---

[18] *CP* 1.634. As is emphasized in Chapter 9, this statement is an exaggeration of Peirce's considered position. He did allow a role for sentiment in logic and in the use of inductive reasoning.

sudden acceptance of a philosophy of religion or who would precipitately change his code of morals at the dictate of a philosophy of ethics . . . is a man who we should consider unwise. (MS 437:14)

Now it is a corollary of this that beliefs have causes which are not reasons for holding them, and for the most part we are not reflectively aware of what these causes actually are. We should guard against the temptation to exercise rational self-control in our practical activities. Once we *believe* a scientific hypothesis, our attitude towards it is affected by this extra-scientific causal nexus as well as by rational self-control. If science is to be the epitome of rational self-control, it requires us to understand the determinants of our attitudes to hypotheses. Belief compromises logical integrity by limiting self-control.

If this is what Peirce has in mind, it seems an over-reaction to a recognizable difficulty; indeed, Peirce's response to his problem seems utopian. It is hard to believe that human inquirers possess the self-control required to immunize their scientific opinions from the sorts of malign forces which would thus threaten their ability to subject these beliefs to rational self-control. But it is also hard to believe that the community of inquirers as a whole is not alert to the sorts of dangers here referred to; one's first reaction is that in most circumstances the result of failing to achieve such immunity is unlikely to block the road of inquiry. Moreover, we can acknowledge the diverse demands upon the judgement of applied scientists without concluding that logical integrity cannot be maintained through self-awareness and self-control.[19]

But what should we make of Peirce's claim that scientific assurances are 'but opinions at most' (*CP* 1.635)? Are they opinions or not even that? In the light of the interpretation offered, I suggest that opinions are beliefs about which we are tentative or uncommitted, in which case the grip of the causal processes which have transformed scientific assent into (weak)

---

[19] Peirce frequently returns to a particular kind of case where the existence of such a blockage may be found. Theologians attempt to use rational controlled inquiry in theorizing about religious matters, and they expect their inquiries to reach substantial conclusions on matters of doctrine. In Peirce's view, the results of their investigations are expected to make a difference to what the believer should believe, and to how he or she should live. Peirce holds that undertaking such projects denies the true character of religious belief and is a betrayal of the scientific or philosophical spirit: it tries to use reason where sentiment should rule. His sense that the resulting outlook is deeply dishonest, and his assurance of the purity of the motives of those possessed of the true scientific spirit, are reflected in his famous observation that he had never heard of someone who 'considerably increased human knowledge' being a criminal 'unless theology be knowledge' (*CP* 1.576).

belief will not be strong enough to inhibit the further operations of rational self-control. We might be psychologically incapable of preventing these processes giving rise to weak opinions, but scientific self-control requires us to be able to withstand processes which would produce anything stronger.

3. The Method of Science and 'The Fixation of Belief'

As we noted in section 1, the claim that 'belief' has no place in science appears to conflict with the views of 'The Fixation of Belief'. I shall now turn to the arguments of that paper. If we read it with the later distinction in mind, we can gain insight into both. We can find the later claim about scientific belief prefigured there; but we shall also be able to locate a deeper and unresolved tension in the earlier discussion. I shall sketch two competing accounts of the strategy employed in that paper. My conclusion will be that both contain a partially correct account of what was going on, and that, *in 1877*, Peirce could not bring them together into a coherently structured whole. I should guard against misunderstanding here. The claim that there were tensions in the earlier position does not entail that Peirce was confused at the time. I suspect that he was fully aware of these tensions, and that they resulted from his inability, in the mid- to late 1870s, to solve some difficult problems about reference and reality. His other work at the time, and especially in the ensuing decade, can best be read as a concerted attempt to solve these problems. As he was aware, until he had solutions to them, his arguments for the position he defended would not be fully satisfying.[20]

In 'The Fixation of Belief', inquiry is described as a process initiated by the disturbance of a previously settled body of opinion. The doubt resulting from this disturbance motivates us to activities which come to an end once the uneasy state of doubt is replaced by the settled state of belief. Peirce evaluates some methods which promise to facilitate this process of inquiry. As is well known, four such methods are examined: three fail, and the method of science triumphs. The method of tenacity—'taking any answer to a question which we may fancy, and constantly reiterating it to ourselves, dwelling on all which may conduce to that belief, and learning

---

[20]   The last three sentences of this paragraph are an addition to my original paper. This is explained in more detail in the Introduction, section 5. The ideas about the development of Peirce's work are taken further in Chapters 4 and 6. A very useful recent discussion of the interpretation of Peirce's intriguing paper is to be found in Anderson (1995: 82–115).

to turn with contempt and hatred from anything which might disturb it'
(W3: 248–9)—fails because we shall not be able to avoid meeting others
with different opinions and that will inevitably shake our confidence. The
method of authority advocates the creation of an institution whose role is
'to keep correct doctrines before the attention of the people, to reiterate
them perpetually, and to teach them to the young; having at the same time
power to prevent contrary doctrines from being taught, advocated or
expressed' (W3: 250). This fails, we are told, for a similar reason: the institution cannot guarantee that we shall never encounter those who are not
subject to our authority and this will lead us to view our opinions as arbitrary, thus unsettling them and producing doubt. Third comes the a priori
method: 'let the action of natural preferences be unimpeded . . . and under
their influence let men, conversing together and regarding matters in
different lights, gradually develop opinions in harmony with natural
causes' (W3: 252). This fails through making the development of inquiry
'a matter of taste', submitting opinion to the dictates of fashion. Reflecting
on differences in (for example) moral standards, Peirce 'cannot help seeing
that . . . sentiments in their development will be very greatly determined
by accidental causes'; and he continues:

Now, there are some people, among whom I must suppose that my reader is to be
found, who, when they see that any belief of theirs is determined by any circumstance extraneous to the facts, will from that moment not merely admit in words
that that belief is doubtful, but will experience a real doubt of it, so that it ceases
to be a belief. (W3: 253)

In view of the discussion of the 1890s, this is a very surprising statement: Peirce appears to be saying that the fact that a belief originates in
sentiment makes right-thinking inquirers doubt it. Twenty years later he
thought otherwise. Surprisingly, appeals to common sense and sentiment
can be found in writings from the 1860s too.[21] But we must not interrupt
the story: we seek a method 'by which our beliefs may be caused by nothing human, but by some external permanency—by something on which
our thinking has no effect'. And so we adopt the method of science, using
methods and rules only if they can be defended by reference to the fundamental hypothesis that:

There are real things, whose characters are entirely independent of our opinions
about them; those realities affect our senses according to regular laws, and, though

----

[21] See note 14.

our sensations are as different as our relations to the objects, yet, by taking advantage of the laws of perception, we can ascertain by reasoning how things really are, and any man, if he have sufficient experience and reason enough about it, will be led to the one true conclusion. (W3: 254)

Reflection on four competing methods of inquiry shows that only one of them is capable of being sustained: it provides a non-accidental source for our opinions, assuring us that any settled belief it provides will be truly stable.

I have presented this argument rather as Peirce himself does: we want secure stable 'fixed' belief, and we compare four methods according to how effective they will be at providing it. So understood, the argument rests upon what appear to be contingent (and not invariable) features of human psychology: meeting others with different opinions tends to shake our confidence in opinions that we hold to 'tenaciously'. It also leads Peirce to make a claim which, there is every reason to think, he did not believe: that sentiment should not be allowed to have a role in settling our opinions; his later work does not suggest that beliefs resulting from sentiment are weak, unstable, driven by fashion, and easily doubted.

If the argument is intended to work in this fashion, it involves another massive weakness. When Peirce's account of science is worked out in full detail, it turns out that by adopting the method of science we postpone the removal of doubt for the sake of a settlement of belief which is truly stable. Adoption of the method of science provides no guarantee that we shall settle belief in the short run: indeed, one of its ethical glories is supposed to be the way in which it involves a subordination of our personal interest to a search for a settlement of belief by a wider community of single-minded scientific investigators. Although settlement of belief on the matters that interest me may not be reached until long after my death, my small contribution to this process ensures that my life has not been in vain. In that case, it is reasonable to protest, I have not obtained what I was looking for. I sought a method for removing the irritation of doubt; and I triumphantly endorse a method which requires me to put up with it in the hope that when, eventually, it is removed, the removal will be permanent. Worse: if we accept the 'no-belief' thesis, it seems, the doubt may be removed but not be replaced by settled *belief at* all.

In practical matters—when we confront 'vital questions'—this seems highly unsatisfactory. In such cases it matters less that we obtain a settlement of opinion that will be permanently settled than that we obtain a reasonably secure verdict soon. Hence the argument of the later papers advocates something like the a priori method in connection with vital questions. But according to the published argument of 'The Fixation of Belief', that ought to yield opinions which immediately succumb to doubt.

Although this way of reading 'The Fixation of Belief' is very common, I doubt that it is the right way to do so. The text itself contains remarks about the strategy adopted in the paper, and these suggest another interpretation which avoids some of the troubling consequences just described. In section II, Peirce addresses the question of how to establish the correctness of logical principles. He proposes that certain guiding principles 'are necessarily taken for granted in asking whether a certain conclusion follows from certain premises'; and he argues that 'rules of reasoning which are deduced from the very idea of the process are the ones which are most essential', claiming that 'so long as [reasoning] conforms to these, it will, at least, not lead to false conclusions from true premises' (W3: 246). There is much evidence that Peirce takes himself to be carrying out such a 'deduction' in 'The Fixation of Belief' and the papers which follow it in the 'Illustrations of the Logic of Science'. His illustration of the 'facts from which logic starts out' begins:

It is implied, for instance, that there are such states as doubt and belief—that a passage from one to the other is possible, the object of thought remaining the same, and that this transition is subject to some rules which all minds alike are bound by. As these are facts which we must already know before we can have any clear conception of reasoning at all, it cannot be supposed to be any longer of much interest to inquire into their truth or falsity. (W3: 246)

When, towards the end of the paper, Peirce summarizes the evidence for the merits of the method of science, different styles of argument are employed. One is empirical: we are invited to be impressed by the triumphs of the method of science, particularly when we have noted that we unthinkingly use it much of the time for everyday investigations. Another is logical or presuppositional: the fundamental hypothesis of the method of science is involved in those facts taken for granted by the 'logical question':

The feeling that gives rise to any method of fixing belief is a dissatisfaction at two repugnant propositions. But here already is a vague concession that there is some one thing to which a proposition should conform. Nobody, therefore, can really doubt that there are realities, or, if he did, doubt would not be a source of dissatisfaction. The hypothesis, therefore, is one which every mind admits. (W3: 254)

One would then expect Peirce to claim that the hypothesis of reality is either itself one of the presuppositions of logic or is deducible from them. The flaws of the other methods all stem from the fact that they deny some feature of the method of science and are thus at odds with the presuppositions of the logical question. In that case, it is not so much the 'social impulse' that overthrows the earlier methods as the fact that they conflict with the underlying presuppositions of both the method of science and the logical question: the social impulse is merely evidence of that fact. If the presupposition of the method of science is indeed a presupposition of inquiry or of 'the logical question', then this would explain the power of the social impulse to constrain our opinions.

The two descriptions of what is going on in 'The Fixation of Belief' treat it as addressing different questions. The first claims that Peirce is asking:

1. Which methods of inquiry is it possible to adopt?

while the second identifies his problem as:

2. Which methods of inquiry can be vindicated by reference to the presuppositions of the logical question?

Peirce's strategy is to assume that the answer to question (1) will provide evidence in support of an answer to question (2). The later lectures suggest that this is a mistake: it is possible, and often desirable, to use methods which cannot be vindicated by reference to the presuppositions of logic.[22] At best, question (2) shares an answer with question (3):

3. Which methods is it possible to adopt in inquiries that are subjected to reflective rational monitoring and control?

So long as we decline to submit our modes of belief formation to reflective, rational monitoring and control, then the methods of tenacity and

----

[22] The position is slightly more complicated than this allows. Peirce probably holds that logical reflection can persuade us that, in connection with vital issues, we ought to trust opinions that are not grounded in logical self-control. Skagestad seems to suggest this when he says 'for the purpose of making decisive practical choices, instinct is a better guide than reason' (1981: 207) and cites Peirce's claim that animals, which never reason about vital matters, 'very rarely fall into error of any kind, and *never* into a vitally important one' (*CP* 1.649). For example, reason may explain that we are wise to *hope* that our sentiments will put us into harmony with truth and reason. Since this view would legitimate reliance on the a priori method only because doing so can receive a vindication which is more properly scientific, the general point stands.

authority and the a priori method might work. The weakness of Peirce's strategy of argument is that, if it works, it appears to be unreasonable (or 'unwise', or indeed impossible) to resist the demand that we exercise rational monitoring and reflective control in connection with all of our beliefs.

A brief digression concerning why Peirce's argument had this character is in order. Part of the story is that at the time of writing the 'Illustrations of the Logic of Science', Peirce was unable to give his philosophical 'system' the systematic grounding in semiotics and the theory of categories that it required: hence, he was still struggling to find satisfying arguments for positions that he was reasonably confident were correct.[23]

Another part of the story concerns Peirce's complex relations to Kant. He saw himself as a broadly Kantian philosopher, who wanted to correct Kant's logic and improve on his system of categories. This makes it unsurprising that he would be interested in hunting down the presuppositions of logic, attaching importance to the fact that some proposition is presupposed by the logical question. In spite of this, however, he wanted to reject the transcendental method: showing that something was a presupposition of logic was no guarantee of its truth.[24] He repudiated the idea of a priori philosophical derivations; he insisted that philosophy had to be, in some fashion, scientific. Yet, we have seen, his project involves identifying what are, in some way, presuppositions. Hence, during the 1870s, he moved uneasily between at least three kinds of claim about their status: they are presuppositions of reasoning; they can be vindicated by a kind of empirical argument; and no proof of them is required because everybody believes them. If he could show that the method of science somehow reflected a presupposition of reasoning, he could hold that it is possible (and indeed wise) to turn one's back on reflective reasoning in some areas of one's life. Everyone (in principle) could acknowledge that if we were to submit some question to an investigation subject to full rational self-control, the method of science would have to be followed. But it might be possible to decline to submit some questions to such an investigation. Even in the 1870s, I suspect, Peirce wanted to say this. But, at that stage, methodological uncertainty prevented him from seeing clearly how he should or could defend this claim. This may also be responsible for the ambivalence exhibited in Peirce's comments, in those papers, about the merits of the other three methods (see W3: 255).

---

[23] See Hookway (1988*a*) and Chapter 4.

[24] For discussion of Peirce's attitudes towards the use of transcendental strategies in philosophy, see Oehler (1987) and Chapters 7 and 12.

4. Belief: Scientific Assent

The special character of scientific acceptance has two related sources. First, as we have seen, someone imbued with the true scientific spirit welcomes the refutation of 'established' views: anything identifiable as the elimination of error is embraced as a contribution to progress. Second, there is the special character of Peirce's logical vindication of the scientific method. Peirce believed he could show that adopting the scientific method, trusting abductive suggestions and submitting them to inductive testing, was a good strategy for contributing to scientific progress. A community of inquirers who proceeded in this fashion was fated eventually to reach the truth about the questions they raised. But logic could offer no reason for supposing that conclusions recommended by the scientific method at any particular time were true. There is no justification of the short-run reliability of induction: at best, we can say that the wealth of human experience over many thousands of years has ensured that the short-run reliability of induction in ordinary affairs of life is an instinctive or common-sense belief. In the short run, induction causes beliefs but does not, properly speaking, justify them: when we trust induction in the short run, the a priori method of fixing belief, trusting what seems reasonable or what it is natural to believe, is ultimately responsible for our believing what we do.

This ought to suggest that we should never cease inductively testing hypotheses; even observational claims should be subjected to endless empirical testing. All we can say of a scientific proposition is that, so far, it has not been refuted. In that case, there would be no such thing as scientific belief, but science would have a very odd character. It is not clear we could ever test a hypothesis, because we have to accept reports of experimental results in order to treat them as refuting current theories. Since experimental design depends upon current theory, experimentation would seem to be impossible too. And we would not be able to decide that a theory has survived severe testing and could be included in the list of 'established truths' to be used in formulating new theories and in constructing experiments. The question of the character of scientific assent concerns what our attitude to a proposition should be when we remove it from the list of propositions currently under test, and include it in the list of propositions that may be relied upon in testing other hypotheses. Ordinary experience suggests that we would then judge that, in all probability, the hypothesis is approximately true, although subsequent developments may lead us to revise or refine it, or to see it as a limited special case of some more inclusive body of laws. The alternative picture is that we make a practical judgement which involves no commitment to the probable or approximate truth of the proposition: ceasing testing this proposition at this stage of inquiry will be the best means of making progress eventually towards the truth. In that case, we take up an 'as-if' attitude towards the possible truth of the proposition: it is now good to treat the world as if this proposition is true; but we have no right to believe that it actually is true. We might hope that it is approximately true, but that attitude shares with the practical as-if response a highly qualified, tentative, and detached relation to the proposition.[25] And, indeed, given the overall flavour of Peirce's philosophy of science, we might think that such a hope is unnecessary: at best we should hope that 'assenting' to the proposition will be useful as a way of making progress towards the truth.

This accords with another theme in Peirce's philosophy that became prominent during the 1890s; his increasing insistence that logical principles have the status of hopes (*NEM* 4: 19). Whenever we attempt to investigate a question, we hope that it has an answer, that convergence on one opinion would result in the long run of such investigations; we hope that we are sufficiently attuned to reality, that investigating hypotheses that seem plausible to us will serve as a useful means to reaching, sooner or later, the truth. We hope that contributing to the growth of knowledge will prove a fulfilling and satisfying project, and so on. Once again, we take a highly detached attitude towards our scientific commitments; and this is of a piece with the claim that science has no place for belief.

This connects nicely with the Kantian streak in Peirce's strategy that was noted in the last section. If showing that something is a presupposition of logic does not justify us in believing it, it can ground the hope that it is true: 'the true presuppositions are merely hopes' (*NEM* 4:19). So not only do current scientific results and currently approved theories function as objects of a kind of assent which is not straightforwardly cognitive, but so do the fundamental commitments which ground our acceptance of the scientific method and our adoption of the project of contributing to scientific knowledge: 'what is properly and usually called belief . . . has no place in science at all' (*CP* 1.635; *RLT*: 112).

---

[25] To avoid misunderstanding, I should point out that adopting an 'as if' attitude towards *current* theories is compatible with scientific realism. In fact, the detached attitude which it involves requires a realist view of theories: the scientist wants to accept a theory only if it is true, and she is aware that the current theory is accepted in the absence of any assurance that it meets this requirement. This issue is discussed further in Chapter 2, 4, and 5.

This seems a very unsatisfactory position. Peirce often speaks of the scientist's commitment to the growth of knowledge in almost apocalyptic terms. Consider a passage from 'The Fixation of Belief':

The genius of a man's logical method should be loved and reverenced as his bride, whom he has chosen from all the world. He need not contemn the others; on the contrary, he may honor them deeply, and in doing so he only honors her the more. But she is the one he has chosen, and he knows that he was right in making that choice. And having made it, he will work and fight for her, and will not complain that there are blows to take, hoping there may be as many and as hard to give, and will strive to be the worthy knight and champion of her from the blaze of whose splendors he draws his inspiration and his courage. (W3: 257)

The problem is that if one's assurance that progress can be made and that one is contributing to it amount to no more than a *hope*, if belief has no role in science, it is hard to see how he can 'know he was right in making that choice'. How can such detached and uncertain commitments motivate someone to continue to try to contribute to scientific activity? To return to a problem raised in our discussion of 'The Fixation of Belief': if we seek a method for removing the irritation of doubt, why should we so readily embrace a method which postpones the satisfaction we seek, holding out no more than the hope that the result of such self-denial will be an eventual settlement of opinion that will be more truly stable. If a hope is genuinely to motivate us to make inquiry our fundamental project, then, we are likely to think, some causal, psychological process must transform the hope into a living belief. And unless we believe that our currently accepted theories are likely to prove approximately correct, it is hard to understand what can motivate us to sustain our commitment to inquiry.

5. Confidence: The Life of Science

One way to challenge this sharp distinction between science and practice would be to deny the autonomy of theoretical science. John Dewey, for example, probably held that we can appreciate the value of theoretical investigations only when we place them in the context of inquiries designed to effect a real transformation in existential conditions, in response to vital concerns. The problem I am concerned with remains even if we grant Peirce the autonomy of pure theoretical inquiry. I want to suggest that his distinction between theory and practice cannot be formulated in the kind of terms he used in the 1890s.

Among the most pressing vital questions confronting an individual are those about what fundamental ends to adopt: which projects should we allow to give shape and meaning to our lives? Failure in such projects will be interpreted as failure in one's life. The questions of whether to be a scientist or philosopher, an engineer or surgeon, whether to live contentedly without ambition, and so on, are clearly among such vital questions. In that case, the decision to seek to exercise maximal rational self-control, using the method of science in order to contribute to our knowledge of reality, is a response to a vital question. In view of our comments about the argument of 'The Fixation of Belief', two difficulties face reflection about whether to adopt this project. We face, first, the question of how it is possible to adopt this project: since our fundamental motivation is to find a method for the settlement of belief, how can we be content with a method which promises very stable eventual settlement of belief but which holds out no assured prospect of stable settlement in the short run. The argument rests upon assumptions about human motivation which are neither stated nor defended. Second, if the argument of 'The Fixation of Belief' can be made to work, and if, as we have seen, it exploits the strategy of showing that only the method of science can be adopted for the stable settlement of belief, then, how is it possible to adopt a fundamental project other than contributing to science and philosophy? Furthermore, if both kinds of project are possible, how are we to choose between them? If the matter is to be settled by self-controlled rational inquiry, then, we might feel, the crucial decision has already been taken before one considers the question of how to live. Moreover, if self-controlled rational inquiry is involved, Peirce was wrong to deny its relevance to vital questions. If he is to be consistent, Peirce ought to hold that it is base and sordid to rely upon self-controlled rational inquiry when we settle such fundamental and vital issues. But if, as with other vital questions, we are guided by sentiment and instinct, then Peirce's denial that sentiment and instinct have a role in science is compromised. One passage in a draft of the 1898 lectures indicates recognition of these problems: if he were prepared to make an exception to his claim that scientific inquiry cannot be vitally important, he would 'make that exception in favour of logic; for the reason that if we fall into the error of believing that vitally important questions are to be decided by reasoning, the only hope of salvation lies in formal logic, which demonstrates its own ultimate subordination to sentiment' (*CP* 1.672). But this important insight is not developed in these writings.

Decisions about fundamental projects can be revoked; we can wonder whether to continue with our current projects, reflecting on their value and on the value of our own contribution to them. And once we have adopted 'the life of science', decisions about which disciplines to work in, which specialities to enter, and which problems to tackle produce vital dilemmas which are not wholly solved by reference to the exigencies of funding. If these are 'vital' questions, then it would be 'intellectual betrayal' to expect scientific reflection to solve them. Such questions call for an answer that produces living belief. In that case, for Peirce, they cannot be answered without the aid of sentiment, instinct, and common sense. The scientist must be *confident* that the life of science is a possible one, that it can be (and will be) a rewarding one, that the contributions he or she is making are of value, and so on: this must be full belief, because it has to determine action in response to vital questions—it determines how the individual decides to live.

We see here, once again, the limitations of the perspective that Peirce had obtained when he wrote 'The Fixation of Belief'. Reading that paper suggests that adoption of the method of science is the only possibility: we (quite generally) cannot sustain use of the other methods. In that case, the question what motivation we might have for devoting our lives to the exercise of the method of science and rational self-control seems to have little sense. From reading that paper, one would think that there was no alternative to adopting the method of science. In his later work, Peirce was forced to take seriously the fact that in many areas of life rational self-control has limited application. But during the 1890s, it seems to me, he had still not fully faced up to the question of how it is possible to live the life of science. How can we have the confidence in our contributions which is required if we are to be able to make a serious commitment to the life of science?

It is, of course, an oversimplification to deny that there is a serious response to these issues before 1900, but we can conclude that they were not addressed in 'The Fixation of Belief' or in the papers in which Peirce defended the 'no-belief' thesis.[26] A number of themes prominent in Peirce's thought after 1900 contribute to a more sophisticated understanding of the 'practice of theoretical science'. Although examining them

---

[26] A striking example of a fusion of sentiment and logic from the 1870s is Peirce's insistence that probabilistic reasoning depends on the logical sentiments of 'faith, hope and charity' (W3: 281–5). But it should be noted that this occurs in the context of a strained (1877) attempt to deal with the relations of theory and practice: it can only be rational for me to rely on probabilities in connection with a particular case (a vital question) if my *sentiments* express my rational identification with the indefinite community of scientists. In 1898, we may suppose, Peirce would have seen this as a misguided attempt to show that rational considerations have a bearing on vital issues. See Chapter 9.

in detail would be a topic for another paper, I shall conclude this chapter by briefly listing some of these themes. In the 1903 pragmatism lectures, Peirce attempted to ground logic in ethics and aesthetics, developing views about the sorts of ends it was possible to adopt and to sustain in any circumstances. At the same time his classification of the sciences was being refined, and he was able to argue that mathematics, phenomenology, ethics, aesthetics, and logic lacked the kind of fallibility which grounded the claim that scientific acceptance should be so tentative. Hence, he was able to discuss the bases on which ultimate aims can be adopted and he had available a fund of certainties on which he could rely in order to do this. Two years later, he was placing most stress on the claims of common sense: we can be certain of a range of vague common-sense certainties which ground the scientific view of the world (*CP* 5.438–52; see also Chapter 8). The approximate correctness of mechanics, dynamics, and 'rational man theory' was part of common sense; the task of science was to replace vague certainties by precise testable laws and to explain these precise laws. Moreover, any scientific hypothesis is offered as a precisification of a vague picture whose vagueness permits considerable assurance that some filling in of its details is correct. So there is a provision for assurance about the value of the scientific enterprise and for considerable confidence in the approximate adequacy of current theory. Finally, during the second half of that decade, we learn that scientific observation is a species of religious experience, and that religious belief transforms the world into a benign and meaningful unity which invites our inquiries and investigation: our experience of the world is then suffused with the sentiment required to motivate inquiry (see Chapter 11 and Raposa 1989). Some of these themes are found in writings of an earlier period, but their prominence in this later work together with their evident relevance to the problem which I have discussed helps to make sense of the pattern of some of his later writing.

2

Truth and the Convergence of Opinion

1. Pragmatism and the Theory of Truth

'Pragmatism' is commonly associated with some views about truth. William James claimed that his form of pragmatism *was* a theory of truth; and when Peirce introduced his version as a technique for clarifying ideas, one of its first applications was to elucidate the meaning of 'true'. Central to Peirce's account was the claim that 'truth' could be defined in terms of a special kind of 'fated' or 'destined' consensus, a long-run convergence of the views of inquirers: 'The opinion which is fated to be ultimately agreed to by all who investigate is what we mean by the truth' (W3: 273). Both James and Dewey endorsed this connection between convergence of opinion and truth: the former accepted it as an account of 'absolute truth'; while the latter agreed with it as an analysis of *truth* before concluding that logic and epistemology would do well to abandon this notion in favour of 'warranted assertibility'. The aim of this chapter is to explain the content of Peirce's account of truth and to identify some themes in his thought which help to provide answers to at least some of the objections that have been presented to his view. Several of these themes are explored more fully elsewhere in the book.

It will be important to bear in mind the vagueness of the expression 'theory of truth'. It might just refer to an account of the meaning of the word 'true' and its equivalents. Alternatively, it could herald an account of the normative role of the concept of truth in assessing beliefs and assertions or keeping track of the progress of our investigations. Or it could offer some heavy-duty metaphysics designed to provide deep philosophical explanations of the relations between thought and reality. Competing theories of truth (correspondence, coherence, redundancy, pragmatist) need not be different answers to the same question. Rather, they may reflect contrasting views about the kinds of theory that philosophers should be looking for when they try to clarify the concept of truth. Even when a philosopher has decided that objective knowledge is indeed a possibility, that there is a world that exists independently of us, that the theoretical entities spoken of in the sciences are as real as tables and chairs, and that there are objective truths about laws and counterfactual possibilities, it remains an open question whether these metaphysical commitments can or should be expressed in the form of a 'theory of truth'. The connection between realism and a correspondence theory of truth (for example) obtains only if we think that 'truth' is a fundamental *metaphysical* concept. If it is not such a concept, then the fact that a commitment to objectivity or realism cannot be read off what a thinker says specifically about *truth* need have no implications about his or her metaphysical views. Thus we must pay close attention to the aims of the theory that Peirce attempted to construct.

This chapter falls into three main parts. The first, 'Truth and Convergence', offers a formulation of Peirce's account of truth before considering some problems that it faces. This is followed by an extended discussion of why Peirce was untroubled by the fact that there appear to be many truths which will forever be beyond our reach. We consider the relevance of Peirce's later realist theory of laws and counterfactuals; and we examine how far his insistence on the indeterminacy of the content of many of our assertions can be used to support the view that, in such cases, there may indeed be no 'truth'. The first part concludes by defending the view that Peirce's analysis is better seen as an account of the commitments we incur when we assert a proposition than as an explanation of the meaning of the word 'true'. 'Truth and Assertion', the second part, attempts to understand the role Peirce assigned to truth, understood in terms of convergence, in normative reflections about the conduct of inquiry and deliberation. The final part, 'Truth and Reality', argues that the Peircean idea of truth is metaphysically neutral: one could accept this account of truth while remaining agnostic about whether realism or an idealist or anti-realist position provided the best explanation of this convergence in opinion.

TRUTH AND CONVERGENCE

2. Peirce's Theory of Truth: Formulations

Peirce's 1877 paper, 'How to Make our Ideas Clear', formulated and defended rules for achieving reflective clarity about the contents of concepts, propositions, and hypotheses. After formulating and defending his favoured rule, Peirce employed it to clarify a concept of fundamental importance to his logic, the concept of reality. Truth and reality were viewed by Peirce as closely related:

D1: The opinion which is fated[1] to be ultimately agreed to by all who investigate, is what we mean by the truth, and the object represented in that opinion is the real. (*CP* 5.407; W3: 273)

This is offered as a further clarification of an abstract verbal definition of reality:

D2: The real is 'that whose characters are independent of what anyone may think them to be'. (W3: 271)

D2 defines 'the real' by providing another expression which is supposed to be equivalent to it. Since such definitions simply move around in a web of words and concepts, Peirce sought a further kind of clarification which related a concept to possible experience. The pragmatist principle was a rule for providing such clarifications: we provide a complete clarification of a concept by listing experiential consequences we would expect actions to have if the concept applies to some specified object. If some proposition is true then any action of inquiring into it (of 'investigating') will have the experiential consequence of leading eventually to a stable belief in that proposition.

The two definitions entail three claims:

1. An object is real if it is represented in a true proposition.
2. An object is real if its 'characters are independent of what anyone may think them to be'.
3. A true proposition is one which is 'fated to be ultimately agreed on by all who investigate'.

It is natural to worry that these form an inconsistent triad: the second explains reality as 'independence of thought'; while the third explains the

---

[1] Sometimes Peirce spoke of an opinion which is 'destined' to be agreed upon rather then 'fated'; and he also spoke of the true opinion as the 'final cause' of inquiry. A footnote to the passage in the text explains that 'Fate means merely that which is sure to come true, and can nohow be avoided'. It continues, somewhat mysteriously: 'It is superstition to suppose that a certain sort of events are ever fated, and it is another to suppose that the word fate can never be freed from its superstitious taint. We are all fated to die.'

related notion of truth in terms of inter-subjective agreement. The tension resurfaces in Peirce's insistence that he is a 'realist of a somewhat extreme stripe', and in the widespread tendency to think that explaining truth in terms of convergence involves a form of anti-realism. As I have argued elsewhere, Peirce may not have been clear about how the different themes in his philosophy hung together in the 1870s.[2] But it is important to note his reference to 'fated' or 'destined' convergence of opinion. However 'fate' is explained, it is clear that he wanted to hold that we come to agree on some proposition *because it is true*; it is not true simply in virtue of the fact that we come to agree on it. The truth draws us toward it, and serves as the 'final cause' of inquiry. Moreover, although explaining truth by reference to thought and inquiry may ensure that it is not independent of 'thought in general', reality can still be independent of what any individual thinks. Many truths are not believed by anyone; and individual realities are not dependent for their existence upon being believed in or acknowledged.

The more anti-realist readings can be challenged too by noting another, later, account of truth, to be found in an entry on 'Truth, Falsity and Error' which Peirce wrote for Baldwin's *Dictionary of Philosophy* (1901; see *CP* 5.565–73):

D3: 'Truth is that accordance of the abstract statement with the ideal limit towards which endless investigation would tend to bring scientific belief.' (*CP* 5.565)

This differs from *D1* in its explicit reference to 'scientific belief'. When we bear in mind that Peirce often used 'investigation' to refer to a particular method for carrying out inquiries, the *method of science*, then it is clear that participating in the fated consensus will depend upon our using the correct methods, upon our conforming to appropriate normative standards in carrying out our inquiries. Inquiry could lead to a convergence on a false proposition if it was conducted in accord with faulty logical standards. Thus we might adopt *D4*:

D4: If a proposition is true, then anyone who inquired into it *using good methods of inquiry* would be fated eventually to accept that proposition.

Of course, this requires an explanation of what makes a method of inquiry 'good', a fundamental concern of Peirce's work in logic and philosophy. So

---

[2] See Chapters 4 and 6.

long as the goodness of a method is not a product of human tastes or human conventions, then the fated convergence of opinion need introduce nothing subjective or mind-dependent into the account of truth.[3]

One more refinement is required, and this will help us to avoid a widespread misreading of Peirce's view. For a particularly clear example of the mistaken reading, consider Crispin Wright's characterization of the notion of 'Peircean truth' (1992: 45) which he takes from Putnam and others. He defines it as 'what is justified at an *ideal limit* of enquiry, when all empirical information is in' (ibid). A true proposition would be assertible in 'a state of information which comprises *all* information relevant to any empirical hypothesis' (1992: 46). On this view, the convergence of opinion has an objective basis because it will occur in epistemically ideal circumstances when all possible evidence is to hand. So long as the totality of the evidence together with the correct epistemic norms require belief in the proposition in question, then we have an explanation of the convergence of opinion which avoids any hint of subjectivism or relativism. As Wright argues, this idea of a state of information comprising *all* information relevant to any empirical hypothesis is extremely problematic. If it were true that we were in this position, then we would possess all the information we require to see that this is our situation; but (especially for a fallibilist such as Peirce) it is hard to see how we could ever be in a position of recognizing that there is nothing more to learn. Fortunately, Peircean truth is not Peirce's view.

There is no doubt that Peirce's theory of truth appeals to what would be believed in epistemic situations which are, in some respect, *ideal*. When James explained his Peircean notion of absolute truth, he referred to 'that ideal vanishing point towards which we imagine that all our temporary truths will some day converge' (1907: 106–7), and *D3* above spoke of 'the ideal limit towards which endless investigation would tend to bring scientific belief'. But the kind of idealization differs from that involved in Wright's 'Peircean truth'. Indeed, it is closer to what Wright calls 'superassertibility' (1992: 48).[4] Peirce often models the convergence of scientific investigation upon the case of statistical sampling. Someone who

---

[3] Peirce normally takes 'good methods of inquiry' to involve the 'scientific method'. Given the views about ethical truth noted in the last section, we must be open minded about whether this is the only kind of 'good' method. It is likely that Peirce understands the 'method of science' sufficiently broadly that he can retain the claim that the method of science is the only good one.

[4] Cheryl Misak has also noticed the analogies between Peirce's conception of truth and Wright's idea of superassertibility (1998: 413).

thinks that the probability that somebody wounded in the liver will die is .75 would expect inferences with true premises of the form:

X has been wounded in the liver so X will die

to yield true conclusions 75 per cent of the time.

As we go on drawing inference after inference of the given kind, during the first ten or hundred cases, the ratio of successes may be expected to show some considerable fluctuations; but when we come into the thousands and millions, these fluctuations become less and less; and if we continue long enough, the ratio will approximate towards a fixed limit. (*CP* 2.650)

As we 'test' our sample of people wounded in the liver we eventually reach a point where we believe that the chance of such a person dying is 75 per cent *and no further evidence will disturb that view*. Peirce's position does not require that we can ever reach, or even make sense of, a state of 'perfect evidence'. It requires only that we can reach a state where no further evidence would disturb the belief that we have arrived at. The verification of non-probabilistic claims has a similar structure: we 'sample' the predictions that can be derived from a proposition and, if it is true, we eventually arrive at a settled opinion which will not be disturbed by further experience. It need not be decidable whether we have actually reached this position, although often, of course, we will reach it very quickly.

This leads to a slightly more precise formulation of Peirce's linkage of truth and convergence.

D5: If it is true that *p*, then anyone who inquired into the question whether *p* long enough and well enough (using good methods of inquiry) would eventually reach a stable belief that *p* which would not be disturbed by further evidence or investigation.[5]

This position has two significant corollaries. First it reinforces Peirce's fallibilism. Although responsible inquirers are destined to reach a point at which their opinions will not be disturbed by further inquiry, there is never any absolute guarantee that this position has been reached. No matter how confident we are that we have the truth, further experience

---

[5] Some of Peirce's claims suggest that he would accept this as a biconditional.

could surprise us. Thus when I claim that some belief of mine is true, I assert fallibly that the proposition I believe is one that would be the object of destined or fated convergence in opinion. Second, recall that in *D3* Peirce defined truth as 'that accordance of the abstract statement with the ideal limit towards which endless investigation would tend to bring scientific belief'. Although this is not a version of the classical correspondence theory of truth, it does suggest that the truth of a current opinion consists in its correspondence to ('accordance of the abstract statement with') something else—the opinion that would be an object of fated convergence of opinion. Thus second, we find an *echo* of a correspondence theory of truth. This will be relevant to understanding the role of truth in Peirce's account of how we evaluate beliefs and methods of inquiry.

3. Some Problems for Peirce's Account

Until this point, we have not ventured far from Peirce's remarks about truth in his 1877 paper 'How to Make our Ideas Clear'. As is explained in the Introduction and in other chapters in this volume, the following decade witnessed important developments in his philosophical views. There were dramatic changes in his logical views and in his account of the kinds of signs that must be employed in a scientific language. From 1880, he was engaged in the metaphysical investigations that yielded the evolutionary cosmology and 'scientific metaphysics' that was presented in a series of papers in *The Monist* after 1890. I have suggested that these developments responded to problems that he faced in the 1870s but which he could not then solve to his satisfaction. In this section, we shall formulate some of the problems that confront the account of truth just described.

First, little has been said about the mechanisms whereby this fate or destiny operates. What is the explanation of the convergence of opinion? And how can we ensure that it occurs? Perhaps there is an algorithm for scientific testing and discovery: properly put into practice, this algorithm or method cannot fail to eliminate false answers to our questions and propose and settle on the correct ones. In that case, there would be no problem. But there seems to be no such algorithm. We depend upon imagination to think up answers to our questions. Bad luck can conceal from us ways in which our evidence has been produced in a biased manner; standards of plausibility and simplicity reflect our background knowledge, education, and aesthetic sensibilities. The fated convergence is simply a metaphysical mystery: there is no reason to think that it can in general be guaranteed.[6]

We need to specify in some detail what is involved in carrying out an inquiry 'well enough'. If we cannot do this, then Peirce's claims about truth become trivial and uninteresting—an inquiry counts as good enough only when it contributes to producing agreement, even if we cannot say in detail what was good about the inquirer's activities. For the claims about truth to be important, we need a detailed account of the scientific method or of the relevant standards of rationality. For many of Peirce's critics, this presents the greatest difficulty. In the present chapter, I am more concerned with a second issue. There seem to be many facets of reality which will be forever hidden from us, no matter how long and carefully we carry out our inquiries. For example, there is the question how many leaves there were on the tree in my garden at exactly 10 a.m. yesterday. Since no observations were made or counts taken at that time, it seems likely that no one could now find out what that number is. Hence there is a true proposition stating the number of leaves that were then on my tree, and, no matter how hard we work at it, it is extremely unlikely that anyone could ever arrive at a stable belief in that proposition. Yet Peirce appears to be committed to the implausible claim that if this proposition is true, then anyone who investigated the matter is destined eventually to believe it. Similar examples can be constructed about events in the remote past, objects very distant from us in space, and so on. Given the close link Peirce forged between truth and reality, would he have to conclude that such cases display genuine indeterminacies in reality?

Towards the end of 'How to Make our Ideas Clear', Peirce discusses these lost facts or 'buried secrets' (W3: 274). Considering 'all the minute facts of history, forgotten never to be recovered, to the lost books of the ancients, to the buried secrets', he asks 'Do these things not really exist because they are hopelessly beyond the reach of our knowledge?' (ibid.).[7] He does not respond by considering counterfactual possibilities or anything like that. His answer is that 'it is unphilosophical to suppose, with regard to any given question (which has any clear meaning), investigation would not bring forth a solution of it, if it were carried far enough'. Pointing to the remarkable and unpredictable growth in knowledge of the previous

---

[6] This topic is discussed further in Chapter 4. Josiah Royce (1885: 426 ff) attacked a view of truth that Peirce recognized as his own on the grounds that truth and objectivity were made to rest upon 'bare possibilities' about the future course of inquiry.

[7] Bear in mind remarks made earlier that the distinction between truth and reality (truth and existence) was not clear in Peirce's mind when he wrote this paper.

century, he responds by asking rhetorically: 'who can be sure' ('who can guess?', 'how is it possible to say?') what we shall be able to find out in a few hundred, a few thousand or a few million years? This response seems wholly inadequate to the problem. Peirce's account of truth seems to entail that properly conducted inquiry is destined or fated to reach these truths. This response encourages a much weaker claim: seemingly lost truths *might* come to light in surprising ways, and we cannot prove that they will not. Although we have no basis for confidence that there *are* truths in these areas, we would be irrational ('it would be unphilosophical') to assert that there are not. Since the evidence for believing that we could never discover how many leaves were on my tree yesterday morning seems as good as my evidence for many other wholly unproblematic truths, it is hard to see why we should find this solution satisfying. Peirce seems so far from recognizing the force of the problem that we may be left with the suspicion that we have not yet reached a full understanding of his position.

4. Nominalism and Realism

One response to our problem is to reformulate the claim about truth and convergence in a subjunctive form. Although no one *will* arrive at the fated opinion about the number of leaves on the tree, it seems clear that if someone had investigated the matter, they *would have* arrived at that opinion. We understand clearly enough how someone could have investigated the matter yesterday morning, and we believe that anyone who had done so who made no mistakes would have arrived at the same view. Although no one now can inquire into the matter long enough and well enough, we can see that people could have done so; and if they had, they would have reached the truth. So long as we can make sense of these claims about what would have happened had that inquiry occurred, the conceptual connection between truth and the convergence of opinion can be preserved.

Some famous passages in Peirce's writings suggest that this is his favoured solution. In 1877, he had difficulty in making sense of these subjunctive conditionals and thus could not arrive at a satisfactory solution to the problem of lost facts. Subsequent developments in his philosophy enabled him to accept the objectivity of 'would-be's and 'would-have-been's, and this provided the required solution. In this section, we begin by considering a passage from 'How to Make our Ideas Clear' which appears to support this interpretation. However, although the point being made is relevant to questions about lost facts, we shall see that it cannot provide a fully satisfying solution to the problem. The closing part of the section argues that this passage is not, in fact, directly concerned with the problem of lost facts at all: it has a different target, and once this is recognized its claims are less absurd than they initially appear.[8]

Having suggested—surely controversially—that 'there is absolutely no difference between a hard thing and a soft thing so long as they are not brought to the test', Peirce introduced the example of a diamond which was 'crystallized in the midst of a cushion of soft cotton' and remained there until it was destroyed. Peirce asked: would it be false to say that the diamond was soft? On the normal reading, his response to his question is: 'There would be no *falsity* in such modes of speech. They would involve a modification of our present usage of speech with regard to the words hard and soft, but not of their meanings. For they represent no fact to be different from what it is; only they involve arrangements of facts that would be exceedingly maladroit' (W3: 267). He seems to be claiming that, in such cases, since nothing will ever show that we are mistaken, it is up to us what we say. Whatever we say will not be false; although, presumably, this does not establish that it is true. We might expect him to say the same thing about other examples of lost facts: so long as the leaves on the tree are not counted, there would be no falsity in any answer that we offer to the question how many leaves there were. This encourages a strongly anti-realist reading of his theory of truth.

Peirce later rejected this solution as too 'nominalistic' (*CP* 8.208). Ten years after composing this passage, he insisted that regularities such as laws must be explained. We explain the hardness of diamonds by reference to their crystalline structure. Hence, we might suppose, hard things and soft things differ in their molecular structure 'before they are brought to the test'. The quotations from the 1877 paper suggest that 'the facts' are somehow exhausted by what can be directly observed. Whether Peirce seriously believed that even then may be questioned, but the changes in his logical and metaphysical writings during the 1880s enabled him more confidently to resist the temptation to make such claims. The realist, non-Humean theory of laws that was developed at that time accounted for aspects of theory choice which, in 1877, he could make little sense of.[9]

---

[8] It is significant that the passage under discussion does not appear when Peirce is applying the pragmatist principle to the analysis of *truth*. It occurs earlier in the paper when he is discussing its application to *hardness*.

[9] See Chapter 6.

Once this is accepted, someone might respond to the problem raised by the diamond crystallized in soft cotton and destroyed before it is tested, by pointing out that according to my explanation of Peirce's position, this fated agreement is limited to those who inquire into the matter 'long enough and well enough'. The lack of agreement on this case is then due to the fact that any inquiry that can actually occur would be inadequate: we could not acquire enough evidence. Since, in the tree example, we could have done so had we made a count yesterday, perhaps the analysis can be rescued by appeal to counterfactuals. And this can be supported by pointing out that anyone who had gone into the garden yesterday, who made a count and did not make any mistakes, would have arrived at the same answer. We preserve the analysis by appeal to facts about what people *would have* believed if they had inquired into the matter long enough and well enough. This is not contrary to the spirit of Peirce's philosophy: in later work he emphasized that his form of pragmatism would only be plausible to someone who took a realist, anti-Humean view of laws and subjunctive conditionals.

Such laws and conditionals may enable us to conclude that anyone who carefully counted the leaves on the tree yesterday morning at 10 a.m. would have come to the same definite answer. On that basis we can accept that it is true that there was a definite number of leaves on the tree yesterday morning at 10 a.m. This shows that a truth which is undiscoverable can be grounded in facts which determine how that truth could have been discovered in other circumstances. And we can agree that our judgement that such a truth is, in fact, undiscoverable is fallible: who knows but that evidence may come to light that will enable us to discover it.

In that case, the explanation of Peirce's 1877 response to the problem is that he then lacked the account of the metaphysics of laws and the logic of counterfactuals that would be required to follow this route. In the 1870s, his philosophy was too nominalistic, insufficiently realist to make sense of this. If realism about laws can be defended, and if a suitable epistemology of laws can be constructed, then it may be possible to extend the range of truths beyond those that could now be discovered by us. Our knowledge of laws may tell us that there was a definite number of leaves on the tree, even if we cannot learn of the truth of any instance of that existentially quantified proposition.

However, this cannot provide a complete solution to the problem. Suppose that one of the branches of the tree is contained within a protective box which would have to be opened before the count could be completed. And suppose that this box is designed so that opening it will trigger a bomb that destroys the entire earth. In that case, nobody could inquire long enough and well enough: trying to inquire well enough would disastrously prevent the inquiry continuing for long enough.[10] Even if the proposal can be revised to make sense of this kind of example, it is hard to see how we should interpret the relevant counterfactuals to deal with propositions about the remote reaches of space or about times before any minds or inquirers existed. Consider the proposition that there was a rock on this spot ten thousand years before minds first acquired knowledge of the Earth. So long as inquiries into this matter are restricted to those that could be carried out after the appearance of such minds, then there is no reason to expect that knowledge of this truth would even have been achieved. If, on the other hand, we think of a counterfactual case where inquiries were carried out by inspecting the rock at the time, then such inquirers would not conclude that the rock was there in the absence of minds. Serious problems face the attempt to solve the problem of lost facts by appeal to counterfactual facts about inquiries. Although there may be ways of solving these problems, we will do better to consider some other strategies.

In fact, I suspect that it is a mistake to read Peirce's discussion of the example of the diamond as a response to the problem of lost facts. After speaking of the diamond, he changes the example: what prevents us from saying that all hard bodies remain perfectly soft until they are touched, when their hardness increases with the pressure until they are scratched? The challenge this case raises is somewhat different from the problem of lost facts. The example concerns a law rather than a particular state of affairs. Moreover, the challenge cuts deep: if we cannot rule out this possibility, how could we ever have evidence which forced us to believe that all diamonds were hard? This raises a problem about induction and the underdetermination of theory by evidence: if one theory fits our evidence, then so will an indefinite number of other theories. Science uses inductive reasoning to obtain knowledge of *laws*: experiments on a sample of diamonds (for example) will lead us to knowledge of the theoretical properties of all diamonds. The problem is that the evidence so far available will always fit a large number of alternative hypotheses; and in that case, it

---

[10] Such counterexamples reflect the fact that pragmatist clarifications of concepts and propositions seem to show that propositions that appear to be categorical (*That object is a magnetic*) have a subject-matter that is most perspicuously displayed as conditional (*If we were to place iron filings close to that object, then they would be attracted to it*). There is a recipe for constructing counterexamples to such analyses: they involve what has been called the 'conditional fallacy' (Shope 1978).

is hard to defend the view that one of these hypotheses is *fated* or *destined* to be accepted if only we continue inquiring for long enough. Indeed, the suggestion here seems to be that, as a matter of principle, there will always be many hypotheses left open. Given our experiences of scratching diamonds so far, consider the following possibilities:

- All diamonds are hard.
- All diamonds are soft until tested, at which point their hardness increases in proportion to the pressure with which they are scratched.
- All diamonds are hard except for the one that was crystallized in soft cotton and destroyed without being tested for hardness.
- All diamonds tested before the year 2010 are hard, and all diamonds not tested before that time are soft.[11]

At any time in the future our evidence will be compatible with the first three of these if it is compatible with the first—and it will also be compatible with a suitably altered version of the fourth. Unless we say that there is no fact of the matter which of the first three is correct (the response suggested in the passage from 'How to Make our Ideas Clear'), Peirce must explain how it is that we are fated to arrive at the correct answer. In this context, the 1877 solution looks rather different. He is saying that since the first three laws stated above are empirically equivalent, the choice between them is not a substantive one. There is no fact of the matter which is true.

The realist emphasis on the role of crystalline structure in grounding the hardness of diamonds then has a different focus. It enables Peirce to claim that these 'laws' are not equivalent according to scientific method. Once we accept that it is laws, above all, that require an explanation, we can note that no explanation is readily available of why or how diamonds steadily become harder when scratched; nor of how the untested and now destroyed diamond can possess the inner structure required to be a diamond yet still not be hard. Peirce's realism allows him to argue that certain law formulations, which he earlier claimed were empirically equivalent, can be distinguished by a sensible pragmatist.

5. Indeterminate Truth, Determinate Reality

Peirce's contribution to Baldwin's dictionary suggests a different response to the problem of lost facts. In such cases, he seems to suggest, there is no

---

[11] This is a straightforward variant on Goodman's 'grue' example from *Fact, Fiction and Forecast*: an indefinite number of variations upon it can be produced by altering the date.

truth; but it is compatible with this that the underlying *reality* is relatively determinate. In connection with a slightly different example, he allows that if there would be no fated agreement on the matter, 'there certainly is no *truth*': 'But whether or not there would perhaps be any *reality* is a question for the metaphysician, not the logician.' The possibility must be taken seriously that there may be realities where there is no truth. Could the precise configuration of leaves on my tree be a determinate feature of reality which is not reflected in any truth?

Consider part of the passage from the *Dictionary*:

Truth is a character which attaches to an abstract proposition, such as a person might utter. *It essentially depends upon that proposition's not professing to be exactly true.* . . . Truth is that concordance of an abstract statement with the ideal limit to which endless investigation could tend to bring scientific belief, *which concordance the abstract statement may possess by virtue of the confession of its inaccuracy and one-sidedness, and this confession is an essential ingredient of truth.* (CP 5.565, italics added)

This suggests that when I make an assertion, claiming that some proposition is true, the content of what I commit myself to can be somewhat indeterminate. In that case, I shall suggest, there need be no fact about what judgement we *would* reach if we inquired for long enough and well enough. Truth may be indeterminate even if reality is not.

This possibility can be made plausible by reference to two kinds of example. The first involves simple semantic indeterminacy or vagueness. We might decide that there is no fact of the matter concerning whether someone is bald without concluding that there is any indeterminacy in the underlying reality, in the arrangement of hairs on their head. The indeterminacy infects how we describe and represent this 'underlying reality'; it does not infect the reality itself. But even if such cases are widespread, there will still be others in which judgement or decision was not required to determine the truth value of a proposition; suppose a question arose about the baldness of someone who was (as a matter of fact) utterly hairless. In that case, there do seem to be determinate facts about what a rational careful inquirer would have concluded. Interesting examples of lost facts will be of this kind.

Now for the second kind of example. If I had counted the leaves on the tree yesterday morning, then I would have faced a number of decisions which would have affected the result. Should I include a brown, gnarled diseased leaf which no longer has a role in sustaining the tree? Should I include a leaf which is suspended from the tree by a thread, about to fall off at any moment? What about new growth just escaping from the bud? In such cases, I must exercise judgement; there is nothing in the semantic content of the question how many leaves are on the tree which determines how I should decide. I cannot be confident that everyone would decide in the same way or even that I would have made the same judgement on another occasion. I may be influenced by reasons for undertaking the count: if it is to be used to assess the health of the tree, the brown gnarled leaf should be excluded; if it is used to assess the shade the tree will produce, it should be included. So long as I exercise my judgement wisely and sensibly, then, we may allow, my count has powers of 'retroactive legislation' (for this concept see James 1907: 107): it can be used to evaluate an earlier guess, for example. So long as the result I reach will stand the test of checking and further observation, it is true; but due to the role of judgement in carrying out the count, there may have been no such fact as to what results I would come up with until I had completed the exercise. There is no suggestion here that the underlying reality is indeterminate; but there is a limited degree of freedom in how to represent it. A different sort of example illustrates the same point. I assert of someone that she has always been very good at arithmetic. I am offered a counterexample: after two bottles of wine in the restaurant last week she could not add up the bill. Is this excluded by an implicit *ceteris paribus* clause? This is a matter for judgement, and we can see how the decision may go either way. We can see too how it will be influenced by reflection on the use that will be made of the information, or about what prompted the question. Whatever decision is made may possess powers of retroactive legislation. Ahead of time there may have been no determinate fact which decreed how the judgement would or should be made.

What do such examples illustrate? Four points are being brought together. First, *truth* and *falsity* are properties of representations, thoughts, and utterances. Second, the contents of such representations are often indeterminate; this might involve vagueness, or the effect of *ceteris paribus* clauses, or even the absence of an explicitly described universe of discourse. Third, these indeterminacies will be resolved by reference to contextual and other considerations which can be loosely described as 'pragmatic': they reflect the role that the representation will have in planning further conduct or carrying out further inquiries. Fourth, resolving such indeterminacy may involve judgement: there may be nothing in the speaker's mind when the original representation was produced which determines that one way of resolving them is correct; yet the judgements made can have a power of retroactive legislation. Now consider a case where judgement has not yet been exercised. Perhaps Peirce could allow that there is no fact of the matter about whether the assertion, belief, or hypothesis is true, even if the corresponding reality is wholly determinate. However, once again, even if there are many cases of this sort, there will be others in which no judgement of the sort described is required to determine a truth value for the proposition. There are lost facts where we do believe there is a determinate, but undiscoverable fact about what a rational careful inquirer would have concluded. Is Peirce committed to saying that even in these cases there is no truth? Since this seems implausible, these considerations cannot provide a wholly general solution to the problem of lost facts.

Moreover, if this kind of indeterminacy is indeed widespread, then we may begin to wonder what weight attaches to the claims about truth and convergence of opinion. There may be no fated convergence on how many leaves there are on the tree, whether someone has always been good at arithmetic, whether atoms are indivisible and so on. Is there a fated convergence upon anything? If not, then it is hard to see how the Peircean conception of truth has any serious normative role in evaluating our beliefs and methods of inquiry. If it is to retain a normative use, then we need to understand what 'the convergence of opinion' amounts to in cases where there is a role for judgement in assessing the bearing of new evidence upon the acceptability of a claim. Our understanding of what the convergence of opinion involves must, at the very least, be sensitive to the sorts of considerations that guide us in resolving semantic indeterminacies, interpreting *ceteris paribus* clauses, and deciding upon the universe of discourse to which a proposition is supposed to apply.

6. Truth, Assertion, and Styles of Philosophical Analysis

This section examines a distinctive feature of Peirce's theory of truth, one that enables us to see some continuities between his account and some more recent analyses of truth that have been described as 'pragmatist'. In the course of doing this, we shall see better why he may be right to be untroubled by the problem of lost facts. The discussion proceeds through two stages. First, as we have seen, Peirce's 'theory of truth' results from applying his pragmatist principle to the clarification of that concept; it tells us what truth 'consists in'. All philosophical analyses provide 'clarifications', but clarifications can take different forms and serve different purposes. Peirce's 'pragmatist' clarifications are distinctive, and they may not be assessable by the standards that are appropriate to more familiar styles of philosophical analysis. Second, once we are clear about what is distinctive in his conceptual clarifications, we shall be able to appreciate an oddity in some of the things he says about truth. His account is not of exactly the same kind as his clarifications of some other concepts. This will have a bearing upon the question of how Peirce's account of truth differs from a minimal or redundancy theory.

In 'How to Make our Ideas Clear', Peirce presented pragmatism as a rule for achieving a complete clarification of what is involved in *believing* a given proposition. Later discussions defend it as providing all the information we need in order to test an hypothesis scientifically and responsibly.[12] The pragmatist principle is defended as a *methodological rule*, and Peirce hopes to show, on the basis of his systematic theory of signs, that it is an adequate rule for its intended purpose. A pragmatist analysis of *hardness*, for example, would tell us what is involved in believing that something is hard, or provide the information we need in order to establish whether something is hard. If I believe or assert a proposition, I commit myself to the expectation that future experience will have a particular character. If this expectation is disappointed, than I will probably have to abandon the belief or withdraw the assertion. Clarification of a concept using the pragmatist principle provides an account of just what commitments I incur when I believe or assert a proposition in which the concept is ascribed to something.

The claim that the pragmatist principle is a methodological rule, which guides us in constructing clarifications that serve distinctive purposes, is important. It means that we would be wrong to describe the principle as capturing Peirce's 'theory of meaning'. If Peirce has a systematic theory of meaning, then this is to be found in his semiotic, in his account of reference and the understanding of thoughts and signs. The pragmatist principle, in that case, captures a methodological consequence of this theory of signs and meaning. Peirce would not deny that meanings are compositional, that the significance of a sentence is a function of its structure and of the semiotic properties of its parts. If pragmatism is a *methodological* principle, then he need not be committed to the view that pragmatic clarifications of particular concepts provide clauses in a recursive specification of the meanings of sentences. It need not itself provide a clarification of

---

[12] In 1903, this is expressed by saying that pragmatism is 'the whole logic of abduction' (*CP* 5.197).

what terms mean when unasserted, when used, for example, in the antecedents of conditional propositions or in contexts of propositional attitudes.

If this is correct, it places the problem of lost facts in a new light. If I am confident that a fact is lost, neither belief nor assertion of the associated proposition is a serious option: there is nothing that asserting it commits me to. I could only turn out to be wrong if the fact turned out not to be lost after all. If the pragmatist analysis of hardness only applies to cases where the hardness makes a difference to future experience, this need not show that it is flawed; it may still be an adequate account of what I commit myself to by asserting or claiming that some object is hard. An account which explained what the hardness of untestable objects consisted in could form part of an analysis that served different philosophical purposes; but the failure to provide such an account is no objection to Peirce's strategy for pragmatic clarification. Similarly, if the result of applying the pragmatist principle to the clarification of *truth* does not explain what the truth of verification-transcendent propositions consists in, this may reflect the goals of the analysis rather than its commitment to a distinctive metaphysical stance. If I am certain that evidence relevant to a proposition p will never be obtained, then believing or asserting that proposition involves no expectations or commitments in accordance with which it can be rationally assessed. Belief in a proposition known to be verification-transcendent is not a rational option. The proposition can have no role as a premise or possible conclusion of responsible inquiry. In that case, it is no loss that the pragmatist clarification assigns it no content that could be relevant to inquiring into it. At best (as Peirce saw in 1877) I can acknowledge kinds of evidence that *might* turn up and which would lead me to revise my previous confidence that the fact was lost. If this is correct, then pragmatist clarifications of concepts are attempts to explain what is involved in (or what commitments would result from) believing or asserting that the concept applies to something.

I am thus agreeing with Cheryl Misak when she denies that Peirce was committed to the claim that there are no lost facts or buried secrets. When I assert a proposition or accept it as true, then I am committed to thinking that it would be a matter on which a fated convergence of opinion would be secured. And when I inquire into a proposition, then I am committed to the hope, to the regulative presumption, that a destined agreement is available (Misak, 1991: 137 ff). But, once we take account of the distinctive character of pragmatist clarifications, there is no need to see Peirce as committed to the stronger claim that all truths are discoverable.

We can now move on to the second stage, the attempt to draw out an odd feature of Peirce's elucidation of *truth*. Like other philosophers of thought and language, Peirce distinguished the force of an utterance from its propositional content. A proposition can be 'affirmed, denied, judged, doubted, inwardly inquired into, put as a question, wished . . .' *Assertion* of a proposition involves 'the deliberate exercise, in uttering a proposition, of a force tending to determine a belief in it in the mind of the interpreter' (*NEM*4: 248–9).[13] Assertion involves 'taking responsibility' for the truth of the proposition (*CP* 2.315). Now, when Peirce tried to analyse a concept like 'hardness', he was concerned with a possible constituent of the propositional content of an assertion: I can assert, deny, etc. that a particular object is hard. Moreover, there are many beliefs and assertions in which the concept of hardness has no role. The case with truth is different: every assertion that we make involves a commitment to the *truth* of the asserted proposition. This is reflected in the common insistence that to assert something is to assert that it is true, to believe something is to believe that it is true. Hence, we manifest our mastery of the concept of *truth* when we make assertions or hold beliefs, even if that concept is not a constituent of the proposition asserted.

This 'internal' connection between belief and assertion, on the one hand, and truth, on the other, means that there are two different routes we could take to an understanding of the cognitive role of the concept of truth. One strategy would focus on occurrences of the concept of truth or the word 'true' in propositions and their expression: what commitments do I incur when I assert a proposition of the form '*p* is true'? Just as my concept of hardness is manifested in the assertions I make about which things are, or are not, hard, so my concept of truth is manifested in my assertions about which propositions are *true*. If this is the route to take, then we are likely to conclude that the concept of truth has no substantive cognitive role. It is hard to see how the assertion that diamonds are hard has a different content from the assertion that it is true that diamonds are hard. This may lead naturally to a minimal or redundancy theory of truth: we could eliminate occurrences of 'true' from our assertions without loss of content.[14]

---

[13]   Peirce's theory of assertion is discussed in more detail in Hookway (1985: 128ff).

[14]   Of course there are technical difficulties in achieving such an elimination. For example, I may want to endorse propositions whose content I cannot specify. Although I cannot tell you all Peirce's claims about Boolean algebra, I may confidently assert that everything Peirce believes about Boolean algebra is true. Even if such occurrences of 'true' are ineliminable, the resulting concept is not substantive or philosophically interesting.

Since to assert a proposition is to put it forward as true (to commit oneself to its truth), I can also express my commitment to its truth without *using* the concept of truth. I commit myself to its being true that diamonds are hard simply by asserting that diamonds are hard. The second route to an understanding of our concept of truth insists that the content of this concept is most directly manifested in our practice of making and evaluating assertions. Once we have explained what commitments we incur through asserting something (or though believing or judging it) we have clarified the concept. We clarify *truth* through explaining, in general terms, the commitments we acquire through asserting or believing something. In that case, an analysis of *truth* need not proceed through an explanation of the use of the word 'true' or of the content of propositions which contain the concept of truth as a constituent. It is easy to see that adopting this second strategy might lead to a richer analysis of truth, one that described substantive commitments involved in assertion. Moreover, the availability of these two different strategies is a special feature of the clarification of *truth*. If our goal is to clarify *hardness* or *force*, we have no alternative but to adopt the first strategy, to describe the use of these words and concepts in propositions. We now see that the most illuminating strategy in elucidating the concept of truth may be to adopt the second strategy, to provide an account of assertoric force rather than an explanation of the use of the word or concept.[15]

We are now in a position to see how Peirce's account of truth is closer than it initially seems to some contemporary ideas about what is distinctive in 'pragmatist' accounts of concepts. In describing 'classical pragmatist' approaches to truth, Robert Brandom identifies a 'performative, anti-descriptive strategy, emphasizing the act of calling something true rather than the descriptive content one thereby associates with what is called true' (1994: 287).[16] This fits a more general 'pragmatist' pattern of analysis, associated with Brandom, Huw Price and others, who offer 'expressivist' analyses of (for example) modal concepts, some ethical concepts and the concept of truth. Describing something as true involves taking up a 'normative stance or attitude towards' it: it is to endorse it and

---

[15] If this is correct, then it would be possible to accept a minimalist or disquotationalist account of our use of the word 'true', while denying that this provided a full philosophical account of truth.

[16] It is striking that Brandom slides from discussing the commitments incurred by 'calling' something true to discussing those I incur by 'taking' something to be true. I can 'take' something to be true without 'calling' it true: all I need do is assert, judge, or believe it.

to incur various normatively grounded *commitments* to it.[17] For example: we commit ourselves to the expectation that future experiment and experience will not require us to withdraw the claim. Peirce's account of truth conforms to this mark of pragmatism: taking something to be true commits me to expecting a long-run fated convergence in opinion.

Although Peirce does not make explicit that this is the character of his account of truth, I suggest that it makes best sense of his views to claim that it is what he is doing.[18] However, this claim must receive one important qualification. 'Assertoric stances' may be of different kinds, and the claim that truth is the 'aim' of judgement or assertion is importantly unclear. We have already encountered evidence that the mature Peirce did not accept that to believe something (or to assert it) is to believe (assert) that it is (absolutely) true; he appears to believe that a responsible inquirer can 'successfully' assert propositions that she thinks are almost certainly not (strictly) true. Recall the passages in the entry on truth for Baldwin's *Dictionary of Philosophy*, in which Peirce wrote of the ascription of truth to a proposition: 'It essentially depends upon that proposition's not professing to be exactly true.' He continued that a proposition may possess the property of truth only 'by virtue of the confession of its inaccuracy and one-sidedness, and this confession is an essential ingredient of truth' (*CP* 5.565).[19] The suggestion seems to be that when an assertion is made by someone who carries out inquiries in the scientific spirit, this does not involve a firm commitment to the *truth* of the proposition. It involves quite a complex propositional attitude, one that uses the concept of truth to articulate an ideal to which the asserted proposition does not fully

[17] This is relevant to Blackburn's identification of the 'conjuring trick' that lures us into accepting a redundancy theory. Truth is '*internal* to judgement in the sense that to make or accept a judgement is to have it as an aim'; 'truth counts as success in judgement' (Blackburn, 1984: 231; cf. Dummett, 1959). It follows from this that believing that *p* is the same as believing that *p is true*: 'Since truth counts as success in judgement, making a judgement and describing it as true are evidently equivalent' (ibid.). But, as Blackburn recognizes, this is compatible with our having a substantive account of what success in judgement is.

[18] Given that his philosophy of language draws a sharp distinction between assertoric force and propositional content, it is surprising that he did not have this point more clearly in focus. It might help to explain why he said relatively little about *truth*. Peirce's account of assertion is examined in more detail in Chapter 5.

[19] The break between assertion and truth may be stronger than this. In Chapter 1 there is some discussion of passages in which Peirce denies that it is proper to *believe* current scientific results, without denying that there can be an intelligible and invaluable practice of making scientific assertions with them. If that is correct, there may be practices of responsible assertion which do not commit the speaker to the truth of her assertion: she is committed only to the proposition being assertible at the current stage of scientific inquiry.

measure up. In that case, asserting a proposition commits me to its 'approximate truth', not to its exact truth. If that is correct, a difference opens up between *asserting that p* and *asserting that it is true that p*. Peirce might argue that if I claim that a proposition *is true*, I go beyond this commitment to approximate correctness: using Wright's terminology, perhaps I think that it is superassertible, not just assertible. The concept of truth would still have a role in signalling that one's commitments extend beyond the 'approximate truth' of the proposition; one is committing oneself to the proposition being defensible in the long run. True propositions are 'indefeasible' (*CP* 6.485).

7. Summary

I have attempted to explain Peirce's account of *truth* in terms of a fated or destined convergence in the opinions of inquirers, arguing that it is less evidently unsatisfactory than is commonly supposed. Much depends upon whether he can come up with a satisfactory account of how well conducted inquiry is expected to lead to the truth. This topic is not discussed in detail here. We have also seen the role of Peirce's realism about laws in dealing with some of the problems faced by his theory of truth during the 1870s. This topic, which is related to the development of his metaphysical ideas during the following decade, is discussed more fully in Chapters 4, 6, and 7. Two other topics have been introduced in order to explain why Peirce was not disturbed by the problem of lost facts, and the remainder of this chapter will examine them in more detail.

One of these topics was discussed in the last section. We can clarify the concept of truth in two ways: by examining the uses of the word 'true' and by studying the commitments we undertake when we *assert* a proposition. We have already noted some of the complexities in Peirce's understanding of assertion. In the second part of this chapter we shall look at these more closely in order to examine the normative role of the idea of convergence that Peirce presents. This will enable us to understand why some other pragmatists took this idea much less seriously than he did and thus begin to see what is distinctive about his particular version of pragmatism. Then we consider the relations between Peirce's account of truth and metaphysical issues about the nature of reality. I shall suggest that although Peirce defended quite an extreme form of realism, his account of truth was metaphysically neutral.

TRUTH AND ASSERTION: THE NORMATIVE ROLE OF CONVERGENCE

8. Truth and Assertion

I have argued above that the concept of truth can be elucidated in two ways: by reference to the use of the word 'true' and by examining the network of commitments we incur when we *assert* a proposition. The discussion relied upon the observation that to assert a proposition is to commit oneself to its truth and suggested, on this basis, that the most illuminating account of truth is likely to come from adopting the second of the two strategies. In that case, the correctness of the Peircean account of truth would depend upon whether, when we assert a proposition, we commit ourselves to its being the object of a fated convergence of opinion. If this is so, then the normative force of ideas about convergence is evident: it follows immediately from the body of commitments that we acquire from the practice of assertion.

We have already seen one reason to question Peirce's adherence to the claim that to assert something is to commit oneself to its truth. This is the passage from Baldwin's *Dictionary*: Truth is a property of propositions which 'essentially depends upon that proposition's not professing to be exactly true' (*CP* 5.565). A statement or assertion of a proposition involves 'a confession of its inaccuracy and one-sidedness'. This passage seems, at first sight, to claim, paradoxically, that a proposition's *being true* is a matter of its not being *exactly* true. If 'exact truth' makes sense, as its surely does, then it is hard to see how this can be part of an explanation of *what truth is*. However it may be more plausible if taken as an account of the commitments one incurs when uttering a proposition assertively: we are committing ourselves to the claim that some suitably revised and adjusted version of this proposition would ultimately be accepted by anyone who investigated the matter long enough and well enough.

Other passages also suggest a view an account of 'scientific assertion' which does not involve putting a proposition forward as actually *true*. In a lecture of 1898, Peirce described current scientific results as 'not matters for belief' but rather as 'established truths', by which is meant 'propositions which the economy of endeavour prescribes that, for the time being, further inquiry shall cease' (*CP* 5.589). Elsewhere (*CP* 1.635 and cf. 5.60), such established truths are described as opinions 'from which no competent man now demurs'. This suggests a weaker notion of scientific assertion than the passage from the *Dictionary* entry: practical ('economic') considerations may make it rational to assert a proposition even if we think it likely that further inquiry will not even recognize it as approximately true. Asserting it now may be merely an effective means for stimulating further progress. It is in line with this that Peirce sometimes says that the word 'belief' 'is out of place in the vocabulary of science', and often emphasizes that all scientific acceptance is 'provisional'.

We initially hoped that we would find evidence for the claim that truth can be explained in terms of a fated convergence of opinion in the fact that when we assert propositions we are committed to their being the objects of such a long-run consensus. We now find that Peirce rejects this view: scientific assertion carries no such commitment. However, this does not immediately refute the convergence thesis: the latter idea can have an essential normative or regulative role in governing those very assertions which commit themselves to less than the truth of the proposition asserted. I shall now argue that that is how we should understand Peirce's view (cf. Misak 1991: 40).

The underlying idea is quite simple. Suppose we grant that the goal of scientific activity is to arrive at law formulations which are as near as possible to being exactly true, to being formulations whose adequacy would be acknowledged by anyone who considered the matter for long enough and well enough. A law formulation, or, indeed, any proposition which has this property, will be described as being T^*. One view that might be ascribed to Peirce is that when we assert a proposition, we commit ourselves to its being T^*. Peirce's theory of truth spells out what we are committed to when we assert a proposition. The passages we have just considered indicate that this is not Peirce's account of assertion. However, even on the views suggested by these passages, we cannot understand what commitments are incurred through asserting some proposition without taking account of the fact that the assertion forms part of a practice of inquiry whose goal is to get as close as possible to propositions that are T^*.

- The asserted proposition is presented as approximately T^*, and revision and reformulation of the proposition can lead to a more precise version which is T^*.
- Asserting such a proposition at this time forms part of a practice of co-operative inquiry which will eventually lead us to propositions that are T^*.

In either case, it is only by virtue of possessing the concept expressed by T^*, that we can understand the commitments that are incurred through making serious assertions. We must appeal to this concept in explaining how assertions are evaluated and revised.

A good way to understand this point is to compare Peirce's views with those of James and Dewey. Each of the latter endorsed the connection between some concept of truth and the idea of convergence. Yet neither believed that this idea of convergence had an important regulative or normative role in our reflections upon our beliefs. After briefly surveying some of their comments on convergence, we shall see how their distinctive views about the nature of scientific inquiry help to explain their disagreements with Peirce.

9. James and Dewey

In 'Abstractionismus and "Relativismus"', reprinted in *The Meaning of Truth*, James discussed truth 'in the pragmatic sense, of an ideal opinion in which all men might agree, and which no man should ever wish to change' (1909: 142). Two years earlier, in *Pragmatism*, he had written:

On the one hand there will stand reality, on the other an account of it which it proves impossible to better or alter. If the impossibility prove permanent, the truth of the account will be absolute. *Other content of truth than this, I can find nowhere.* (1907: 120)

In the same book he wrote of the 'absolutely true', by which he meant 'what no further experience will ever alter, in that ideal vanishing point towards which we imagine that all our temporary truths will some day converge' (1907: 106).[20]

As James acknowledged, the 'absolutely true' is a 'regulative notion', the idea of 'a better truth to be established later ... and with powers of retroactive legislation' (1907: 107). This suggests that it can have a role in responsible reflection upon our current opinions; it reminds us that we may be forced to abandon them in the light of further information. However, the passage from *Pragmatism* makes a telling qualification:

---

[20] Note the qualification to James's identification of truth with what it is expedient to believe: 'expedient *in the long run and on the whole*, of course' (italics added).

'Meanwhile, we have to live today by what truth we can get today, and be ready tomorrow to call it falsehood.'

In Dewey's *Logic: The Theory of Inquiry*, there is only one discussion of *truth*: a footnote attached to the claim that 'In scientific inquiry, every conclusion reached, whether of fact or conception, is held subject to determination by its fate in further inquiries'. The footnote cites 'the best definition of *truth*' known to Dewey: Peirce's account from 'How to Make our Ideas Clear'. This is accompanied by a quotation of the definition in Baldwin's *Dictionary* which is described as 'more complete (and more suggestive)' (1938: 345 and fn.). As with James, the point of linking truth and long-run convergence is to encourage us to moderate or qualify our attitudes towards current (scientific) views: it is always possible (and frequently likely) that further inquiries will exercise their powers of 'retroactive legislation' and thus require us to abandon our current conclusions. All beliefs (especially scientific ones) are provisional and fallible. So far there is little disagreement between the three pragmatists. Even James's qualification would be acceptable to Peirce: he would agree that we cannot look on our current views as the absolute truth. Moreover, he denied that we should rely on the results of scientific investigations in connection with vital matters; we should live today by something other than beliefs which are ordered and regulated by reflections governed by thoughts of long-run convergence.[21]

Let us review the current state of play. The three pragmatists seem to agree that:

1. Truth (or 'absolute truth') can be defined in terms of a long-run convergence in the opinions of responsible inquirers.
2. Current opinions are revisable, and are answerable to subsequent experience and to the beliefs and responses of other people. Subsequent inquiry can have powers of retroactive legislation.
3. The Peircean conception of truth provides a way of capturing this idea that a belief is 'held subject to determination by its fate in further inquiries'.
4. When we assert a proposition, we do not necessarily fully commit ourselves to its truth (or its 'absolute truth').

They differ over their responses to a further claim:

---

[21] See Chapter 1.

5. Our reflections about how we ought to test our opinions and carry out our inquiries should make use of this concept of truth. The concept of truth as convergence has an indispensable normative role.

How are we to understand and resolve this difference?

10. Belief, Assertion, and the Demands of Objectivity

Although Peirce thought that the concept of truth as convergence ('absolute truth') was of major importance for our evaluations and revisions of our beliefs, both Dewey and James thought that its role was relatively limited. And even in Peirce's case, as we shall see, its role in scientific discourse was far more important than its role in dealing with everyday matters. We should bear in mind that using this concept in regulating our beliefs and inquiries requires sensitivity to a range of competing opinions which extends along two different dimensions: I should be sensitive to the judgements of 'anyone who investigates the matter in hand'; and I should be sensitive to judgements that would be made as inquiry extends into the remote and indefinite future. My judgements are not just answerable to those who belong to my community or to those who live at the present time; I am addressing an unlimited community of inquirers.

The pragmatists emphasized that one element in the progress of inquiry, in the growth of knowledge, was the development and clarification of hypotheses: in the course of collecting and weighing the evidence for or against our hypotheses, we are making adjustments in our concepts, making judgements about the interpretation of *ceteris paribus* clauses, and so on. Although the standards that guide these changes can be thought of as logical or cognitive, they are not truth-relevant. When I think about whether to include the diseased brown specimen in my count of the leaves, I am not trying to work out whether including that leaf will lead to a *false* answer to my question. I am guided by what are often called 'pragmatic considerations', wondering which kind of refinement in my understanding of the question will lead to an answer which is best suited to my further goals and purposes. Other reflections will be truth-relevant: I may, for example, consider strategies for counting that reduce the chances of double counting or missing one branch completely.

Consider a different example. Imagine someone in the fourteenth century who assertively utters the sentence 'All swans are white'. The content of the assertion is, in many ways, indeterminate: he has not fully specified a universe of discourse, since there has been no need to do so; he may not even have determined what he should do if it turned out that young swans were not snowy white. Now let us suppose he hears that explorers have encountered black swans. It seems clear that he has a choice: he can admit that he was wrong, or he can decide that he was only concerned with swans in his own vicinity. Which choice he makes may not be determined by the content of his original assertion, and he may never have considered what he should do if this situation arose. His goals will be a determining factor. If he is a proto-scientist seeking fundamental laws of bird life, he may be more ready to admit error than if he is simply teaching his children about local fauna. We may be reminded here of a phrase of James's. One strategy 'preserves the truth' that we now possess; the other sacrifices this for the sake of something much better. Moreover, on the pragmatist view, there is no need to assume that the *content* of the assertion, the meaning of the proposition expressed, determines that we should take one route rather than the other. Refinement and clarification of different kinds are available, and a sensitivity to a range of possible cognitive goals can explain how, in different circumstances, we might make different decisions.

Suppose that the assertion is defended by limiting its universe of discourse: we are concerned with swans that live *around here*, and *at the present time*, maybe even excluding domesticated examples in zoos. The concept of 'absolute truth' *may* still have application, but it is normatively irrelevant. If my judgement is true, then any rational agent who understood the content of my claim, was aware of my cognitive needs, and was fully informed about the contextual and other matters that influence my judgement and about the results of observations that I have not actually made, would acknowledge either that I should have made the judgement that I did or that it was cognitively permissible for me to make that judgement. But it is hard to see why the verdict of such agents has any authority over my own judgements. Indeed, we would expect such remote beings to defer to me as a more reliable source of information over these matters. Their opinions could challenge mine only if they dealt with swans in my vicinity while I am alive, and their authority about that would be very limited. If they disapproved of judgements which I take to be sound, I will be not be wrong to question their understanding of the needs and interests that have shaped my judgements. This fits the view of James and Dewey: there is a conceptual connection between the concept of truth and a fated convergence of opinion among an unlimited community of competent inquirers; but reflection on the judgements that would be made

by members of such a community rarely has a role in my critical reflections upon my own views. I need to take account of the information available to, and the judgements made by, those who occupy the same cognitive
niche as myself.

So is there any reflection in which the concept of truth as a fated convergence of opinion *does* have a role? Peirce thinks that there is: reflection
which is internal to scientific research. Given the preceding discussion, this
requires that scientific work seeks laws or generalizations which do not
merely serve the practical interests of a limited group but which possess a
sort of universal applicability. What does Peirce say about the character of
scientific inquiries? He distances himself from the view that 'science is
systematized knowledge', and rejects the idea that science is distinguished
from other bodies of knowledge by its subject-matter. Instead, he insists:

Science is to mean for us a mode of life whose single animating purpose is to find
out the real truth, which pursues this purpose by a well considered method,
founded on thorough acquaintance with such scientific results already ascertained
by others as may be available, and which seeks co-operation in the hope that the
truth may be found, if not by any actual inquirers, yet ultimately by those who
come after them and who shall make use of their results. (*CP* 7.54)

By emphasizing that science is an *activity* (indeed, a 'mode of life', an activity that has importance for its practitioners' sense of who they are) Peirce
distinguishes scientific inquiry from other kinds of inquiries by pointing
to the goals and ambitions which influence how judgement is exercised in
testing opinions. The idea that science is an inquiry carried out in a
distinctive *spirit* recurs on many occasions. Elsewhere, he claims that one
component of this spirit is an 'unwearied interest in testing general propositions' (*CP* 1.34). Not content to save a useful generalization by restrict-
ing its intended universe of discourse, counterexamples are welcomed as
clues to more complex generalizations; the encounter of black swans elsewhere simply prompts an investigation into why there should be this
colour variation.

This activity is reflective, and it should not be influenced by our current
practical needs or concerns.[22] It is co-operative, and anyone imbued with
this scientific spirit can be viewed as a potential collaborator. If this is
indeed the 'spirit' in which we carry out our inquiries, reflection about
what other potential inquirers possessed of the same spirit would make of

---

[22] See Chapter 1.

our results will be of fundamental importance. We seek the broadest generalizations, to understand their limits and to explain them, so the Peircean conception of truth has a genuine normative role. We are alert to the possibility that our opinions may need to be replaced by *better* ones. The evaluation expressed by 'better' relates to an activity which involves a search for laws and generalizations which would be acceptable to any inquirer and which are not limited in their application to a specific context. If that is our goal, then our reflections on how to improve our opinions may reasonably make use of a concept which possesses the marks of Peircean truth.

However, there may be other ways to make sense of this 'better'. Suppose that we hold to a body of scientific theories. Perhaps they are accepted because they make good sense of puzzling phenomena or offer considerable technological benefits. It may be reasonable to expect that further use of these theories will present us with problems: phenomena will occur that they cannot explain; some of their predictions may fail; logical incoherence may emerge. When this occurs, we hope we can revise the theories, replacing them by others which serve these purposes rather better than the original. A theory that solves all our current problems may need to be revised to meet problems that arise in the future. Understanding the future improvement in our understanding in this way does not require appeal to the idea of a body of theory that would pass all tests, whose correctness could be acknowledged by all inquirers in all contexts. If Dewey and James had different ideas about the goals that direct scientific activity, then we could understand why they did not think that we were required to appeal to Peircean truth in order to describe our attitudes towards our current theories or reflect upon how to continue our inquiries into them.

The views of science that we find in the work of James is very different from Peirce's. For example, James wrote:

Scientific logicians are saying on every hand that these entities and their determinations, however definitely conceived, should not be held for literally real. It is *as if* they existed; but in reality they are like co-ordinates of logarithms, only artificial short cuts for taking us from one part to another of experience's flux. We can cipher fruitfully with them; they serve us wonderfully; but we must not be their dupes. (1907: 92)

Theories are valuable instruments, and their value lies in their uses. Comparing common-sense and scientific views of the world, he concludes:

There is no ringing conclusion possible when we compare these types of thinking, with a view to telling which is the more absolutely true. Their naturalness, their intellectual economy, their fruitfulness for practice, all start up as distinct tests of their veracity, and as a result we get confused. Common sense is *better* for one sphere of life, science for another, philosophic criticism for a third; but whether either be true absolutely, Heaven only knows ... They are all ways of talking on our part, to be compared solely from the point of view of their *use*. (1907: 93)

There is a clear admission here that the uses to which scientific opinions are put will provide a basis for assessments of better and worse which makes no reference or appeal to the idea of absolute truth.[23]

TRUTH AND REALITY

11. Logic and Metaphysics

The papers of 1877–8 introduce discussions of truth and convergence at two different stages. The first in the series, 'The Fixation of Belief', defends the *method of science*, which is identified by reference to its 'fundamental hypothesis':

There are real things, whose characters are entirely independent of our opinions about them; those realities affect our senses according to regular laws, and, though our sensations are as different as our relations to the objects, yet, by taking advantage of the laws of perception, we can ascertain by reasoning how things really are, and any man, if he have sufficient experience and reason enough about it, will be led to the one true conclusion. (W3: 254)

The first part defends a realist conception of scientific knowledge; and the remainder asserts that scientific inquiry will take us to the truth about these 'real things'. The passage is not presented as an analysis of either *real* or *true*, as is evident from the fact that it *uses* these concepts in presenting its claims. The pragmatist principle is adopted as a tool for clarifying ideas to be employed as part of the scientific method; and among its first applications is the explanation of these key concepts. At this point, the claims about convergence are transformed from an assertion about scientific inquiry into a clarification of what we mean by 'true'.

---

[23] Dewey's position is more complex than James's. I have compared his view of science with Peirce's elsewhere: see Hookway (2000).

In 'How to Make Ideas Clear' Peirce presents his pragmatic clarification of 'true' and 'real': The opinion which is fated to be ultimately agreed to by all who investigate, is what we mean by the truth, and the object represented in that opinion is the real, (*CP* 5.407, W3: 273). He also offers a verbal definition of 'real': The real is 'that whose characters are independent of what anyone may think them to be' (W3: 271). Since this verbal definition of 'real' appears to be realist in character, and since he regards 'true' and 'real' as correlative notions, this seems to suggest that the realism that we find in the fundamental hypothesis is also entailed by the pragmatist account of truth. However, as I argue in Chapter 4, at this time he had difficulty providing a defence of realism that was sufficiently robust. The view of reality contained in these definitions seems weaker than the view expressed in the fundamental hypothesis. Indeed we might expect to find a convergence of opinions onto a 'true' propositions in cases where we are not attempting to describe a wholly independent reality.

When he wrote the definition of 'Truth, Falsity and Error' for Baldwin's *Dictionary* (1901), Peirce emphasized the importance of distinguishing truth from reality: an analysis of truth leaves metaphysical questions about the nature of reality open.[24] While truth is 'that concordance of an abstract statement with the ideal limit towards which endless investigation would tend to bring scientific belief', reality is 'that mode of being by virtue of which the real things is as it is, irrespectively of what any mind or any definite collection of minds may represent it to be' (*CP* 5.565). The definition of truth just offered does not itself explain how or why convergence upon the truth will occur. Use of the concept of truth may commit us to believing that some explanation of this is possible, but it does not prescribe what form that explanation should take. Peirce considers the proposition that Caesar crossed the Rubicon. Its truth 'consists in the fact that the further we push our archaeological and other studies, the more strongly will that conclusion force itself on our minds forever'. An idealist metaphysician may hold that the corresponding reality consists in—or is constituted by—the fact that the inquiry is fated to take this path. Where opinion will not converge, reality would be indeterminate. But we might also explain convergence by showing how experimental interaction

---

[24] The verificationist character of Peirce's pragmatism, together with his proud claim that it will put an end to 'ontological metaphysics', may lead the reader to conclude that his identifying a problem as 'metaphysical' is a prelude to dismissing it. His objections were to a priori ('deductive') metaphysics; from the mid-1880s, the search for a system of 'scientific metaphysics' was central to his philosophy. See Chapter 7.

with an independently existing reality will suffice to ensure that reality makes itself manifest to us. Indeed, from the 1880s, Peirce was insisting that experience provides direct contact with external things, which become the referents of demonstrative or indexical expressions, and whose characteristics are further investigated by exploiting our physical or 'dynamical' relations to them.[25]

We can also note Peirce's insistence that there may be truth where there is no reality. He considers several examples. Suppose a moralist describes an ideal of a *summum bonum*, and suppose that 'the development of man's moral nature will only lead to a firmer satisfaction with the described ideal'. It may be a consequence of this that, with time, anyone who thinks about the matter long enough and carefully enough will be led to share this view of the good (*CP* 5.566). With one qualification (to be noted below), this appears to be enough to render propositions about the good and bad *true*. There may be a fated consensus on the acceptability of such claims. But what, then, is the *reality* which such propositions deal with? The metaphysical account we provide of the 'mode of being' of such states of affairs may insist that they are not 'mind-independent': their truth is in part a function of our sentimental dispositions and moral nature. We need not conclude that there is no reality corresponding to such truths; but we may decide that they do not share the 'realist' mind-independent character which scientific entities and properties possess. Different kinds of explanations of the metaphysical bases of different kinds of truth may be called for. In similar vein, although it is uncontroversial that many statements of mathematics are true, the supposition that mathematics deals only in hypothetical structures leaves room for it to be controversial whether a realist understanding of the subject-matter of mathematics is defensible (*CP* 5.567). Peirce himself was a realist about empirical science, but his view of the objectivity of mathematical discourse and some ethical discourse assigns them a rather different metaphysical status.[26]

The 'slight qualification' concerns the reference to 'scientific belief' in the quotation from Baldwin's *Dictionary*. We might suppose that Peirce is offering a limited definition, one that characterizes 'scientific truth' rather than simple 'truth'. His remarks about ethical propositions indicate that this is not correct. Rather, he appears to believe that the 'method of

---

[25] There is a more detailed discussion of the route from pragmatism to this set of views in Chapter 4.

[26] These themes are discussed at length in Hookway (1985).

science', broadly understood, is applicable to all respectable subject-matters. If we suppose that different methods of inquiry may be appropriate in connection with different subject-matters, we do better to say simply that the truth is a fated convergence among well-conducted inquiries, while allowing that what makes an inquiry *good* may vary in systematic ways from case to case.

If this interpretation of Peirce's mature position is correct, then it follows that his account of truth is metaphysically neutral. It can be held in conjunction with a realist or an anti-realist metaphysics. The most plausible view may be that some truths can be understood in a 'realist' manner, as dealing with a mind-independent reality, while others deal with matters whose character bears more marks of our interests, sentiments or constructive activities. What, then, are the indications that a philosopher treats a subject-matter in a more 'realist' manner? We can cast useful light upon Peirce's views by taking note of some of the marks of realism discussed by Crispin Wright in *Truth and Objectivity*.

Peirce's theory of truth links the normative function of the concept to the fact that in forming a belief or making an assertion we are aware of the possibility that a subsequent 'better' opinion may force us to reconsider our current view. Although most of Peirce's examples concern the growth of scientific knowledge, there is no reason why subsequent opinions may not possess powers of 'retroactive legislation' in other areas too: for example, in mathematics, ethics and aesthetics and in dealing with the practical concerns of life. If that possibility is admitted, we have to acknowledge that our account of what makes a later opinion better than an earlier one—or our explanation of how convergence in opinion is to be achieved—may not be the same for all cases. The marks of scientific truth need not be the same as the marks of other kinds of truth. For example, the objects of scientific truths may possess a kind or degree of mind-independence which is not found in those of ethical or even mathematical ones. This will become important when we turn to Peirce's reasons for thinking that his account of truth is neutral between realism and idealism. At the present stage, we shall merely use some concepts from Wright's discussions of objectivity to describe what Peirce takes to be some of the marks of scientific truth.

According to Wright, an area of discourse displays 'cognitive command' when disagreement must be explained by reference to a 'cognitive shortcoming' of at least one of the people involved. Perhaps one lacks evidence that others possess; perhaps one has been careless in evaluating evidence or carrying out inferences; perhaps one is the victim of prejudice or some other cognitive 'malfunction'.[27] One reason for thinking that judgements about whether mushrooms taste pleasant, or whether a particular joke is funny, are less than fully objective is that they do not meet this condition. Differences in food preferences, or differences in sense of humour, need not be viewed as always involving cognitive failings. The texts we have considered so far suggest that Peirce believes that scientific discourse displays cognitive command, and this is supported by his observation that 'all the followers of science are fully persuaded that the process of investigation [i.e. properly conducted scientific inquiries], if only pushed far enough, will give one certain solution to every question to which they can be applied' (W3: 273). Differences of opinion will disappear so long as we do not lack relevant information, and so long as we process this information in the right way. This adds to Wright's characterization only the (over?) optimistic assurance that we need only persevere in order to overcome all cognitive shortcomings.[28]

An important difference between science and mathematics emerges immediately. Cognitive shortcomings, obstacles to our reaching the truth in science, are of two kinds. Some are subjective or internal to the inquirer: we may be careless, inattentive, or simply lacking in imagination or understanding. But others are objective: through no fault of our own we can lack relevant evidence or information. There is always the possibility that the future will provide unanticipated new evidence that causes us to revise our views. The structure of Peirce's map of human knowledge ensures that the only sources of error in mathematics are of the first 'subjective' kind: having constructed and understood a proof or calculation, we need not fear that it will be undermined by 'further evidence'. Indeed, Peirce suggests that although normative reflection using the concept of truth has an ineliminable role in empirical science, it can be dispensed with in mathematics.[29] And this is because we do not need to bear constantly in mind the possibility that what currently *seems* to be true to reasonable inquirers may subsequently, in the light of further evidence, turn out to be mistaken. In mathematics, we do not risk discovering that our evidence is misleading because it is unrepresentative.

Some take it as a mark of a belief having a mind-independent subject-matter that we must appeal to the object of the belief in order to explain

[27] A more careful definition is provided in Wright (1992: 92–3).

[28] Some of these remarks will be qualified below. Peirce observes that convergence on the truth could be held up by failures of *imagination*. Whether Wright would describe these as 'cognitive shortcomings' is not fully clear.

[29] Peirce's philosophy of mathematics is discussed in detail in Hookway (1985: ch. 6).

the fact that someone holds it. I believe that the ash tree in the garden is losing its leaves because those falling leaves cause me to have distinctive experiences; if the leaves were not falling, then I would not believe that they were. We saw above that Peirce thought that the convergence of opinion secured through the method of science has this character: there are real things existing independently of us; they interact with our senses in systematic ways; and by exploiting the laws of perception we can discover the real mind-independent properties that those things have. The method of science secures convergence of opinion by seeking the best explanations of our experiences. In discussing the role of explanatory dependencies as a mark of realism, Wright plausibly claims that a fundamental notion is what he calls 'width of cosmological role': this is a measure of the range of things which a state of affairs can explain *in addition to* the attitudinal states we might hold towards it (1992: 196). To illustrate this point, he suggests that the idea that the wetness of rocks is mind-independent is strengthened when we realize that as well as explaining my belief that the rocks are wet, it also explains my slipping and falling when I step on the rocks, the abundance of lichen growing on them, and so on (p. 197).

When defending realism about scientific discourse, and illustrating his theory of truth, Peirce is always anxious to emphasize that the fated convergence of opinion will occur among investigators who have observed a wide range of different phenomena:

One man may investigate the velocity of light by studying the transits of Venus and the aberrations of the stars; another by the oppositions of Mars and the eclipses of Jupiter's satellites; a third by the method of Fizeau; a fourth by that of Foucault; a fifth by the motions of the curves of Lissajous; a sixth, a seventh, an eighth, and a ninth, may follow the different methods of comparing the different measures of statical and dynamical electricity. They may at first have different results, but, as each perfects his method and his processes, the results will move steadily towards a destined center. So with all scientific research. (W3: 273)

Unless the subject-matter of scientific discourse possessed a relatively wide cosmological role, there is no reason to expect that investigation will lead to a convergence upon the truth. Indeed, when we test an hypothesis scientifically, our first task is to clarify its content, reflecting upon the range of experimental phenomena that it would explain.[30] Scientific progress depends upon our confidence that once some of these experimental tests

---

[30] This is the 'abductive' phase of scientific inquiry, an important prerequisite for subsequent inductive testing.

have been passed, we can provisionally accept it: we must hope that anyone else who tested the hypothesis by focusing on other putative explananda would come to a similar verdict.[31]

The account of truth as convergence requires that inquiry be disciplined and constrained; there should be an explanation of how effective inquiry will ensure that there will be a fated convergence upon the truth. Such explanations are likely to have metaphysical consequences: they will say something about the 'modes of being' of the realities which true opinions describe. We have just noticed some themes that will enter into the explanation of the convergence of scientific belief, themes that support Peirce's realism. However, these claims about cognitive command and width of explanatory role do not form part of the account of truth. Instead they are part of the explanation of convergence that is offered for a specific class of truths—those of empirical science. As we have seen, Peirce's theory allows him to offer different explanations of how convergence occurs for inquiries with different kinds of subject-matter (compare the discussion of pluralism in Misak 1998). The account of truth does not require a uniform account of the metaphysical character of all truths. Indeed, it is compatible with being a realist about some truths and an anti-realist about others. The account of truth is metaphysically neutral, but, with respect to any subject-matter or field of inquiry, it gives rise to metaphysical questions about the mode of being of the objects of study.

12. Conclusion

The main conclusion of this chapter is that it is possible to hold a position that combines the following claims.

1. If we seek an account of the role of the word 'true' in discourse, a minimalist or redundancy theory of some kind is adequate.
2. Any evidence that a proposition would not be the object of a stable long-run consensus among competent inquirers should be taken as evidence that the proposition is not true.

---

[31] Once again, the objects and structures of mathematics are less robustly real than those of empirical science. They have no causal impact upon us and do not behave in accordance with nomological laws: although, of course, we do stand in nomological relations to instances of mathematical structures. Hence their explanatory role is far more limited. But it is compatible with this that there will be a fated convergence of opinion among those who understand a proof upon whether it establishes its conclusion: there *is* mathematical truth even if reflection upon mathematical practice which uses that concept has little importance.

3. If we seek to elucidate the normative commitments that are expressed through our practice of scientific assertion, then we should conclude that our goal is to arrive at a body of propositions which are such that any responsible investigator who inquired into the matter long enough would eventually rationally accept these propositions.

4. When we explain why and how this convergence of opinion occurs, we must appeal to a *realist* account of laws, theoretical entities, and so on.

The first two claims hold in connection with any subject-matter that can be the subject of rational investigation. The third is a reflection of Peirce's distinctive conception of science. Both the second and third capture a role for the idea that truth, assertion, objectivity, and consensus are related concepts. When an area of inquiry does display convergence towards a final opinion, we require an explanation of how this occurs. Meeting this explanatory demand calls for a metaphysical investigation. Realism is one such explanation, but we can allow that other kinds of explanation may be appropriate in some circumstances. Acceptance of the first three claims does not logically commit us to realism. I am suggesting that Peirce could have accepted the first of these claims, although there is no real evidence that he did. He did accept the other three.

3

Truth and Correspondence

1. Truth and Correspondence

The correspondence theory of truth is both defended as a platitude and attacked as a source of philosophical illusion. It is possible for both views to be correct. There are ways of understanding 'True propositions correspond to reality' which turn it into an uncontroversial truism which any theory of truth must accommodate. But it can also become the slogan of a distorted metaphysical perspective which underpins what I shall call 'the classical correspondence theory'. Debates about it are often unsatisfactory: defenders of the truism confront opponents of the distorted perspective. This chapter explores both sides: we examine the ways in which Peirce's theory of truth allowed for the platitudes of correspondence; and we identify his reasons for rejecting the substantive and controversial metaphysics of the classical theory.

According to William James, true propositions 'agree with reality', they fit the facts. In Aristotle's words, they 'say of what is that it is, or of what is not that it is not'. If it is true that snow is white, then this is because snow is, in fact, white. Such claims are simple truisms and like many truisms they are vague. The philosophical task is to understand them, to explain what it means for a proposition to agree with reality or to fit the facts. Thus James introduced his version of the pragmatist theory of truth as an attempt to elucidate just what agreement with reality amounts to. Different philosophical theories of truth should be seen, not as denying these platitudes, but as offering alternative theoretical accounts of just what they involve.

From this perspective, it is easy to conclude that the claim that a true proposition 'corresponds to the facts' is just one more uncontroversial platitude about truth, and that the 'correspondence theory of truth' is merely an expression of a truism. Correspondence and pragmatist theories may not then be in competition: a pragmatist explanation of truth would be one explanation of this correspondence relation rather than a denial that truth is a matter of correspondence. Evidence for this is provided by some claims of Peirce's that were mentioned in Chapter 2. In a manuscript from 1906, he endorsed Kant's definition of truth: 'the correspondence of a representation with its object'. His own account was then presented as an answer to the question: 'What does this correspondence or reference of a sign, to its object, consist in?' (*CP* 5.553; see also 5.565 ff). Further evidence is provided by the claim that 'Truth is that accordance of the abstract statement with the ideal limit towards which endless investigation would tend to bring scientific belief' (*CP* 5.565). Peter Skagestad argues that Peirce saw the claim that truth was correspondence with facts as uninformative rather than actually wrong (1981: 76, 82–3), and Robert Almeder contends that Peirce provided a novel version of the correspondence theory, one which effectively bypassed the philosophical perspective from which correspondence and coherence were viewed as rival perspectives on truth (1980: 79). In the same spirit, Paul Forster (1996) has claimed that Peirce has shown us how the relations between truth and such ideas as correspondence, coherence, instrumental success, and consensus can be brought into mutually supportive harmony.

The previous chapter discussed a number of themes in Peirce's writing about truth which support the idea that he endorsed many of the intuitions about truth which lead naturally to a correspondence theory. We now examine two further issues about the relations between Peirce's theory of truth and what we might call 'classical correspondence theories'. Those who reject the correspondence theory of truth must view it as something other than a platitude. They will hold that the claim that true propositions *correspond* to *facts* makes a substantive claim about how the platitudes are to be explained. Any satisfactory account of truth must enable us to understand the vague platitude that true propositions correspond to facts. But theorists can differ about how far concepts like *correspondence* and *fact* have a role in providing such explanations. In sections 2 and 3, we shall use some of Peirce's ideas about reality to identify a metaphysical picture which encourages a substantive correspondence theory of truth, a picture which all of the pragmatists reject. The aim is to identify a philosophically interesting correspondence theory of truth which is in competition with Peirce's pragmatist theory. Indeed, we shall see that Peirce's view grew directly out of his rejection of this picture.

A correspondence theorist may hold that reality is composed of entities such as facts or states of affairs: these are structured unities composed of objects, properties, and relations. Thus the fact that Sheffield is to the east of Manchester is made up of those two cities, and the relation of *being to the east of,* structured in a distinctive way. If Manchester had been to the east of Sheffield, the fact would have contained the same elements put together in a different way. Moreover, there is an isomorphism between the structure of thoughts, utterances, and perceptions, on the one hand, and the structure of these facts or states of affairs on the other. Just as a map can adequately portray the spatial relations between cities if it contains dots indicating the locations of the cities and is so constructed that the relations between the dots are systematically related to the spatial relations between the cities, so an utterance expresses the fact that Sheffield is to the east of Manchester only by containing elements that refer to Manchester, Sheffield, and the relation of being to the east of, and these are connected in the proposition in a way that parallels the arrangement of these elements in the fact. This idea may be expressed by saying that true propositions provide pictures of, or iconic representations of, reality. From the 1880s, Peirce agreed that thoughts and representations can be vehicles for thought and deliberation about reality only if they involve iconic representations: he agreed that thoughts and propositions provide logical pictures of reality. Indeed, he thought that the predicates employed in a natural language, expressions such as '. . . is to the east of . . .', function as iconic signs. The remainder of this chapter explores this theme in Peirce's thought, attempting to understand what was distinctive about his use of an idea which is often supposed to be characteristic of substantive correspondence theories.

As we saw in the previous chapter, Peirce's account of truth results from applying his pragmatist principle to the elucidation of that notion. When his principle was introduced in 'How to Make our Ideas Clear', he contrasted three grades of clarity that can be achieved in our understanding of a concept. The first grade is reached when an idea 'is so apprehended that it will be recognized wherever it is met with, and so that no other will be mistaken for it' (W3: 258). And we advance to the second when we can give a 'a precise definition of it in abstract terms' (ibid.). Applying the pragmatist principle requires us to relate the idea to possible experience. We ask what experiential consequences we would expect our actions to have if the idea or concept applied to some given object. As Cheryl Misak has emphasized, those passages in which Peirce seems to defend a correspondence theory of truth are concerned with reaching the second grade of clarity, with finding 'a precise abstract definition' (1991: 37–41). The pragmatic construal, which related truth to the convergence of opinion, results from showing how we understand and apply that abstract definition. It tries to show what correspondence of an idea to its object amounts to in practice. The idea that the correspondence theory tells us all there is to know about truth involves resting content with a non-pragmatist explanation. As Misak notes, this involves defending what Peirce called a 'transcendental' account of truth, one that sees the truth as a matter for *metaphysical* inquiry—'spurious metaphysics, not pragmatically legitimate metaphysics' (1991: 38–9). Sections 2 and 3 explore and defend this idea.

Gottlob Frege attacked the correspondence theory of truth by challenging this suggestion that propositions correspond to reality in the same way that maps, pictures, or diagrams match external things. He pointed out that while maps or pictures can be assessed as more or less accurate representations, propositions were either true or false; resemblance, unlike truth, is a matter of degree (1984: 352–3). In a similar spirit, Wilfrid Sellars complained that while it is fundamental to the representational properties of propositions that they can be the objects of logical operations such as disjunction, conjunction, conditionalization, and so on, the same does not hold for maps and pictures. Sellars, in particular, is very anxious to hold on to the insights to be gained from an analogy between propositions and maps. But he would agree with Frege that the natural and straightforward way in which we can make sense of a correspondence between maps and reality does not carry across to propositions (Sellars 1963: 50 ff; 1968: 134 ff). If Peirce is to retain the idea that propositions are, or involve, iconic representations of reality, he must do so in way that avoids these objections. The analogy between maps and propositions cannot tell the whole story about how thoughts are related to their objects. Sections 4–6 explore Peirce's use of such analogies.

A third theme in debates about the correspondence theory of truth is relevant to these discussions, and we should introduce it at the outset. It concerns the nature of the *facts* to which true propositions correspond. Facts are often taken to be language-and-thought-independent entities whose elements and structures match those of propositions, thoughts, and sentences. Propositions are answerable to these entities: they are true if the matching entities are components of mind-independent reality. Talk of facts as truth-makers can seem attractive, as it appears to flow naturally from some platitudes about truth and reality. These platitudes capture a kind of minimal *realism*: whether our beliefs and utterances are *true* is not up to us. Although we want to change the world to fit our desires, we want our beliefs and utterances to fit the world. If, on waking up, I form the belief that it is raining because of the sound I hear on the window, then the truth or otherwise of my opinion depends upon the state of the weather:

the world will deliver its verdict when I draw the curtains and look outside. So if my belief is true, this is '*because* something in the world is a certain way' (Horwich 1990: 110–11); it is true 'in virtue of something' (Wiggins 1987: 148). Indeed, we might suppose that the truth of 'It is raining outside' *is explained* by the fact that it is now raining; the sentence is *made true* by that fact.

These platitudes can almost certainly be accommodated without adopting the idea that a *fact* is a special ontological category, a portion of reality to which true propositions correspond. According to Frege, facts are simply *true thoughts or propositions*: there is no difference between saying that it is a fact that snow is white and saying that it is true that snow is white. In that case, we cannot appeal to facts in order to *explain* what truth is. The same worry is found in Peirce's work. Referring to Mill's apparent assumption that a fact is 'the very objective history of the Universe for a short time, in its objective state of existence in itself', Peirce responded: 'But that is not what a fact is. A fact is an abstracted element of that. A fact is so much of reality as is represented in a single *proposition*. If a proposition is true, that which it represents is a fact' (*CP* 6.67). The concept of a *fact* lacks the metaphysical weight required for an informative account of truth as a correspondence between proposition and *fact*.[1] We shall see in section 3 that this idea is fundamental to Peirce's 'realist conception of reality'. On the view ascribed to Mill, it might be reasonable to think of reality as a unity which is composed of ultimate parts called 'facts'. Frege and Peirce would both reject that view.

The aims of this chapter are thus twofold. We shall explore some more ways in which Peirce's theory of truth captures the platitudes which help to make the correspondence theory of truth attractive. But we shall also explore how some of Peirce's fundamental philosophical commitments involve rejecting a philosophical picture that is required if we are to transform claims about truth and correspondence from uncontroversial platitudes into an explanatory theory of truth.

---

[1] Another passage suggests—although less clearly—that the identity of facts depends upon our practice of representing reality in abstract conceptual terms: 'A *state of things* is an abstract constituent part of reality, of such a nature that a proposition is needed to represent it. There is but one *individual*, or completely determinate, state of things, namely, the all of reality. A *fact* is so highly a precissively abstract state of things, that it be wholly presented in a simple proposition, and the term "simple", here, has no absolute meaning, but is merely a comparative expression' (*CP* 5.549; see also *CP* 1.427).

2. Comparing Propositions with the Facts

Truth is a normative notion: we want our beliefs to be true; methods of inquiry are evaluated according to how well they lead to truth; self-criticism looks for reasons for suspecting that our opinions may not be true after all. The correspondence theory of truth seems to suggest that our evaluations of beliefs, methods, and reasons employ principles such as:

If a proposition q provides reason to believe p, then it does so because it provides reason for thinking that p corresponds to a fact.[2]

Any assessment of beliefs, utterances, and reasons involves, explicitly or implicitly, comparison between propositions and facts. One apparent problem for the correspondence theory may then be that we have little experience of actually making such comparisons. We know how to evaluate beliefs: we consider reasons for or against them, see how well they cohere with other beliefs and experiences, look for explanations of our holding them which show that we would have held them even if they were not true. Moreover, we learned the distinction between truth and falsity— we learned how to tell what the facts are—in the course of acquiring these skills. But in order to feel confident that we were in contact with the truth—as understood by the correspondence theory—we need to do something else: to inspect facts, understand their properties, and compare them with beliefs. It is not enough that we simply test one belief against others.

In *Spreading the Word*, Simon Blackburn offers a diagnosis of the appeal of the correspondence theory:

When people first start to sympathize with the correspondence theory, they are apt to seize upon some homely, immediate, truth, a truth which 'leaps to the eye'. I consider, say, the fact that my typewriter is on the table, and say 'well, *that's* a fact, *that* is what my judgement that the typewriter is on the table is made true by'. This seems as pure a case of sheer acquaintance with a fact as can be got (nobody with this kind of experience is going to deny that my typewriter is on the table). The instinct behind such a choice of case is sound. The critic is pressing for a conception of 'the facts' which is not wholly derivative from an antecedent conception of true judgement. So it is right to turn to a good case where we might talk of

---

[2] Skagestad's claim that Peirce thought the correspondence theory of truth 'methodologically empty' engages with it at this point: although truth *is* correspondence with the facts, this has no normative weight.

acquaintance with the facts, where the facts leap to the eye. For then that acquaintance might give us an understanding of one end of the relationship (the facts), and then we look forward to building correspondence in the light of that. (1984: 233)

The acquaintance Blackburn refers to here serves two roles: it provides contact with 'facts' which is not mediated through beliefs about them; and it also introduces a forum in which comparison of facts and propositions can occur. We *encounter* facts in experience; and our beliefs are true so long as they fit the facts that we encounter. It also promises an account of how we are *constrained* by the facts: once I open my eyes I have no control over what I see.

As Blackburn observes, this argument is flawed. It rests upon the discredited idea that experience confronts us with the *given*, with a content that is wholly untainted by our beliefs, prejudices, expectations, and concepts. The objects of experience are the-facts-as-they-strike-us; so we do not have this forum in which our beliefs can be compared with pure unadulterated fact. This is not to deny the importance of sensory experience as a point of contact with external things in explaining how we are constrained to believe as we do. But it does challenge the claim that comparing propositions with experience gives content to this special philosophical notion of correspondence. Instead, perhaps we should simply say that we grasp the concept of truth through an understanding of the ways in which we can be led to recognize that some of our beliefs are mistaken.

A different line of thought, which seems to support the idea that we compare propositions with facts, can also be accommodated within the pragmatist's story. Suppose I find myself disposed to believe that the book on the table in the kitchen has a red cover. This proposition has a complex structure: it involves reference to a book, which it identifies by reference to the table in the kitchen; and these are linked through the relations expressed by 'on' and 'in' and through the predicate expression 'has a red cover'. My attempt to evaluate this proposition will exploit a corresponding complexity in reality: I first go to the kitchen; I then find something which meets the conditions of being a table and being *in* the kitchen; I then look for a book with the property of being *on* that table; and finally I make a judgement about the colour of the book. This plainly involves 'comparing the proposition with reality' and the comparison is guided by the logical complexity of the proposition. I identify and then inspect the elements of the corresponding facts; indeed, I can pick the elements of these facts up and announce to which parts of the proposition they correspond. How can this be true and yet the correspondence theory of truth be false?

Those who reject the correspondence theory of truth would find little to dispute in the description of how this proposition is compared with reality. For example, William James begins his book *The Meaning of Truth* by telling us that truth is a 'relation' that may obtain between an idea and its object, and he reminds us of his earlier claim: 'Truth is a property of certain of our ideas. It means their "agreement" as falsity means their disagreement, with "reality". Pragmatists and intellectualists both accept this definition as a matter of course' (James 1909: 3). This prompts the question: what does agreement with reality mean?[3] And we receive an answer: '*True ideas are those that we can assimilate, validate, corroborate and verify. False ideas are those we cannot.*' And this is supplemented by the claim: 'To "agree" in the widest sense, with a reality *can only mean to be guided either straight up to it or into its surroundings, or to be put into working touch with it as to handle either it or something connected with it better than if we disagreed*' (1909: 4; emphasis in original). My ideas of the kitchen and the table guide me up to them, putting me into 'working touch' with the book, and I am thus put in a position to verify the proposition that the book on the table in the kitchen has a red cover. Belief in the proposition will be true ('expedient to believe in the long run and on the whole') so long as it continues to meet all relevant future experience. James would take it as a point in pragmatism's favour that it makes good sense of this sort of comparison between propositions and reality.

Similar views can be found in Peirce. My experience of external things, and my beliefs about them, typically enable me to locate them spatially relative to myself; my understanding of general terms and relations enables me to see how interventions in the world or experiments upon my surroundings will have results which provide a clue to whether the term applies to the objects on which I act. So my understanding of our proposition specifically guides me in locating the book on the kitchen table and establishing through observation and experiment whether it is red. If it fails these tests, then I shall probably conclude that it is false, that it does not agree with reality; if it is true, it will continue to pass any tests to which I subject it. The pragmatist theory of truth may even be *better* placed than a correspondence theory to make sense of the way in which we compare propositions with reality.

[3] In raising this question, James qualifies it in a telling manner: 'where our ideas do not copy definitely their object, what does agreement with that object mean?'

We have yet to see how claims about truth and correspondence to reality might represent a substantive and controversial account of what truth is. Having suggested that the weakness of the correspondence theory lies in its suggestion that we can 'compare propositions with facts', we have come up with what seems to be an innocent and neutral formulation of *that* idea, a version with which no one could reasonably disagree. This helps to explain the opinion of Skagestad, Almeder, and Forster: Peirce did not reject the insights of the correspondence theory of truth; he provided a framework which enables us to understand them more fully. Should we therefore conclude that no serious issue is raised by the idea that we should accept a correspondence theory of truth? No. To see this, we must turn to Peirce's discussion of how we should think about the concept of reality.

In 1871, in a review of a new edition of Berkeley's writings (W2: 462–87), Peirce contrasted two ways of thinking about reality: the Nominalist conception, embraced by Descartes, Berkeley, and most philosophers in the tradition; and the realist conception, defended by Kant, and favoured by Peirce. The nominalist view is suggested by the position discussed by Blackburn: we think of reality as 'the thing out of the mind, which directly influences sensation, and, through sensation, thought'. We think it is real because 'it is out of mind, is independent of how think it' (W2: 468). Reality is composed of the things that are causally responsible for our experiences. Our beliefs are true if they correspond to those things; our methods of inquiry must provide ways of reasoning from experienced effects to their unknown causes. If our only contact with reality is through its impact on experience then, especially if our experience is shaped by our beliefs and expectations, we may become sceptical about our abilities to reach the truth (see Misak 1991: 133 ff). Peirce's favoured realist story is introduced by observing that there is a fated convergence in the process of inquiry (see Chapter 2): 'Everything ... which will be thought to exist in the final opinion is real, and nothing else' (W2: 469). Realities and facts are the things we would believe in if we eliminated error through a process of critical examination. Note that this conception of reality already leads us to endorse something like the Fregean conception of a fact: facts are what are expressed in objectively true propositions. There is no need to evaluate reasons and methods by showing that they enable us to compare beliefs with facts. Instead, the very notion of a fact is explained by reference to inquiries that use sound rules to eliminate error and test hypotheses.

Of course, there is a problem of explaining just what makes an inquiry good.[4] But since we learn the concepts of truth and reality as we learn to identify sources of error, it is not an absurd suggestion that this is *our* concept of truth (see W2: 202–3). Moreover, it can retain at least some features of correspondence. It is not up to us what we would believe if we eliminated errors and effectively criticized our beliefs. And any adequate account of how our beliefs are assessed will allow for the role of experience in constraining our opinions. Indeed, by the 1880s Peirce was ready to insist that external things were encountered in experience: we experience them directly, and our ways of thinking about them are anchored through their role in experience. Experience does not, however, present us with *facts*; rather, our techniques of inquiry provide ways of refining our grasp of the facts about the things that we experience.

On a realist conception of reality, it is easy to understand how a pragmatist account of truth may tell us all we need to know about how beliefs correspond to reality. We must now ask whether the same would hold on a nominalist conception: can that require us to appeal to forms of correspondence which are distinctive and problematic?

3. Correspondence and The Nominalist Conception of Reality

The suggestion is that what Peirce calls the 'nominalist' conception of reality embodies a metaphysical picture which supports the claim that talk of correspondence and facts can have a fundamental role in explaining the nature of truth. It is extremely hard to arrive at a clear formulation of this nominalist conception of reality. This is not surprising, since it seems to be a consequence of Peirce's pragmatism that it actually makes no sense and cannot be clarified. We do better to think of it as an expression of an attractive and tempting philosophical picture which, for a pragmatist, is subtly incoherent and cannot receive a satisfactory formulation. But if this picture did make sense, it would offer a way of defending a substantive and controversial form of the correspondence theory of truth. Peirce supposes that this view of reality leads naturally to nominalism, an anti-realist doctrine about laws and universals, and, indeed, to scepticism.

The relations between the two conceptions of reality are not very clear. They 'define' reality according to different characteristics. An element of reality can be:

---

[4] Blackburn addresses just this question when he considers the weaknesses of 'methodological' accounts of truth.

- something out of the mind, which directly influences sensation, and, through sensation, thought;
- something which will be thought to exist in the final opinion.

Why should we suppose that these characterizations are in conflict? Someone like Peirce, who insists on the priority of the second of these formulations, need not deny that the first is *true*. The fundamental hypothesis of the method of science (discussed in Chapters 1 and 2) seems to incorporate just this idea into a view of truth and inquiry which belongs with the realist conception. And there is no obvious contradiction in supposing that someone who favoured the nominalist conception of reality could acknowledge the truth of the second claim. The difference between the two positions must lie in their views about the relative priority of the two characterizations.

One way to approach this issue is through the distinction between primary and secondary qualities. Locke distinguished primary qualities such as shape, size, and location, which are 'utterly inseparable from a body', from secondary qualities such as colour and sound, which 'in truth are nothing in objects themselves but powers to produce various sensations in us' (1690, II.viii.10). If two objects are red, they are alike in how they affect us, in the colour sensations they produce. If they share a shape or location, the resemblance is somehow intrinsic, it is not just a disposition to affect us in the same way. For Locke, the dispositions which comprise secondary qualities are explained by reference to the primary qualities of the objects that possess them. The shared redness of our two objects could have different bases in their respective primary qualities: objects that are 'really' different can appear to be similar. Are there differences in the ways in which the two conceptions of reality would encourage us to think about this distinction?

They could agree that primary qualities have a sort of generality or even objectivity which is lacked by secondary qualities—or, at least, a higher degree of such generality. First, we expect the primary qualities to feature in laws with a wide range of explanatory application and with the ability to unify much of our knowledge. Primary qualities of objects explain more of their behaviour than their secondary qualities do. Second, secondary qualities involve similarities which are relative to our sensory apparatus, our ways of responding to colours. We would expect them to be of interest primarily to creatures who see things as we do. It is easier to imagine inquirers for whom it is of no interest what colour something is, than it is to imagine ones for whom primary qualities are similarly irrelevant. We can think of many other qualities that resemble secondary qualities in being relative to some feature of the inquirer's life: to her sensory apparatus, her way of life, the specific context in which she lives, her point of view upon the world, and so on. Culinary concepts such as *fruit* or *vegetable*, concepts like a garden *weed*, perhaps concepts that relate to particular professions or to aesthetic traditions—these all resemble colours in being more idiosyncratic or parochial than primary qualities.

Similar points can be made about the ways in which we individuate objects. The principles of individuation by which we identify particular chunks of matter as 'objects' or 'individuals' may reflect our interests or concerns: for different purposes, we might draw the boundaries in Sheffield in a different place; and so on. So the principles of individuation which determine what chunks of matter count as objects, like the systems of classification by which we trace resemblances and differences between them, reflect our interests and ways of life. It is not obvious that all sentient creatures, however they lived, would find a need for the same principles of classification and individuation. There is nothing in these observations which should threaten the philosophical thesis of realism, nor, so far as I can see, is there anything that should disturb many contemporary defenders of the correspondence theory of truth. For all that we have this role in shaping principles of individuation and classification, the objects individuated and the resemblances we notice exist independently of our noticing them. Even if the concept of a fruit reflects our interests and needs, it is still a fully objective matter whether a particular item in the supermarket is a fruit.

There are two views we can take of these differences. We might hold that both primary and secondary qualities are fully real properties of their objects, while recognizing that the former possess the special kinds of generality that I described. Even if they differ in interest and importance, shared possession of any of these qualities constitutes a genuine similarity. Alternatively—and this view is suggested by the quotation from Locke— we could hold that only primary qualities are *real* properties of objects. Indeed, it is arguable that Locke thought that the real essence of something is determined by its primary qualities. Classifications employing secondary qualities embody our ways of coping with the world, grouping things in ways that are relevant to our purposes rather than by reference to their 'real properties'. This combination of views combines realism about primary qualities with nominalism about secondary qualities. Defending it would require a metaphysical theory which explained what makes a property real. It also creates the possibility of a distinctive kind of error, thinking that a predicate expresses a real property of an object when, in fact, it is the product of our ways of coping with our experience.

Peirce's realist conception of reality seems to require him to take the first view: both primary and secondary qualities are equally real. Each can be ascribed to things in propositions that would be a matter of fated belief for anyone who investigated the matter long enough and well enough. It is compatible with this that primary qualities may have an importance for science which secondary qualities lack. For a pragmatist, it is important that a property's relativity to our sensory apparatus, interests, or way of life need not diminish its 'reality'. When we clarify a concept using the pragmatist principle, we explain its whole content by reference to the patterns in experience that would result from our interventions in the world. The relativity that Locke ascribes to secondary qualities may then be features of all real properties.[5]

The nominalist conception of reality allows for the second view. Indeed, its title admits that there is room for the view that classifications that seem satisfactory for our practical purposes may not correspond to real properties in objects. Real objects exist independently of us, and we are aware of them through their effects on our sensations. Most of our classifications reflect patterns in these effects. But the objects may also contain forms or properties intrinsically, and our scientific aim may be to identify these. Since our beliefs about the objects will exploit the patterns we find in our experience and applications of our methods of inquiry, room seems to exist for the view that there could be a fated convergence of opinion of beliefs about these objects which misrepresent their 'real' properties.

There are instructive parallels between Peirce's treatment of the nominalist conception of reality and some more recent discussions of 'metaphysical realism' by philosophers such as Hilary Putnam and Mark Johnston. The description of the same position as 'realism' and as 'nominalist' need not disturb us. Even Locke's view of real properties appears to have the consequence that knowledge of real essences is beyond our capacities and that all the understanding that we possess involves classifications that may not correspond to anything 'real'.

A metaphysical story would be needed which explained what makes properties 'real'. A vivid explanation of metaphysical realism is provided by Mark Johnston. He draws on ideas from medieval natural theology:

---

[5] It is compatible with this that there are differences in the 'mode of being' of these different realities (see Chapter 2 section 11).

God is a being who created the world by realizing one of his own consistent and complete conceptions of how things might go. The world is then a divine artefact. The real structure of this divine artefact is therefore the structure that God represented to himself when he made the world. So God is, among other things, the solution to the problem about what makes one of the many alternative accounts of the world the account ascribing the right structure to the world. The privileged cognitive task is therefore set in advance: it is to rethink God's thoughts, or equivalently to know the real structure of the world.

Metaphysical realism holds that there is an independent privileged structure 'constituted independently of our cognitive activity' (Johnston 1993: 85–6; cf. Craig 1987). This metaphysical story explains why one version of the world, one system of classifications, is 'correct'. Other systems of description may be useful even if they do not reproduce the terms of the divine plan. Whether this metaphysical distinction can be maintained (or even understood) after we abandon this theological story may be an open question. Can we provide a secular metaphysics that warrants us in favouring some classifications as fully real? There may also be questions about whether we really understand the theological story. Since Peirce's pragmatism invites us to clarify concepts by showing what difference their application to something would make to possible experience, and since the facts which lead us to favour one set of classifications as fully 'real' lie outside possible experience, a pragmatist should surely reject the story.

This suggests that a pair of views about the status of the nominalist conception of reality is common ground between Peirce and contemporary pragmatists such as Hilary Putnam.[6] First, many philosophers are drawn to it: they believe that within the slogans and formulations we have offered, there lies a philosophical position which can be clarified and which could turn out to be true. And, second, this is an illusion. The only conception of reality that we can make sense of, *our* concept of reality, is closer to the realist conception.[7]

[6] In *Reason, Truth and History*, Putnam suggests that metaphysical realism is committed to the view that reference—the relation between signs and their objects—must be seen as 'metaphysically unexplainable' and 'magical' (1981: 3–5, 46). The suggestion that the doctrine cannot really be explained or defined is found in Putnam's more recent work, such as *Realism with a Human Face* (1990) and *Words and Life* (1994).

[7] This would also explain why those who resist attacks on the correspondence theory of truth and on metaphysical realism often seem to be defending a position which is different from the target of their opponents. As I shall suggest in the final section of this chapter, there may be a position which can endorse most of the slogans that are associated with the correspondence theory of truth and with metaphysical realism but which is in harmony with the realist conception of reality.

If the metaphysical story were true, then there would be no a priori guarantee that effective responsible inquiry would take us to the truth. No contradiction is involved in the thought that God may prefer that his divine plan be hidden from us. This is because what privileges some set of beliefs as a correct account of reality is something independent of our practices of inquiry. We could be confident that we could reach the truth only if we had some (presumably divine) guarantee that our cognitive faculties are adequate for grasping the truth.[8] In that case one mark of the nominalist conception of reality is that it calls for an additional argument which demonstrates that our methods of inquiry will take us to the truth about reality.

Now let us return to the correspondence theory of truth. If the kind of view we have just described is correct, this has important implications. First: one version of reality, or one set of properties, is picked out as privileged on non-scientific metaphysical grounds. We do not explain what is distinctive about these properties by pointing to their role in our scientific or descriptive practices. Their privileged character is fixed by something external to those practices. This means that if our goal is to arrive at a theory of reality which is based upon these privileged descriptions, then we seek a correspondence between our beliefs and something which is independent of our normal procedures for evaluating and revising them. In that case we arrive at an account of truth—or of the virtues we primarily want our beliefs to possess—which assigns a fundamental role for a notion of correspondence. Our beliefs should correspond to the elements of this privileged version of the world. But admitting this possibility depends upon rejecting what Peirce called the realist conception of reality. Hence Peirce's rejection of the nominalist view of reality involves turning his back on something which might reasonably be called a correspondence theory of truth. And of course, it is compatible with this that he can continue to endorse all of the truisms that seem to make the correspondence theory of truth compulsory.

There is one other respect in which we might think that Peirce rejects a correspondence theory. The example of the book on the kitchen table illustrated one way in which a proposition may correspond to reality. But truths are not all concerned with the observable properties of everyday objects. We might agree that mathematical propositions, ethical propositions,

---

[8] 'Consequences of Four Incapacities' offers a diagnosis of the errors of the Cartesian philosophy which, in effect, traces them to acceptance of the nominalist conception of reality. Peirce concludes that Cartesianism inevitably renders some facts 'absolutely inexplicable, unless to say that "God makes them so" is to be regarded as an explanation' (W2: 212).

propositions from the more theoretical reaches of science can all be assessed as true or false. Each, we might suppose, can be tested or 'compared with reality'. This might involve looking for a proof, considering how the ethical proposition would appeal to someone who took up a distinctive disinterested viewpoint on things, or making explanatory inferences about what best systematizes our other theoretical beliefs and experimental results. So different are these kinds of 'comparison with reality', some might argue, that there is nothing significant to be said about 'correspondence to a fact' at the wide level of generality required for it to apply to all of them. In that case, we should adopt a minimalist account of truth: once we accept that each instance of the schema 'p is true if and only if p' is correct, we have all that is required for understanding the concept. The details of how propositions are compared with reality can then be left to the study of particular ranges of concepts—empirical concepts for describing everyday objects, mathematical concepts, scientific concepts and so on. This is the view of Ramsey, the later Wittgenstein, and, more recently, Paul Horwich (1990). William James's reliance on vague slogans in giving his definition of truth probably has a similar motivation. Telling us that true propositions are those that it is good to believe does not get us very far: it requires to be supplemented by accounts of the functional roles of different kinds of concept which enable us to see how the virtues of different propositions can be evaluated. Equally, it could be suggested that Peirce's claim that true propositions are those that would be a matter of stable long-run consensus may also be seen as a way to characterize truth at level of generality at which something substantive can be said (see Misak 1998: 409–12).

Both in the last chapter and in this one, we have noticed ways in which pragmatist theories of truth can do justice to different aspects of what we might call the 'correspondence intuition'. In this section we have been looking for a way of characterizing a *substantive* correspondence theory of truth, an account of truth in which talk of correspondence has a fundamental and potentially controversial role. Through discussing the nominalist conception of reality and the related doctrine of metaphysical realism we have found a position which appears to do this and which is inconsistent with a pragmatist theory of truth.

4. Iconic Representation: the Accuracy of Maps and Diagrams

We now turn to a second theme in philosophers' talk of truth as correspondence. This is the idea that thoughts and utterances are logical

pictures of reality, that there is a kind of isomorphism between propositions and facts. This view is generally assumed to lead directly to the correspondence theory of truth: indeed, Frege, as we saw, attributed the appeal
of the correspondence theory to a mistaken belief in a parallel between the
truth of a proposition and the accuracy of a picture. This makes it surprising that Peirce's rejection of the classical correspondence theory is tied to
the claim that the representative function of propositions has a substantial
iconic component. If we think of beliefs and utterances as analogous to
maps or diagrams of reality, we shall be able to identify one further place
at which Peirce parts company with the traditional correspondence theory
of truth. In order to avoid the complexities of notions like 'picturing', we
shall focus on two related claims:

1. There is a significant analogy between the ways in which maps and
   diagrams represent the world and the ways in which natural language
   represents the world.
2. The best way to express this analogy is through saying that both involve
   iconic representation: language, thought, and inference are only possible
   through the use of ideas and other signs which function iconically.

We need to introduce the most famous of Peirce's classifications of
signs or representations: that between icons, indices, and symbols.
Understanding a sign involves recognizing what its object is. What
features of the sign are relevant to arriving at this understanding or interpretation? If the sign is a *symbol*, then whether something is its object
depends upon there being a practice of using similar signs (other 'tokens'
or 'replicas' of the same 'type') to signify just that object. The role of
symbols in language is evident: the meaning of a word or phrase is fixed
(at least in part) by the conventions or rules that govern its use. Had the
conventional practice of using the sign been different, it would have had
a different meaning or object. If a sign is an *index*, then whether something is its object depends upon the relations—physical, causal, spatial, or
temporal—which hold between the two. A natural sign provides one kind
of example: my scream is a sign of my pain because it is produced in me
by that pain. There appear to be examples in language too. Something is
the object of a demonstrative (such as 'this' or 'that') only if stands in
appropriate spatial relations to the user of the sign, perhaps being picked
out by her pointing finger. A moment or interval is the referent of a
temporal indexical such as 'now' only if the utterance is appropriately
related to that moment or that interval. Finally, if a sign is an *icon*, then

whether something is its object depends upon there being a resemblance between the two. They share a property which each could have possessed even if the other had not done so. Photographs, maps, and portraits all seem to provide iconic representations of their objects. In interpreting representations, we are guided by information about the conventions that govern their use, about real relations between them and aspects of the context in which they are uttered, and about similarities that hold between the representation and its object. During the 1880s, Peirce argued that an adequate language for reasoning, description, and communication must exploit all three of these forms of signification. Indeed, all three will be involved in any proposition that we can put forward as true: ordinary English sentences involve symbolic, indexical, and iconic representations.[9]

To guard against misunderstanding (and to avoid a sense of paradox), we should note that there may not be any 'pure' symbols, icons, or indices. A demonstrative pronoun, for example, is an expression with a conventional or symbolic role in our language. But the conventions governing the word 'this' do not specify what it represents directly; rather, they provide rules for interpreting it as an indexical sign.[10] Similarly, my ability to understand a map as an iconic representation of some terrain depends upon a grasp of the conventions governing the use of maps. Indexical or iconic signs are normally 'hypoindices' (conventional devices for indexical representation) and 'hypoicons'.[11] The claim under discussion is thus that both propositions and maps are conventional representations of reality which have a substantial iconic component.[12]

---

[9] This chapter is primarily concerned with the role of iconic representations in cognition. Chapter 4 will discuss Peirce's reasons for thinking that the most fundamental form of reference to external things involves using indexical signs such as demonstratives.

[10] The same holds for proper names such as 'Winston Churchill'. See Brock (1997) and Dileo (1997).

[11] Peirce uses the term 'hypoicon' in this way at *CP* 2.276 and 3.320. I am not aware that he actually uses the word 'hypoindex' with the meaning I have suggested here. However, it would be fully consistent for him to do so, and the idea I am using this word to express is one that he has to take seriously.

[12] The need to combine these forms of signification in informative signs is very clear when we consider photographs. Peirce often insists that photographs are indices of their objects—as well as depicting them. When we treat something as a photograph, we interpret it as representation which is produced *by* the object: it is the effect of light from the object striking the photographic plate or film. In a passage from around 1902, Peirce wrote: 'Photographs are very instructive: because we know they are in certain respects exactly like the objects they represent—this is because they were produced in such a way that they were physically forced to correspond point by point to nature' (*CP* 2.281).

It is easy to see how a street map is an iconic representation of a town. We might even expect that we would see a clear resemblance between the map and the streets of the town if we were to view them from the appropriate direction and distance. It is less easy to see how the word 'give' can be an iconic representation of the act of giving, or the word 'atom' can be an iconic representation of a fundamental constituent of matter. Before we can tell whether this is a decisive objection to Peirce's suggestion, we must explore his views of how maps, diagrams, and other iconic representations work. We can then consider whether there is an analogy between these representations and those used within a natural language or in inference.

Peirce discusses diagrams and maps in *The Critic of Arguments* (1892):

Diagrams . . . are intended to be applied to the better understanding of states of things, whether experienced, or read of, or imagined. Such a figure cannot, however, show what it is to which it is intended to be applied; nor can any other diagram avail for that purpose. The where and when of the particular experience, or the occasion or other identifying circumstance of the particular fiction to which the diagram is to be applied, are things not capable of being diagrammatically exhibited. (*CP* 3.419)

Before discussing how diagrams are 'applied to the better understanding of things', we must consider the issues raised by the later parts of this passage. Imagine a diagram on the page, representing the locations of the troops at the beginning of the Battle of Waterloo. There is nothing in the marks on the page which determine that *this* line is the British infantry, and that *that* point is the location of Napoleon's command post. The significance of the dots and marks and of their locations must be independently fixed before we can use and understand the diagram. We cannot use a map as a representation of a set of 'localities' until 'the law of projection is understood, nor even then unless at least two points on the map are somehow previously identified with points in nature' (ibid.).

A map or a diagram is an arrangements of marks on paper. When we *use* this arrangement of marks as a map of the battlefield, it is not enough simply to inspect these marks to see what battlefield is displayed and to see what the significance of the different symbols and their arrangement is. The system of representation that we employ has a number of elements:

1. The map or diagram: the arrangement of marks and lines on paper.
2. A system of rules or conventions which fix how the symbols are to be understood: this may require knowledge of conventional symbols, of the scale of the map, of the method of projection employed, and so on.

3. An anchoring of the map: an indication that *this* dot is the village we can see to our left, or that *that* line is the coast just above Bruges, and so on.

4. We may also need information about which features of the map are essential to its functioning and which are accidental: could we change colour, or omit certain lines and marks without turning it into a wholly different map.

A diagram or map cannot serve all these functions unaided. Most important, as Peirce insists, the anchoring function (3) cannot be achieved through the use of a diagram or iconic representation. The use of iconic representation requires us to use a different kind of sign: an index such as a demonstrative expression. As Peirce puts it: 'the diagrammatization is one thing and the application of the diagram quite another' (ibid.).

This has an important implication for any attempt to find analogies between 'diagrammatization' and ordinary thought and language. I can use a map (for example) to communicate information: I could show you the best route from Sheffield to Manchester by pointing it out on a map. But I cannot do this simply by waving the map at you. The map is an instrument of communication, but its use depends upon other forms of expression. I could show you the map and say: '*This* is Sheffield, and *that* is Manchester, and this route between them will be shorter than that one.' Once the initial identifications are accepted, inspection of the map will show that the claim about routes is correct. The map is thus a vehicle or instrument for communication and thought; but it can serve this role only if other kinds of representation are employed too. The example usefully illustrates the respect in which iconic or diagrammatic representation is valuable. Since the map bears certain similarities to the terrain, then once I have 'anchored' the map, and once I am aware that it is accurate, then I can learn more about the terrain by investigating the map. I can compare the distances of different routes, take account of likely obstacles such as hills or busy junctions, without having to make any observations of the terrain.

We should note that the spatial resemblance between map and terrain (they look the same shape) is inessential to this iconic role. If we were aware of the conventions used in reading it, we could use a map which was the mirror image of the familiar kind: we would know to turn right when the road on the map branched to the left of the one we were currently driving along (for example). Already a more abstract kind of correspondence between map and terrain is being employed. Second, we can notice that in contrast with a three-dimensional map in which the shape of a mountain is matched by a three-dimensional feature of the map's surface, a contour map already depicts the structure of the mountain in a much more abstract fashion. The key to iconicity is not perceived resemblance between the sign and what it signifies but rather the possibility of making new discoveries about the object of a sign through observing features of the sign itself. Thus a mathematical model of a physical system is an iconic representation because its use provides new information about the physical system. This is the distinctive feature and value of iconic representations: a sign *resembles* its object if, and only if, study of the sign can yield new information about the object.[13]

Before we consider how these ideas can be applied to the case of linguistic representation, we should note their importance for a response to the objections made by Sellars and Frege to the suggestion that the truth of a proposition is analogous to the correctness of a picture, map, or diagram. Sellars objected that pictures cannot be made the objects of logical operations: they cannot be disjoined, included in conditionals, negated, and so on. In fact, Peirce's response to this problem would be similar to Sellars's own. A map or diagram does not *embody* any propositions: it can do this only when supplemented by an indexical anchoring. Thus the isomorphism between the map and the terrain turns it into an *instrument* of thought and communication: it can serve as part of the expression of a proposition. In that case, maps can be used to formulate thoughts along the lines of: 'Given that *this* is Manchester and *that* is Sheffield: either this (highlighting one route) is the shortest distance between them or *that* (highlighting another route) is.' The map then has an essential role in the expression of a thought which involves logical complexity, one which exploits its role as an iconic sign. Any plausible development of the idea that propositions are analogous to diagrams or logical pictures must employ this idea.

Frege's objection was that the truth of a proposition cannot be viewed as analogous to the goodness of a picture because the latter, unlike the former, is a matter of degree. It is a corollary of this observation that the notion of the 'correctness' of a picture is not well defined. We can discuss whether a likeness is good enough for certain specified purposes, but without reference to a purpose, or to a way of using the picture, the bipolar notion of a picture being correct has no application. Although this seems

---

[13] This topic is discussed more fully in Hookway (1994*a*). This paragraph borrows a few sentences from that paper.

correct, it does not follow that a bipolar evaluative notion does not apply to iconic representations such as maps, representations that are constructed as instruments of thought and action. A map is correct, or accurate, so long as all the information we obtain from it is reliable: a road map that omits minor roads is accurate so long as it is only used in order to plan journeys that make no use of such roads. The accuracy of a map is a function of the purposes that guide its interpretation and its use.

Whether this is a response to Frege's argument depends upon exactly what the target of the latter was. If Frege took the correspondence theory of truth to be committed to the claim that *truth* could be explained *solely* in terms of resemblance or similarity, then his objection is effective. Moreover, he could reasonably complain that the account of the accuracy of maps just sketched *uses* the notion of truth: a map is accurate so long as it is a source of true information about the terrain. This helps explain why recognizing that linguistic representation involves logical picturing or iconic signs need not entail a substantive correspondence theory of truth. The view of maps and diagrams as largely conventional suggests a way of retaining the idea that there is an isomorphism between thought and reality without a commitment to metaphysical realism as we described that position above: classification and individuation can still be shaped by our interests, purposes, and concerns. We can retain the correspondence intuition without accepting the classical correspondence theory of truth.

5. From Maps to Propositions

The bearing of these ideas upon linguistic representation should now be fairly clear. First, the distinction between a map (or diagram) and its application is analogous to the distinction between a predicate or concept and its application to some element of experience. And the claim that the anchoring of a map depends upon indexical (non-iconic) representation is analogous to Peirce's claim that the subject of a proposition must be picked out indexically, normally with a demonstrative expression.[14] Moreover, once we know that a predicate or general term (a 'rhema' (*CP* 3.421) or 'rheme', sometimes called a 'propositional function' (*CP* 2.95)) applies to some object, then this triggers much new and relevant information that can add to our knowledge of the object: reflection upon how the object can be represented yields new information about the object

---

[14] This theme will be discussed in more detail in Chapter 4.

through inference. Thus the claim that we find Peirce defending is that the only account of the understanding of predicate expressions that can make sense of the fact that deliberation can provide new information about familiar objects requires us to interpret predicate expressions as iconic representations. This is evident from a further section of *CP* 3.419:

The meanings of words ordinarily depend upon our tendencies to weld together qualities and our aptitudes to see resemblances, or, to use a received phrase, by means of associations of similarity; while experience is bound together, and only recognisable, by forces acting upon us, or, to use an even worse chosen technical term, by means of associations by contiguity. Two men meet on a country road. One says to the other; 'That house is on fire'. 'What house?' 'Why the house about a mile to my right.' Let this speech be taken down and shown to anybody in the neighbouring village, and it will appear that the language by itself does not fix the house. But the person addressed sees where the speaker is standing, recognizes his right hand side (a word having a most singular mode of signification) estimates a mile (a length having no geometrical properties different from other lengths), and looking there, sees a house. It is not the language alone, with its mere associations of similarity, but the language taken in connection with the auditor's own experiential associations of contiguity, which determines for him which house is meant. It is requisite then, in order to show what we are talking or writing about, to put the hearer's or reader's mind into real, active connection with the concatenation of experience or of fiction with which we are dealing, and, further, to draw his attention to, and identify, a certain number of particular points in such concatenation. (*CP* 3.419)[15]

In a map, the spatial relations between two cities are represented through the relations in the diagram between dots that serve as indexical signs for those cities. Peirce describes a 'rhema' as 'analogous to a chemical atom or radicle [*sic*] with unsaturated bonds':[16] '—is a man' has one unsaturated bond, '—loves—' has two unsaturated bonds, '—takes—from—' has three, and so on. (*CP* 3.421, 469) We form complete propositions[17] by 'saturating' them: an indexical expression can serve this role; or a quantifier phrase which, perhaps, links bonds in different rhemata. This is a fundamental idea underlying Peirce's various attempts to construct

---

[15] Emphasizing the role of context and indexical reference in anchoring our representations, Peirce notes that although 'extravagant', it is 'quite true' that 'we can never tell what we are talking about'.

[16] He develops this chemical analogy by using the term 'valency' to refer to the number of terms (or unsaturated bonds) of such expressions.

[17] When being careful about his terminology, Peirce often calls propositions 'dicent signs'.

systems of logical notation. For our purposes, it provides one way to capture the diagrammatic character of the proposition: we express some relations between two objects by using indexical expressions which refer to those objects to saturate the bonds of some appropriate 'rhema'.

The 'rhema' itself will be a conventional sign, a type whose tokens will occur in many propositions that I accept. Suppose I believe that:

1. John is the brother of a bachelor.

This contains two rhemata: '—is a brother of—' and '—is a bachelor'. The first bond of '—is a bachelor' is filled by the name (a variety of indexical sign) 'John'; the second is linked to the unsaturated bond of '—bachelor' by an existential quantifier.[18] In effect, we construct the complex rheme '—is a brother of some bachelor' through 'indefinitely identifying' one bond of each, and then the remaining bond is filled by 'John'. Suppose I also believe such propositions as:

2. Bachelors are unmarried.
3. All John's brothers are lawyers.
4. All lawyers are rich.

Then I can conclude that there is at least one rich unmarried person. This is achieved through transforming our initial representation in accord with laws of deductive logic and transformations licensed by our other beliefs. The rhema '—is a bachelor' would be correctly applied to John so long as the pattern of inferences thereby licensed provides a good cognitive model of the appropriate sector of John's life. Very roughly: John serves as a nexus for a body of laws and tendencies, and the rhema or predicate occupies a distinctive conceptual or inferential role in our practices of sign interpretation. Whether John is correctly described as a bachelor depends upon whether there is a similarity between the nexus of laws and tendencies and the inferential or conceptual role.

6. The Correspondence Theory of Truth

Although it accommodates the platitudes behind the 'correspondence intuition', Peirce's account of truth does not fall into place as a version of

---

[18] Peirce's account of quantification is discussed in more detail in Chapter 5.

the 'classical correspondence theory'. In section 3 this was traced to his defence of a realist rather than a nominalist conception of reality, and we have subsequently explored some of the issues raised by his claim that propositions involve iconic representations of reality. In this concluding section, we consider how Peirce's use of the idea that propositions resemble reality differs from that classical correspondence theorists.

The two conceptions of reality differ in the role they attach to *time* in describing the relations between thought and the world. On the nominalist view, reality either does, or does not, contain the *fact* whose presence determines the truth value of a given proposition *p*. We might think of some elements of the proposition as *denoting* objects and others as expressing properties and relations; so long as there is a fact which is appropriately composed of those objects, properties, and relations, the proposition is true, and its objects are real. It is noteworthy that little is said here about *how* the elements of the proposition have the semantic properties they do. When we understand the proposition, we somehow discern what those objects and properties are; understanding involves recognizing an independent fact about what these semantic properties are. Our subsequent use of the proposition, the way we understand it and apply it in the future, is unanswerable to these independent semantic facts. The proposition marks out a possible fact; and understanding the proposition involves identifying what possible fact that is.

The realist view characterizes *reality* by reference to the future: whether a proposition is true, and what is real, is characterized by reference to what we will or would believe were we to inquire into the matter long enough and well enough. Meaning and understanding also point towards the future: the meaning of a proposition is a function of how it would or should be used or interpreted. One of the fundamental ideas in Peirce's philosophy of language is that semantic or semiotic relations are essentially triadic: the relation between a sign and its object is mediated through its 'interpretant', through the way in which it is used and understood in thought and discourse. That 'Paris' stands for Paris is not independent of how that name is understood, used, or interpreted; rather, the name stands for the city only because it is interpreted or understood as a name for it. The connection between the two 'goes through' interpreting thoughts.

Consider a map of France. We may ask how accurate it is. This cannot be answered without taking account of how it will be used or understood. If Paris is shown as a perfect circle, this will be a flaw if the user will expect the shape of the cities to match the shapes of the marks that represent them; it is not a flaw if users have no such expectation. Similarly, whether a sentence is true will depend upon how it is used and understood. If my desk were inspected through powerful lenses, its surface would appear to be ridged and pitted. So is it flat? That depends upon whether 'interpreters' form expectations about how it would appear when inspected in this manner: if they would, then it is not flat; if they would not, we might suppose, then it would be. Comparing a map with the terrain is an act of interpretation; it involves judgement about which similarities are salient, which are not. The same might hold of 'comparing a proposition with reality'. Which similarities are salient or relevant is always affected by interests and purposes, by the goals which lead us to make the comparison and interpret the representation. This holds even if the goal is to find an economical and elegant account of the mechanisms that underlie some physical process. The realist conception of reality, by allowing interpretation an essential role in fixing whether a proposition is true, allows little room for the idea, constitutive of metaphysical realism, that some privileged representations are true because they *really resemble reality* or because they describe and classify things *as they really are*. The result is a form of realism which allows little room for the heavy-duty metaphysics of correspondence.

Which is not to deny, of course, that true propositions correspond to reality. Thoughts and propositions are isomorphic to reality, and their structures guide us in comparing them with their subject-matter to settle whether they are true. We refer directly to external things using indexical expressions, and our beliefs are answerable to the facts: we try to ensure that we accept them only if they are true. There is no reason to cast any doubt on our robust common-sense commitment to realism, or to deny that many truths may be 'buried secrets', likely to be for ever hidden from us. The truisms about correspondence all seem to be secure, even if they are explained along pragmatist lines.

4

Truth and Reference: Peirce versus Royce

1. The Possibility of Error

In the early 1880s, Peirce made a discovery of vital importance for the
further development of his thought: reference to external things is primarily
indexical or demonstrative. This discovery provided solutions to problems
that he had struggled with throughout the previous decade. It helped
him to bring his logic of science into harmony with the systematic theory
of reference and understanding that he always took to be fundamental to
his work. Indexical signs put us in contact with external independent
things ('dynamical objects') which constrain our opinions and whose
properties we try to discover through inquiry. This promised a way of
reconciling pragmatism with a robust form of realism.[1] One aim of this
chapter is to explain the role of demonstrative or indexical signs in ensuring
the fated or destined convergence of opinion required for Peirce's
account of truth.

The occasion of his setting out these views about reference was the
publication of Josiah Royce's book *The Religious Aspect of Philosophy* in
1885.[2] In chapter 11, 'The Possibility of Error', Royce raised some problems
about reference and false belief, offering a solution to them which
supported absolute idealism. One section of the chapter criticized an

[1] The role of Peirce's account of dynamical objects in his defence of realism has been
stressed by Carl Hausman (1993: passim, especially ch. 4).

[2] It would be difficult to exaggerate the importance of the stimulus he received from
Royce's work for the development of Peirce's philosophy during the 1880s. It is very plausible
that his turn to metaphysics and evolutionary cosmology was stimulated by the problems
raised by his reading of Royce. Nathan Houser suggests that the publication of *The
Religious Aspect of Philosophy* was the 'most influential factor' in Peirce's return from formal
logic to philosophy in the summer of 1885. Houser comments: 'There is no doubt that
Royce's book, in conjunction with his own recent discoveries in logic and his revised theory
of signs, had a profound effect on Peirce. It was then that Peirce returned to his categories
and to a reassessment of Kant' (W5: xxxv). The first commentator to attach major importance
to this work in explaining the development of Peirce's thought was Karl-Otto Apel
(1981, especially ch. 7).

account of truth (ascribed to 'Thrasymachus') which Peirce recognized as his own.[3] Hence, in a review of Royce's book (entitled 'An American Plato' and not published at the time) Peirce used these views about indexical reference to answer these criticisms and to discuss in detail the problems about reference and Royce's own solution to them.[4] The second aim of this chapter is to explain the role of Royce's challenge in the development of Peirce's thought.

As a first step in evaluating the impact of Royce's book upon Peirce's philosophical development, we should notice some significant similarities between their intellectual projects. In 'The Fixation of Belief' Peirce undertook to formulate the norms or 'guiding principles' we should use in carrying out inquiries, in trying to replace doubt by settled belief. He claimed that the only fully defensible norms carry a commitment to realism. 'There are real things, whose characters are entirely independent of our opinions about them; those realities affect our senses according to regular laws . . . yet, by taking advantage of the laws of perception, we can ascertain by reasoning how things really are' (W3: 254). Early in the paper he proposes a method for identifying the most fundamental or essential guiding principles. These can be derived from those facts which 'are necessarily taken for granted in asking whether a certain conclusion follows from certain premises'. If there are facts which 'we must already know before we have any clear conception of reasoning at all' or which form 'the assumptions involved in the logical question', then 'it cannot be supposed to be any longer of much interest to inquire into their truth or falsity'. Norms derived from such facts will be 'the most essential'; if we conform to these, reasoning will 'not lead to false conclusions from true premises'. Thus it is part of Peirce's argument for the principle of realism that *doubt* would only be possible if we already accepted it, if we conceded that 'there is some *one* thing to which a proposition should conform' (W3: 254).

This strategy is analogous to what is sometimes called a *transcendental*

---

[3] It would not be surprising if Royce was reacting to Peirce's views. Royce's argument was developed in his Ph.D. thesis at Johns Hopkins University, where Peirce taught from 1879 (Murphey 1961: 104). Indeed, Peirce was present in 1880 for a discussion of a paper by Royce at a Metaphysical Club at Johns Hopkins. On this occasion, the paper (on 'Purpose in Thought') was read in Royce's absence.

[4] Peirce took Royce's philosophy very seriously, describing him as the 'pragmatist' whose views were closest to his own and subsequently noting that he could believe most of the claims made in Royce's Gifford Lectures *The World and the Individual* (1900). Royce's late book, *The Problem of Christianity* (1913), explicitly drew upon the ideas about communities and sign interpretation that were fundamental to Peirce's thought from the beginning

argument: fundamental norms and principles are shown to be presuppositions of uncontroversial cognitive achievements, in this case of the possibility of reasoning and inquiry. In the passage from W3: 254, cited above,
he investigates the necessary conditions for the possibility of *doubt*, for
entertaining the possibility that we may be in error. Royce's position shares
these features. He, too, offers a sort of transcendental argument against
scepticism. Since sceptical arguments typically suppose that all or most of
our beliefs may be false, they presuppose that *error is possible*. If we can
identify the conditions that must obtain if error is to be possible, then, it
seems, the 'actual existence of those conditions' is assumed by 'our wildest
doubts'. '*The conditions that determine the logical possibility of error must
themselves be absolute truth*' (Royce 1885: 385; italics in original). But
where Peirce identifies the principle of realism as one of the conditions of
the possibility of error, Royce prefers to conclude that 'there is an infinite
unity of conscious thought to which is present all possible truth' (1885:
424). (But we should beware of exaggerating this difference. Since Peirce's
account of truth entails that erroneous beliefs are those that fail to accord
with the fated convergence of opinion among an indefinite community of
rational inquirers, 'infinite unities of thought' may have a place in his story
too.[5])

There is one important difference between these two philosophical
strategies which reflects the fact that Peirce's philosophy was shaped by his
reading of Kant, while Royce was deeply influenced by Hegel. For Royce,
philosophical reflection reveals that our common-sense conception of
cognition is incoherent and that adhering to it leads inevitably to scepticism from which Royce's metaphysics offers us an escape. We turn to
absolute idealism as the only alternative to the confusions of our
common-sense views. Peirce, by contrast, is a 'critical common-sensist':
realism is part of our common-sense view of things; and philosophical
reflection reveals that many of our common-sense ideas about mind and
reality can be sustained.[6] Important as this difference is, we should not
allow it to conceal deeper similarities. Royce and Peirce give very different

---

[5] Peirce's attitude towards transcendental arguments is a complicated matter,
discussed in Chapter 7. He was generally sceptical of arguments that used the fact that *p* is
a presupposition of logic or of rational inquiry as a premise in an argument that would
demonstrate the truth of *p*—although such arguments may provide good grounds for
hoping that *p*. I trust that the strategic analogies I am calling attention to here do not
depend upon a controversial interpretation of Peirce as a 'transcendental philosopher'.

[6] Although, as we shall see, defence of this common-sense view of things does commit
Peirce to the construction of a system of evolutionary cosmology, which tells us that the
Universe is a vast mind perfecting itself through time.

accounts of the common-sense view, and there are many similarities between the view Peirce *ascribes* to common-sense and the view that Royce proposes to put in its place. Thus Royce asserts that an atomistic account of understanding is part of common sense but must be replaced through philosophical reflection by a more holistic theory. Peirce, by contrast, finds an holistic picture within the common-sense view of cognition and attributes the attractions of atomism to a set of purely philosophical prejudices that he calls 'nominalism'. Despite their differences, there can be important similarities in the positions that each adopts. [7]

2. Reference and False Belief: the Problem

Section III of Royce's chapter 11 starts with a supposedly uncontroversial definition of *error*: it is 'a judgment that does not agree with its object'. Suppose I judge that 'That purse contains money'. The 'object' of the judgement is the purse; unless the purse exists, the judgement is neither true nor false. So long as the object does exist, the judgement is true or false according to whether it contains money or not. Royce's problem concerns 'the *assumed relation between a judgement and its object*': 'What then is meant by *its object*?' (1885: 397; italics in original). Answering this question requires a theory of reference or of the intentionality of thought, and Royce believes that this task is especially difficult when it is allowed that there can be false judgements: a judgement can pick out a particular object as its own even if it does not agree with (or correctly describe) that object. In this section we shall try to identify the problems about reference that Royce claims he has identified. We shall restrict our attention to simple singular judgements about external things such as:

Josiah Royce was an American.
The book on my desk has a red cover.
That car is red.

---

[7] Peirce was not the only pragmatist to be influenced by *The Religious Aspect of Philosophy*. James, too, reviewed the book when it appeared and he discussed some of its conclusions in 'The Function of Cognition', a paper delivered to the Aristotelian Society in December 1884, and reprinted in *The Meaning of Truth*. When Peirce's response was written, James was unable to see his way around Royce's argument, commenting in his review that '[We] are inclined to think him right, and to suspect that his idealistic escape from the quandary may be the best one for us all to take' (James 1920: 281). He was later persuaded that there was a way to avoid this consequence by the argument of Miller (1893). The relations between James and Royce have been discussed by Sprigge (1993: 25 ff; 1997)

In each case, as Royce notes, we can divide the judgement into two parts, subject and predicate (p. 402). 'Josiah Royce', 'The book on my desk', and 'That car' all represent the subject of the judgement. Royce claims that they are 'accompanied by a sense of curiosity', while the other predicative components are tinged by a sense of satisfying this curiosity. How should we understand this? The first of our judgements can be understood as answering a question:

What nationality was Josiah Royce?

Royce's existence is presupposed by this question: it is the object about which the question arises, the object about whose properties we are curious. The predicative term, 'was an American', offers an answer to the question which is meant to satisfy our curiosity. The judgement is true or false according to whether the presupposed object actually possesses the property expressed in the predicate. Thus we would expect an account of how the objects of our judgements are identified to focus upon the role of subject terms in doing this.

In that case, it is initially difficult to see why false beliefs create any special problems. Suppose that the book on my desk does not, in fact, have a red cover. This provides no impediment to my identification of the book: I pick out the book by looking for the unique object which has the properties of being a book and being on my desk. So long as the descriptions contained within the subject term apply to the object, I can identify it successfully even if my other beliefs about it are false. Although Royce makes a functional distinction between subject and predicate, he does not consider this solution to his problem.

I can see two reasons why he may be correct. First, there are familiar cases where a judgement succeeds in picking out any object through using a description which fails to fit that object. For example, someone can be referred to successfully as 'the man drinking martini' even if he is really drinking water from a martini glass (Donnellan 1966). We have no difficulty deciding who the judgement or utterance is *about*. Once we allow that our beliefs about our surroundings are fallible, then it would be unsurprising if we often refer to objects using descriptions that fail to fit them. Hence an adequate account of reference and false belief must explain what is going on: if someone else is, in fact, drinking champagne, why is it the water drinker rather than the champagne drinker that we are talking and thinking about?

Second, let us return to the example of the red book on the desk.

Suppose it turns out that among the items on the desk are a blue book which is visible but in shadow and a red box which, from a distance, looks like a book. In this case it would be natural to invoke the description contained in the predicate in order to determine that the object is the box, not the book. Predicate characterizations can have a role in determining reference.

We can now introduce some Peircean terminology. Having made the judgement, someone may be asked: what are you talking/thinking about? The answer offered will provide a characterization of the object:

1. The book on the desk.
2. The red book on the desk
3. The red copy of *The Critique of Pure Reason* on the corner of the desk.

The answer offered articulates what the speaker or thinker takes the object to be. The first repeats the mode of presentation of the object contained in the subject term; the second presents the object under a mode of presentation which adds nothing to the information present in the judgement itself. The mode of presentation of the object employed in the third answer contains extraneous information. Following Peirce, we will say that the first gives the 'immediate object' of the subject term; the second gives the immediate object of the judgement as a whole; and the third gives what we will call the *informed object*. Royce's problems arise from the fact that the immediate object of a sign, utterance, or judgement may employ a characterization which only *appears* to fit the object.

This problem about false belief is a special case of more general problems about reference. The only information that a particular judgement carries about its object will be contained in the *immediate object*. Moreover, different judgements may present the same object in different ways. My judgement that the book on the desk is red may have the same object as your judgement that the copy of *The Critique of Pure Reason* next to the glass of water has a damaged spine. Once it is recognized that they have the same object, then we can infer, for example, that the book with a damaged spine is red. Explaining such inferences requires an account of how judgements with different immediate objects can still refer to the same thing. Similar issues arise even if the immediate objects are superficially similar: I can judge that the book on the desk is red, and then judge ten minutes later that the book on the desk has a damaged spine. The conclusion that there is a red book with a damaged spine can be drawn only if the books have not been changed during that time. Learning from experience depends upon being able to establish when judgements at different times have the same object; learning from testimony (and engaging in discussion) depends upon being able to tell when judgements made by different people have the same object; and Royce's problems about false belief provide the additional twist that we can be in cognitive contact with an object through a misdescription of it. How do 'immediate objects' mediate between signs, thoughts, and utterances on the one hand, and their 'real' objects on the other hand?

This terminology helps to clarify two features of Royce's argument. According to 'common sense', the object of a judgement is 'what it intends to have as its object' (p. 397). Moreover, 'any judgment has by itself its own object, so that thereby alone, apart from other judgments, it stands or falls' (p. 405). The only information relevant to identifying the object of a judgement is information *about that judgement itself.* That I also believe that the book is a copy of the *Critique of Pure Reason*, and that I believe that I can now see it are irrelevant to fixing the object of my judgement. Royce concludes, in effect, that the only information relevant to determining the object of my judgement is contained in the *immediate object*: the immediate object must somehow determine what the object is. Once we allow that the immediate object may misrepresent the 'real' object, then this 'common-sense' assumption threatens to render the problem of reference insoluble.

In a famous passage, Royce discusses a conversation between two people, John and Thomas. His insists that six people are involved: the real John, the real Thomas, John's idea of Thomas, Thomas's idea of Thomas, Thomas's idea of John and John's idea of John. In order to see how John's idea of Thomas can be mistaken, it has somehow to be brought into connection with the real Thomas (pp. 408 ff). But how? Let us reformulate this slightly: as well as the 'real Thomas', there is the immediate object of John's thoughts about Thomas, and the immediate object of Thomas's thoughts about Thomas and so on. These immediate objects are their respective 'modes of presentation' of Thomas. Royce tends to reify these ideas or immediate objects: they are things of which we are immediately aware, which represent distinct real objects to us. If the immediate object is present in my thought, then the real object cannot be, but must, instead, be inferred. Royce tends to treat these different objects (the real Thomas, John's idea of Thomas, etc.) as if the former were the inaccessible cause of the latter. For both Peirce, and for Dickinson Miller, this is to place things in the wrong light. We *are* directly aware of external things: the awareness does not depend upon our immediate knowledge of intermediary entities.

The immediate object of my thought is a specification of *how* I think about the external thing. As Miller put it: 'So far then from apprehending only my ideas, I apprehend only a world of objects; the ideas *are* the apprehension' (1893: 411).

Royce's argument suggests that I am only indirectly in contact with the object of my thought: the object is something that fits or corresponds to a conceptual content that I am immediately aware of when I make a judgement. For Peirce and Miller, by contrast, I am in direct cognitive contact with the real thing—with the book or sheep or whatever. However, when I think of an object, I think of it as possessing certain properties and characteristics, not all of which it may actually possess. I am not thinking of it as 'whatever possesses those properties', for that would make my cognitive contact with it indirect. My cognitive grasp of the object is not exhausted by the list of properties contained 'within' the immediate object. The immediate object is not some object distinct from the external thing which serves as an intermediary between me and the latter; rather, it *is* the real object as it is characterized in the thought.

3. Co-reference: Two Pictures

The discussion in the last section suggests that the fundamental issue concerns when we can say that two judgements have the same object. Using Peircean terminology, we can also express this as an issue about when two singular terms with different immediate objects have the same real object. The special case that arises from Royce's paper concerns when, having discovered that two judgements have the same real object, we can conclude that the immediate object of one of them involves an erroneous characterization of that object.

It is important that there are two different ways in which two judgements can have the same object. First, they can quite independently stand in a relation of reference to that thing. We can imagine two people viewing a mountain from different directions.[8] Each forms a description of the mountain which is used in formulating thoughts; perhaps each introduces a proper name for the mountain, fixing its reference through their descriptions. One forms the judgement (J_1) that *the mountain is covered in cloud,*

---

[8] This example is suggested by the example of 'aphla' and 'ateb' from Frege's discussion of his *Sinn–Bedeutung* distinction: see Frege's 1914 letter to Philip Jourdain in Frege (1980: 80).

the other forms the judgement (J_2) that *there is snow on its northern face*. In this case, the fact that J_1 has the same object as J_2 would be the sum of the two independent facts that the object of J_1 is the mountain and the object of J_2 is that very same mountain. In order to show that these judgements shared an object, we would need to provide separate explanations of why each has the object that it does. One possible such explanation would show that the mountain was the object that best fitted the descriptions that each employed. We have already seen that this cannot be the whole story. A second possibility would be to point to the role of the mountain in each agent's acquiring his or her capacity to form the judgements in question: perceptual contact with *that* mountain led each to arrive at particular descriptions or adopt the practice of using a name.

Second, the fact that two judgements have the same object can be guaranteed by the relations between the judgements; it is not the product of independent facts concerning the relation of each judgement to some external thing. Here are some straightforward examples.

1. Suppose I learn of the existence of Montserrat from the testimony of a journalist writing in a newspaper. Then the fact that my Montserrat thoughts and the journalist's Montserrat thoughts have the same object is not the product of independent relations between our thoughts and a Caribbean island. My understanding of the term is deferential to that of the journalist; I intend to refer to whatever he refers to by the use of the term. Hence the fact that our thoughts about Montserrat have the same object is guaranteed by the relations between our thoughts—by the fact that I learned of the existence of that island through learning that name from the journalist.

2. Suppose that having formed J_3, *Peirce reviewed Royce's 1885 book*, I wonder whether the latter ever read or commented upon the review. I carry out an inquiry, checking letters, books, and manuscripts, reflecting on the matter and form a judgement J_4 that *Royce was never aware of Peirce's review*. J_3 and J_4 have the same objects: each is about both Peirce and Royce. Yet this is not the product of independent facts about the two judgements. Rather, since J_4 is obtained through inference, and since reference is transmitted forward from premises to conclusions from various other premises, the relations between J_3 and J_4 in the inquiry guarantee that these judgements will refer to the same objects. Co-reference is not the product of independent facts about the two judgements.

3. Similar examples can be constructed where judgements are linked through explicit anaphora. 'The traffic warden is approaching the car

. . . and now she has reached for her notebook . . . and now she is giving it a ticket.' The structure of the sequence of thoughts ensures that 'she is giving it a ticket' is about the traffic warden and the car; the pronouns secure their reference through reference back to earlier stages in the discourse.

We can now anticipate the story to be told in subsequent sections. Royce took the problems that false beliefs pose for the idea that reference is always determined by the descriptions of the object contained within a proposition to leave no alternative to admitting that all questions about reference concern co-reference of our second kind. Questions of reference can *all* be solved by examining the relations *between* judgements. Peirce's earliest writings (from the 1860s) suggested a position of the same general kind: reference to objects is *always* dependent upon earlier thoughts of the same thing. By the 1870s, Peirce's work in logic faced difficulties about reference that can be traced to his tendency to regard all co-reference as explicable in terms of relations within thought. Responding to Royce, Peirce began to articulate a possibility that Royce had not considered. Although a purely atomistic picture must be rejected, the ways in which we use judgements in inference and revise our grasp of the objects of our judgements makes essential use of judgement–world relations. Taking indexical expressions (such as demonstratives) rather than descriptions as our paradigms of subject terms, we can see how we can be in cognitive contact with objects even if the immediate objects of our judgements present those objects in an erroneous way. Moreover, the resulting cognitive contact will put us into a position to expose and correct our errors. Thus Peirce wrote that Royce's argument ignored a truth which had been noticed by Kant 'in a celebrated passage of his cataclysmic work' and which had been 'put in a clearer light' through 'one of the most recent discoveries' in formal logic. Royce's error was 'to think that the real subject of a proposition can be denoted by a general term of the proposition; that is, that precisely what you are talking about can be distinguished from other things by giving a general description of it' (W5: 224).

4. False Belief and the Rejection of 'Atomism'

I have said that for Peirce in the 1860s and for Royce in his 1885 book, questions of co-reference are explained in terms of how judgements or thoughts are connected in the mind. The relations between two judgements can help us to see that they possess the same object and also to see that one of them is *better* than the other—that any disagreement in the claims that are made about the object can be taken to show that the other judgement is false. The two thinkers disagree about the relations between judgements that serve this role. In each case, my awareness that I may be mistaken places my judgement in a wider context, which contains other judgements that could correct it: these other judgements constitute the 'Beyond' to which I want my thoughts to correspond. For Peirce, my current errors can be exposed by judgements that will or may occur in the future. This is 'Thrasymachus's' view that Royce attacks later in his chapter 11 (1885). He himself insists that this wider context consists of judgements that already actually exist.

In 'Some Consequences of Four Incapacities' (1868), Peirce asked how we acquired the concept of reality, a concept we can take to be correlative to 'true':

It is a conception that we must first have had when we discovered that there was an unreal, an illusion; that is when we first corrected ourselves. Now the distinction for which alone this fact logically called, was between an *ens* relative to private inward determinations, to the negations belonging to idiosyncrasy, and an *ens* such as would stand in the long run. The real, then, is that which sooner or later, information and reasoning would finally result in, and which is therefore independent of the vagaries of me and you. Thus the very origin of the conception of reality shows that this conception essentially involves the notion of a COMMUNITY, without definite limits, and capable of an indefinite increase of knowledge. (W2: 239)

In order to make sense of false belief, Peirce places my thoughts in a more inclusive context of thought. The other thoughts that make up this whole are all thoughts of actual or possible thinkers who make up a community of inquirers: my thoughts can thus be compared with those of other people and with thoughts that are produced or developed in the future. Moreover, this community is not limited to those thinkers who actually exist or *will* exist: it is a community 'without definite limits' and 'capable of an indefinite increase of knowledge': there are no finite limits to the capacities and inquiries that could be relevant. Furthermore, the community is not just a collection of individual thinkers standing in *external* relations to each other. There is no philosophically significant difference between intersubjective thought, discussion, and inquiry, and those processes of thinking that take place within an individual consciousness. In 1905, having noted that 'a person is not absolutely an individual' and commented that his thoughts are just what he is saying to 'that other self that is just coming into life in the flow of time', Peirce observes that someone's 'circle of society (however widely or narrowly this phrase may be understood), is a sort of loosely compacted person, in some respects of higher rank than the person of an individual organism' (*CP* 5.421).[9]

A judgement is in error if properly conducted inquiry is 'destined' or 'fated' to lead to a stable consensus on some other opinion about the same object. My erroneous thought is exposed as an error when placed within a wider context of all that any responsible inquirer *would* think on the matter, once various contingent limitations to carrying out that inquiry are removed. This depends upon having a characterization of what makes an inquiry a good one, of the rules we should follow in interpreting, developing, and correcting our thoughts. Many of these norms were to be grounded within semiotic, the systematic study of signs and their relations to their objects. Thus the Peircean model hopes to account for false belief and reference by placing an individual judgement within an indefinitely large inclusive context of thoughts within which other (actual or possible) thinkers can correct and revise our current fallible opinions. If properly conducted inquiry is destined to decide that what appeared to be a book was in fact a box, then the object of my 'book' thought was, in fact, the box. Of course, it remains to be explained *how* properly conducted inquiry can make this discovery. We shall return to this question below.[10]

Now for Royce's story. Consider a student who is judged to have given the wrong answer to an examination question. In this case, we need not appeal to future discoveries and corrections. So long as we have an examiner whose knowledge includes both information about the student's opinion and expert knowledge of the relevant facts, then the required comparisons can be made straightaway. The examiner's expertise reveals that the particular answer given by the student was wrong; and the expert can even see and explain *why* it is wrong. So long as we can appeal to a present expert who has knowledge both of the subject's beliefs and of the subject-matter of those beliefs, then there are present facts which determine that the student's opinion is false. Just as the first model insists that a thought can be false *relative to possible future correction*, the second

---

[9]   This 'social view of the self' is especially pronounced in Peirce's early writings. See, for example, the closing pages of 'Some Consequences of Four Incapacities' (W2: 211–42). Such passages ground Apel's description of Peirce's position as 'logical socialism'. They are also the views that were found congenial by the later Royce.

[10]   Dealing with this issue fully would require a detailed examination of Peirce's logic and metaphysics. The discussion in this chapter is restricted to Peirce's views about reference.

model urges that a thought can be judged false *relative to the opinions of someone with expertise, with wider and better knowledge.*

Leaving aside problems about how expertise is recognized, this model will only get us so far. Plenty of facts are possessed by no experts—especially those that relate to the remote past or remote future. We can, it seems, always conceive of a wider perspective from which even the confident assertions of experts may be questioned. Royce suggests how to avoid these difficulties. We can 'declare time once for all present in all its moments to an universal inclusive thought':

And to sum up, let us overcome all our difficulties by declaring that all the many Beyonds, which significant judgments seem vaguely and separately to postulate, are present as fully realized intended objects to the unity of an all-inclusive, absolutely clear, universal, and conscious thought, of which all judgments, true or false, are but fragments, the whole being at once Absolute Truth and Absolute Knowledge. Then all our puzzles will disappear at a stroke, and error will be possible, because any one finite thought, viewed in relation to its own intent, may or may not be seen by this higher thought as successful and inadequate in this intent. (1885: 423)

The only way to make room for error, Royce believes, is to posit the ultimate expert, an Infinite Knower. The possibility that my thought '*This is blue*' could be erroneous makes sense only when it is viewed as 'one moment or element in a higher truth' (p. 424) which contains, for example, 'This colour now before me is red, and to say that it is blue would be to make a blunder' (p. 423). Without reference to such all-inclusive thoughts, reference, truth, and falsity are all impossible: 'Thus we are driven to assume an infinite thought, judging truth and error' (p. 425). This provides the more inclusive systematic context for my thoughts, in which they are linked to other thoughts which are not thoughts of *mine*.

In spite of the similarities between Peirce's and Royce's positions, they differ in four important respects. They agree that we can make sense of truth and falsity only by understanding individual judgements as parts of more inclusive systematic structures of thought. They also agree that these systematic structures of thought have no finite limits: Royce appeals to the Infinite Knower, and Peirce speaks of a community with 'no definite limits' and capable of an 'indefinite growth of knowledge'. But since Royce posits an Infinite Knower who already knows everything, we find:

1. Royce need appeal only to a systematic structure of *actual* judgements, while Peirce must also appeal to possible or hypothetical ones.

2. Royce need appeal only to *present* thoughts, which are already contained in some mind, while Peirce must appeal to thoughts that will or would enter a mind at some time in the future.
3. For Royce, the mind in which these thoughts are present is that of an Infinite Knower, while Peirce need appeal only to the actual or possible thoughts of *actual or possible agents of scientific inquiry.*

The fourth difference is that Peirce believed he was articulating our everyday or common-sense conception of truth and error, while Royce was proposing a metaphysical replacement for that common-sense view which he took to be deeply confused.

A reader may be tempted to emphasize another difference. Royce is clearly anxious to show that the Universe has a spiritual character and to find room for God in his account of empirical truth and error. Peirce's story seems more secular, especially to those who associate him with a kind of scientistic neo-positivism. Although Peirce was scathing about the attempt to use philosophical reasoning to *prove* the existence of God, it is very plausible that he thought that responsible use of the scientific method was possible only for those for whom scientific observation is a species of religious experience providing us with direct perception of the Deity.[11] He described the Universe as a vast mind perfecting itself through time, and there is reason to think that Royce's book stimulated more rigorous work on these topics. He commented in his review that 'the existence of God, as well as we can conceive it, consists in this, that a tendency towards ends is so necessary a constituent of the Universe that the mere action of chance upon innumerable atoms has an inevitable teleological result', and further suggests that God's omniscience 'consists in the fact that knowledge in its development leaves no question unanswered'.[12] Both Royce and Peirce may thus have seen the possibility of error as a manifestation of God's omniscience.

In the next section we shall examine Royce's arguments against the view he attributes to Thrasymachus. According to this view, a judgement may be in error 'to a *possible* critical thought that should afterwards undertake to compare it with its object': '*if* a critical thought *did* come and compare it with its object, then it *would* be seen to be false'. Whether Royce had Peirce in mind is not clear. Having noted that Royce declines to name the defender of this view 'perhaps to spare the family', Peirce commented: 'But

[11] This interpretation is discussed and defended in Chapter 11.
[12] For further discussion, see Chapter 6.

I must with shame confess that if I understand what the opinion of this Royce-forsaken Thrasymachus is, I coincide with it exactly' (W4: 222). We shall also look at the difficulties Peirce himself faced in trying to sustain his view while trying to write a logic text in the early 1870s. We can then examine how Peirce's new ideas about reference provide an answer to Royce and help with his own earlier difficulties.

5. Thrasymachus

Why does Royce reject Thrasymachus's position? He complains that 'No barely possible judge who *would* see the error, *if* he were there, will do the job', commenting that 'Bare possibility is blank nothingness' (1885: 427, 430). Why would the possibilities be '*bare*'? And what would be wrong with them being so? To focus the discussion, consider a Peircean claim about truth that would, presumably, be acceptable to Thrasymachus:

If it is true that *p*, then anyone who inquired into the matter long enough and well enough would come to the conclusion that *p*.

This concerns the judgements of possible or hypothetical judges as well as the actual judgements made by actual judges. It is natural to ask for an explanation of why this convergence in opinion is to be expected: what ensures that we will all eventually arrive at the truth? I think Royce supposes that Thrasymachus (and Peirce) must simply refuse this demand for an explanation. But if they do refuse the demand, then it is hard to see how they have made sense of an objective notion of truth and error. If, on the other hand, they *do* try to meet the demand for an explanation, then there is more to their theories of truth than has been advertised. They must have a further more fundamental account of what truth and falsity consist in.

In the background is an assumption that Peirce would share. Inquiry is a process of *discovery*: we are finding things out that were already true anyway:

Here is this stick, this brick bat, this snow flake, there is an infinite amount of error possible about any one of them, and notice, not merely possible is it, but actual ... You cannot in fact *make* a truth or falsehood by your thought, you only find one. From all eternity that truth was true that falsehood false. Very well then, that infinite thought must somehow have had all that in it from the beginning. (1885: 431–2)

When an error is exposed, we *discover* what was the case all along: we judge a proposition to be false because it is false. So if our hypothetical inquiry concludes that *p*, this must be because *p* was true anyway. The inquirer isn't constituting or creating the truth that *p*. Statements about what will be judged about present facts, or about what *would* be judged about present facts in various hypothetical circumstances must somehow be grounded in facts about the actual present. By ensuring that all true propositions are already known by an actual Infinite Knower, Royce's theory allows this condition to be met. If the present truth *consists in* what will or would be judged, then it is more difficult to see how the condition is met. What sense can we attach to the idea that these future or hypothetical inquirers would be discovering rather than inventing facts?

One response would involve suspect metaphysics: facts about what would happen in various hypothetical circumstances are metaphysically basic, they are *barely true*. No explanation of why they are true is to be expected or sought. We can agree that this would be unsatisfactory—not least because reconciling objectivity with Thrasymachus's theory of truth requires a realist view of these 'would be's.[13]

What is the alternative? What kind of explanation might be offered? If it is indeed a fact that *p*, then, like other facts, we would expect this to have causal powers. When we inquire into the matter, we conduct tests which attempt to produce manifestations of those powers, events whose best or only explanation involves reference to the fact that *p*. If it is now raining outside, we can see how anyone who looked out of the window or walked out of the door would obtain the evidence that would lead them to discover this truth. If that is how we explain why competent inquirers are fated to arrive at a true belief, then it does not seem to be a 'bare possibility' that the true opinion will be reached. The destined convergence is *grounded* in facts about the world and about human capacities for investigating our surroundings.

Royce is considering Thrasymachus's theory as the answer to a *constitutive* question: what does the truth of a proposition consist in? In virtue of what is it true that *p*? Thrasymachus's theory holds that even a proposition about the past of the actual world would, if true, be true in virtue of what hypothetical judges would say in various hypothetical circumstances. To appeal to the causal powers of the historical *fact* in order to explain why these hypothetical judges would decide as they do seems to take for

---

[13] Compare Peirce's claim that his pragmatism could only be taken seriously by someone who accepted realism about laws and counterfactual conditionals.

granted another account of what the truth of the proposition actually consists in. The circularity becomes apparent when we consider our example of the rain. What makes it true that it is raining? The fact that the rain affects people's senses in ways that ensure that so long as they are responsible in the way that they think about the matter, they will believe that it is raining. The answer appeals to the fact that it is raining in order to explain what the truth of the proposition that it is raining consists in. Any such explanation, it appears, must rest upon a prior account of what facts consist in.

Thrasymachus's account of truth in terms of the fated convergence of opinion is a fundamental principle of *metaphysics*: it tells us what the truth of a proposition or the obtaining of a reality *consists in*. So understood, it may be difficult to escape from the problem that Royce presents. In that case, the agreement between Peirce and Thrasymachus may be less than he supposed. During the late 1880s, Peirce was developing his metaphysics in some detail—probably under the stimulus of Royce's argument. Once it was fully in place, it is clear that his account of truth is *not* a fundamental metaphysical doctrine: it elucidates our *concept* of truth, but the metaphysics is called for to explain how it is possible to have this concept. Indeed, the scientific metaphysics is used to explain how the convergence of opinions will occur. Peirce was not clear about these issues when he responded to Royce; and he was even less clear about them when developing his pragmatism during the previous decade.

During the early 1870s, Peirce made an unsuccessful attempt to write a book on logic. The surviving drafts contain much material that subsequently appeared in the series of papers that included 'The Fixation of Belief' and 'How to Make our Ideas Clear'. However, while Peirce's systematic theory of signs and his account of the categories was used to structure the material in the book drafts, these doctrines are absent from the later papers. This is surprising, since there is no reason to think that Peirce ever questioned their importance for his work in logic and philosophy. Perhaps Peirce was merely sensitive to the needs of the readership of the *Popular Science Monthly*, the journal where the papers were published. It is more plausible that, while writing his logic text, he faced problems about reference—similar to those discussed by Royce—which he could not solve to his satisfaction.

There are just two themes from the logic drafts that I shall discuss here. First, Peirce distinguished two ways to pin down 'reality': nominalist and realist (see Chapter 3, section 3). Nominalists emphasize that reality is the cause of our opinions: we are constrained by its impact upon us.

Hence 'there is no objection to saying that . . . external reality causes the sensations, and through sensation has caused all that line of thought which has finally led to the belief' (W3:19). However, although 'there is no objection' to this, it can seduce us into such philosophical errors as nominalism, scepticism, and the Lockean picture of reality as the unknowable cause of our sensations. Philosophical insight flows from stressing the realist picture which emphasizes the 'permanence and fixity of reality', and identifies it with what is described in an opinion that would not be overthrown no matter how long inquiry should continue. The real object is the object which is described in that final opinion. Second, struggling to reconcile these two perspectives on reality, Peirce notes a paradox (W3: 30):

1. The real object is what we would believe that object to be if we were to inquire into it long enough and well enough.
2. The real object of a judgement is always or usually involved in constraining or producing that judgement through, for example, its causal impact upon us.

Although Peirce insists that there is no inconsistency between these claims, his attempts to bring them into harmony during the early 1870s were not satisfying.

Consider a passage from the same manuscript:

We say that a diamond is hard. And in what does its hardness consist? It consists merely in the fact that nothing will scratch it: therefore its hardness is entirely constituted by the fact of something as rubbing against it with force without scratching it . . . But though the hardness is entirely constituted by the fact of another stone rubbing against the diamond, yet we do not conceive of it as beginning to be hard when another stone is rubbed against it; on the contrary, we say it is really hard the whole time, and it has been since it began to be a diamond. And yet there was no fact, no event, nothing whatsoever, which made it different from any other thing which is not hard, until the other stone was rubbed against it. (W3: 30)

The hardness 'exists only in virtue of a condition, that something will happen under certain circumstances; but we do not conceive it as first beginning to exist when these circumstances arise' (W3: 30). Similarly, the existence of realities 'depends upon the fact that opinions will finally settle in belief in them. And yet . . . these realities existed before the belief took rise, and were even the cause of that belief' (W3: 31). Peirce was struggling with exactly the problems that Royce was raising against Thrasymachus's view of reality and false belief. He suggests that reality constrains inquiry through 'final causation' (W3: 8); and he complains:

Is not the fact that investigation leads to a definite conclusion of so different a character from ordinary events in the world to which we apply the concept of causation that [an ordinary causal explanation of it] fails nevertheless to bring into due prominence the real peculiarity of its nature? (W3: 45)

But Peirce does not provide a full explanation of how to acknowledge the truth of the idea that reality causally constrains our beliefs while defining truth and reality in terms of the convergence of opinion.

6. Signs, Interpretation, Inquiry

Before we turn to the details of Peirce's claims about reference in his review of Royce, some preliminary comments are in order. The first concerns the fundamental shape of Peirce's ideas about meaning and signification. From the 1860s, he claims that 'means' or 'signifies' is a triadic relation. A thought, utterance, or other sign denotes an object only because it can be interpreted in subsequent thought as a sign of that thing: 'each former thought suggests something to the thought that follows it, i.e. it is a sign of something to this latter' (W2: 224). What something means is what it is interpreted or understood as meaning; its meaning is manifested in its role in inference, inquiry, and planning and guiding activity. Thus an account of the relations between judgements and their objects will inevitably look to the future, to the inferences that can be drawn from the judgements, to the expectations they license, and to the ways in which they are sensitive to further perceptual information. In that case, it is unsurprising that Peirce's account of cognition has a temporal dimension which is absent from Royce's.

To make the second point let us introduce a simple example of a false belief that still manages to secure an object. Looking at a distant hillside in the evening gloom, I judge that the sheep next to the tree has not moved for a long time. The immediate object of my judgement is the sheep next to the tree. Suppose that in fact I am looking at a bush on the hillside which I falsely take to be a sheep: the immediate object misrepresents the real object of my judgement. In spite of this error, there is a sense in which I know what I am thinking or talking about, I am in cognitive contact with it. This is because my judgement is sensitive to further information about the object, that is about the bush which I take to be a sheep.

To illustrate what this involves, consider the process through which I come to recognize my error: how does the fact that the object is a bush constrain inquiry? I might walk up to the 'sheep' in order to see it better; I may focus my binoculars on it, or try to improve the illumination with a torch. Even if I do not know what the object really is, I can act upon it; I can keep track of it as I approach; or I can grab hold of it in order to inspect it more carefully. If I could not be confident that I was approaching or holding the right thing, I could not be sure that the new information I acquired was relevant to the reassessment of the original opinion. Thus the object causally constrains my developing opinions because I can deliberately inspect it and experiment upon it. An adequate account of the relations between judgements and their objects must thus explain how this is possible. How can a judgement which embodies a flawed characterization of its object put me into cognitive contact with it so that I can investigate it further and revise my understanding of what it is?

One might think that such cases are unusual and peripheral. Peirce thought otherwise. Consider part of his account of 'Truth' for Baldwin's *Dictionary of Philosophy*:

Truth is that concordance of an abstract statement with the ideal limit towards which endless investigation would tend to bring scientific belief, which concordance the abstract statement may possess by virtue of the confession of its inaccuracy and one-sidedness, and this confession is an essential ingredient of truth. (*CP* 5.565)

Elsewhere in the entry he writes that truth 'essentially depends upon that proposition's not professing to be exactly true'. If this is to be taken seriously, then the sort of inquiry that involves maintaining cognitive contact with things in spite of having a flawed understanding of what they are may be fundamental to the processes of inquiry by which we converge on the truth. If a proposition can correctly be said to be true, then inquiry is fated to arrive at a version of it which is more accurate and less one-sided.

7. Singulars and Indexical Reference: the Dynamical Object

It is common to distinguish general propositions from singular ones. *All planets circle some star*, is a general proposition which ascribes a property to everything meeting some general condition. *The Earth circles a star*, by contrast, is about a particular object, referred to by name. We naturally think of demonstrative propositions as singular too: *That planet is circling a star*. Modern formal logic encourages this assumption by assigning different logical forms to general propositions and singular ones. *All planets circle some star* would have the logical form ∀x (Fx ⊃ Gx), while *The Earth circles a star* has the form Ga. Within Aristotelian logic, all propositions are understood as general: this distinction is dismissed as mere appearance. In the 1860s, Peirce was still in the grip of the traditional approach to logic: 'Every cognition we are in possession of is a judgement whose subject and predicate are general terms' (W2: 180).[14] In 'An American Plato', he claimed that Royce's argument 'overlooks one of the most important recent discoveries' in formal logic (W5: 224). This was the invention of quantifiers by Peirce and his pupil O. H. Mitchell in 1884, which enabled him to change his mind and to reject Royce's assumption that the subject of a proposition is picked out by a general description.[15]

Peirce's work in the 1860s considered what kind of description can pick out a particular object, criticizing the idea that there are 'determinate individuals' that can be identified though their properties. 'Singular' propositions concern what he there called 'singulars'. His example was Hermolaus Barbarus: his idea of Hermolaus is very general, but he thinks of him as someone who 'can be but in one place at one time'. Once my description of him locates him at a particular place at a particular time, I need not fear that more than one object will fit this general description. *Hermolaus Barbarus translated Aristotle* may be seen as having the form *All possessors of characteristic HB translated Aristotle*, but the content of *HB* ensures that there is at most one such thing.[16] By the time he reviewed Royce, Peirce was ready to embrace the lesson of 'Kant's cataclysmic work' that locations in space and time cannot be identified in wholly general terms.

[14] This is from 'Questions of Reality', a preliminary draft of material which appeared in 'Questions Concerning Certain Faculties Claimed for Man' and 'Some Consequences of Four Incapacities'.

[15] These studies were published in a book edited by Peirce: *Studies in Logic, by Members of the Johns Hopkins University* (1883). The first presentation of Peirce's approach to quantifiers is in a paper by O. H. Mitchell in that volume. Kant's anticipation of the view defended here may thus lie in his famous argument, in the *Critique of Pure Reason*, that existence is not a predicate. As we shall note below, some arguments from the Transcendental Aesthetic may also be what Peirce had in mind.

[16] This all assumes that our paradigm examples of singular propositions concern existing, extended concrete objects. This appears to be Peirce's view. He admits that there are abstract objects such as numbers, sets, and properties. This is because there are sentences which contain grammatical singular terms such as 'seven', 'the empty set', and 'greenness'; but he also thinks that these are 'second-rate' objects. Numbers as objects are constructed by 'hypostatic abstraction' from the use of numerical quantifiers; terms like 'redness' are similarly constructed from predicative uses of terms with 'unsaturated bonds' such as 'is red' (*CP* 4.234 and 4. 464; *NEM*4: 162). The only singulars that are not constructed by hypostatic abstraction are 'existing' concrete things with which we can 'react'.

This thought may acquire some plausibility from noting that we can be in error about the location of some object that we perceive as well as being in error about the nature of the object. Deceived by a mirror, I form a judgement about what I take to be a book on a desk in front of me, but is, in fact, a box on a desk behind me. But Peirce is most impressed by the Kantian thought that 'One instant of time is, in itself, exactly like any other instant, one point of space like any other point; nevertheless dates and positions can be approximately distinguished' (W5: 225). The conclusion to draw from this seems to be that we can identify places only by reference to either objects that occupy them or their relations to other places which are occupied by objects. But this would require us to refer to objects without possessing prior descriptive specifications of the places that they occupy. The moral is that there must be non-descriptive reference to either positions or objects if reference to external things is to be possible at all.[17] Thus Peirce must provide an account of how we refer to locations in space and time and to the objects which occupy them, which denies that this ability is *wholly* mediated through general descriptions of these things and locations.

Peirce's work in logic had provided another reason for believing that there must be non-descriptive reference. Interpretation and evaluation of quantified propositions require a specification of a universe of discourse or domain of quantification.[18] This cannot be specified by a general term *within the proposition itself*, since the interpretation of that very description will itself be relative to the universe of discourse. Peirce had argued that *indexical* signs must be used to fulfil this function; and thus they were available as a theoretical device for handling problems about singular reference too.[19]

In 1868, in 'Some Consequences of Four Incapacities', Peirce introduced the idea of the 'pure demonstrative application' of a sign: 'the real physical connection of a sign with its object, either immediately or by its connection with another sign'. Thus the usefulness of a weathercock 'consists

---

[17] There are close connections between this idea and Kant's claim that space and time are forms of intuition rather than products of the understanding.

[18] 'The real world cannot be distinguished from a fictitious world by any description. It has often been disputed whether Hamlet was mad or not. This exemplifies the necessity of *indicating* that the real world is meant, if it be meant. No reality is altogether dynamic, not qualitative. It consists in forcefulness. Nothing but a dynamic sign can distinguish it from fiction' (*CP* 2.337).

[19] An extensive and useful discussion of the importance of indexical reference in Peirce's philosophy can be found in the work of Armando Fumagalli (1995, 1996)

wholly in [its] being really connected with the things that [it signifies]'. However, this 'real physical connection' is not to be confused with the 'representative function'. Peirce denies that semantic or semiotic notions can be reduced to 'real physical connections'. The semiotic property depends upon how the weathercock is to be used and understood, perhaps upon our practices of interpretation. But this use *exploits* and builds on the 'real physical connection' between the orientation of the weathercock and the direction of the wind. The fact that a sign like a weathercock exploits these real physical or 'existential' relations between sign and object is later captured by calling it an *index* of the direction of the wind. In 1868 it is referred to as the 'pure demonstrative application' of the sign.

Do our thoughts, utterances, and judgements have 'pure demonstrative application'? Given our explanation of Peirce's early theory of truth and error in section 4, it will be no surprise that his 1868 position was that the 'pure demonstrative application' of a thought or judgement was always to another thought or judgement of the same object: the only 'existential' relations exploited in cognition were *between* judgements. When we leap forward ten years to 'The Fixation of Belief', we learn that independent external objects 'affect our senses according to regular laws' and that 'by taking advantage of the laws of perception, we can ascertain by reasoning how things really are' (W3: 254). This suggests that, like the weathercock, my perceptual judgements have 'pure demonstrative application' to external things, and that I can exploit these 'physical' or 'existential' connections to objects in interpreting and using perceptual information. As noted before, Peirce's otherwise ubiquitous concern with semiotic questions is absent from 'The Fixation of Belief'. But this is the direction that his thought was clearly taking by the time he wrote 'An American Plato'. One of the lessons of modern formal logic was that at least one index 'must enter into every proposition, its function being to designate the subject of discourse' (W5: 224).

In the Royce review, there are few examples of indexical expressions. It is clear that a perceptual experience is an indexical sign of what is seen, and discussions elsewhere reveal that demonstrative expressions ('this', 'that', 'here', 'now') and proper names are conventional devices for indexical representation. Peirce does remark that an index 'like a pointing finger exercises a real physiological *force* over the attention . . . and directs it to a particular object of sense'; and that it designates the object of a proposition 'without implying any characters at all' (W5: 224). The index can signify an object because it stands in a real 'existential', 'physical' relation to its object; but the user of the index need not know or understand exactly what that physical or existential relation is.

The emphasis on the role of indexical representations in (for example) visual experience has at least three roles in Peirce's thought on these topics. It illuminates the phenomenology of visual experience; it explains how we perceive external things *directly*; and it promises a satisfying explanation of how we revise and correct our beliefs. 'A blinding flash of lightning forces my attention and directs it to a certain moment of time with an emphatic "Now!" ' (W5: 224). Developing the example slightly, we can say that I make indexical reference to a time and to an event in a judgement which is phenomenologically irresistible: '*That* is lightning *now*.'

In an attempt to understand this indexical anchoring further, Peirce suggests that:

it is by volitional acts that dates and positions are distinguished. The element of feeling is so prominent in sensations, that we do not observe that something like Will enters into them, too. . . . [S]trong, clear, and voluntary consciousness in which we act upon our muscles is nothing more than the most marked variety of a kind of consciousness which enters into many other phenomena of our life, a consciousness of duality or dual consciousness. (W5: 225)

This phenomenological feature of our conscious experience involves 'the sense of action and reaction, resistance, externality, otherness, pairedness. It is the sense that something has hit me or that I am hitting something; it might be called the sense of collision or clash.'[20] This is intended to challenge the common assumption that experiences are subjective pictures, their objects known only by inference to the external causes of these internal impressions. It is intrinsic to the phenomenological character of the experience that it is of something other, that it involves a direct confrontation with another, with 'that'.

This theme is a common pragmatist one.[21] We will understand reference and false belief only if we acknowledge that experience is far richer than traditional empiricists had supposed. Our language contains indexical devices (demonstratives, quantifiers, proper names) which reflect this rich phenomenology, articulating the thoughts that it makes possible. Thus Peirce insisted that we directly (albeit fallibly) perceive external

---

[20] In later work, this phenomenological feature of our experience was referred to as 'secondness'.

[21] In later work, Peirce suggested that James's 'radical empiricism' was Peirce's pragmatism under another name. This is discussed more fully in Hookway (1997).

things—they are present in our thoughts rather than being merely represented by aspects of our feelings and ideas.[22]

We have already encountered Peirce's notion of the *immediate object* of a thought or utterance: the object as it is presented in the thought or utterance itself. We noted that judgements with the different immediate objects could have the same real object. Once the importance of indexical reference is noted, Peirce began to express the point by saying that two judgements with different immediate objects could have the same 'dynamical object'. Thus Peirce wrote that 'a sign has two objects, its object as it is represented and its object in itself' (*CP* 8.333).

His later writings tell us more about the dynamical object. It is the 'really efficient but not immediately present Object' (*CP* 8.343), indeed 'the Reality which by some means contrives to determine the sign to its Representation' (*CP* 4.536). In a review of Lady Welby's *What is Meaning?*, he identifies the dynamical object as 'the Object as it is regardless of any particular aspect of it, the object in such relations as unlimited and final study would show it to be', and justifies his use of the term 'dynamical' by saying that it is 'the Object that Dynamical Science . . . can investigate' (*CP* 8.183). A further clue to Peirce's use of the term 'dynamical' is provided by a comment about indices in his entry in Baldwin's *Dictionary of Philosophy*, in which he remarks that 'If A points his finger to the fire, his finger is dynamically connected with the fire' (*CP* 2.305), and argues that interpretation of indices exploits these dynamical relations in order to arrive at a fuller specification of the object of the sign.[23]

To summarize these points. When I see an object (or think about it indexically), I am aware of the object as external and as acting upon me. My cognitive contact with the object need not commit me logically to any

---

[22]   These aspects of Peirce's position were explored in much greater detail around 1903, especially in the lectures on pragmatism then delivered at Harvard. (*CP* 5.14–134, especially lectures IV, VI, and VII) For further discussion see Hookway (1985, ch. 5). Soon after 1880, Peirce was emphasizing a further element of the richness of experience. Since, as he argued later, his pragmatism would be unacceptable to anyone who rejected realism about laws and generality, he tried to show that 'would be's were manifested in the phenomenological character of our experience. He hoped to vindicate a non-Humean 'empiricist' but realist account of laws and subjunctive conditionals.

[23]   While reluctant to commit myself to the claim that the distinction between immediate and dynamical object is the same as Frege's distinction between *Sinn* and *Bedeutung*, we should note that in every case where Frege would discern a difference in *Sinn* between expressions with the same *Bedeutung*, Peirce could find two expressions with different immediate objects but the same dynamical object. Moreover, in spite of the word 'dynamical' Peirce applies his distinction quite generally, to expressions other than singular terms and to terms for (for example) abstract objects.

beliefs about exactly where the object is located or about the causal process by which it has insinuated itself into my thoughts. However, these are matters that I can investigate further: the object has many properties which I do not yet know, and physical investigations can provide further knowledge of the object of my indexical thought. This independently existing external thing is the dynamical object: an object which can act on me and which is spatially related to me. Moreover, as we have seen, this direct object is something which 'from the nature of the thing the sign *cannot* express but only *indicate* and leave the interpreter to find out by *collateral experience*' (*CP* 8.314). As Carl Hausman has emphasized in defending a Peircean kind of 'metaphysical' realism, it is the aspect of the object which 'functions as an external constraint' and 'manifests resistances encountered in the process of interpretation' (1993: 9; see also pp. 72 ff, 166–7). Study of the dynamical object of my judgements is thus a way of eliminating error and increasing my knowledge of what I am thinking about, of what I first pick out indexically.

This is the key to Peirce's answer to Royce. Recall the example of my observing the lightning. 'Directly following it, I may judge that there will be a terrific peal of thunder, and if it does not come I acknowledge an error' (W5: 225). If it had been lightning, I would soon hear thunder. If I don't, then the flash that I saw was misrepresented when I thought of it as thunder. So I begin to look for other kinds of flash that might have been the dynamic object of my judgement. Discovering a photographer nearby may suggest that the best explanation of my experience was that his flash-gun produced the dynamic object in question.[24] As Peirce insisted in the passage from *CP* 8.314 quoted above, I exploit collateral information to arrive at a fuller description of the dynamical object of the indexical sign.

A similar pattern is involved when we investigate whether two different judgements (made by different people or by the same person at different times) have the same object. It might be asked 'how two different men can know they are speaking of the same thing' (W5: 225–6). Peirce's answer is brief but instructive:

Suppose, for instance, one man should say a flash of lightning was followed by thunder and another should deny it. How would they know they meant the same

---

[24] Royce himself observed that a 'feeling of dependence' formed part of the phenomenology of judgement: the value of a judgement lies in its 'agreement with a vaguely felt Beyond that stands our there as Object.' Since he does not incorporate this into a systematic account of indexical reference, it is unsurprising that he finds it too indeterminate to solve his problem about reference (1885: 402).

flash? The answer is that they would compare notes somewhat as follows. One would say, 'I mean that very brilliant flash which was preceded by three flashes, you know.' The second man would recognize the mark, and thus, by a probable and approximate inference they would conclude they meant the same flash. (W5: 226)

To a first reading, this is an endorsement of a sort of description theory: they each associate the same description with the flash—it was brilliant and preceded by three flashes. The remark that the inference involved is 'probable and approximate' suggests a more plausible interpretation. Their agreement on these descriptive features is evidence that they were confronting the same flash. We could imagine one of the men claiming that it was preceded by only two flashes. If we can explain why he missed one of them (perhaps he was briefly indoors at the time), then the precise nature of the disagreement could itself be evidence that they were talking about the same flash. This fits Peirce's realist principle: we exploit the laws of perception to decide whether they are confronting the same object or event.

Peirce's unpublished review contains more interesting material than I have discussed here. There is a discussion of Royce's general strategy of seeking philosophical truth through undermining our common-sense view of things and allowing the strongest scepticism to destroy itself. And he also makes specific criticisms of Royce's objections to Thrasymachus that have not been covered here. My aim in this chapter has been to use the engagement between Peirce and Royce as a way of exploring Peirce's philosophy at a crucial stage of its development. He was beginning to develop his metaphysical views, and his logical and semiotic theories were undergoing major changes. His responses to Royce are valuable for bringing out the problems he was facing at this time, the challenges he was having to deal with, and for helping us to understand the background against which most of these other changes occurred.

5

Vagueness, Logic, and Interpretation

1. Vagueness, Natural Language, and Logic

For many analytic philosophers, the presence of vague predicates constitutes, in Michael Dummett's phrase, 'an unmitigated defect of natural language' (1981: 316). According to Frege, when we are concerned with reasoning or 'if it is a question of the truth of something', 'we have to throw aside concepts that do not have a meaning [*Bedeutung*]'. He continues: 'These are . . . such as have vague boundaries. It must be determinate for every object whether it falls under a concept or not; a concept-word which does not meet this requirement on its meaning is meaningless' (1979: 122). Similar passages could be found in the works of many other writers, all affirming that vagueness is an imperfection. Some attempt to conclude that there is only an appearance of vagueness in natural languages; most call for linguistic reform, or for the use of artificially constructed languages which are free from imperfection whenever 'it is a question of the truth of something'.

Analytic philosophers who deny that vagueness is an imperfection mostly call for a revision in logic. They look for a system of deductive logic which systematizes inferences involving vague predicates. Such a logic would show which arguments involving vague predicates are valid; and, presumably, would help us to see how their logical behaviour differs from that of precise terms. They seek a formal logic of vagueness; and many would hold that only the construction of such a logic could convince us that vagueness is not an imperfection. In the following section, I shall set out some of the themes involved in these arguments by examining Frege's claims about vagueness more closely.

Wittgenstein, in his later writings, looks upon vagueness much more kindly. For example, in *Philosophical Investigations*, he describes some bizarre possibilities which our familiar notion of a chair leaves us uncertain how to describe: an apparent chair disappears when we approach it, only to reappear with all its familiar properties, and then to disappear again. We have no rules which determine whether it is a real chair or an illusion: 'But do we miss them when we use the word 'chair'; and are we to say that we do not really attach any meaning to this word, because we are not equipped with rules for every possible application of it?' (1953: §80) It is not a defect in a concept that it does not equip us to describe situations that will never arise. This theme recurs in Wittgenstein's writings, and he connects our tendency to view 'inexact' as a term of reproach, and 'exact' as a term of praise with a mistaken view of logic; this is the view that logic is 'something sublime', that it penetrates beneath phenomena to uncover a precise structure which provides 'the basis, or essence, of everything empirical' (1953: §88–9).

It is a commonplace that Wittgenstein's later work has a 'pragmatist' flavour, due to the influence of Frank Ramsey upon his work around 1930. These views of vagueness—which contrast with the more Fregean position of his *Tractatus Logico-Philosophicus*—are one manifestation of this pragmatism. His discussion of 'chair' is followed by an examination of Ramsey's view of logic, which contrasts with his own earlier position. Moreover, Ramsey characterized his own view as differing from that of the *Tractatus* largely in the 'pragmatism' he had learned from Russell and his reading of an early anthology of Peirce's papers, *Chance, Love and Logic.* He accused the *Tractatus* of '*scholasticism*, the essence of which is treating what is vague as if it were precise and trying to fit it into an exact logical category' (1931: 269). Elsewhere, he described the 'essence of pragmatism': 'the meaning of a sentence is to be defined by reference to the actions to which asserting it would lead, or, more vaguely still, by its possible causal effects' (1978: 57; 1931: 155). With its suggestion that the meaning of an expression is to be explained by its importance for (or effects upon) our practices, and the verificationism which it probably suggests, we can see further links with the themes from the *Investigations* which are described as 'pragmatist'. What is less clear, however, are the relations between these themes. Does a determination to take vagueness seriously form a unified whole with a kind of functionalist theory of meaning, and the rejection of an essentialist account of logic? Is the resulting set of views usefully described as 'pragmatist'?

I mentioned above that Ramsey was influenced by one of the classic American pragmatists, Charles Peirce. As well as defending a theory of meaning fitting Ramsey's description of pragmatism, Peirce complained that 'logicians have been at fault in giving Vagueness the go-by, so far as not even to analyze it' (*CP* 5.446). He denied that vagueness was a 'defect in thinking or knowledge' and, in a suggestive comparison, insisted that it 'is no more to be done away with in the world of logic than friction in mechanics' (*CP* 4.344, 4.512). Not only is 'a determinate sign an impossibility', but excessive precision, like excessive vagueness, is an *impediment* to the pursuit of truth. Although he claims to have 'worked out the logic of vagueness with something like completeness' (*CP* 5.506), the systems of *formal* logic that he constructed do not seem to reflect this. He appears to deny that taking vagueness seriously requires us to construct special formal systems.[1] He used the word 'logic' more widely than is now common, to cover the ground he also described as 'semiotic': the general theory of signs and interpretation. His investigations in the logic of vagueness are primarily semantic accounts of the use of vague predicates and classifications of the different kinds of vagueness.

In Wittgenstein, Ramsey, and Peirce, there seem to be connections between a readiness to take vagueness seriously, a 'pragmatist' perspective upon issues of meaning, and some distinctive views of the nature or role of formal logic. I am sympathetic to the view that vagueness is not an imperfection, and I am attracted by broadly 'pragmatist' accounts of meaning. However, in view of the prevalence of the contrary view—and of the view that we can only take vagueness seriously by developing a special logic—my focus is upon whether it is possible to hold to this position. I shall mostly discuss Peirce, but my concern is with understanding some of the pragmatist tendencies present in analytic philosophy and with the underlying assumptions about meaning and logic which underlie the opposing positions.

2. Frege, Wittgenstein, and 'Pragmatism'

What reason has Frege for claiming that vague predicates lack meaning, and are no concern of logic? In section 56, volume 2 of the *Grundgesetze*, we read:

[A] concept that is not sharply defined is wrongly termed a concept. Such quasi-conceptual constructions cannot be recognized as concepts by logic: it is impossible to lay down precise laws for them. The law of excluded middle is really just

---

[1] This needs slight qualification. There are a few manuscript pages in which Peirce sketches a three-valued logic, and suggests that this might have application in accounting for the logic of vagueness (Fisch and Turquette 1966). The reprint of this paper in Fisch 1986 lists eight papers in which Turquette has extended his study of this system (Fisch 1986: 183, note 29). The fragmentary nature of this material means that the claim made here still stands.

another form of the requirement that the concept should have a precise boundary. (1970: 159)

And in a letter to Peano:

But logic can only recognize sharply delimited concepts. Only under this presupposition can it set up precise laws . . . Just as it would be impossible for geometry to set up precise laws if it tried to recognize threads as lines and knots in threads as points, so logic must demand sharp limits of what it will recognize as a concept unless it wants to renounce all precision and certainty. (1980: 11–15)

The comparison with geometry occurs elsewhere too, in 'The Law of Inertia':

If something fails to display a sharp boundary, it cannot be recognized in logic as a concept, just as something that is not extensionless cannot be recognized in geometry as a point, because otherwise it would be impossible to set up geometrical axioms. The technical language of any science must conform to a single standard: does it enable the lawfulness of nature to be expressed as simply as possible and at the same time with perfect precision? (1984: 133)

The central point is that simple, precise logical laws could not be obtained if logic 'recognized' vague concepts; and the law of excluded middle is apparently an example of a fundamental logical truth which holds only for 'genuine' concepts. Frege offers no extended demonstration that no such logical laws are available—it seems to be accepted without much argument.

When Wittgenstein objects to Frege's denial that vague concepts have meaning, he does not respond directly to the challenge to find precise logical laws. Instead, he employs two different strategies. First, he examines the ways we actually use concepts, the needs to which they answer, and reminds us that vague concepts can often answer to these needs far better than precise ones. For example, when uncertainty is expressed about whether a 'blurred concept' is a concept at all, he responds: 'Is an indistinct photograph a picture of a person at all? Is it always an advantage to replace an indistinct picture by a sharp one? Isn't the indistinct one often exactly what we need?' And when Frege compares a concept to an area, denying that an area with vague boundaries is an area at all, Wittgenstein asks: 'But is it senseless to say: "Stand roughly there"?' (1953: §71). The 'pragmatist' flavour of the remarks is evident: the meanings of our words, the character of our concepts, reflect the relations of their uses to our practical concerns and projects. Linguistic behaviour is a form of behaviour, and its tools can only be judged by their contribution to our achieving our communicative ends.

Second, Wittgenstein attempts a diagnosis of what has gone wrong. Logicians construct formal systems which provide idealizations of our ordinary practice. These systems can prove useful tools in evaluating reasoning and studying arguments. Of course, since they are idealizations, there will sometimes be a lack of fit between the model and our ordinary practice of argument—for example, in connection with some arguments involving vague predicates. Examination of our practice of evaluating arguments shows that we are aware of this, and that it rarely leads to error. But the logician misunderstands the nature of his formal system, and claims that his ideal pattern either is implicit in ordinary untidy usage, or, like Frege, that it should be. The conclusion is that logic can only take seriously forms of discourse which do not risk exposing the idealizations involved in our logic. Once again there is a pragmatist flavour: we are to view logical systems as normative frameworks, whose meaning is to be understood by considering their role in our practices. They are not to be seen as capturing fundamental truths about some underlying or ideal reality.

In at least one respect, these arguments may fail to engage with Frege's concerns. Frege employs 'concept' and 'meaning' in a technical fashion, and the claim that vagueness is no concern of logic is compatible with the view that vague expressions are very useful for many practical purposes. He admits that the 'softness and instability of ordinary language' is 'necessary for its versatility and potential for development'. Its inadequacies only intrude, we might suppose, 'if it is a question of the truth of something' (1972: 86; cf. Dummett 1981: 33). It is only then that logic comes into its own and vagueness should be spurned. We could imagine a Quinean holding that vague predicates have no role in a canonical notation for serious science, while being invaluable in the home and marketplace: this may be close to Frege's position. It is at this point that I wish to turn to Peirce. His pragmatism, and his stress upon the importance of vagueness, emerge in the course of an extended attempt to justify the claim that serious inquiry, properly conducted, will take us to the truth about reality. The core of this argument is an approach to the philosophy of language and mind which provided philosophical foundations for his pragmatism, and also (through Ogden and Richards's important book *The Meaning of Meaning* (1923)) influenced Ramsey and Wittgenstein. I hope that an examination of this will help us to see how the Fregean perspective upon vagueness can be avoided.

3. Pragmatism and Science

The term 'pragmatism' can be taken in a narrow and a wide sense. According to the former, it applies to a rule for clarifying the meanings of words and concepts. Peirce almost invariably uses the term to refer to such a rule, which he first defended in 'How to Make our Ideas Clear', published in 1878, and returned to on many occasions. If we wish to clarify a concept, he tells us, we should 'Consider what effects, which might conceivably have practical bearing, we conceive the object of our conception to have. Then, our conception of these effects is the whole of our conception of the object' (W3: 266).

As his examples and later formulations make clear, we clarify the claim that some object *o* is F by deciding which claims of the following form we take to be true:

If *o* is F, then if action A were to be performed, experience *e* would result.

Thus:

If this powder is salt, then if we were to place it in water and stir vigorously, we would observe it dissolve.

If this object is hard, then if we were to make many attempts to scratch it, employing different objects to do so, few of our attempts would be successful.

and so on. (For further discussion, and more examples, see Hookway 1985: 49–51, 234–40).[2]

In its wider sense, we can think of pragmatism as an approach to philosophy which places stress upon the facts that human beings are agents, and inquiry and investigation are forms of activity. Scientific activity, for example, is understood as an attempt to put human agents into some sort

---

[2] In order to prevent misunderstanding by readers who are familiar with the positivists' approach to meaning, two points should be stressed. First, there is no suggestion that the conditionals we arrive at in applying the principle should be *analytic*: they reflect our theoretical understanding of the concept in question; and they will he revised (and their number grow) as this scientific understanding develops. Second, Peirce is increasingly emphatic that his view would have no plausibility if we lacked a realist understanding of the subjunctive conditionals, (the 'would-be's), that these formulations contain (see, for example, *CP* 5.453, and Hookway 1985: 239–46).

of harmonious relation with their environment; and it is to be understood in terms of the goals of the activity and the means we have available for pursuing them. Questions of meaning and language are to be resolved by exploring the role of thought and speech in these activities. What kinds of concept do we need for such purposes? What practices of linguistic behaviour are called for by serious science? It accords with this broader conception of pragmatism that Wittgenstein replaces questions about truth in mathematics with questions about the use of mathematical propositions (1967: 3). It encourages a broadly 'functionalist' approach to questions of thought and language. We approach them through an understanding of the contributions of concepts and utterances to the achievement of our aims. This is vague, and can only serve as a general characterization of the pragmatist flavour of much recent philosophy by remaining so. Hence, I shall descend to a particular example, examining two features of Peirce's philosophy which fit this pattern.

The first involves the underlying insight of his work on thought and language. One philosophical approach to meaning talks simply of expressions and their referents, or of sentences and the propositions they express. Little is said about how names can denote their bearers, or of how sentences can express propositions. Since the underlying concern is with describing (say) the truth-conditions of sentences, and with explaining the validity of inferences, it is supposed that we can abstract from the psychological details of how these dyadic relations are set up, and from the social framework which sustains them. While it is acknowledged that the relations of denotation and expression are mysterious in the absence of such explanations, philosophy of language can get on without them.

According to Peirce, by contrast, the fundamental semantic relation is triadic. A name denotes an object only by being *interpreted* as denoting the object; a sentence expresses a proposition only by being understood or interpreted as expressing it. In general, something is meaningful by virtue of having the power to enforce a particular interpretation; and the relation between a sign (linguistic expression or thought) and its 'object' is mediated through an interpreting thought or utterance. In consequence, we can understand the contents of thoughts only by taking into account their interpretation in subsequent thoughts or their expression in utterances; and we can understand the meanings of utterances only by examining their interpretation through the thoughts and utterances of those who attend to them.

Interpretations are various, and Peirce has written extensively on the nature of interpretation and the different kinds of 'interpretant'. I shall very briefly mention a very few relevant considerations. The simplest kind of interpretation, I suppose, consists, in the thought that (for example):

That utterance of 'snow is white' expresses the proposition that snow is white.

or

That utterance of 'Brutus' refers to Brutus.

But an interpretation can 'develop' a thought through inference. I manifest my understanding of an utterance of 'snow is white' by inferring from it that snow is not red, or that snow is the same colour as flour, etc. Similarly, thoughts are typically interpreted through inference, in this fashion. Finally, a thought or utterance can be interpreted in a habit of expectation: my understanding of my thought that salt is soluble is manifested in my expecting any sample which is placed in water to dissolve—I am surprised if this does not happen. These different elements can be combined. For example, my understanding of the proposition that heavy clouds are forming over the mountains may be manifested in my expecting a thunderstorm tonight—this expectation reflecting the impact of other beliefs about such cloud formations through inference. It follows from this that how I interpret a thought or utterance will depend upon the interests and concerns which occupy me at the time.

The second element of Peirce's thought that I wish to consider is his picture of *science* as a distinctive kind of activity, which involves the interpretation of thoughts and utterances through deliberation and discussion. Scientific activity is not directed at solving practical problems in the short run. The true scientist devotes his life to contributing to the eventual discovery of the truth. Peirce believes that methods are available which will ensure that, unless we are distracted by the search for personal glory or by the short-run demands of practice, the community of scientists will eventually reach the truth on all questions which are raised There is supposed to be a proof that the scientific method will take us to the truth in the long run, although there is no reply to sceptical doubts about its short-run effectiveness. Our use of induction, for example, for the practical affairs of life is grounded in unquestioned common sense, but can receive no logical vindication. The method of science involves proposing hypotheses, testing them experimentally by deriving predictions from them, and modifying or abandoning them when our expectations about the results of experiments are surprised. The assurance that we shall eventually reach the truth is attributed to the logical character of certain patterns of statistical inference, and to the justified hope that our gradually developing standards of plausibility will equip us to propose, and take seriously, the theories which experience will eventually reveal to be true.

My concern here is not with Peirce's attempted *vindication* of the method of science: the argument is complex, and is entwined with his defence of a complex metaphysical framework which appears to involve a form of objective idealism. His account of how science proceeds—how we behave when 'it is a question of the truth of something'—is largely independent of this wider framework, and reflects his many years of experience as a practising scientist. I am interested in what can be said about the interpretative practices of serious scientific researchers. The pragmatist principle arises in this context. In order to function as a scientist efficiently, it is important that we do so in a reflective or self-conscious fashion. One thing that this involves is that we be reflective about how our 'scientific assertions' and beliefs can be interpreted: it is good methodology to seek a reflective clarity about those interpretations of our beliefs and utterances which could have a bearing upon scientific practice. Peirce claims that, if we apply the pragmatic principle, we become completely aware of the relevant features of the meanings of our terms: the principle is a rule for determining the 'ultimate logical interpretant' or content of our beliefs and concepts.

Once again, my primary concern is not with the thorny issue of how successful Peirce was at 'proving' his pragmatist principle. Rather, I want to point out some of the strategies he employs in arguing for it. One of these is familiar from writings on meaning by empiricists like Moritz Schlick. Peirce appears to think that a habit of expectation is the only kind of interpretation that takes us beyond the web of thoughts and words, enabling a thought or expression to be interpreted by something which gives it a definite content without itself needing to be interpreted. More interesting are arguments which appeal to what goes on in scientific practice and consider what kinds of interpretant we should favour to participate in these practices. I shall mention two of these.

First, the scientific method involves deriving testable predictions from hypotheses and seeing whether they are surprised by the results of experiment or observation. The pragmatist principle guides us to a reflective understanding of which experimental results we should anticipate if an hypothesis were true. If all that there is to science is experimental testing, the claim runs, then the pragmatist principle reveals all the interpretations of an hypothesis which we would judge to be relevant to our scientific activity. If it is 'a question of the truth of something', that is all that we could need.

Second, a community of scientists is held together by a practice of *assertion*. If I assert something to you, then I am attempting to get you to believe it. I do so by producing an utterance which is conventionally recognized as a sign that I think it reasonable to believe that proposition. I expect your inference that I think it reasonable to hold this belief to be grounded in the fact that there is a practice of penalizing assertions of propositions which are false—unless the asserter has a reasonable excuse for being mistaken. Assertion provides the means for transmitting information from one member of the scientific community to another. It also provides the vehicle for scientific debate: once an assertion is made, another can criticize it, providing considerations which suggest that the assertion was improperly made or should be withdrawn. A cautious asserter should ensure that he is not likely to incur penalties before making an assertion. And the auditor of an assertion should be wary of the risks to which he is exposed when he accepts some testimony as something he will assert himself. In each case, what we need to know is what experimental results or observations would show the assertion to be unjustified. Once again, the pragmatist principle provides the information we need in order to participate in the practice of assertion in a reflective and cautiously scientific manner.

Peirce took these arguments to show that the pragmatist principle provided a valuable methodological rule for clarifying concepts, for those involved in the activity of science. The arguments rest upon examining scientific practice, and considering the semantic needs of someone who participates in it. His own worries about pragmatism—which occasioned most of his philosophical efforts during the first decade of the twentieth century—turned on whether he could prove that no further clarification was important for science. He was worried that we may have concepts available that would enable us to prefer one hypothesis to another empirically equivalent one on the grounds that it provided a 'better explanation' of the facts, entering into a more coherent or intelligible framework of theory. Whether he ever satisfied himself on this score is uncertain; and it would take us beyond the concerns of this chapter to examine it more fully.

4. Vagueness and Assertability

In one of his contributions to Baldwin's *Dictionary of Philosophy*, Peirce wrote that 'a proposition is vague when there are possible states of things concerning which it is intrinsically uncertain whether, had they been contemplated by the speaker, he would regard them as excluded or allowed by the proposition.' His disposition to accept the proposition is indeterminate simply because the question whether to apply it in these cases did not present itself. It is left 'doubtful just what [the sign's] intended interpretation was, not between two or more separate interpretations, which would be ambiguity . . . but as to a greater multitude or even a continuum of possible interpretations no two of which differ without the doubt being extended to the intermediate interpretations' (MS 283, 1906).

It is helpful to distinguish some different 'phenomena of vagueness' here. Much work by logicians has been concerned with the *semantics* of vagueness, examining predicates such as 'heap', 'red' and so on which admit of borderline cases. The meaning we attach to 'red', does not entail that it effectively partitions any domain of objects into those that possess the associated property and those which lack it. Semantic vagueness gives rise to logical puzzles such as the Sorites paradox. This underlies the project of revising formal logic to avoid such paradoxes, or giving an account of the meanings of vague predicates which reveals that they do not really give rise to such paradoxes.

If I am using the predicate to describe a domain in which no borderline cases are to be found, then, although I use expressions which are semantically vague, the content of my assertions may well be fully precise. The sentence is vague but, in some contexts, the assertions it is used to make are perfectly precise. One target for a study of the *pragmatics* of vagueness would be the description of the contextual circumstances in which assertions made using vague expressions have fully determinate contents. A vague assertion, by contrast, would be one whose content left us unclear how it should be evaluated in circumstances which, we allow, could actually arise. Someone could intelligibly announce that they would buy a small car while aware that many possible purchases would leave it unclear whether their announcement was true.

Peirce's work on the 'logic' of vagueness is mainly concerned with issues of this second kind, issues concerning how we deal with vague or indeterminate assertions. These too are of several kinds, and he does not always distinguish them carefully. In the example we have just considered the vagueness of the assertion results from the use of a vague predicate, 'small', in a situation where the possibility of encountering borderline cases has not been ruled out. We can also find cases where vague assertions are made through the use of predicates which are semantically precise. For example, when the authorities announce that 1,000 people attended a political demonstration, their claim is not shown to be mistaken when a more precise count reveals that there were 995. Rather, contextual clues alert us to the fact they commit themselves only to the approximate truth of the sentence they had uttered.[3] In different cases, different explanations will be offered of why no determinate proposition is expressed in a proposition: it may result from the semantic vagueness of expressions such as 'red', 'heap', or 'bald'; it may reflect the use being made of a sentence, perhaps to the fact that the speaker commits herself only to its approximate truth.

Peirce himself offers a variety of examples, including colour predicates (*CP* 5.448, n.1). Unsurprisingly, he is especially interested in cases drawn from the history of science, where we use a vocabulary which, we are sure, will be improved upon, or even rejected, in the light of further progress. This has implications for our understanding of the force of 'scientific assertions' which were discussed in Chapters 1 and 2. Their relations to issues of vagueness and approximate truth are discussed further in the following section. For the present, we can note an example from a draft of a logic text, *Reason's Rules*:

To the question whether a certain newly found skeleton was the skeleton of a man rather than an anthropoid ape, the reply 'Yes and No' might, in a certain sense, be justifiable. Namely, owing to our conception of what a man is having formed without thinking of the possibility of such a creature as that to which this skeleton belongs, the question really has no definite meaning. (MS 596)

Peirce insists that the question of whether this skeleton is of a man has no definite meaning, but he has no doubts about the propriety of more familiar questions involving the concept *man*. By contrast, Frege seems to be committed to a more extreme claim: no sentences involving 'man' express thoughts or can be used in inference.

Peirce often compares vague propositions to quantified ones, and it is natural to do so. Semantic accounts of vague expressions which exploit supervaluations, for example, do so explicitly (see Fine 1975). A predicate M is a sharpening of 'man' if it agrees with 'man' concerning all those

---

[3] Grice's theory of conversational implicatures may provide a plausible account of how we pick up on the contextual clues (see Grice 1989, ch. 2). On the assumption that the authorities are intending to be co-operative in contributing to this conversation, we can see (and they can predict that we shall see) that they could only be truthful and sincere in their contribution if they were committed to no more than the approximate truth of what was said. Grice's discussion of 'speaking loosely' (p. 44) may also be relevant to the understanding of some of those cases where we are not committed to some of the strict entailments carried by the sentences we assert.

objects which are definitely either men or not men, and is, in addition, precise, yielding definite verdicts where 'man' yields none. A proposition containing vague predicates is then said to be true (false) if it is true (false) according to every sharpening of the vague predicates contained. So, the skeleton is of a man if it satisfies *every* sharpening of 'man'. We understand the truth-conditions of vague predicates when we see that they function analogously to universally quantified expressions. We should expect this picture to be attractive to Peirce. Since he thinks that a proposition is true only if inquiry is destined to reach an unforced consensus upon its truth, he is surely committed to the view that it is true only if we should agree on its truth however it is sharpened. Up to a point, this is correct: he would agree that only in these circumstances does the question have a 'definite meaning'. However, it is important to understand that, whenever he makes a comparison between vagueness and quantification, the analogy he stresses is with *existential* quantification.

The point of the analogy emerges when we consider the assertability conditions of vague and existentially quantified propositions. Under which circumstances is the assertion that some book on my desk is green successfully challenged? How can it be defended? According to Peirce, the speaker (the 'defender') reserves the right to stipulate the member of the universe of discourse by which it is to be judged. Perhaps better, he is sanctioned when it is shown that he cannot find a defensible instance of the quantified expression. Similarly, an assertion of a universally quantified proposition is defeated when the person addressed (the 'opponent') can find an instance of the quantified expression which is not defensible. In another words, the evaluation of the proposition depends upon a subsequent interpretation which renders it more determinate: an existential quantifier leaves it up to the speaker to fix the more precise assertion by reference to which it is to be evaluated; a universal quantifier assigns this role to the person addressed, who is concerned with whether to accept the testimony that he is offered (MS 9, MS 515). (The speaker is described as *defending* his utterance against the challenge that would expose him to sanction; the hearer, or opponent, will be anxious to refute the utterance if he can, since he desires to accept it only if he will not himself incur sanctions when he repeats the assertion.)[4]

Turning to vague expressions, the analogy with existential quantification emerges: if the speaker can produce a sharpening of the original

---

[4] There are marked similarities between Peirce's approach to quantification and Hintikka's 'game-theoretic semantics': they are discussed by Hilpinen (1982) and Brock (1980).

predicate which accords with past usage and delivers an unequivocal verdict on the present case, then he has successfully met any challenge to his assertion. In that case, in the case described, both:

This is a human skeleton

and

This is not a human skeleton

may be defensible. The speaker reserves the right to determine which sharpening should be employed in evaluating his utterance. His assertion is criticized only if he selects a sharpening which renders it indefensible, or if the opponent can show that no sharpening of the assertion is defensible at all. Thus:

[Vagueness] is the antithetical analogue of generality [sc. universal quantification]. A sign is objectively *general,* insofar as, leaving its effective interpretation indeterminate, it surrenders to the interpreter the right of completing the determination for himself . . . A sign is objectively *vague,* insofar as, leaving its interpretation more or less indeterminate, it reserves for some other possible sign or experience the function of completing the determination. (*CP* 5.505)

While it is false that 'A *proposition whose identity 1 have determined* is both true and false,' yet until it is determinate, it may be true that a proposition is true and that a proposition is false. (*CP* 5.448)

We have already encountered this in the speaker's willingness to countenance the answer 'Yes and no' to the question 'Is this a human skeleton?'

The distinctive pragmatist approach to semantic issues is evident in the style of argument used here. When Frege expresses doubts about the coherence of vague predicates, this is because he thinks that there are no precise laws of logic which explain their logical behaviour. When Peirce defends their coherence, this is through showing that they do not prevent our interpreting the utterances in which they occur: the focus is on the practice of interpretation, and upon how we can make them more precise through such a process.[5] Our two remaining tasks are to consider the

---

[5] Hence, Peirce's 'logic' of vagueness consists in a classification of the different kinds of vagueness and an exploration of how sentences containing vague expressions are interpreted. Brock (1979) discusses some of these claims in more detail, and they are also considered in Nadin (1980).

views about the nature of logic which enable Peirce to remain unimpressed by the sorts of considerations which disturb Frege, and to understand the importance of these interpretative practices when we are concerned with discovering the truth.

5. Vagueness and Science

I shall take the second of these questions first: why does Peirce believe that vagueness is a virtue? He sometimes argues that vagueness is unavoidable by reference to the semantics of singular terms, but I shall not discuss these arguments here (see, for example, *CP* 3.93, 5.448 fn.). More immediately relevant here are three respects in which science calls for vague predicates.

As is well known, Peirce holds, by and large, to a hypothetico-deductivist account of the growth of science; one element in his realism is his assurance that any false theory would eventually be refuted by the test of experience, while only a true theory can survive the test of time. When we formulate an hypothesis for testing, we put it forward as approximately true: although ad hoc adjustments of theories to avoid empirical falsification are frowned upon, our initial hypothesis is only that some more precise theory grounded in the vague one proposed will turn out to be true. We hope that an unforced consensus will be secured on some precisification of our vague hypothesis. The refutation of some formulation of the hypothesis is not taken to refute the initial vague hypothesis: it refutes the formulation and sends us back to find a new better formulation of the hypothesis. Thus, when the tentative hypothesis is first put forward, it is understood that its precise interpretation is undetermined: it is suggested only that there is a way of interpreting it according to which it is defensible; and it is left to subsequent research to fix on how the hypothesis should be interpreted.

The familiar history of the kinetical theory of gases well illustrates this. It began with a number of spheres almost infinitesimally small occasionally colliding. It was afterward so modified that the forces between the spheres, instead of merely separating them, were mainly attractive, that the molecules were not spheres, but systems, and that the part of space within which their motions are free is appreciably less than the entire volume of the gas. There was no new hypothetical element in these modifications. They were partly quantitative, and partly such as to make the formal hypothesis represent better what was really supposed to be the case. (*CP* 7.216)

Second, Peirce allows a role for common-sense certainties in grounding our claims to knowledge. Justification comes to a halt upon propositions which function as the 'bedrock of truth' which are accepted without grounds or justification. We regard them as 'the very truth' (*CP* 5.505): 'if you absolutely cannot doubt a proposition . . . it is plain that there is no room to desire anything more' (*CP* 6.498). Although these claims are, in fact, fallible, they are 'acritical'. This is an important concept for Peirce's philosophy (as well as being another point where his views strongly resemble those of Wittgenstein (see Wittgenstein 1969: passim)): an acritical belief is one of which we are certain, which does not issue from the kind of process of deliberation or reasoning which can be subjected to critical monitoring. We do not know why we believe these things; we cannot imagine being able to doubt them; and they have a foundational role for our practices of inquiry and justification.

When he discusses how a fallibilist can accept that there are such certainties, Peirce writes: 'It is . . . easy to be certain. One has only to be sufficiently vague' (*CP* 4.237). He claims that he can offer an a priori proof that 'veritably indubitable beliefs are especially vague' (*CP* 5.507). If a belief is formulated precisely, 'a suitable line of reflection, accompanied by imaginary experimentation, always excites doubt of [it]'. Once we can specify experiential results which would successfully challenge a claim, we can admit the possibility of its being false. So long as we do not specify what is burned by fire, and in what circumstances, little can falsify the vague common-sense claim that fire burns (*CP* 5.498). And, although no laboratory experiment could leave the proposition that there is an element of order in the Universe 'more certain than instinct or common sense leaves it', still, 'when anyone undertakes to say *precisely* what that order consists in, he will quickly find he outruns all logical warrant' (*CP* 6.496).

Finally, it seems plain that Peirce thinks that perceptual judgements are unavoidably vague. These too are acritical: they are theory-laden judgements, which are fallible in the light of subsequent experience; but at the time of making them, we find them absolutely compelling while having no sense of any grounds upon which they are made. At *CP* 5.448, note 1, Peirce suggests that precision is not required of observational predicates. Considering two people discussing the colour of Charles II's hair, he points out that in spite of the facts that neither is a trained observer of colours, and that 'colors are seen quite differently by different retinas', 'if one of them says that Charles II had dark auburn hair, the other will understand him precisely enough for all their possible purposes; and it will be a determinate predication'. Colour predications work well enough for practical purposes although we lack any precise sense of what a particular colour attribution excludes. All that is required, to defend our claim, is that we can make a case for our attribution being a defensible interpretation of the pattern of use which has determined the meaning of the term. If the vagueness and variation is such that we do, in practice, find different observers making different judgements, then the term must be made more precise. There is no point seeking greater precision if this does not occur. When the term is more precise, we have to be more careful, more painstaking, in deciding whether it applies in any particular occasion; and it becomes less suited for casual reports of observation.

So, the practice of science is better served by vague predicates than by precise ones. It is compatible with this that we should aspire to greater precision, that one of the tasks of science should be the gradual elimination of vagueness from its theories. I suspect that Peirce believes that scientists properly, and naturally, attempt to remove the vagueness from their hypotheses. I suspect, too, that Peirce believed that science was approaching, as a limit, a point at which such vagueness was wholly eliminated. However, there is nothing internal to his account of the scientific method which guarantees this; and his assurance reflects other philosophical doctrines which are involved in his defence of objective idealism.

6. Logic and Bivalence

We have seen that Peirce offers an account of the use of vague predicates. He explains how we interpret them by describing their assertability-conditions, and he stresses their importance for the practice of science. However, Frege's challenge remains: can Peirce respond consistently to the charge that vague language is incoherent because otherwise no logical laws can be laid down. Frege insists that 'the law of excluded middle is really just another form of the requirement that the concept should have a precise boundary' (Frege 1970: 159). What is Peirce's view of the law of excluded middle? The question is especially pressing since, as has been mentioned above, Peirce's systems of formal logic are mainly classical.

Peirce's discussion of the example of the skeleton occurs in the course of a critique of some common false logical presumptions. We naturally suppose that any proposition, or its negation, is determinately true: in fact, we assume that the negation of a proposition's being true is the 'same fact' as the proposition's not being true. Vague propositions show that this is incorrect. The fact that it is not destined that 'This skeleton is a man' would occur in the final consensus is compatible with it not being destined that 'This skeleton is not a man' would appear in the final consensus: and, equally, the fact that the former sentence could feature in such an unforced consensus is compatible with the claim that, the facts being as they are, the other could equally legitimately do so. The mistaken presumption rested upon an erroneous conception of facts which leads us, mistakenly, to accept the principle of bivalence. We conclude:

P is an ultimately defensible assertion (it will not be successfully challenged), if and only if not-*P* is not an ultimately defensible assertion.

However, when vague predicates are involved, a statement and its negation may both be ultimately defensible. Unless we adopt a convention to sharpen a vague term in one way rather than another, neither is destined to be part of the final consensus.

It is natural to see in this a challenge to accepted logical principles: the law of excluded middle fails, because there is no reason to suppose that either *P* or its negation is actually true. Peirce seems to insist that vagueness is a source of counterexamples to the law of excluded middle. Many arguments formulated in everyday language (or, indeed, in scientific language) appear to fail to conform to the 'laws' of classical logic. The common insistence in that case, that some adjustment is required, seems irresistible: either we seek an improved formulation of the laws, or we despair of ordinary language and its limitations. The legitimacy of this demand, however, depends upon how the calculi developed by logicians are to be interpreted: how do those who develop systems of deductive logic contribute to the pursuit of truth? It is instructive to note the analogies that Frege and Peirce use to describe the lack of fit between logical 'laws' and the practice of inference employing ordinary vague predicates. While Peirce tells us that vagueness can no more be eliminated from language than 'friction can from physics', Frege insists that for a logician to take vagueness seriously would be like a geometer recognizing 'threads as lines and knots as points'. Both are aware that the laws formulated by logicians idealize the patterns of argument found in ordinary reasoning employing vague expressions: 'external reality' fits the theories only imperfectly. Frege seems to conclude that the theory is really about ideal objects—which fit the laws perfectly—and hence logic deals only with arguments involving precise predicates; he is happy to remark that 'the task of our vernacular languages is essentially fulfilled if people engaged in communication with one another connect the same thought, or approximately the same thought, with the same proposition' (1980: 115). He insists that logical laws apply only to sentences in which concepts are expressed and, as we have seen, vague concepts are not really concepts. Peirce is impressed with how we use theoretical idealizations in order to understand less ideal occurrences—a physical theory which abstracts from the effects of friction can provide us with understanding of ordinary physical occurrences, so long as we are careful about how we apply it.

If, as Peirce appears to think, bivalence does not hold in all cases, how can he justify employing a classical logic?

Logic requires us, with reference to each question we have in hand, to hope some definite answer to it may be true. That *hope* with reference to each case as it comes up is, by a *saltus* stated by logicians as a *law* concerning *all* eases, namely the law of excluded middle. (*NEM4*: xiii)

When I commit myself to investigating a proposition, to determining whether it is true, I assume (or hope) that this is one of those propositions with a determinate truth value. I should not undertake the investigation if I thought that both it and its negation were assertable. Thus, I take it for granted that if it is assertable, its negation is not assertable; I take it for granted that this is one of those propositions for which bivalence holds. I can express the presupposition of my inquiry by saying:

Either this skeleton is a man or it is not.

This reflects my acceptance that a genuine question is at issue on this *occasion*. It does not reflect my acceptance of a general logical law: in general, (1) below is true but (2) is false.

1. *(P)* If I investigate whether *P*, then I hope that if *P* is assertable the negation of *P* is not assertable.
2. I believe that *(P)* if *P* is assertable, then the negation of *P* is not assertable.

Peirce criticizes an illicit move whereby (2) is endorsed by logicians on the basis of a confused awareness of the facts underlying (1). He appears to suggest that I can rely upon any instance of the law which becomes relevant in the course of inquiry, although I am not justified in accepting the law as, in general, true.

So long as I am aware of the dangers, I can use classical logic as a tool in my inquiries, for the propositions that I make use of will generally be ones for which I believe bivalence holds. Even if classical logical laws are not in general valid, the instances of them which I actually deal with will normally be true. I use classical logic while sensitive to its limitations. I may occasionally be misled by this, just as my predictions may fail when I apply my elegant physical theory to concrete situations which involve frictional forces not taken into account by my theory. But the risks are worth taking for the elegant simplicity of the framework that is employed. The moral to be drawn from this seems to be that a system of formal logic can answer to our needs—we can interpret its formulae and exploit them in ordering our inquiries—without providing a set of exceptionless laws which apply to all meaningful propositions. We should look at the uses to which logical calculi are put, rather than jumping too rapidly to the claim that they purport to reveal exceptionless laws.

Another example will illustrate the point. One symptom of the curious logical behaviour of vague predicates is the Sorites paradox: so long as we employ classical logical principles, we can 'prove' that evidently red objects are blue, that enormous piles of sand are not heaps, and so on. The argument forms we use are wholly satisfactory when they are not strung together in sequence: thus, given that one object obviously looks the same shade as another plainly red object, we *do* know that it is red. We are deceived by classical logical inferences only if we exploit the transitivity of entailment and construct a lengthy demonstration composed of many such arguments. Insofar as we never have to consider such lengthy proofs, we can retain our elegant classical formalism. If we rarely have to consider arguments which can be undermined by the logical oddities of vagueness, we may once again stay with our classical logic, confident that, if we are led into error, the mistake can be corrected when we check the result of our inference against casual observation. This is wholly parallel to the way in which we might rely, for practical purposes, upon physical theories which abstract from considerations of friction: we know that, in practice, ignoring this complication is unlikely to make much difference; and when this does lead us astray, we have a ready explanation of what has gone wrong, and we allow observation to override the predictions made by our idealized theory. The theory is not *refuted,* because it only offers an idealization, a simplified model, of the physical facts to which it applies.

Sluga has argued that the prevalent nineteenth-century view of formal logic placed it as a branch of applied mathematics: it employed mathematical techniques for the study of argument (1980: ch. 1). This is Peirce's view. Deductive logic is descriptive of our practice of mathematical inference: it may also try to explain it, but it has no normative or justificatory role.[6] Formal logic provides an idealized model or diagram of patterns of valid inference. To this end, it can have a heuristic role in avoiding slips or in carrying out inferences in a more rigorous fashion. But when an inference that all agree is (in)valid is not certified as such by the logical theory, this indicates the limits of application of the idealized theory rather than a fault in our practice. In wholly analogous fashion, a geometrical theory begins as an idealized modelling of some physical state of affairs (knots and strings). As a mathematical theory it develops autonomously—the mathematician is not constantly thinking of the intended application. But its value lies in its possible applications as iconic representations of other phenomena. So logical laws idealize the structure of ordinary argument and inference: and the application of logical systems must be accompanied by a sense of the limits of application of the formal model as well as a sense of the model's value.

Classical logic does not lead us into error when we employ arguments involving vague predicates, because its limitations can be respected: just as experience can teach us where we have failed to take into account the effects of friction in making a predication on the basis of a physical theory, so we can tell that we were wrong to rely upon a classically valid argument. We have a system of checks and balances which alerts us to the limitations of our formalism.

This argument appears to assume that there are no *truths* containing vague predicates which can *only* be known by methods which essentially rely upon possibly suspect logical principles: experiential checks arc always available. However, suppose that there was a sphere of reality which dealt with abstract objects which were looked upon as just as real as (for example) ordinary physical objects. We have no experience of them, nor do we enter into any kind of causal interaction with them. In fact, our canonical means of acquiring knowledge of them is through constructing formal proofs, which are not constrained by experience or by other 'checks'. It seems to be common ground between Peirce and Frege that unless we have

---

[6] There is danger of confusion here. Peirce insists that logic is a 'normative science' (see, for example, *CP* 1.577). He holds, for example, that deductive logic is a scientific investigation of the norms or standards that govern our practice of mathematical reasoning. It does not purport to criticize that practice. Mathematical reasoning needs no justification. A revision in logic can arise when we arrive at a better characterization of what is involved in deductive validity. But this is answerable to our mathematical or deductive practice: there is no suggestion that logic could be normative in the sense of prescribing a change in our deductive practice (for further discussion, see Hookway 1985: ch. 6 and, especially, pp. 182–3).

an accurate non-classical logic which accounts for the logical behaviour of vague predicates, we can have no reliable knowledge of such objects if our proofs contain propositions involving vague predicates.

Frege's philosophy of mathematics appears to embody just this picture. Logic is not an application of mathematics, but is, rather, a pre-mathematical discipline with a role in justifying mathematical knowledge. Frege speaks of a distinct 'logical' source of knowledge. Arithmetical knowledge depends upon the proofs that Frege offers in the *Grundgesetze*: unless the laws of logic are exceptionless, we can have no assurance of the truth of arithmetic. The logical source of knowledge can only be a source of *knowledge* if the laws of logic are exceptionless in their application to sentences that genuinely express thoughts. Since such truths are only known through proof we obtain knowledge of them only through absolutely secure proofs from absolutely secure basic truths.

7. Realism

Peirce often describes himself as a 'realist'. He repudiates nominalist accounts of law and generality. And, especially in his later works, he rejects idealism, holding that we investigate an independent reality whose character is not determined or constituted by our opinions about it. Indeed, one of the tasks of logic is to guide us in conducting our investigations in pursuit of the goal of discovering the truth. Since vagueness is often seen as a problem for realism, I shall close this chapter with some comments on Peirce's realism.

Peirce's philosophy of mathematics seems wholly constructivist. Mathematical theories grow out of idealizations of models designed for the solution of 'practical' problems. As idealizations, they are not answerable to the physical 'facts' and are interpreted as autonomous, mathematicians soon losing sight of the practical problems which initially prompted their activities. Since we have no 'logical source of knowledge', it appears to follow that mathematics does not take us to knowledge of an independent reality. Mathematical objects—numbers, points, propositions—lack the independent reality that physical objects have. It accords with this that mathematics is pre-logical: whereas we may be forced to revise methods in the natural science because logic teaches us that they will not lead us to knowledge of reality, there is no scope for comparable logical criticism in mathematics. We can attach no sense to the thought that mathematical reality may be other than we take it to be. Thus, Peirce repudiates realism about mathematics. He denies that it studies an external reality, and insists that mathematics is a pre-logical science which 'needs no foundations'. It is arguable that unless he took this position, his relaxed attitude towards classical logic would be untenable and his use of logical laws which were admitted to be idealizations of the logical relations of everyday beliefs and utterances could not be sustained.

However, he resists a similar constructivism about empirical knowledge: here there is room for logical dispute about the methods of inference and inquiry which are best designed to take us to the truth. Peirce's position is often called 'convergent realism'. The 'investigation-independence' of reality—the fact that its character is independent of what it is taken to be—is supposedly captured by the claim that it is 'fated' or 'destined' that serious, efficient inquiry will eventually arrive at the truth. We now seem to find Peirce claiming that, in the course of inquiry, the meanings of concepts are enriched; vague concepts are replaced by more precise ones: we decide on more precise classifications of things like colours that fall on a continuum. Insofar as it is up to us how we make these adjustments— convention or decision has a role in the development of concepts—it is hard to take seriously the idea that all inquirers will eventually assent to just the same sentences. If it is up to us how we make vague concepts more precise, it must be (at least in part) up to us which propositions would be accepted at the end of the inquiry. How can we make sense of Peirce's talk of convergence and destiny?

Consider an investigator, concerned with the pursuit of truth, considering a statement which contains a vague predicate. How are we to account for his understanding of it? One caricature of what occurs would be as follows: he must establish what proposition is expressed by the statement, and his investigation is then directed towards establishing whether that proposition is true. The statement introduces a proposition, a putative candidate for inclusion in the ultimately true account of reality. Since the statement involves vague predicates, it seems highly problematic just which proposition the statement expresses. Yet unless we can account for the identification of this proposition, we have no account of what putative truth is expressed; and the investigator lacks a target for his investigation. If we hold to the 'dyadic' account of understanding described in section 3, some such picture can seem very attractive. In that case, unless we hold that reality itself is vague, vagueness can appear to be an impediment to the kind of understanding that is required for serious pursuit of the truth.

We can contrast with this the picture of such understanding suggested by pragmatism. The investigator's goal is to contribute to our arriving at an adequate account of the laws that govern the world he encounters through perception. How should he interpret and develop the statement, in the light of this overarching goal? What role have the assertion, criticism, and defence of the statement in the broader project of arriving at an adequate account of the laws which comprise reality? He can seek a fuller description of the objects of indexical expressions contained in the statement. He can criticize and enrich the habits of expectation that he links to the predicate expressions. Vagueness can be removed, or unwarranted precision can be mitigated. An account of practices of interpretation which is guided by this overarching goal threatens to bypass the difficulties discussed in the previous paragraph. It is not required that this statement be understood now as expressing a definite candidate for the final consensus. If a statement does not express a 'definite question', it still has a role in the pursuit of truth: it is interpreted as a gesture towards a definite question; or we understand how to recognize that no definite question is raised and to respond accordingly.

There is much more to be said of the details of the views of Peirce and Frege on vagueness, and there are many similarities in their approaches to issues of language and meaning on which I have not touched. My concern has not been to suggest a sharp opposition of approaches to meaning where there is much in common. Rather, I hope to have clarified something of what is distinctive in pragmatist accounts of meaning and understanding, and to have done so in a way which will help us to understand the role of pragmatist ideas in the developments of analytical philosophy which can be traced to the influence of Ramsey and Wittgenstein. The stress upon the practice of interpretation, and upon the respects in which this is sensitive to the goals which guide our activities, provides a perspective from which we can understand the role of language in our lives without feeling constrained to search for pristine logical structures which are somehow present in our ordinary assertions.[7]

---

[7] There is a further link between Peirce's views on vagueness and his realism which I have not discussed. An important theme in his philosophy is his 'synechism', a philosophical outlook which stresses continuities in thought and nature. We have already seen that Peirce holds that vagueness is a characteristic of language used to describe phenomena which vary continuously along a dimension such as colours. He also holds that that the reality of continua, and our experience of them, provide the key to a realist account of universals. Discussion of the difficult interpretative issues which this raises would take us beyond the concerns of this chapter. There is a brief discussion of them in Hookway (1985: 172 ff); and see Potter (1967: passim) and Engel-Tiercelin (1986).

6

Design and Chance: the Evolution of Peirce's Evolutionary Cosmology

1. Introduction

In 1886, Peirce wrote:

We must . . . suppose an element of absolute chance, sporting, spontaneity, originality, freedom in nature. We must further suppose that this element in the ages of the past was indefinitely more prominent than now, and that the present almost exact conformity to law is something that has been gradually brought about . . . If the universe is thus progressing from a state of all but pure chance to a state of all but complete determination by law, we must suppose that there is an original elemental tendency of things to acquire determinate properties, to take habits. This is the third or mediating element between chance, which brings forth First and original events, and law which produces sequences or Seconds . . . [T]his tendency must itself have been gradually evolved; and it would evidently tend to strengthen itself . . . Here then is a rational physical hypothesis, which is calculated to account, or all but account for everything in the universe except pure originality itself. (W5: 293)

This passage outlines a metaphysical programme which Peirce developed in a series of six papers published in *The Monist* between 1890 and 1893. It offers a general account of the Universe, finding pattern in its development and overall structure. This pattern is of an evolutionary structure: Peirce's approach combines his 'tychistic' insistence on the importance of absolute chance with an appeal to a tendency to 'take habits' or to reinforce chance patterns. For some early commentators, the whole idea of a Peircean system of metaphysics was a puzzling embarrassment. Since his pragmatism resembled the verificationism of the logical positivists, and was credited with disposing of 'ontological metaphysics', such metaphysical speculations seemed anomalous. Although we now recognize that Peirce's own metaphysics was supposed to be 'scientific' and empirically grounded (and was thus expected to avoid pragmatic criticism), there are still some deep puzzles about its role in Peirce's thought.[1] This chapter examines the emergence of these cosmological ideas in Peirce's writings: why did he suddenly start addressing these topics some twenty years after his first philosophical publications appeared?

We might explain Peirce's new interest in metaphysics by appeal to external factors. As Nathan Houser has noted, Peirce's energies turned to metaphysics after his professional duties at Johns Hopkins came to an end: perhaps he now had time to pursue interests that his professional obligations had previously distracted him from. He may also have supposed that a reputation as a metaphysician would improve his chances of university employment. Joseph Brent has emphasized that Peirce's interest in 'different manifestations of the real' was stimulated by his father's lectures on *Ideality in the Physical World*, delivered in Baltimore in 1880 (1993: 204 ff); and Max Fisch has traced the form taken by the metaphysics to Peirce's intensive reading of Aristotle and Hellenic philosophy in the early 1880s (1986: ch. 12). But this cannot be the whole story. As late as 1878, Peirce's attitude towards such cosmological endeavours was ambivalent: if it were possible to construct one, this would be of great philosophical and logical interest, but it was rational to be sceptical about the feasibility of doing so. So perhaps exposure to his father's writings or to Greek philosophy enabled Peirce to overcome what had previously seemed to be insuperable problems. Or perhaps problems internal to his work in logic made it important at least to hope that these metaphysical questions could be answered. Murray Murphey (1961: 299 ff) has argued that the new logical discoveries of the early 1880s required revisions in his theory of categories which in turn made it necessary to construct a system of evolutionary cosmology. He has also suggested that Peirce's theory of inquiry ran into problems which could only be met with the aid of these metaphysical doctrines. In a similar vein, Karl-Otto Apel (1981: 134 ff) argues that metaphysics was required to rescue Peirce's account of reality. Are there questions which became pressing for Peirce in the early 1880s which can only be answered with the aid of a system of metaphysics?

Our best source for understanding the origins of Peirce's metaphysics lies in some unpublished papers which prefigure the views published in *The Monist*. The most important texts are:

1. 'Design and Chance' (1884): a manuscript which was used as the basis of a talk to the Metaphysical Club at Johns Hopkins University (W4: 544–54).

---

[1] These topics are discussed further in Chapter 7.

2. 'An American Plato' (1885): a review of Josiah Royce's *Religious Aspects of Philosophy*, commissioned by the editor of the *Popular Science Monthly* who declined to publish it (W5: 221–34).
3. 'One, Two, Three: Kantian Categories' (1886): some drafts towards a systematic treatment of Peirce's categories (W5: 292–302).
3. 'A Guess at the Riddle' (1887–8): an extended manuscript, developing Peirce's theory of categories.[2]

We must also take account of a paper from 1878:

5. 'The Order of Nature': published in the *Popular Science Monthly* as the fifth of the 'Illustrations of the Logic of Science' (W3: 306–22).

Some of the key arguments of this paper are repeated in 'A Theory of Probable Inference' (W4: 408–50), published in 1883, a year before 'Design and Chance' was delivered.

In his introduction to volume 5 of *Writings of Charles S. Peirce*, Nathan Houser emphasizes that Peirce's metaphysical ideas developed throughout this period, his full metaphysical vision not being in place until 'A Guess at the Riddle'. The papers contain developments of two kinds. In 'Design and Chance', the main focus is on the introduction of evolutionary ideas into logic and metaphysics: Peirce sketched an evolutionary explanation of laws which claimed that the Universe had become more regular and law governed through time, and this was refined in some of the later papers. In addition, especially in 'A Guess at the Riddle', Peirce developed a 'long list of categories'. Where earlier discussions of the three categories had concentrated upon their role in logic and semiotic, Peirce now began to trace the characteristic forms of firstness, secondness, and thirdness in metaphysics, psychology, physiology, biology, physics, sociology, and theology. These two developments both form part of Peirce's evolving metaphysical system, but my main interest here is with his insistence that a metaphysical cosmology should have an evolutionary structure.

After noting some of Peirce's early remarks about the current state of metaphysics and its prospects (section 2), we introduce some themes in the development of Peirce's thought during the late 1870s and 1880s.

---

[2] The best current source of this text is *The Essential Peirce* (*EP*1: 245–79). This volume contains all of the listed papers. Murphey was aware of 'A Guess at the Riddle', but he wrongly dated it as 1890. This understandable error, together with his apparent ignorance of 'Design and Chance', explains his belief that Peirce's work on metaphysics began around 1890, representing a sudden fundamental shift 'following five years of very slight philosophical activity' (1961: 323).

Section 3 contrasts Peirce's pessimism about the possibility of finding a characterization of the Universe in general in 1878 with his attempt to develop one just six years later, and section 4 chronicles his growing stress upon the role of innate ideas over the same period. This is followed by an attempt to analyse the chief argument for Peirce's metaphysics, which is linked to his insistence that we should doubt the absolute truth of fundamental logical and metaphysical axioms. The final section discusses how far pressures facing the theory of inquiry Peirce had developed during the 1870s forced him to address these metaphysical questions.

2. Peirce and Metaphysics before 1884

Although Peirce had happily called himself a metaphysician since the 1860s, his early writings contain many negative remarks about the subject. A typical example is a footnote to 'On the Natural Classification of Arguments' (1867), which records that 'almost all men think that metaphysical theories are valueless, because metaphysicians disagree so much among themselves' (W2: 45n). Such remarks did not reflect a positivist rejection of a whole area of knowledge. Peirce's aim, rather, was to lament the poor state of contemporary metaphysical writing, and to attribute it to the assumption that an a priori system of metaphysics was a possibility: 'It is of no avail that philosophers adopt strictly demonstrative forms of argument as long as they cannot, after all, come to agreement on conclusions' (W2: 187). He also criticized the widespread belief that metaphysics could contribute to our understanding of practical (especially religious) matters.[3] In this section we shall note some of his early claims about how metaphysical inquiry *should* be carried out. The business of metaphysics, Peirce later wrote (in 1903), 'is to study the most general features of reality and real objects' (*CP* 6.6).[4] The early remarks we shall look at will concern the means to be employed in such a study.

---

[3]　This attitude was present throughout his career. It is most prominent in the first of the Cambridge Conferences Lectures of 1898, where Peirce exposes the intellectual folly of supposing that philosophy can help with the solution of 'vital questions'. These lectures are published in *Reasoning and the Logic of Things*. I have examined the grounds of Peirce's view in Chapter 1.

[4]　Of course, 'metaphysics' is a technical term of philosophy, and it is far from clear that his usage of the term was the same in 1868, 1884, and 1903. But we can certainly draw from these remarks the conclusion that Peirce supposed that progress in metaphysics depended upon use of the scientific method and that the discipline was not, in 1868, in a position to make rapid progress.

Peirce's pessimism about progress in metaphysics has limits. Indeed, due to the clarification of various 'indistinct conceptions', disagreement has diminished over the centuries (W2: 127). His attack on a priori approaches to metaphysics in 'Potentia ex impotientia' (1868), leads to the suggestion that progress will depend upon using 'hypothetic and inductive reasoning' (W2: 187). But in the 1860s he was sceptical that there would be rapid progress even if the scientific method were employed: the current state of metaphysics reflected its immaturity.

Every great branch of science has once been in the state which metaphysics is in now, that is when its fundamental conceptions were vague and consequently its doctrines utterly unsettled; and there is no reason whatever to despair of metaphysics eventually becoming a real science like the rest; but at present that is not the case. (W2: 127)

Suggesting that 'dynamics just before the time of Galileo was in a state not dissimilar to that in which philosophy now is', he recommended that:

If metaphysics has the happy future before it which dynamics then had, it must be content to rest upon tangible external facts and to begin with theories not supported by any great multitude of different considerations or held with absolute confidence. When these first theories have been systematically traced to their consequences, we can see how many facts they serve to explain, and which are the ones that require to be retained. (W2: 188)

So metaphysics should be investigated using the method of science, but, in the 1860s, it was in a rather primitive 'pre-Galilean' state. By the 1880s, Peirce was more confident that he saw the way ahead.

There is a second theme in Peirce's early responses to metaphysics. In 1865 and 1866, lecturing on 'The Logic of Science', he claimed to follow Kant and Aristotle in accepting that 'the Analytic of Logic is the foundation of metaphysics' (W: 302). He endorsed the view 'of several great thinkers' that progress in these areas requires 'adopting our logic as our metaphysics' (W1: 490). Bearing in mind the claim that metaphysics aims to describe the most general features of reality, we can understand these claims by recalling Kant's metaphysical deduction of his categories. Since reality is what is described in a true proposition, an account of the general formal features of propositions—an account of their *logical* forms—will tell us about the most general features of reality.

This theme *appears* to be in conflict with the first: it suggests that metaphysics should be an a priori discipline rather than one which employs the

method of science. But this is only appearance. First, Peirce would probably have advocated the use of observation and experiment in constructing
logical systems and in deriving systems of categories from them. Second,
the questions discussed in metaphysics are not exhausted by the search for
a system of categories, and, as we shall see, there are more complex and
indirect ways in which logic can guide our inquiries in metaphysics. In his
later work, for example, we discover that one task of metaphysics is to
provide a scientific account of reality which explains the truth of various
propositions that logic adopts as regulative ideals or hopes. Although the
metaphysics of the 1880s is clearly intended to be empirical and scientific,
Peirce often emphasized that it grew out of his work in logic.

3. The Order of Nature

'The Order of Nature' (1878), the fifth of Peirce's *Illustrations of the Logic of
Science*, examines some broad questions about the nature of reality which
are clearly relevant to the metaphysical writings of half a decade later. The
introductory section alludes to the traditional argument from design for the
reality of God: the only evidence we could imagine for the reality of God, he
supposes, would arise out of 'the universal subjection of phenomena to laws'
or out of 'the character of those laws themselves' (as being benevolent, beau-
tiful, economical, etc.) (W3: 306). Peirce himself supposed that religion does
not require grounding in 'evidences' of this kind, and indeed found religious
belief which *was* so supported rather distasteful. But he retained an interest
in whether there was any 'general characteristic of the universe', because, if
there was, it 'would be of such singular assistance to us in all our future
reasoning, that it would deserve a place almost at the head of the principles
of logic' (W3: 307). So there are logical reasons for investigating: 'what sort
of conception we ought to have of the universe': 'how to think of the *ensem-
ble* of things, is a fundamental problem in the theory of reasoning.'

This issue—in the form of the question whether there is 'a general plan
or design embracing the whole universe'—is taken further in the final
section of the paper. Peirce supposed that there could be such a plan only
if the material Universe was 'of limited extent and finite age'. If it is infinite,
in time or space, then 'there is no *whole* of material things, and consequently no general character to the universe' (W3: 319). If, on the other
hand, 'there are certain absolute bounds to the region of things outside of
which there is mere void, then we naturally seek for an explanation of it,
and, since we cannot look for it among material things, the hypothesis of

a great disembodied animal, the creator and governor of the world, is natural enough'. According to Peirce, 'the universe ought to be presumed to be too vast to have any character.' It is rational to be prejudiced against general cosmologies which account for the Universe as a whole—especially if they purport to explain the Universe in non-mechanical terms. Once again, note that 'important questions of *logic*' (my italics) depend upon whether the Universe is bounded or not.

'General plan or design' is a vague phrase, but it is reasonable to suppose that Peirce's scepticism about this idea soon diminished. Indeed, the cosmological views we saw expressed at the beginning of this paper suggest that the Universe is not too vast to have a general character: indeed, it has directions and limits in time and space. Moreover, by the time he wrote 'An American Plato', his view of God was not of a 'great disembodied animal', but clearly linked to his cosmological ideas. Discussing Royce's view that the real existence of God consists in his imaging or positing Himself, Peirce commented:

For my part, I hold another theory, which I intend to take an early opportunity of putting into print. I think that the existence of God, as well as we can conceive it, consists in this, that a tendency toward ends is so necessary a constituent of the Universe that the mere action of chance upon innumerable atoms has an inevitable teleological result. One of the ends so brought about is the development of intelligence and of knowledge; and therefore I should say that God's omniscience, humanly conceived, consists in the fact that knowledge in its development leaves no question unanswered. (W5: 229)

Belief in God, then, goes together with confidence in a kind of progress or development in human life and inquiry (see Chapter 11). The evolutionary cosmology (with its appeal, on occasion, to the 'mere action of chance') is plainly of a piece with this account of religious belief. Our question about the relations between the evolutionary cosmology and Peirce's logical views then becomes, in the light of these views, a question about the logical significance of this 'cosmic optimism'. In view of the last sentence of the quoted passage, this will presumably concern the logical significance of the claim that 'knowledge in its development leaves no question unanswered'.

One focus of Peirce's review of Royce is the latter's criticisms of a view of reality which is recognizable as Peirce's own. This is the view that:

Reality, the fact that there is such a thing as a true answer to a question, consists in this: that human inquiries,—human reasoning and observation,—tend toward the settlement of disputes and ultimate agreement in definite conclusions which are independent of the particular stand-points from which the different inquirers may have set out; so that the real is that which any man would believe in, and be ready to act upon, if his investigations were to be carried sufficiently far. (W5: 222)

One plausible interpretation of Peirce's argument views it as an attempt to show that his conception of reality is compatible with a religious outlook that finds room for God's omniscience. It is required to block objections which challenge this conception of reality by suggesting that things may be knowable to God which could never be a matter of unforced consensus among human inquirers. This does not provide a very strong argument in favour of Peirce's evolutionary cosmology. Indeed, the text of 'An American Plato' strongly suggests that the cosmological picture is supported by other arguments, not stated there. However, we do receive strong confirmation for the view that these ideas are linked to problems with Peirce's account of reality. The older view of God's omniscience tended to think of the limits and fallibility of *our* knowledge by contrasting it with the information available to this omniscient God. Once the evolutionary cosmology is in place, Peirce is able to describe our limits and fallibility in terms that are internal to the process of human inquiry: our beliefs are measured against what *would be believed* after sufficient inquiry.

4. Innate Ideas

Some philosophers have turned to the uniformity to be found in nature in order to find a premise from which they can demonstrate various conclusions from the existence of God to the soundness of inductive reasoning. According to a much discussed argument in 'The Order of Nature', this premise is too trivial to yield such interesting conclusions: even a wholly chance world would be uniform. More significant, Peirce argues, is the fact that there are regularities which are salient to our senses and intelligence, and relevant to our concerns.[5] It is not interesting that nature is uniform; but it is significant that we can discover what these regularities are. It is easy to imagine a world governed by regularities which were so recondite,

---

[5] This argument is retained in the 1883 'A Theory of Probable Inference': 'That there is a general tendency toward uniformity in nature is not merely an unfounded, it is an absolutely absurd, idea in any other sense than that man is adapted to his surroundings' (W4: 446).

so remote from our everyday concerns, that the prospects of their being discovered were close to zero. Peirce illustrates this by an example. Having completed a statistical induction, for example that one half of all births are of male children, we can search for a description of which births are of male children. He supposes that one can always be found: this reflects the principle *that every event must have a cause*. But, he continues:

[I]f there be nothing to guide us to the discovery; if we have to hunt among all the events in the world without any scent; if, for instance, the sex of the child might equally be supposed to depend upon the configuration of the planets, on what was going on at the antipodes, or on anything else—then the discovery would have no chance of every being made.[6] (W3: 317)

It is then a short step to being impressed by the ease with which human beings (and even animals) arrive at extremely sophisticated and complex concepts and hypotheses—space, time, and force are offered as examples—and to then concluding that such concepts must be innate. Peirce does just this, proposing that the innateness of concepts like space, time, and force is due to natural selection: creatures with such concepts would possess great advantages in the struggle for life.

This notion of 'innateness' covers a range of phenomena. As well as concepts such as space which 'take possession of the mind on small provocation', it is also required to account for the fact that some concepts and hypotheses, which are not themselves produced in us by natural selection, appeal to our sense of plausibility or simplicity. Peirce uses gravity as an example of a concept which 'the mind is particularly adapted to apprehend with facility'. In general:

[T]he mind of man is strongly adapted to the comprehension of the world; at least, so far as this goes, that certain conceptions, highly important for such a comprehension, naturally arise in his mind; and, without such a tendency, the mind could never have had any development at all. (W3: 318)

---

[6] Similar remarks occur in 'A Theory of Probable Inference' (1883): 'Nature is a far vaster and less clearly arranged repertory of facts than a census report; and if men had not come to it with special aptitudes for guessing right, it may well be doubted whether in the ten or twenty thousand years that they may have existed their greatest mind would have attained to the amount of knowledge which is actually possessed by the lowest idiot' (W4: 447). In 1883 too, Peirce appeals to innate or instinctive belief: 'all human knowledge, up to the highest flights of science, is but the development of our inborn animal instinct' (W4: 450).

Peirce seems to be convinced that such an innate aptitude is required to explain the possibility of science: unless we possessed it, progress in science would be so slow as to be indiscernible. But he is aware that natural selection cannot account for all of the innate predispositions which guide scientific inquiry. Since it is implausible that natural selection would favour creatures well equipped to be good at the most abstract theoretical physics, 'it is probable that there is some secret here which remains to be discovered' (W3: 319). The cosmic optimism grounded in an evolutionary cosmology which posits additional mechanisms of evolutionary change besides natural selection has a role in his attempt to probe this secret.

In a version of 'One, Two, Three' written in the summer of 1885, a related appeal to innateness is used to motivate the search for a 'long list' of categories. After offering the logical analyses of signs and arguments which he had long used to defend his categories, Peirce concludes that 'the whole organism of logic may be mentally evolved from the three conceptions of first, second, and third' (W5: 245). He continues:

But if these three conceptions enter as we find they do as elements of all conceptions connected with reasoning, they must be virtually in the mind when reasoning first commences. In that sense, at least, they must be innate ideas; and consequently they must be capable of explanation, psychologically;—there must be in the consciousness three faculties corresponding to these three categories of logic.

We can ignore the details of his demonstration that 'the true categories of consciousness' are (i) consciousness of quality, (ii) consciousness of an interruption into the field of consciousness, and (iii) synthetic consciousness. These, he insists, 'afford a psychological explanation of the three logical conceptions of quality, relation and synthesis or mediation' (W5: 246). But we should notice his immediate observation that 'Three such fundamental elements of consciousness must be capable of a psychological explanation from three fundamental properties of the nervous system' (W5: 247—the manuscript comes to an end in unfinished speculation about the behaviour of cells). Although nothing in this passage introduces the evolutionary cosmology, it is significant that—for the first time in his writings—Peirce's reflections on his categories lead from logic to psychology and physiology on the basis of considerations about *explanation*. Peirce tells us that the three categories (and our grasp of them) *must* receive such explanations: if our grasp of the categories is not 'innate', they must be inferred from something *more* fundamental, in which case the categories would not be truly fundamental. The 'must' here suggests that unless such explanations are forthcoming, Peirce's arguments for his logical categories would be unsatisfactory.

These two uses of innateness are both concerned with explanation: we can only explain why people have concepts such as space, time, and the categories by appealing to structures which are innate in the mind. But they are crucially different in a way that ensures that the innateness of the categories must receive a 'metaphysical' explanation. Peirce agrees with Berkeley that the concepts of space and time are acquired through inference. The focus of his puzzlement is that these complex concepts are acquired so easily, even by those of little education or by animals. The task is to explain why our inductive habits lead us to favour some hypotheses so strongly and so unreflectively.

The cases of the categories is different. Since these concepts are fundamental and are involved in all inference and inquiry, it would be absurd to see our knowledge of them as the *result* of inference and inquiry. If we acquire them on the basis of an inference from something else, then they are not manifested, as he supposes they are, in the different forms of inference. Once we are capable of reflective inference, on Peirce's view, we already possess the categories. They must be present as forms of the mind, as forms of understanding. Metaphysics must explain the correctness of our rational hope that the categories reflected in the forms of the mind will fit reality. This explains why Peirce believes that, having identified the role of the categories within mental phenomena, he must continue to explore the forms they take in biology, physics, and metaphysics. The developing theory of categories is meeting an explanatory demand: a confidence in our skills as investigators depends upon our trust that we are attuned to the structure of reality, and we must explain why and how this can be so.[7]

5. Doubting the Exact Truth of Axioms

The earliest paper which is a clear ancestor of Peirce's evolutionary metaphysics was given to the Metaphysical Club at Johns Hopkins in 1884:

[7] The difference noted here between Peirce's attitude towards the 'innateness' of time and space and of the categories is relevant to the difficult issue of how his philosophy relates to Kant's. By treating space and time as a priori forms which supplement the categories—rather than as concepts which can be learned through observation and inference—Kant is committed to seeing the cases as parallel. Peirce's pragmatist insistence that the only a priori forms we require are the categories of the understanding commits him to distinguishing two kinds of 'innateness', as suggested here.

'Design and Chance'.[8] It will be useful to begin with a sketch of its contents. Peirce mentions two fundamental characteristics of the intellectual life of the time at which he was writing: Darwin's work and 'the tendency to question the exact truth of axioms' (W4: 544). And he expresses the view that the development of this second idea in mathematics, science, and philosophy is 'likely to teach us more than any other general conception'. Having mentioned some uses already made of this idea, especially in non-Euclidean geometry, he continues: 'What I propose to do tonight is, following the lead of those mathematicians who question whether the sum of the angles of a triangle is exactly equal to two right angles, to call in question the perfect accuracy of a fundamental law of logic'. Related comments occur in 'One, Two, Three': 'This is the day for doubting axioms. With mathematicians, the question is settled; there is no reason to believe that the geometrical axioms are exactly true. Metaphysics is an imitation of geometry, and with the geometrical axioms the metaphysical axioms must go too' (W5: 292).

The 'metaphysical axiom' questioned in 'One, Two, Three' is identical to the 'logical axiom' of 'Design and Chance'. In 1884, Peirce offers four formulations which are not obviously equivalent.

1. Real things exist (W4: 545).
2. Every intelligible question whatever is susceptible in its own nature of receiving a definitive and satisfactory answer, if it be sufficiently investigated by observation and reasoning (W4: 545–6). (This is Peirce's preferred formulation.)
3. 'In Mill's formulation': Nature is uniform (W4: 546).
4. Every event has a cause[9] (W4: 546).

The 1886 formulation is:

5. Every thing that happens is completely determined by exact laws (W5: 293).

The earlier paper also cites (5) as a corollary of the more basic principle:

6. Every fact has an explanation, a reason.

---

[8] William Davenport's account of the links between Peirce's evolutionism and his logic concentrates upon the arguments to be discussed here (Davenport 1981).

[9] This is 'not one of the most scientifically accurate statements of the axiom'.

The consequence of denying these fundamental logical principles is the admission that '*chance*, in the Aristotelian sense, mere absence of cause, has to be admitted as having some slight place in the universe' (W4: 547).

As before, it will be useful to begin with 'The Order of Nature', where Peirce enunciated a 'logical principle' involved in our inductive practice:

When we have drawn any statistical induction—such, for instance, as that one-half of all births are of male children—it is always possible to discover, by investigation sufficiently prolonged, a class of which the same predicate may be affirmed universally; to find out, for instance, *what sorts of* births are of male children. The truth of this principle follows immediately from the theorem that there is a character peculiar to every group of possible objects. The form in which this principle is usually stated is, that *every event must have a cause*. (W3: 316–17—note this principle is the same as (4) above)

But he concluded that, although there is always such an exceptionless regularity, our attempts to discover it will be thwarted without 'something to guide us'. As well as the claim about innateness that we have discussed, Peirce discovers another supposed corollary of this observation. It concerns the fallibility of our inductions: we have no right to assume that 'any induction whatever is entirely without exception' or that 'we ever do discover the precise cause of things'. Indeed, 'every empirical rule has an exception'.

It is evident that Peirce's views changed between 1878 and 1884. In 1878, he was happy to accept the absolute truth of the principle that every event must have a cause—where he understood this to entail that every event conformed to an exceptionless deterministic law. Although we often use statistical regularities to explain and predict phenomena, there will always be a law accounting for those phenomena which is not statistical. But he was sceptical than we would ever arrive at knowledge of such a law: our knowledge will be limited to laws and regularities which, whether statistical or deterministic, are approximately correct. By 1884 he admitted the existence of absolute chance, and questioned the absolute truth of the logical or metaphysical principle that every event must have a cause.

When we ask why Peirce was so confident of this principle in 1878, his reasons appear to involve a nominalistic conception of law. He relies upon a 'highly-important logical principle', probably first stated by De Morgan: 'any plurality or lot of objects whatever have some character in common (no matter how insignificant) which is peculiar to them and not shared by anything else' (W3: 310, 316–17). Such laws need not be 'operative in nature', and there need be no interesting explanation of why the law takes the form that it does: coincidence or accident could have a role in the determination of character which is appealed to in formulating this universal law. Its explanatory value could be extremely limited.

Let us now turn to Peirce's reasons for questioning his logico-metaphysical 'axiom'. For the present, we shall focus on the formulation: every fact has an explanation, a reason. What does Peirce gain from questioning it? Once this 'axiom' is accepted, we face considerable explanatory demands: the axiom would be refuted by the existence of a single fact that could receive no explanation. When we explore the range of facts that require explanation, the axiom faces a *reductio ad absurdam*: if it is absolutely true, we are forced to acknowledge that some facts cannot be explained. Once we accept that it is only *approximately* true, then our explanatory capacities are enhanced and we escape from the threatening *reductio*. Unless we acknowledge the existence of absolute chance—unless we accept Peirce's 'tychism'—there is a gap between what ought to be explained and what can be explained. Tychism is to be accepted because it provides the best explanation of a range of important phenomena.

How does the *reductio* work: what facts require explanations, but cannot receive them, if the axiom is absolutely true? In 'The Architecture of Theories' (1891), Peirce famously argued:

Uniformities are precisely the sorts of things that need to be accounted for. That a pitched coin should sometimes turn up heads and sometimes tails calls for no particular explanation; but if it shows heads every time, we wish to know how this event has been brought about. Law is par excellence the things that wants a reason. (*CP* 6.12)

Evolutionary theory shows how to explain many of the laws and uniformities of biology. Although such explanations make it probable that 'organisms and worlds have taken their origin from a state of affairs indefinitely homogeneous [they] all suppose essentially the same basis of physical law to have been operative in every age of the universe' (W4: 548). But, Peirce supposes, it is irrational to think that biological laws require explanations while physical laws do not:

Among the things that demand explanation, then, are the laws of physics; and not this law or that law only but every single law. Why are the three laws of mechanics as they are and not otherwise? What is the cause of the restriction of extended bodies to three dimensions? . . . And then the general fact that there are laws, how is that to be explained? . . . I maintain that the postulate that things be explained extends itself to laws as well as to states of things. (W4: 547–8)

So we need to explain why the laws of physics (and other disciplines) are as they are. And we also need to explain why the world is law-governed at all. These are the explanatory demands that force Peirce's metaphysics to take its distinctively evolutionary turn.

The route from these explanatory demands to evolutionary metaphysics can be set out by appeal to a trilemma. Explanations are sought which provide answers to 'why' questions such as:

1. Why are the laws of physics not different?
2. Why are there any laws of nature at all?
3. Why is the world governed by laws to the degree that it is?

One's first thought is that three kinds of response are possible to these questions, all of which Peirce would find unsatisfactory. First, we could deny that these questions have answers at all. This involves a straightforward rejection of the fundamental logical axiom, since it acknowledges that some facts have no cause or reason. Second, we could offer naturalistic answers to these questions, ones that appeal to laws of nature. This looks circular: what laws are we to appeal to when we try to explain the laws or uniformities appealed to in the proffered explanations? Third, these facts have explanations which do not appeal to laws of nature: perhaps we explain them by invoking the power of a transcendent God. Peirce frequently ridiculed such explanations, and adopting this strategy would threaten the integrity of his system of categories: it appeals to something other than law (mediation or thirdness) in order to understand the relations between laws and the individual events which they govern. If the second and third answers are to be rejected, then we are thrown back on the first and we are obliged to reject the fundamental axiom.

Peirce needed to find a way out of this trilemma. His evolutionary cosmology provides a way of doing so. It frees the second strategy of the circularity that it appeared to face. How does this work? Peirce addresses this issue on a number of occasions. Since we are interested in the development of his thought during the 1880s, it will be useful to consider several examples from that period.

a) 'Design and Chance' (1884)

This is the paper in which Peirce proposed that 'on excessively rare sporadic occasions a law of nature is violated in some infinitesimal degree' (W4: 549). Once we take into account that chance is governed by the laws of the probability calculus, it becomes possible to argue that chance 'has the property of being able to produce uniformities far more strict than those from which it works' (W4: 551). Peirce's first illustration of this concerns a gambling game:

A million players sit down to play a fair game. Each bets one dollar each time which he has an even chance of winning or losing . . . [Suppose] that the dice used by the players become worn down in the course of time. Chance changes every-thing and chance will change that. And we will suppose that they are worn down in such a way that every time a man wins, he has a slightly better chance of winning on subsequent trials. This will make little difference in the first million bets, but its ultimate effect would be to separate the players into two classes: those who had gained and those who had lost with few or none who had neither gained nor lost and these classes would separate themselves, more and more, faster and faster. (W4: 549–50)

Having illustrated the same point by indicating how certain laws of nature—he mentions Boyle's Law, Charles' Law, and the Second Law of Thermodynamics—are 'statistical facts' or the results of chance, he ventures that perhaps all known laws are statistical results:

Now I will suppose that all known laws are due to chance, and repose upon others less rigid themselves due to chance and so on in an infinite regress, the further we go back the more indefinite being the nature of the laws, and in this way we see the possibility of an indefinite approximation toward a complete explanation of nature. (W4: 551–2)

This is vague, but a supplement to 'Design and Chance' (W4: 552–4) takes a further step forward. In 'The Order of Nature', discussing innate ideas, Peirce had argued that our innate tendencies had to be treated with caution. His example was the 'tendency to personify everything, and to attribute human characters to it' (W3: 318), an innate predisposition which was 'very soon overcome by civilized man in regard to the greater part of the objects about him'. If that is taken as warning against thinking of material things in anthropomorphic terms, Peirce soon ceased to heed his own warning. For his next step was to build on his dice-playing exam-ple to construct an analysis of '*Design* or *Intelligence*': the principles of probability enabled us to explain 'some of the main laws of cerebration and particularly the formation of habits' (W4: 553). And he then concluded that the laws of physics may be 'habits gradually acquired by systems'. This anthropomorphic suggestion that the processes whereby we acquire habits of conduct provides a model that can be used for understanding laws of nature was already explicitly endorsed in a manuscript of 1881, 'Methods of Reasoning':

When, in consequence of receiving a certain sensation, we act in a certain way by force of habit, which is a rule operative within the organism, our action cannot be said to be an inference, but it conforms to the formula of Barbara. So when an effect follows upon its cause by virtue of a law of nature, the operation of causation takes place in Barbara. These instances give us an inkling that logic is far more than an art of reasoning: its forms have psychological and metaphysical importance. (W4: 252)

And we find similar claims that metaphysics should adopt anthropomorphic categories when he reasons from the premise that philosophy seeks to explain or 'to show what there is intelligible or reasonable within' the universe at large to the conclusion ('a postulate, which however may not be completely true') that 'the process of nature and the process of thought are alike' (*EP1*: xxix; *NEM4*: 375).[10]

b) Subsequent formulations

Both in 'One, Two, Three' and in 'A Guess at the Riddle', the idea suggested in 'Design and Chance' is further developed. Having put forward the suggestion that 'the universe is progressing from a state of all but pure chance to a state of all but complete determination by law', Peirce draws out the consequence that 'there is an original, elemental tendency of things to acquire determinate properties, to take habits'. This tendency to take habits is 'the mediating element between Chance, which brings forth First and original events, and law, which produces sequences or Seconds' (W5: 293). In 'A Guess at the Riddle', this idea is developed in a way that shows clearly its promised route out of our trilemma. 'Habit-taking' does not introduce something which is categorially distinct from law. This tendency is itself a law which explains the evolution of laws, including itself:

This tendency itself constitutes a regularity, and is continually on the increase. In looking back into the past we are looking towards periods when it was a less and

---

[10] This passage suggests a kind of justification for 'making our logic our metaphysics', which is significantly different from the kind employed in Kant's metaphysical deduction—and is also different from what Peirce had in mind during the 1860s. A parallel formal structure between thought and the external world is proposed as an explanatory hypothesis: it is not an a priori claim.

less established tendency. But its own essential nature is to grow. It is a generalizing tendency; it causes actions in the future to follow some generalization of past actions; and this tendency is itself something capable of similar generalization; and thus, it is self-generative. We have therefore only to suppose the smallest spur of it in the past, and that spur would have been bound to develop into a mighty and over-ruling principle, until it supersedes itself by strengthening habits into absolute laws regulating the action of all things in every respect in the indefinite future. (*EP*1: 277)

Chance may account for the 'small spur', and once this is in place, Peirce's metaphysical hypothesis explains the evolution of law. So far, however, it is only an hypothesis and requires to be refined and tested before it forms part of a properly scientific metaphysics. What we need to understand is why it was a plausible hypothesis; why is it an abductive suggestion that Peirce thinks should be taken seriously? And, most important, what is the role of *logical* considerations in all this?

6. Logic, Hope, Causation, and Reality

Peirce often claimed that his metaphysical system responded to demands generated by his work in logic. This concluding section offers some brief remarks about why this should be. Recognizing that axioms might not be absolutely true and thus admitting a role for chance, and exploring the role of evolutionary explanations in biology, may have helped Peirce to see that a general account of the constitution of the Universe was possible. Bearing in mind his qualified scepticism about such projects in 'The Order of Nature', we need to be clear about why he came to think that it was desirable.

It will be useful to bear in mind a strategy that Peirce formally enunciated only several years later. Inquiry is governed by a body of regulative principles: norms whose truth cannot be established within logic, but which rationality enjoins us to hope are true.[11] There is no guarantee that human inquiry can find the answer to every question that arises; but declaring a question beyond our cognitive grasp threatens to 'block the road of inquiry'. Rationality requires us to hope that each question we encounter is capable of being answered eventually by responsible human inquiry. A metaphysical hypothesis deserves to be taken seriously if it enables us to see how these hopes might be true—although, of course, it

---

[11] I have discussed this aspect of Peirce's metaphysics in Chapter 7.

should only be accepted if it survives rigorous empirical testing. If logic enjoins us to accept (or to hope) that laws can be explained—and that law in general can be explained—then a metaphysical theory that enables us to escape the trilemma outlined in the last section deserves our attention. If it seems that only a system of evolutionary cosmology offers an escape route, then we have a priori reasons for hoping that such a system of cosmology can be attained. Of course, the details of the cosmology will then call for serious scientific investigation.

Can we see how developments in Peirce's logic around 1880 could have forced him to take this line of thought seriously? A useful clue is provided by a puzzling feature of 'Design and Chance'. Recall that Peirce offered four different formulations of the fundamental logical axiom whose absolute truth he wished to challenge:

1. Real things exist.
2. Every intelligible question whatever is susceptible in its own nature of receiving a definitive and satisfactory answer, if it be sufficiently investigated by observation and reasoning. (This is Peirce's favoured formulation of the principle.)
3. Nature is uniform. (This is offered as Mill's favoured formulation of the principle.)
4. Every event has a cause. (This is 'one of the most popular although not one of the most scientifically accurate statements of the axiom'. Peirce claimed that it entailed that every fact had an explanation.)

The suggestion that (1)–(4) are necessarily equivalent would be interesting and controversial. But Peirce claims that they are alternative formulations of *the same axiom*: why? Note that the route from questioning the axiom to evolutionary metaphysics focuses on (4) and its entailment about explanation, while (1) and (2) are concerned with the nature of reality. This offers support for the suggestion that problems about reality are at the source of Peirce's concern with these problems, but, to see why, we need to explore some relations between these different formulations. Sympathetic interpretation will be required: (1) is barely intelligible as it stands and should be taken only as pointing us towards questions about reality better articulated in (2); and we must not ignore Peirce's avowed dissatisfaction with the formulations (3) and (4). Our question must concern how the metaphysics allows us to accept (2) while denying that it is exactly or absolutely true. To that end we must consider two separate issues. What is involved in denying the exact truth of (2)? And why does the truth of (2) depend upon there being explanations of laws and of law in general?

One might suppose that (2) entails (4) (or its entailment) fairly immediately. Since 'Why are the laws of dynamics as they are?' and 'Why are there laws of nature?' are obviously intelligible questions, then (given (2)) it must have a discoverable answer; and the truth of (4) (or of some principle related to it) is a necessary condition of this being so. But this argument would establish, at best, that (2) entails (3)—it would not establish the two-way entailment which is a necessary condition of their being formulations of the same axiom. And it is not *obvious* that these abstract and strange questions are intelligible. Peirce's linking of these apparently distinct formulations must go deeper than this proposal would allow. We need to find a connection between the formulations about causation and explanation and the application of (2) to less arcane, more everyday questions. If we could find this connection, then we would have an account of how problems facing Peirce's account of truth and reality (the account formulated as (2)) forced him to seek a metaphysical explanation of the nature of law. How might there be such a connection? To pick up another clue, the presence of the garbled formulation (1) suggests that we are concerned with Peirce's struggle to defend *realism*.

When Peirce defends the method of science in his 1877 paper 'The Fixation of Belief', he ties use of this method to accepting a fundamental hypothesis:

There are real things, whose characters are entirely independent of our opinions about them; those realities affect our senses according to regular laws, and, though our sensations are as different as our relations to the objects, yet, by taking advantage of the laws of perception, we can ascertain how things really are, and any man, if he have sufficient experience and reason enough about it, will be led to the one true conclusion. (W3: 254)

Starting from the assertion that 'there are real things', he arrives at the claim that (in effect) any intelligible question possesses an answer that can be discovered through sufficient inquiry. The bridge between these two rests on his belief that 'realities affect our senses according to regular laws'. In other words, the link between the first and second formulations of the 'axiom' depends upon propositions which are closely related to the views about causation, uniformity, and explanation expressed in the other formulations.

We can now ask what would be involved in each of these axioms being only approximately true. For the later formulations, this is clear: there are random or chance deviations from laws and regularities. What effect has this upon the second formulation? In 'An American Plato', Peirce considers what it would show if it turned out that 'some questions eventually get settled, and that some others, indistinguishable from the others by any marks, never do' (W5: 227–8). If this were the case then, at best, (2) would be only approximately true. In that case, Peirce avows, his conception of reality 'was rather a faulty one, for while there is a real so far as a question that will be settled goes, there is none for a question that will never get settled'. If we agree that there are questions which will never get settled, 'we ought to admit that our conception of nature as absolutely real is only partially correct' (W5: 228). It is tempting to conclude that denying the absolute correctness of the logical axiom we are concerned with involves admitting this possibility: some intelligible questions will not get settled and it is only approximately true that nature is absolutely real.

The equivalence of these different formulations requires that there are chance deviations from laws if, and only if, there are questions that will never get settled. Given the pattern of argument we have been examining, it also entails that allowing that there are some questions which will never get settled enables us to understand how, in general, questions do get settled. These connections are probably straightforward: if some events occur by chance, some intelligible 'why' questions have no determinate answer; and if some intelligible 'why' questions have no fully satisfactory answer, it follows that some events are not fully determined by law.

The deeper issue concerns the intelligibility of these very general 'why' questions: why are the laws of physics as they are? why is there lawfulness in the Universe at all? It will be useful now to turn to Apel's and Murphey's arguments. According to Murphey, 'The theory of inquiry of the 1870s had by 1890 led to problems which are answerable, if at all, only by cosmology' (1961: 323). He begins from the arguments discussed above where Peirce appeals to instinctive or 'innate' common-sense beliefs in order to explain how we are able to arrive at plausible hypotheses about nature surprisingly quickly. These instincts originate, we may assume, through natural selection, and Peirce's 'critical common-sensism' requires us to question instinctive beliefs critically before taking seriously their recommendations about which hypotheses to take seriously. Once we move away from the contexts in which these instincts have evolved, their reliability is open to question: 'a significant change in the nature of either man or the environment can alter the desirability and utility of belief or the effectiveness of our ways of seeking it' (p. 326). Although Murphey does not do so, we could note that our cognitive instincts did not develop because they were effective at meeting the very special needs of post-Galilean theoretical science: 'it is quite conceivable that evolution could take a course which would make our current adaptation positively dysfunctional' (ibid.). For this reason, we need to 'determine the future course of evolution', to estimate 'what sorts of laws, if any, we may expect nature to follow in the future and in areas as yet little explored': 'we need a method for finding methods so that we may be able to deal with such situations as may arise' (ibid.). This need is met by the evolutionary cosmology.[12]

Apel's interpretation focuses on Peirce's struggles with nominalism. The review of Royce forced Peirce to distinguish between 'the final opinion "which would be sure to result from sufficient investigation" and the empirically conditioned circumstances that the final opinion "may possibly, in reference to a given question, never be actually attained" ' (1981: 140). This distinction between what *would* occur and what *will* happen calls for a realist conception of modalities and laws: it requires Peirce to attach weight to a distinction between real laws and accidental generalizations which he neglected when he appealed to De Morgan in 'The Order of Nature'. The first step towards introducing this distinction, we might suppose, is to recognize that laws, unlike accidental generalizations, can receive explanations: we expect an account of why water expands on freezing. The evolutionary cosmology is suited to meeting this demand. As Apel has insisted, the most striking tensions facing Peirce's theory of inquiry stem from his reluctance, in the 1870s, to adopt a realist theory of laws (1981: 76 ff). The most famous of these is the problem of the diamond from 'How to Make our Ideas Clear'.[13] Would it be false to say that nothing is hard until it is touched or tested, its hardness increasing with the pressure until it is scratched (W3: 267)? If a diamond were crystallized in a bed of soft cotton and then destroyed before being touched, would it be false to say that it was soft (W3: 266)? Peirce's nominalistic response is to say that while such descriptions would revise current usage, they contain nothing *false*. Despite some later protestations, it is implausible that these passages were simply a loose expression of issues about which Peirce had a better understanding than he revealed. Nominalist ideas about the nature of law are too widespread in his writings at this time for that to be the explanation. The evolutionary

[12] We noted above Peirce's insistence in 1883 that 'all human knowledge, up to the highest flights of science, is but the development of our inborn animal instinct' (W4: 450). This appears to be in tension with the views of Murphey's discussed here. If so, his account of the sources of Peirce's evolutionary cosmology are doubtful.

[13] Apel traces a number of discussions of this problem from writings earlier in the decade. These passages are also discussed in Chapter 2, section 4.

cosmology offers the tendency to take habits as something that mediates between laws and particular events, whereas the nominalist view does not regard laws as separate entities whose relations to events require mediation.

By the 1880s Peirce had materials available for a better understanding of laws and their relations to the events which they explain.[14] Murphey's analysis finds the motivation for developing a system of evolutionary cosmology in the need for more help with inventing laws than instinct and common sense can provide, whereas Apel focuses on the need to take seriously realism about laws and 'would be's. The emphasis, in 'Design and Chance' and elsewhere, upon how laws are to be *explained*, together with Peirce's attempt to explain how the tendency to take habits mediates between laws and particular events makes Apel's kind of interpretation more plausible. Although, as William Davenport has noticed, Peirce asserted in 1898 that the considerations emphasized by Murphey had provided the 'living motive' for his evolutionary inquiries, there is little trace of it in the writings of the early 1880s. Davenport's view was that it would have been 'insufficient ground for investigating evolutionism, had he not seen supporting considerations of a more theoretical character' (1981: 308). Peirce's own account of his motivation in 1884 appeals to the issues about explanation and law that we have stressed above.

But even if the problems about laws and nominalism which Apel emphasizes were in the background, it is striking that they receive little explicit recognition in the papers under discussion. Peirce's emphasis is on the need to answer extremely general 'why' questions which seek explanations of particular laws and of lawfulness in general. The method of science carries a commitment to explaining laws and patterns: this commitment cannot be met without exploiting evolutionary explanations to escape the trilemma I outlined above. If these general 'why' questions make sense, then, unless the evolutionary cosmology can be defended, there are intelligible questions which will receive no 'definitive and satisfactory answer'.

Peirce does not say, in these papers, that the intelligibility of 'why' questions applied to laws is tied to the question of realism about laws. However, since possessing an explanation of a law will enable us to predict that and how it would operate in cases which are not observed or experienced by human beings, it seems certain that struggles to avoid nominalistic doctrines and formulations during the 1870s would have encouraged the sorts of philosophical development we have been examining here.

---

[14] However, as Apel notes, Peirce was unable to embrace such realism fully (or else unable to grasp its full implications) in papers such as 'An American Plato'.

7

Metaphysics, Science, and Self-Control

1. Peirce and Metaphysics

Questions about Peirce's metaphysics can be raised at a number of levels. We could consider the details of his answers to particular metaphysical questions such as:

- Is there any real possibility or impossibility?
- Is time a real thing, and if not, what is the nature of the reality that it represents?
- What external reality do the qualities of sense represent, in general?
- Are time and space continuous? (see *CP* 6.6)

But we can also raise the question of how metaphysical knowledge is possible at all. What methods of inquiry are appropriate for answering metaphysical questions? How can Peirce's respectable metaphysics avoid the destiny of the 'ontological metaphysics' whose fate is sealed through application of the pragmatist maxim (*CP* 5.423)?

This question is, in fact, easily answered. Since Peirce espoused a 'scientific metaphysics', its methods did not differ in kind from those used in the special sciences—except that the latter make more use of special observations and controlled experiments, while the former normally draws its data from frequently unnoticed features of everyday experience. This characterization invites an investigation of how far Peirce's metaphysical practice conformed to this description. But such an investigation is not our concern here. For a further question that is raised is: just what distinguishes metaphysical investigations from those which belong to the special sciences? And also, why did Peirce believe that he needed a metaphysics at all? What is the role of metaphysics within his philosophical system?

He described the business of metaphysics as the 'study [of] the most general features of reality and real objects', and as 'the completing department of philosophical science (coenoscopy) which in places welds itself into idioscopy or special science' (*CP* 6.6). A philosopher like Russell or Quine would be content to allow physics to describe for us 'the most general features of reality and real objects'. We shall understand why Peirce supposed he needed a scientific discipline which was more general that physics (one of the special sciences) if we attend to its role in his classification of the sciences. Peirce's mature classification of the sciences saw mathematics as the 'first' science, needing no foundations and supporting the phenomenological elucidation of the categories which succeeds it in his ordering. The three normative sciences follow: aesthetics, ethics, and logic, in that order. Metaphysics then falls into place, belonging with the philosophical disciplines and somehow effecting a bridge from them to physics and the rest.

Why, then, did Peirce think that we required a system of 'scientific metaphysics'? What role does it have in his system as a whole? According to the influential interpretations of Karl-Otto Apel, the place occupied by metaphysics is central to the Peircean solution to some fundamental epistemological issues (see, in particular, Apel 1995). He claims that it promises a way out of a dilemma which destroyed the system of Kant's first *Critique* and which was ducked by subsequent philosophical movements. When Apel presents this view, he is anxious to place Peirce within the tradition of post-Kantian philosophical debate: Peirce's great contribution was to trigger a development from 'transcendental logic' to 'transcendental semiotic'. Although I am very sympathetic to Apel's underlying view of the importance and role of Peirce's metaphysics, I believe that embedding it in this Kantian framework of ideas can be an obstacle to getting it into a proper focus. Furthermore, while describing Peirce's work on logic as '*transcendental* semiotic' may not be strictly false, it threatens to distort our understanding of his philosophy. Hence this chapter is an attempt to articulate this insight about the role and importance of Peirce's metaphysics in a rather different vocabulary. Section 2 discusses the dangers involved in describing Peirce as a 'transcendental philosopher', taking account of his own reasons for explicitly disavowing the description. Then (in sections 3 and 4), I attempt to formulate the important underlying thought about the role of Peirce's metaphysics. One conclusion that Apel draws from his view of the structure of Peirce's thought is that his logic is metaphysically neutral: none of his explicitly logical work, including his clarification of truth in terms of the fated convergence of opinion, embodies assertions with a metaphysical content. In section 5, I shall offer reasons for treating this claim with caution.

Peirce often commented on the 'deplorably backward condition' of metaphysics (*CP* 6.2), finding it a 'puny, rickety, and scrofulous science' (*CP* 6.6). Such remarks occur in the context of denying that this relative immaturity results from the fact that metaphysics is more difficult than physics, psychology, and the other special sciences. It is the result, rather, of the fact that 'those who pretend to cultivate it carry not the hearts of true men of science in their breast' (ibid.). Most were theologians who were unwilling or unable to strive 'with might and main to find out what errors they have fallen into'. Because they could not exult 'joyously at every such discovery, they are scared to look Truth in the face' (ibid.). Peirce anticipated that his scientific metaphysics would be 'somewhat more difficult than logic, but still on the whole one of the simplest sciences' (*CP* 6.4). Indeed, since he thought that logic required metaphysics to be developed earlier than the more concrete special sciences (*CP* 6.1), its 'main principles' being 'settled before very much progress can be gained either in psychics or in physics' (*CP* 6.4), it was important for him that scientific metaphysics should not be a difficult field of inquiry. The final section of this paper considers Peirce's reasons for making such claims.

2. Peirce and Transcendental Philosophy

As noted above, Karl-Otto Apel has defended a distinctive interpretation of Peirce's writings in logic and semiotic. All would agree that Peirce was much influenced by Kant and that this influence was evident throughout his writings. Apel makes the further claim that his strategy is Kantian through and through. Peirce is credited with effecting a transformation of the critical philosophy from 'transcendental logic' to 'transcendental semiotic', and Apel's exegesis of his writings in logic and epistemology focuses upon finding correspondences between stages in Peirce's argument and stages of Kant's argument in the first *Critique* (Apel 1980, 1981). Few can doubt that this reading has yielded insight into the structure of Peirce's thought, and it has been valuable in focusing attention upon his emphasis on the relations between the different sciences. But my aim here is to articulate the points about the role of metaphysics in the system without relying upon this framework of interpretation. I shall now explain why it is valuable to restate the points in this way. Since our central concern is with Peirce's metaphysics rather than with the relations of his philosophical approach to Kant's, I shall be brief.

Like Kant, Peirce aimed to explain the possibility of empirical scientific inquiry and to explain the legitimacy of the rules we use in subjecting our inquiries to rational self-control. And like Kant, he thought that it was inappropriate to use materials drawn from such self-controlled inquiries into the nature of reality while attempting to vindicate this practice of self-control. In earlier writings, the resemblances go further. Consider the avowed argumentative structure of the *Illustrations of the Logic of the Sciences*. In the 'Fixation of Belief', we learn that some facts are taken for granted by the very posing of the logical question; and the most fundamental logical rules are those that can be derived from these presuppositions of logic (W3: 246). The demonstration in that essay that the methods of authority and tenacity and the a priori method cannot be sustained in all circumstances is intended to reveal that the fundamental hypothesis of the method of science (there are real things whose characters are independent of our beliefs about them, but whose characters can be discovered through empirical investigation (W3: 254)) is itself one of the presuppositions of the logical question. Hunting out such presuppositions of thought, experience, and logic is commonly taken to be one of the marks of so-called 'transcendental' approaches to philosophy.[1]

In a paper from 1902, Peirce denied that he was a transcendental philosopher: 'I am not one of those transcendental apothecaries, as I call them—they are so skilful in making up a bill—who call for a quantity of big admissions, as indispensable *Voraussetzungen* of logic' (*CP* 2.113). We might suppose that Peirce was criticizing those who *misuse* the 'transcendental' method by identifying far too many 'indispensable postulates'. However, Peirce is making a more substantial point: 'I do not admit that indispensability is any ground for belief.' Suppose it is established that some proposition is a presupposition of inquiry: this fact does not legitimate my *believing* it to be true; although it does explain why I am warranted in *hoping* that it is true.

For example, when we discuss a vexed question, we *hope* that there is some ascertainable truth about it, and that the discussion is not to go on forever and to no purpose. A transcendentalist would claim that it is an indispensable 'presupposition' that there is an ascertainable true answer to every intelligible question. I used to talk like that, myself; for when I was a babe in philosophy my bottle was filled from the udders of Kant. But by this time I have come to want something more substantial. (*CP* 2.113)

---

[1] This interpretation of the argumentative structure of 'Fixation of Belief' is defended more fully in Hookway (1985: 43 ff). It is explored further in Chapter 1 above. Chapter 8 argues that some of these 'presuppositions' are transformed into common-sense certainties in Peirce's later thought. There are further discussions of the role of 'transcendental' moves in Peirce's philosophy in Chapters 4, 6, and 12.

A passage from the 1903 'Lowell Lectures' shows that he distinguished his logic from Kant's on the grounds that where the latter viewed logical principles as 'Constitutive Principles', for Peirce 'every principle of logic is a Regulative Principle [i.e. a hope] and nothing more. Logic has nothing to do with existence' (*NEM*3: 371). Peirce and the transcendentalists differ on the logical status of the 'presuppositions of logic'. The Kantian believed that showing that something is a precondition of experience or of inquiry somehow (and sometimes) legitimates our assurance of its truth. Peirce denied that *belief* in fundamental commitments can ever be legitimated in this fashion: at best we are warranted in hoping that they are true.

André de Tienne has recently argued that 'antitranscendentalism' characterized Peirce's writings as early as the 1860s, claiming that Peirce objected to a Kantian demand 'for a justification of what the mind does "normally" ' (de Tienne 1988: 256). This accords with the above suggestion that what is at issue is the possibility of a legitimation of our practices which is independent of, or prior to, experiential knowledge. For Peirce, all justification and legitimation must occur within consciousness or within experience. It is such considerations which have led Klaus Oehler to denounce any description of Peirce as a transcendental philosopher (Oehler 1987); and it is also the source of Apel's admission that Peirce's attempt to vindicate his categories phenomenologically by testing them against *experience* is an embarrassment for his transcendental reading (Apel 1995: 385 ff).

The fundamental issue involved in evaluating the transcendental characterization turns on the relations between the methods employed in philosophical inquiry and empirical science. The Kantian terms suggest a methodological dualism: logic and semiotic make no use of the scientific method, their results being in some sense known a priori. As I shall illustrate, avoidance of various circles requires some sort of distinction between philosophical method and the method of science. We might put this by saying that the materials used in logic must be acquired through investigations that are pre-logical: logical reflection can have no role in the inquiries whose goal is to justify the tools of logical reflection. This is enough to justify the thought that such inquiries possess a kind of priority or a 'relative a priority'. Whereas this may be enough to give the term 'transcendental' some application, its use can conceal the fact that this dualism rests upon a deeper unity. The pre-logical sciences use observation, experiment, deductive and abductive inference, and even a form of inductive reasoning: the knowledge they provide all rests upon experience.

Kant's transcendental framework provides a model or diagram which can be applied to Peirce's philosophy and provide insight into the relations of its parts. This is useful only insofar as we understand the limits of the analogy as well as the positive points of resemblance. Indeed, it is worth noting that Apel admits that the Peircean 'transformation' of Kantian transcendental logic transforms Kant's constitutive principles into regulative ones and does not permit the deduction of any synthetic principles as knowable a priori: the passage quoted above from *CP* 2.113 need not disturb Apel's interpretation. His sense that the resemblance between the strategies of Kant and Peirce is only partial is evident from his occasional use of the term '*quasi*-transcendental' to describe Peirce's strategy (Apel 1980: 88). Working exhaustively with such a picture or diagram can lead us to raise questions about the relations of the parts of Peirce's philosophy which can encourage us to distort Peirce's intentions. Since he explicitly disavowed the epithet 'transcendental', we can take it that he felt that such a representation of his thought could conceal some of his fundamental commitments.[2] But it is compatible with this that those who approach Peirce's thought from a different intellectual background may find that the benefits of the Kantian analogy outweigh these dangers. At the very least, since I think that Apel's chief point is detachable from this transcendental perspective, it is useful to illustrate this by reformulating it in terms closer to those that Peirce favoured. This will enable us to sidestep the debates over the permissible use of the term 'transcendental'.[3]

3. The Problem

I shall now present some epistemological problems which are (at least) analogous to those emphasized by Apel. In the background is the thought that logical reflection must provide confidence that empirical investigation of reality is possible and that we can control our inquiries using

---

[2] Peirce's criticisms of transcendentalism have to be interpreted carefully. An attack on 'transcendental apothecaries' only challenges transcendental approaches to philosophy in general if *all* transcendental philosophers are guilty of the excesses which Peirce describes. And an attack on 'occult transcendentalism' (*CP* 3.422) may just be directed at a subset of transcendental approaches: the context does not suggest that Peirce believed that *all* transcendentalism was 'occult'.

[3] I should confess to being more tolerant of stretching the use of 'transcendental' than some of Apel's critics—see Hookway (1985:113 ff; 1988*b*). Varying degrees of tolerance of this may be due to the different roles of Kant (and post-Kantian German philosophy) in both philosophical education and philosophical thought in Britain and on continental Europe.

normative standards whose legitimacy we can trust. We aspire to a sort of autonomous and responsible self-control: we monitor and control our activities; and in order to avoid a sceptical sense of alienation from our practice of evaluation, we need to be sure that the standards we use are accepted because they are right. We are not constrained to use certain standards whether they are correct or not; we actively endorse them rather than, in pyrrhonist fashion, passively acquiescing in what seems right to us.

There are two problems. The first is a simple difficulty about circularity and justification. If we make use of results obtained through logically monitored empirical (or metaphysical) inquiry in carrying out investigations into the legitimacy of methods of inquiry, then we risk incorrigible error: we might use an incorrect empirical theory which leads us to adopt mistaken procedures of inquiry which, in turn, confirm our acceptance of that empirical theory. For Peirce at least, the fundamental principles of the method of science must receive a vindication which avoids that danger. If we adopt the method of science, we face no risk that our best efforts at inquiry will ultimately be thwarted.

But the second problem is that the belief that we are capable of such autonomous self-control appears to involve a substantive conception of the self. If we are products of natural selection, equipped with a battery of instincts—inferential practices, standards of plausibility, broad views of the nature of reality, or tendencies to seize on some similarities and ignore others—we may judge that our position is that of the pyrrhonist alluded to earlier. We are the prisoners of our cognitive apparatus, unable to rise above it to achieve the autonomous self-control which prompts our interest in logic.

The fundamental dilemma is this: The second problem appears to entail that our logical investigations require a distinctive metaphysics of the person, one that entails that we are not just the victims of our natural instincts. But if we do rely upon a metaphysics of the person in carrying out our logical investigations, then we face the circularity posed by the first problem.

This can suggest that logic is impossible. I agree with Apel that the structure of Peirce's mature philosophy—and particularly the role of his metaphysics—provides an ingenious response to this difficulty. The claim that his pre-logical sciences all use the scientific method themselves may make it hard to see how this can be. Therefore I shall next try to explain the character of pre-logical inquiries which enables him to do this. How can these sciences use techniques of confirmation and observation ultimately analogous to those used in reflective empirical inquiry without themselves requiring legitimation from logic?

4. The Role of Metaphysics

How can the Peircean logician make use of material which results from applications of the scientific method (in a broad sense) without facing circularity? Space is insufficient for a full answer to this question, but we can indicate the character of Peirce's answer by describing three strategies available to the Peircean logician or semiotician. Logic attempts to explain the validity of the inferences we use when we carry out investigations, and it guides us in our attempts to exercise self-control in our inquiries. Peirce's claim is that critical self-control, employing standards defended within logic, has a fundamental role in inquiry in the special sciences, in sciences which attempt to describe the laws governing objects and events in the empirical world. Although pre-logical inquiries employ the scientific method, they do not require the kind of critical self-control which makes use of logical principles.

Although mathematics uses observation and experiment to arrive at results, it makes no claims about the nature of *reality*. Its results are hypothetical, and are not answerable to anything independent of the diagrams and structures used in constructing proofs and calculations. There is only limited scope for fallibility in mathematics: we may make slips or blunders in evaluating proofs or carrying out calculations, but we cannot discover that misconceptions about method in mathematics have led us to radical misunderstandings of the referents of mathematical terms. In physics, even if we carry out our inquiries as well as possible, current scientific 'beliefs' can be false: subsequent experience can refute them. Peirce denies that this is possible in mathematics: the only source of mathematical fallibility is our propensity to make blunders (these claims are documented and defended in Hookway 1985: ch. 6). Phenomenology and the normative sciences similarly make no claims about the nature of reality. Although they rely upon observation, experiment, and mathematical reasoning, they investigate the categorial structure of all possible appearance and ask: what is it *possible* to admire? what is it *possible* to adopt as an ultimate end? what is it *possible* to adopt as an ultimate principle of reasoning? The notion of 'possibility' employed here is not limited to what is possible in reality: we are to take into account whether our ultimate aims could be sustained in worlds which conform to laws of nature other than those which obtain in reality. Once again, we are not concerned with the nature of reality, and reflection on whether our methods will take us to the truth about reality have no place (Hookway 1985: 58 ff).

The second component is a broad range of common-sense beliefs about inquiry, inquirers and the objects of inquiry (*CP* 5.438 ff; see also Chapter 8). Unlike the first component, these beliefs do concern the nature of empirical reality. They result from experience, but they are not the products of deliberate self-controlled inquiry. When asked what supports them, we can only say: 'Everything counts for them and nothing counts against them.' It does not occur to us that we can question them: their extreme vagueness renders them immune from straightforward falsification. Once again, relying upon them appears not to introduce any immediate circularity into logic. Like the results of mathematics and the normative sciences, these beliefs are acritical: logical assessment has no role in their acquisition and retention.

In later writings, Peirce insisted that some of Kant's constitutive synthetic a priori principles are interpreted by pragmaticists as such commonsense certainties. These are not—like the principles of logic—transformed into regulative ideas or hopes. They are *believed*, and this belief has withstood the test of an enormous amount of uncontrolled observation. Hence, such beliefs are not known a priori; but since they are acritical commonsense certainties they do not require legitimation by logical investigations or *defence* by further metaphysical investigation (*CP* 5.452).

But these materials are accompanied by a third component: a battery of regulative ideas or hopes (*CP* 2.113; and see section 2 above). We aspire to logical self-control. This is only possible if we can trust our ability to carry out the normative sciences (and thus possess the required autonomy); and it is only possible if our common sense, which gives sense to key terms in inquiry, will continue to be trustworthy; and it is only possible if we can expect our abductive instincts to lead us to the right hypotheses as inquiry develops. We cannot know these things are true, but since we shall not otherwise achieve rational self-control, Peirce proposed that we should *hope* that they are true. We rely upon a Pascalian practical judgement rather than the product of self-controlled empirical inquiry. But where common sense and mathematics provided an acritical *certainty*, these hopes introduce a tentative *contingent* character to our assurance that empirical science and self-control are possible.

Peirce wrote that metaphysics tells us how the world must be if the hopes that guide our logical investigations are absolutely true (*CP* 1.487).

It is required by logic, but metaphysical investigations and results have no role in carrying out logical investigations. And here I agree with Apel: unless metaphysics can explain how minds possess the powers required for logical self-control, the results of logic are vitiated; but our logical investigations can be (must be) completed *before* metaphysical investigations begin. The interplay of practically grounded hopes and subsequent metaphysical confirmation enables us to hold:

1. Logic places certain requirements upon an adequate metaphysical theory.
2. Metaphysical investigations do not need to be carried out *before* logic can be completed.[4]

My main difference from Apel consists in my employing here as the fundamental distinction one between beliefs produced by the scientific method in a broad sense which calls for no logical monitoring and self-control, and beliefs resulting from reflective investigations of the nature of reality. Apel's talk of the 'transcendental' *suggests* a more radical methodological dualism. Although, as indicated in section 2, I am unsure how far this suggestion is correct.

5. Logic and Metaphysical Neutrality

I shall now introduce and dispute one of the conclusions that Apel draws from the line of argument we have just described. This is that, for Peirce, no 'metaphysical' assertions are made in the course of doing logic. I shall suggest that the preceding argument does not establish that this is so. Clearly if, within logic, I express the hope that there will be a metaphysics which will explain how I am indeed capable of autonomous self-control, then I *assert* no metaphysical proposition. Equally, my hope that metaphysics will underwrite the objectivity of subjunctive conditionals or my hope that it will explain why we are likely to be good at thinking up plausible hypotheses does not involve the assertion of a metaphysical hypothesis. Equally clearly, an assertion arrived at through reflective metaphysical investigation has (for Peirce) no place in logic.

---

[4] Peirce's use of metaphysics to explain or ground logical principles emerged before he became clear about the 'regulative' character of the principles of logic. William Davenport has traced his evolutionary cosmology to 'Design and Chance', a manuscript dated 1884 (MS 875; Davenport 1981). These views are discussed more fully in Chapter 6.

The possibility has not yet been excluded that assertions with a metaphysical subject-matter (albeit not defended through self-controlled metaphysical inquiry) may yet have a place in logic. For logic does make use of assertions about reality: the vague, acritical certainties which make up common sense. So long as we make every effort to doubt such propositions, Peirce thinks that we are not at fault in using them as the basis of self-control. The relation of such common-sense propositions as have a metaphysical subject-matter to metaphysics is different from that of the regulative ideas or hopes. Although they call for further investigation in postlogical metaphysical inquiry, they are genuinely assertions with a metaphysical subject-matter. The task of metaphysics here is to arrive at a precise and testable version of such vague common-sense certainties. So if some of these common-sense certainties do have a metaphysical subject-matter, then the metaphysical neutrality of logic has not been established.

What is required for a belief to be 'metaphysical' may be somewhat indeterminate. But suppose that it is part of the common-sense background to logic—linked to Peirce's doctrine of the dynamical object—that we have direct perceptual knowledge of external things. Many of Peirce's remarks suggest that this is his view, and although vague, it would appear to be a metaphysical claim. Indeed, we might suppose that unless some such vague metaphysical commitments are involved in logic, the question whether theories are to be interpreted realistically or (say) instrumentally would be left open. And, on pain of circularity, *that* question could not be resolved by a 'realist' metaphysics which could, in principle, itself be interpreted instrumentally.

I have nothing to say in response to the complaint that these common-sense certainties do *not* have a metaphysical subject-matter. 'Metaphysics' is a term of art, and the boundaries of its application are not clear. Moreover, I could agree that no metaphysical *hypotheses* are employed in logic. Acritical common-sense certainties are not correctly described as (testable) 'hypotheses'. But that does not contradict the claim that assertions with a metaphysical subject-matter are made in the course of logical investigations. Peirce's claims about the structure of the different sciences do not eliminate that possibility. However, it is important not to attach too much significance to these remarks. They suggest that logic is not necessarily metaphysically neutral. But this does not threaten the claim, argued in Chapter 2, that Peirce's account of truth leaves open substantive metaphysical questions about the 'modes of being' of different kinds of truth. Even if logic may have *some* metaphysical implications, it is silent about most interesting metaphysical issues.

6. How Easy is Metaphysics?

At the beginning of this chapter, we noticed Peirce's insistence that metaphysics was quite an easy subject: it is more difficult than logic but easier than any of the special sciences. Two distinct points were at issue. The first is that metaphysics' place in Peirce's classification of the sciences explains why it is fairly easy: Peirce believed that the closer a discipline was to mathematics (the foundational discipline), the easier it would be. And, second, he held that unless metaphysics made progress, the special sciences (especially psychology) would be checked, this being 'a great disadvantage to all the other psychical sciences' (*CP* 6.2). These doctrines follow from a principle announced in 1898:

Logic requires that the more abstract sciences should be developed earlier than the more concrete ones. For the more concrete sciences require as fundamental principles the results of the more abstract sciences, while the latter only make use of the results of the former as data; and if one fact is wanting, some other will generally serve to support the same generalisation. (*CP* 6.1)

Experience of mathematics (the most abstract science) suggested that what logic required was in fact forthcoming: the more abstract a discipline, the less difficult it is (*CP* 6.2).

Peirce thus claimed both that it was possible to develop metaphysical theories before carrying out investigations in the special sciences and that it was necessary to do so. In concluding this chapter, I shall make some comments about both of these claims. The analogy with mathematics offers very weak support for the claim that it is possible to develop metaphysics before physics. It appears to equivocate on what is involved in a science being 'abstract', suggesting that the relation of more fundamental to less fundamental sciences is always the same. Mathematics is abstract because it does not deal with *existing* objects; it is relatively easy because it is an ideal and hypothetical science. It provides tools to be employed in less fundamental sciences but makes no claims about reality. Once we turn to the special sciences, the more 'general' ones are expected to *explain* the laws of those sciences which are subordinate to them. Peirce's suggestion appears to entail (very implausibly) that the relation between logic and metaphysics (say) is analogous to that between physics and chemistry.

Peirce sometimes explained the structure of his classification of the sciences by saying that sciences employ principles from those sciences to which they are subordinate and draw data from (or apply those principles to) sciences which are subordinate to them (*CP* 6.1). It is natural to complain that this finds more uniformity in the relations between sciences than is warranted by experience. The advice that empirical science hopes to receive from logical or methodological investigations seems different in kind from the input that chemists expect from physics. Moreover, we might think that progress in chemistry would be obstructed by constantly looking over one's shoulder to ensure that physical principles were being correctly applied. Before qualifying this judgement, however, we should explore some of Peirce's other comments about why metaphysics is supposed to be easier than the special sciences.

The claim that metaphysics draws data from physics (or psychology) might suggest that the special sciences must be developed *before* metaphysical theories can be tested. However, when discussing the relations between the metaphysics of mind and scientific psychology, Peirce remarked that it had never been proved that 'metaphysical psychology stands in need, in any degree worth consideration, of the scientific results of positive psychology'. He continued:

We must distinguish between results which depend upon the scientific method of psychology—scientific discoveries—and those rough facts about the mind which are open to everyone's observation, and which no sane man dreams of calling into question. As a matter of fact, it is upon these latter facts, and upon a series of similar facts about the outer world, that every man actually and really bases, first, his general metaphysics, and then his metaphysics of the soul. Even modern conceptions of the nature of intelligence, although facts of physiology have aided their development, can be more logically defended without resort to anything but those general facts about which nobody ever simulates a doubt, and never did do more than simulate one. (*NEM*3: 49; for a useful discussion, see Colapietro 1989: 51ff)

There are similar remarks about our common-sense physics (*CP* 8.198; see also Chapter 8). They suggest that metaphysics is easy because it does not use sophisticated experimental techniques. 'The data of metaphysics are not less open to observation, but immeasurably more so, than the data of the highly developed science of astronomy, to make any important addition to whose observations requires an expenditure of many tens of thousands of dollars.' We fail to see this only because metaphysical observations are of a kind 'with which every man's experience is so saturated that he usually pays no particular attention to them' (*CP* 6.2).

Other passages conflict with this. 'The Architecture of Theories' recommends that our metaphysics should borrow conceptions from the latest and best scientific theories (*CP* 6.9); and in 'Man's Glassy Essence' Peirce found it useful to refer to equations from recent doctoral theses in order to state his conception of the nature of matter (*CP* 6.238–45). These writings date from the early 1890s, while the passages in the previous paragraph were written at least five years later. However, since *CP* 6.1 (from 1898) retains the claim that metaphysics draws data from the special sciences, we should not conclude simply that the development of Peirce's thought led him to reject his earlier insistence that metaphysics should exploit scientific results. I shall suggest that a more interesting theme in Peirce's thought is involved. To formulate this, we must ask why it was *necessary* for metaphysics to be developed before physics and the other special sciences.

One answer is suggested by the earlier sections of this chapter: unless we have some positive reason to suppose that metaphysics will provide the concept of the self (and the view of reality) required to vindicate the regulative ideas we adopt in constructing our logic, those hopes might fade. It accords with this that the current discussion suggests that the materials for constructing this conception of the self and reality are available in everyday experience and common sense. But the source of Peirce's insistence that metaphysics be developed before the special sciences lies elsewhere. If metaphysics was ignored, he believed, progress in physical science and (especially) psychological science would be impeded. Metaphysics is 'applied' to physics and psychology in two distinct ways. As a more general science, it is required to explain the obtaining of physical laws: Peirce's evolutionary cosmology explains fundamental physical law by showing how such laws evolved over time. But metaphysical knowledge is applied in physics in a different way as well: just as the approximate truth of our commonsense understanding of dynamics 'is assumed by everybody who devises an experiment, and is therefore more certain than the result of any laboratory experiment' (*CP* 8.198), so our common-sense conception of mind serves as background for all scientific psychology. Reflection on this common-sense conception of nature or mind can prevent our taking seriously theories which conflict with it: it guides us in constructing hypotheses, and in deciding which are interesting enough to be tested experimentally. It is clear that Peirce thought that inattention to our common-sense metaphysics of mind was responsible for the popularity of psychological approaches which are familiar to us from the writings of Hume and other empiricists. Attention to metaphysics would have convinced us that they ignored features of mind which were potentially evident to all.

So understood, Peirce's insistence that psychological research had been 'checked' by the backward state of metaphysics (*CP* 6.2) is of a piece with Wittgenstein's insistence (in the *Philosophical Investigations*) that the 'confusion and barrenness of psychology is not to be explained by calling it a "young science" ': rather, 'in psychology there are experimental methods and *conceptual confusion*' (1958: §232). Unless a metaphysical theory is developed, the wrong framework of concepts may be used to formulate psychological theories and evaluate their plausibility.

I suggested that an interesting feature of Peirce's thought explained his apparent uncertainty about the role of information from the special sciences in metaphysics. It relates to his insistence that common sense changes, although it does so very slowly (*CP* 5.444). Since he acknowledged that 'modern science with its microscopes and telescopes' (*CP* 5.513) showed that we inhabit a world which the 'old beliefs' do not fit 'except in extended senses', our 'common-sense' metaphysical view will lose its methodological value as scientific inquiry develops. Physical inquiry in the late twentieth century is guided by a conception of reality which may be enshrined in the 'common-sense' and unreflective experience of trained physicists, but which is foreign to our everyday common-sense 'folk-physics'. The common-sense view of the world has developed with the progress of physical inquiry—except that it is now the possession of only a few, and thus not properly described as 'common sense'. But it is now this scientifically refined conception of reality which is relevant to our attempts to formulate and evaluate hypotheses.

When Peirce was writing (and to this day), physics was a flourishing research programme which had already escaped the confines of our everyday conception of the physical world, while psychology was still attempting to forge the concepts that were required for experimental research to be possible at all. In that case, we should expect his investigations of the metaphysics of the self to focus upon elucidating the psychological views implicit in ordinary common-sense and everyday experience; but when he turned to the metaphysics of the physical world, we should expect attention to the physical concepts manifested in the beliefs and practices of physicists. It seems to me that this is what we do find. Hence the uncertainty about whether scientific information is relevant to metaphysics is a reflection of the different states of development of different sciences.

This interpretation does not conflict with Peirce's insistence that metaphysics should be 'developed' before physics and psychology. 'Developed' need not mean 'completed'. Peirce may only have intended to stress that progress in physics or psychology (at a particular time) would be checked if we lack a clear understanding of the metaphysical conception of mind and nature which is available at that time. Metaphysical pictures of mind and nature have a role in evaluating hypothesis, so science will suffer if the task of articulating them is postponed.

In this section, we have examined Peirce's reasons for thinking it important to develop a metaphysics sooner rather than later. It turns out that these reasons rest upon a role for metaphysics distinct from the one that emerges from Apel's work and which was discussed in the earlier sections of this chapter. The themes we have just discussed are likely to prompt metaphysical investigations with a different focus from those examined earlier. Of course, that does not diminish the importance of the considerations which concerned Apel; but it helps us to understand the variety of roles which Peirce's metaphysics was intended to fill. Moreover, the arguments discussed in this section help to explain why Peirce needs a metaphysics in addition to the special sciences.

8

Common Sense, Pragmatism, and Rationality

1. Common Sense and Philosophy

We begin doing philosophy against the background of our common-sense view of things, a set of often inchoate and unformulated assumptions about the nature of mind and the physical world, about the scope of our knowledge and its sources, and about values and rationality, which forms the background to our everyday actions and inquiries. In modern jargon, we begin with a folk physics and a folk psychology, and a common-sense view of morality and rationality which are more often embodied in our habits of belief, action, inference, and evaluation than in a carefully set out body of principles. Since Plato, philosophical theories have often questioned these common-sense views, contrasting them with the better articulated and defended views contained in some favoured philosophical theory. Having identified possible sources of error in the ways in which our common-sense views were acquired, Descartes viewed them with suspicion. His method of doubt required us to suspend judgement in any belief that could conceivably be mistaken. Familiar sceptical arguments suggested that the epistemological position of common-sense beliefs is unsatisfactory and in need of philosophical foundations. When philosophical theory confronted common-sense opinions, the latter were held to be defensible only if they could be underwritten by the former.

Another philosophical tradition, with roots in Aristotle's respect for common ways of talking, questioned this view of the relations between common sense and philosophical theory. Members of the Scottish school of common sense, for example Thomas Reid (1710–96), saw common sense as a body of ill-defined but self-evident and certain principles which guide our actions and our beliefs, including our philosophical ones. Being self-evident, these principles are more certain than any philosophical argument or theory. If a philosophical theory challenges some self-evident certainty, for example that we have reliable knowledge of a world of independently existing things, we are rational to embrace the self-evident certainty and question the philosophy. If a philosophical theory conflicts with habitual belief and inference, it should be rejected. Since the suggestion that all might be a dream does not shake any of my everyday certainties, it has no more relevance to philosophy than it does to my attempts to organize my domestic life. Philosophers' sceptical doubts are 'unreasonable' or 'unnatural'. I know that I am awake, that I can see my hand, that fire burns, that murder is wrong; and since philosophical scepticism does not shake my confidence in any of these beliefs, it is reasonable to rely upon them in developing an adequate understanding of how I am able to investigate my surroundings.[1]

In this spirit, Reid remarked that

[when philosophers] condescend to mingle again with the human race, and to converse with a friend, a companion, or a fellow-citizen, the ideal system vanishes; common sense, like an irresistible torrent, carries them along; and, in spite of all their reasoning and philosophy, they believe their own existence, and the existence of other things. (Quoted in Coates 1996: 16)

Impressed by the danger of an infinite regress if the legitimacy of beliefs depends upon our ability to offer reasons in their support, Reid insisted that justification 'must stop only when we come to propositions which support all that are built upon them, but are supported by none themselves—that is, to self-evident propositions'. These self-evident propositions are not absolutely indubitable; nor do they form part of a philosophical theory. Sceptical challenges to them, once accepted, cannot be defeated; but this, it is argued, does not touch their self-evidence. Some of the first principles of contingent truth are: that memory is generally reliable; that things which we 'distinctly perceive by our senses' generally really exist and conform to our perceptions; that observed regularities will probably fit future experience; that testimony is generally reliable; and that 'certain features of the countenance, sounds of the voice, and gestures of the body, indicate certain thoughts and dispositions of the mind'. In general, 'the natural faculties, by which we distinguish truth from error, are not fallacious' (Reid 1975: 266–84 passim). We could not test such beliefs through an empirical investigation: if we genuinely doubted these propositions, we would lack confidence in our ability to carry out such an investigation into them. Yet since they express contingent truths, we would not

---

[1] The first chapter of Coates (1996) contains a clear account of some of these themes in philosophy.

expect to be able to establish their truth a priori. The fact that they form part of 'common sense' is supposed to ensure that these observations do not lead us to question our right to rely upon them. They form part of a collection of self-evident certainties, manifested in our unthinking habits of belief formation. Only a mistaken attachment to the need for a *theoretical* underpinning leads us to find them unsatisfactory.

Philosophical investigation can identify the beliefs which have this foundational role, and describe the marks of a proposition being self-evident. The claim that something is a true first principle can be supported by pointing to 'the consent of the ages and nations, of the learned and the vulgar'. Support comes, too, from observing that something was believed from a very early stage of human development, 'before we could reason, and before we could learn it by instruction'. That belief in the proposition is necessary for action and conduct is also relevant. But our acceptance of such propositions does not rest upon the observation that they are universally accepted. Rather, as we have seen, they are *self-evident*: they are irresistible; our nature will not permit us to doubt them; once they are understood, they cannot be doubted. When we perceive something, we have 'an irresistible conviction and belief in its existence', which is immediate:

it is not by any train of reasoning or argumentation that we come to be convinced of the existence of what we perceive; we ask no argument for the existence of the object, but that we perceive it; perception commands our belief upon its own authority, and disdains to rest its authority upon any reasoning whatsoever. (Reid 1975: 163–4)

Although Reid invokes the benevolence of God to explain why our faculties are naturally attuned to the nature of reality, acceptance of this explanation is not required to justify our confidence in them. Indeed, justification and explanation are quite distinct. Reid holds that memory provides immediate, reliable information about the past; but 'how it provides this information . . . is inexplicable'. Indeed, knowledge of the past through memory is 'as unaccountable as an immediate knowledge would be of things to come; and I can give no reason why I should have the one and not the other' (Reid 1975: 209; and see Duggan 1984). Self-evidence can be a kind of brute, unintelligible evidence or plausibility.

This common-sense tradition shaped the philosophy taught at Harvard during the middle of the nineteenth century. Although Kant was a more direct influence upon his early thought, insights from this tradition were embraced by Peirce from very early in his career. For example, a manuscript from 1872 reminds us that common sense 'usually hits the nail on the head' (W3: 10). Peirce's disdain for theology (the attempt to subject religious belief to *theory*), and his suspicion of philosophical ethics both stem from the respect he had for common sense. Its subtle sensitivity to the richness of phenomena, and the confidence we feel in its demands, compare very favourably with the crude oversimplifications and controversial character of the philosophical theories that are offered in its defence.[2] In Chapter 1 we saw that Peirce's view of the proper approach to 'vital questions' in the late 1890s also reflected these views. My concern in this chapter is with the role of the idea of common sense in his approach to epistemological issues, in his work on logic.

In 'Some Consequences of Four Incapacities' (1867), Peirce opposed the Cartesian recommendation that 'philosophy must begin with complete doubt':

We cannot begin with complete doubt. We must begin with all the prejudices which we actually have when we enter upon the study of philosophy. These prejudices are not to be dispelled by a maxim, for they are things which it does not occur to us *can* be questioned. Hence this initial scepticism will be mere self-deception, and not real doubt ... A person may, it is true, in the course of his studies find reason to doubt what he began by believing; but in that case he doubts because he has a positive reason for it, and not on account of the Cartesian maxim. Let us not pretend to doubt in philosophy what we do not doubt in our hearts. (*CP* 5.265)

Similar remarks are found in 'The Fixation of Belief' (1877): inquiry must proceed from 'real and living doubt' (*CP* 5.377); and sceptical doubts are not real and living. Although these passages endorse the common-sense suggestion that avowals of doubt are often insincere or self-deceived, that our actions show what we doubt better than the sentences we write in philosophy books, they contain few signs of the common-sense claim that there are fundamental self-evident 'first principles'.[3] However, it cannot be denied that they reveal a sympathy for themes from the common-sense tradition.

---

[2] Chapter 11 cites a number of passages which support this claim.

[3] The discussion of the structure of the argument of 'The Fixation of Belief' in Chapter 1 suggests that the discussion of the facts already taken for granted when we ask how we ought to carry out inquiries may reveal a deeper commitment to the common-sense tradition than is allowed here.

In 1905, in 'Issues of Pragmaticism', Peirce's common-sensism is explicit. He argues that 'critical common-sensism' is a consequence of his pragmaticism (as he then began to call his own distinctive version of pragmatism in order to distinguish it from less palatable rivals. The new name, he said, was 'ugly enough to be safe from kidnappers' (CP 5.414).) Care is taken to list the respects in which 'critical' common-sensism differs from Reid's version of the doctrine. He argues that it stands in a complex and subtle relation to the philosophy of Kant, suggesting that critical common-sensism is the doctrine which Kant ought to have adopted, had he taken pains to remove inconsistencies from his position. Why does he see this doctrine as a consequence of pragmaticism? And what role does common sense have in his mature theory of critical rationality?

The philosophical use of appeals to self-evident principles of common sense can seem straightforward in the hands of a thinker such as Thomas Reid, but it presents a number of problems. It seems too easy to assert that fundamental principles form part of common sense, and Reid says little about how we are to settle debates over exactly what common sense requires. In the face of widespread disagreement over fundamental philosophical issues, this is disturbing. Even if we could show that some proposition appeared self-evident to everybody, there are questions about why we should take that as a sign of its truth. The method of doubt is grounded in a living awareness of the extent to which the general assumptions that guide our inquiries (particularly those resting on the testimony of our teachers) may involve undetected prejudice. We need an explanation of why the fact that something seems self-evident should not be viewed as an instinctive compulsion which influences our cognition, but which may not be a vehicle of cognitive progress. By the time that Peirce was writing, scholars were ready to explain instincts by reference to natural selection. The instincts that form common-sense certainties may have been advantageous to our forebears, whose ways of life were less complex than our own. Why should we expect them to be applicable once we move away from primitive forms of life? Coates cites Kant's complaint that the Scottish philosophy of common sense is a kind of 'intellectual Luddism': 'To appeal to common sense when insight and science fail . . . this is one of the subtle discoveries of modern times, by means of which the most superficial ranter can safely enter the lists with the most thorough thinker and hold his own' (Coates 1996: 1–2; Kant 1950: 7). It can seem like a force for intellectual conservatism: appeal to our common-sense certainties can always be used to question new ideas and conceptual innovations.

Peirce's critical common-sensism acknowledges these and other difficulties. Indeed, there are signs of this in some later annotations to a passage in 'The Fixation of Belief', in which he had challenged some 'erroneous conceptions of proof'. These rested on the twin assumptions that we have only to formulate a question to start an inquiry and that we should begin by questioning everything. The original text (*CP* 5.376)[4] urged:

1. But the mere putting of a proposition into the interrogative form does not stimulate the mind to any struggle after belief. There must be a real and living doubt, and without this all discussion is idle.

Then, after introducing the suggestion that proofs must rest on 'ultimate and absolutely indubitable premises', he continued:

2. But, in point of fact, an inquiry, to have that completely satisfactory result called demonstration, has only to start with propositions free from all actual doubt. If the premises are not in fact doubted at all, they cannot be more satisfactory than they are.[5]

And finally:

3. When doubt ceases, mental action on the subject comes to an end; and if it did go on, it would be without purpose.

Subsequently (in 1893 and 1903), Peirce added notes to each of these passages. Commenting on (1), he wrote that 'so long as we do not put our fingers on our erroneous opinions, they remain our opinions still', and recommended a general survey of the origins of our opinions, many of which were acquired before we possessed the ability to distinguish truth from error. 'Such reflection may awaken real doubts about some of the propositions'; but if it does not, the search for reasons to believe them is an 'idle farce' (1893). In his reaction to (2) we read that we can never eliminate the possibility that a doubt will emerge later, and that we ought to construct theories to minimize that risk, relying upon a wide range of evidence and leaving room for subsequent modification (1893). And (3) too is qualified: mental action can continue to have role in 'self-criticism'

---

[4] This passage is also at W3: 248. The later comments are included as footnotes in the *Collected Papers* version; they are not in the *Writings*.

[5] This passage could be read as a rejection of the common-sense philosopher's appeal to self-evident first principles.

and 'rational self-control' (1903). It thus seems that we should try to doubt propositions that seem self-evident; and, even if they escape criticism, we must allow that they could still succumb in the future. In these remarks we find the germs of 'critical' common-sensism.

Talk of rational self-control here is related to epistemic responsibility. When Descartes invokes errors he has received from his teachers, the moral is that it would be irresponsible to hold on to opinions that may be infected by falsehood through having such a source. Questions arise about how stringently this should be taken. Descartes's method of doubt appears to conclude that unless I can demonstrate conclusively that a belief has not been so infected, intellectual responsibility requires me to suspend judgement. Peirce, by contrast, seems to think that further inquiry or suspension of judgement is required only if a 'general review of the causes of our beliefs' offers positive reason for thinking that infection has occured. Common-sense beliefs will generally fail the first test but pass the second. Continued trust in them requires an account of the rationality of belief and inquiry which can leave us confident that adopting the less stringent test will not lead us down a blind alley from which there will be no escape.

The underlying difficulty concerns the interplay of psychological and normative considerations in explaining and evaluating inquiries. Rationality requires us to subject our reasoning to control according to defensible standards. Our accepting such standards can often receive a psychological explanation, and we understand how humans can find beliefs compelling which are not true. When it is claimed that we cannot but find certain beliefs reasonable, we ask whether that 'cannot' expresses psychological impossibility or whether it indicates that to do otherwise would contravene rationality.[6] When Kant asserts that fundamental principles are synthetic a priori, and when Wittgenstein insists that it is improper to claim knowledge that one sees a hand, each is attempting to establish that putative 'common-sense' claims have a *constitutive* role: they are involved in specifying the aims of our inquiries and the question whether they are *true* does not arise as it does for propositions whose truth is investigated against the background of such a framework. The common-sense response to scepticism appears to hold both that

---

[6] David Wiggins (1987: 348) has emphasized that sometimes we express the correctness of a belief using phrases such as 'There is nothing else for us to think'. This appears to involve a 'cannot' which fuses psychological and normative considerations: the psychological 'cannot' is a reflection of our rational capacities. Common-sense philosophers require something similar—although it should be emphasized that Wiggins is not concerned with common-sense beliefs in the papers in which he discusses this.

common-sense propositions are objects of knowledge and that their status as knowledge is untouched by our refusal to respond to the challenge of explaining how we know these things.

2. Making Common-Sensism 'Critical'

In 'Issues of Pragmaticism', Peirce lists six characteristics which distinguish his critical common-sensism from the position of Reid and his followers (*CP* 5.438 ff; see also 5.498, 5.523).[7] Before turning to those which explain his use of the word 'critical' to describe the position, we should consider four claims about the nature of our common-sense view of things. First, where Reid's examples of common sense are all beliefs, Peirce insists that we should also take account of instinctive or indubitable *inferences* (*CP* 5.440). This is probably a minor shift. My acceptance of the reliability of testimony (to take one of Reid's examples) may be manifested only in my disposition to infer *p* from the premise that *A* said that *p*. If common sense is a matter of instinctive habits of inference, however, this would help to explain why it can often be difficult to identify what is included in common sense. Arriving at a theoretical understanding of our inferential habits need not be an easy task.

Second, one of Reid's identifying marks for common-sense is common acceptance; he held that it was the same for all people at all times. In early writings, Peirce probably believed that it changed quite quickly.[8] By 1905, he took an intermediate view: common-sense beliefs 'vary a little and but a little under varying circumstances and in distant ages' (*CP* 5.444). Common sense does change, but very slowly. Third, Reid and Peirce agree that common sense is a matter of instinct. This means that it relates to relatively 'primitive' areas of life: it is accepted by both 'the learned and the vulgar'; and it is acquired at an early stage of development, 'before we could reason, and before we could learn it by instruction'. But Peirce drew a moral from this which Reid failed to notice: 'the original beliefs only remain indubitable in their applications to affairs that resemble those of a

---

[7] Another useful account of the distinctive features of critical common-sensism is found in an entry that Peirce wrote and the editor rejected for the 1906 supplement to the *Century Dictionary*. The number of the manuscript is L10; it is quoted in full in Brent (1993: 299–300).

[8] This would explain the somewhat cavalier insistence that we should trust anything that we do not doubt in some of the passages from 'The Fixation of Belief' that we have considered.

primitive mode of life'. Once we turn to questions of theoretical science, common sense may provide an unreliable guide: 'It is, for example, quite open to reasonable doubt whether the motions of electrons are confined to three dimensions' (*CP* 5.445).[9] Finally, common-sense beliefs and inferences are 'very vague indeed (such as, that fire burns) without being perfectly so' (*CP* 5.498). So we possess set of slowly evolving habits of belief and inference, which are indubitable in their application to everyday matters and which are 'invariably vague' (*CP* 5.446).

The first step to seeing what makes Peirce's position 'critical' is to ask why and how we accept common-sense beliefs and inferences. He explains that they are 'original': we cannot 'go behind them' in order to ask what reasons and rules license us in accepting them. But more important is his attempt to explain how they are indubitable by saying that they are 'acritical' (*CP* 5.440–5): they are not subject to reflective rational self-control:

[According to pragmaticism] . . . to say that an operation of the mind is controlled is to say that it is, in a special sense, a conscious operation; and this no doubt is the consciousness of reasoning. For this theory requires that in reasoning we should be conscious, not only of the conclusion, and of our deliberate approval of it, but also of its being the result of the premiss from which it does result, and furthermore that the inference is one of a possible class of inferences which conform to one guiding principle. (*CP* 5.441)

Reflective control of beliefs and inferences involves going beyond them, seeing them as the products of processes of reasoning whose soundness depends upon the truth of premises and the correctness of guiding principles. When a belief or inference is *acritical*, this kind of reflective control is missing: the belief is unshakeable, but there are no premises or rules we can question in order to check the belief's credentials; or although we are aware that a conclusion is produced in us by a particular premise, we are not reflectively conscious of a rule of guiding principle upon whose adequacy the inference is conditional. Acritical beliefs and inferences provide stopping points for rational reflection: perceptual judgements, common-sense beliefs, acritical inferences can all be used in justifying other beliefs and inferences but are not themselves grounded in rational reflection.

Sometimes Peirce describes common-sense beliefs as 'original (i.e.

---

[9] Common-sense beliefs 'resemble instincts . . . in relating to matters of life, in being beneficial, especially for the stock, in coming up into consciousness only on occasions of applicability, in being accompanied with deep unaccountable feeling' (Brent 1993: 300).

indubitable because uncriticized) beliefs of a general and recurrent kind' (*CP* 5.442). Quite how being 'uncriticized' enhances a belief's epistemic status may be unclear: it may be uncriticized merely through inattention or carelessness. Peirce occasionally prefers a rather better term: such beliefs are 'uncriticizable' (see *CP* 5.497). If a belief cannot be criticized, we would have a good reason for holding on to it. But he is clearly uneasy about this second term, and investigating the sources of this unease provides a clue to what is distinctive about his position. The only evidence we normally have that a proposition cannot be criticized is the fact that we have so far failed to criticize it. Recall Peirce's 1893 comment on the passage from 'The Fixation of Belief': 'We have to acknowledge that doubts about them may spring up later; but we can find no propositions which are not subject to this contingency' (*CP* 5.376 fn.). Thus the critical common-sensist embraces the 'critical acceptance of uncriticizable propositions' (*CP* 5.497). According to Peirce, Reid himself was 'insufficiently critical': he is 'not critical of the substantial truth of uncriticizable propositions' (ibid.). Comparing his own pragmatism with that of Schiller, Peirce talks of its dependence upon 'critical acceptance of a sifted common sense of mankind regarding mental phenomena'. Our common-sense folk psychology may be uncriticized and even uncriticizable, but the critical common-sensist accepts it 'critically' and is ready to be critical of its truth What does this mean? And why does Peirce's thought take this direction?

In one passage, Peirce expresses the points we have just examined by saying that a *critical* common-sensist, disclaims any 'infallible introspective power into the secrets of his own heart, to know just what he believes and what he doubts' (*CP* 5.498). We may not be very good at identifying common-sense certainties; and this brings with it some intellectual risks.

1. We may think we doubt something which we really believe.
2. We may really doubt what we *ought* to believe.
3. We may believe what we *ought* to doubt.
4. We may think we believe what we really doubt.

Two kinds of error are involved: (1) and (2) involve a misidentification of our own psychologico-cognitive states; and (2) and (3) involve cognitive states which are normatively inappropriate to our circumstances. There is another way of classifying the cases: (3) and (4) involve an excess of belief, while (1) and (2) involve an excess of doubt. Interestingly, while all four of these conditions could be 'disastrous for science', Peirce saw (3) and (4) as the more serious impediments to rationality. Elsewhere he warned that 'the danger ... does not lie in believing too little but in believing too much' (*CP* 5.517). He is clearly alert to the problems that face a common-sense philosopher.

We must discuss below why 'believing too much' can be so disastrous. The moral Peirce draws is to embrace something like the method of doubt and to make his common-sensism truly critical:

A philosopher ought not to regard an important proposition as indubitable without a systematic and arduous endeavour to attain a doubt of it, remembering that genuine doubt cannot be created by a mere effort of will, but must be compassed through experience. (*CP* 5.498)

With such sentiments, the Critical Common-sensist sets himself in serious earnest to the systematic business of endeavouring to bring all his very general first premises to recognition, and of developing every suspicion of doubt of their truth, by the use of logical analysis, and by experimenting in imagination. (*CP* 5.517)

These remarks explain Peirce's apparent unease about whether common-sense beliefs owe their status to being 'uncriticized' or 'uncriticizable'. Their special status stems from being 'uncriticizable', to their depending upon no other assumptions or principles through which they can be challenged. But our capacity to identify such beliefs and inferences is limited. Our best evidence that a belief is uncriticizable is fallible: it has not been criticized in spite of a rigorous attempt to doubt it. 'Critical acceptance' recognizes this possibility of error.[10]

The need for critical acceptance has another source too. Propositions which 'really are indubitable, for the time being' can turn out to be false. Hence, although we are obliged to think of anything we find indubitable that it is true, 'we may and ought to think it likely that some one of them, if not more, is false' (*CP* 5.498). Common sense itself is fallible. There are thus two respects in which Peirce's common-sensism is 'critical'. First, it calls for systematic criticism of any candidate for a common-sense certainty. And second, even if a proposition has passed this test, we should view it with a degree of critical detachment: we cannot help believing it, but we are aware that this does not rule out the possibility that it is false. We must try to criticize apparent common-

---

[10] Peirce's submission to the *Century Dictionary* usefully describes them as 'uncriticizable by the ordinary trained and well-matured minds of one generation' and grants that we may learn to criticize them later (Brent 1993: 299).

sense certainties; and our acceptance of them should be wary and critical.[11]

So marked is the critical common-sensist's 'high esteem for doubt' (*CP*
5.514) that we may suspect that Peirce has sunk back into a Cartesian mire
from which his common-sensism was supposed to offer escape. Indeed, he
has an imagined critic complain that 'so passionate a lover of doubt would
make a clean sweep of his beliefs' (*CP* 5.519). Peirce and the Cartesian
agree on the importance of trying to doubt beliefs and inferences; they
differ on how easy it is to find a reason to doubt. The common-sensist's
'hunger [for doubt] is not to be appeased with paper doubts: he must have
the heavy and noble metal, or else belief' (*CP* 5.514). Cartesians have a
picture of 'the adult's [mind as] a school slate, on which doubts are written with a soapstone pencil to be cleaned off with the dab of a wet sponge'
(*CP* 5.520). The Cartesian fault is not to try to doubt our most confident
beliefs, it is to have too lax a view of when the attempt has succeeded. The
Cartesian believes she doubts what she really believes; and she may also
doubt what she ought to believe. Reference to evil demons may satisfy her,
but lacking any reference to the possibility of refutation through future
experience, it does not provide a pragmatist with grounds for doubt.

We might understand the difference by asking: why is it such a cognitive disaster to believe what we ought to doubt? According to Peirce, the
greatest logical sin was to 'block the road of inquiry', to place impediments
in the way of cognitive progress. This could involve preventing us from
eliminating error or standing in the way of the discovery of truth.
Presumably the value of systematic doubt lies in its contribution to eliminating such blockage; and our current question calls for an examination of
the ways in which 'believing what we ought to doubt' can be an obstacle to
progress. Under Peirce's conception of truth and the aims of inquiry,
obstacles could be of two kinds: they might slow progress towards a fated
consensus; or they might potentially block it altogether. It is easy to see
that doubting what we ought to believe can slow things down: we might
waste time inquiring into the truth value of some proposition which could
have been better spent on some other cognitive activity. If, by contrast, we
believe what we ought to doubt, whole lines of research may be based on

---

[11] This explains the 1893 note to 'The Fixation of Belief' mentioned above. Peirce's
attitude towards the Cartesian project of seeking foundations for science through systematic doubt or scrutiny is endorsed: we should question our beliefs, hunting out those which
have been acquired on an insecure basis. Peirce's objection to Descartes is simply that he
too readily believed that he was able to doubt propositions (or ought to doubt propositions) which should not be doubted.

propositions that will subsequently have to be abandoned. This seems to be Peirce's line of thought.[12] Modern historiography of science suggests that it is controversial: dogmatically continuing to believe an otherwise attractive theory which has failed in some of its predictions may prove the best strategy for improving our understanding. But the strong claim about the dire effects of such dogmatism is probably not a deep feature of Peirce's position.

Descartes too sees the method of doubt as a methodological tool for removing prejudices and dogmas that may provide blocks to cognitive progress. A major difference between the two comes from their contrasting pictures of reality: Peirce, a 'realist', defines reality as the object of a fated convergence of opinion, but Descartes presumably sees it as the external cause of our ideas and experiences.[13] For the former, no sense attaches to the idea that there might be a fated permanent consensus on some proposition which is not true. Descartes, by contrast, can take seriously the idea that an evil demon could set things up so that there would be a fated convergence upon an opinion which gave a false description of reality. This gives sense to doubts which the critical common-sensist will not allow. The Cartesian thinks he can doubt what he should not doubt and, indeed, what he does not really doubt. This can easily lead to the conclusion that scientific inquiry is wholly illegitimate, to an acceptance of scepticism. Peirce's method of doubt, if we can only understand the principles by which real doubts are distinguished from unreal ones, avoids this difficulty.

We should now collect our thoughts and raise some questions for further discussion. Critical Common-sensism is distinguished from earlier forms of common-sensism by a package of commitments: it exploits common-sense beliefs and inferences which are vague, instinctive, and slowly evolving, and which are accepted in spite of a careful attempt to doubt them. Although sharing the common-sense philosophy's opposition to Cartesianism, it respects a modified version of the Cartesian method of doubt. As we shall see below, there is another distinctive 'critical' feature: a critical attachment to many ideas of the Kantian or critical philosophy. Moreover, as has already been noticed, the position is intimately related to Peirce's pragmaticism (*CP* 5.439). If critical common-sensism cannot be sustained, pragmaticism must be abandoned. In the

---

[12] Related matters have already been discussed in Chapter 1 when we considered Peirce's reasons for denying (in 1898) that belief had any place in science at all.

[13] See the discussion of nominalist and realist accounts of truth and reality in Chapter 3.

next section, we explore some examples of common-sense beliefs, and ask how what unifies these different elements of Peirce's package. Why does the 'critical' stance fit together with common-sense certainties that are vague and, instinctive? Why is it important that they be permitted to evolve? And why must such evolution be slow? We then consider their role in rational inquiry, preparing the way for an examination of the relations between critical common-sensism and pragmaticism.

3. Common Sense: Some Examples

First, 'Fire burns' (*CP* 5.498). Peirce uses this example to illustrate the vagueness of common-sense propositions: the statement leaves open which things fire burns and under what circumstances. While we know what kind of experience would falsify 'Fire burns all kinds of dry wood at normal temperatures', and can therefore test it empirically, almost any experience can be rendered compatible with the vague statement 'Fire burns'. It is not 'perfectly vague': if fire never burned anything, then this proposition would be false.[14] It also illustrates how common-sense beliefs are instinctive. A habit of expecting fire to burn things it comes into contact with may have a biological basis; the likelihood of our remote fore-bears surviving to reproduce was enhanced by an instinctive disposition to fear fire. The exceptions were, perhaps, unimportant for their lives: falsely expecting fire damage has better consequences than falsely expecting things to be fireproof. In a modern environment, this may not be so: we need more carefully worked out (and hence fallible) beliefs about incendi-ary properties. The general instinctive or common-sense belief was a more valuable cognitive instrument in the more 'primitive' mode of life in which it developed than it is in many areas of modern life. The more specialized our lives, the less valuable the common-sense belief. Common-sense beliefs about fire may evolve, slowly incorporating vague qualifications which identify important classes of exceptions.

The example illustrates the role of criticism too. Suppose that the vague statement 'Fire burns' is indeed an 'original' belief, encoded in our genes or the product of many generations of shared experience. In most of us, it will become mixed with more explicitly grounded empirical information which reduces the vagueness. Our *expressions* of the vague common-sense certainty may thus involve propositions which we do know how to falsify

---

[14] For further discussion of Peirce's view of vagueness, see Chapter 5.

or criticize. The only way to challenge true common sense would involve confirming a negative existential proposition about experience: it is not the case that there is something that fire burns. Everyday experience quickly shows that this is not so; and, if it did not, no finite sequence of experience would establish that the doubt was justified. The attempt to doubt it is then an attempt to identify the mix of common sense and empirical achievement and this can help us to identify the true deliverance of common sense. And critical acceptance is required because we should always be wary when we apply it in particular cases: unexpected exceptions may turn up at any time.

The role of critical acceptance is more evident from a second kind of example: moral beliefs.[15] Recent defenders of evolutionary psychology have suggested that many of our instinctive beliefs evolved to meet the needs of our hunter-gatherer ancestors. If this were true, then it would be unsurprising that some elements of common-sense morality should be remarkably ill-suited to the demands of a complex capitalist society. In that case, some would conclude, the discovery that some components of our 'folk morality' were 'original' or instinctive would be grounds for suspicion about our ready endorsement of them. If we reject a wholly biological understanding of instinctive belief and recognize that common sense is largely an historical cultural achievement, we may still expect a time-lag: inherited assumptions about the capacities of men and women derive highly fallible authority from their entrenchment in common sense.

If we are interested in the role of common sense in guiding belief fixation, two other sorts of example become important. First, common-sense beliefs influence our abductive sense; they shape our ideas about what sorts of theory should be taken seriously in trying to explain phenomena. A striking example is provided by dynamics, the discipline on which, Peirce suggests, all of physical science depends. In contemporary jargon, his view is that dynamics forms part of a common-sense 'folk physics':

[It] neither is nor ever was one of the special sciences that aim at the discovery of novel phenomena, but merely consists in the analysis of truths which universal experience has compelled every man of us to acknowledge. Thus the proof by Archimedes of the principle of the lever upon which Lagrange substantially bases

---

[15] Peirce's views about the role of instinct and common sense in morality was introduced in Chapter 1.

the whole statistical branch of the science, consists in showing that that principle is virtually assumed in our ordinary conception of two bodies of equal weight. Such universal experiences may not be true to microscopical accuracy, but that they are true in the main is assumed by everybody who devises an experiment, and is therefore more certain than any result of any laboratory experiment. (*CP* 8.198)

Our common-sense beliefs about bodies and their dynamical properties form a framework for research in physics. The common presumption of their 'truth in the main' is not challenged by experimental results; theories develop through attempts to make these principles precise, to apply them in new contexts. Theories that accord with these principles are more plausible than those which do not. A similar role is assigned to the analytical economics of Adam Smith and David Ricardo in providing a common-sense framework within which research in the human sciences can proceed: social science grows out of our common-sense views about rational action (*CP* 8.199). In philosophy, the same work is to be done by pragmatism and common-sensism.

If this is correct, then the need for critical acceptance of common-sense views is further clarified. When physics studies the microstructure of matter or the broad properties of the Universe, then we will not be surprised if our common-sense physics must be revised more than we initially hoped. Peirce says 'while they never become dubitable insofar as our mode of life remains that of somewhat primitive man, yet as we develop *degrees of self-control* unknown to that man, occasions of action arise in relation to which the original beliefs, if stretched to cover them, have no sufficient authority' (*CP* 5.511). It is, for example, quite open to reasonable doubt whether the motions of electrons are confined to three dimensions, although it is good methodology to presume that they are until some evidence to the contrary is forthcoming (*CP* 5.445). Critical acceptance of these common-sense views when we move beyond a 'primitive' context involves regarding them as a fallible guide to the underlying nature of matter; we are to have confidence in our sense of plausibility which is largely shaped by these common-sense certainties.

The second kind of common sense beliefs relevant to our practice of belief fixation reflects fundamental epistemological principles and harks back to Reid's first principles of contingent truth. For example: 'There is order in the universe' (*CP* 8.208). This illustrates the vagueness of common-sense propositions: 'everybody's actions show that it is impossible to doubt that there is an element of order in the universe, but the moment we attempt to define that orderliness we find room for doubt' (ibid.). Another illustration is provided by the argumentative strategy of ' The Fixation of Belief'.[16] Peirce compares four methods for arriving at opinions. Three are found wanting, and the paper recommends adoption of the method of science, the fundamental hypothesis of which is:

There are real things, whose characters are entirely independent of our opinions about them; those realities affect our senses according to regular laws, and, through our sensations are as different as our relations to the objects, yet, by taking advantage of the laws of perception, we can ascertain by reasoning how things really are. (*CP* 5.384; W3: 254)

Peirce may have thought that this was a common-sense indubitable belief, a vague proposition, presupposed by our methods of inquiry, which we accept critically because it cannot be criticized. The 'critical' component of his common-sensism requires him to attempt to doubt it, perhaps by considering the adoption of methods of inquiry which conflict with this hypothesis. If it were part of common sense, then we should be unable to sustain the use of such methods: the role of the hypothesis in our instinctive 'primitive' practices would, quite simply, disrupt the attempt to take alternative methods seriously.[17] And this is just what happens: when we adopt the method of tenacity, choosing any opinion which suits us and sticking to it through thick and thin, we are defeated by finding that others have different opinions; and so on with the other methods. Our implicit, common-sense adherence to the hypothesis underlying the method of science emerges when we subject it to rigorous criticism. Our responses show that the hypothesis is indubitable. This interpretation fits Peirce's claim to be searching for those facts which 'are already assumed' when we ask what methods of inquiry we should adopt, which 'we must already know before we have any clear conception of reasoning at all, it cannot be

---

[16] These arguments are discussed in more detail in Chapter 1.

[17] It is a matter of controversy how far 'critical' common-sensism was a component of Peirce's philosophy in the 1870s. Douglas Anderson is sceptical about how important it then was (1995: 92), but he notes that it was emerging by 1893 when an annotation to 'The Fixation of Belief' emphasized that 'that which there is a very decided and general inclination to believe must be true' (*CP* 5.382n). The need to *criticize* common-sense views is present in the original paper: 'The truth is that common-sense, or thought as it first emerges above the level of the narrowly practical, is deeply imbued with that bad logical quality to which the epithet *metaphysical* is commonly applied; and nothing can clear it up but a severe course of logic (W3: 246). Peirce is concerned, as later, with the fact that what appears to be self-evident and common-sensical may result from harmful logical reflection.

supposed to be any longer of much interest to inquire into their truth or falsity' (*CP* 5.369).[18]

4. Kantian Affiliations

As we have seen, common-sense beliefs and inferences include 'the first principles of logic and philosophy' (*CP* 5.521). Why are we entitled to make use of them? As we saw, Kant objected to the view that the mere fact that we have not been able to challenge them gives them any legitimate authority. The fact that I have no positive reason to doubt the uniformity of nature or the reality of the external world gives no reason to believe these things. In 'Consequences of Common-Sensism', Peirce considers the suggestion that they might be defended by 'scientific experimentation'; his response illuminates the complex relations between his pragmaticism and Kant's critical philosophy.

The first reason offered for rejecting the suggestion is that to adopt it would be to risk circularity. Any scientific inquiry 'must proceed upon the virtual assumption of sundry logical and metaphysical beliefs; and it is rational to settle the validity of those before undertaking the operation that supposes their truth' (*CP* 5.521). If confidence in our sense of plausibility, faith in the 'uniformity in nature' (*CP* 5.22) or in the presence of 'order in the universe' (*CP* 8.208), and belief that 'there are real things whose characters are entirely independent of our opinions about them' (*CP* 5.384) are 'virtual assumptions' of any use of the scientific method, it will not be wise to trust scientific inquiry to underwrite our dependence upon them. Peirce agrees with the Kantians that many fundamental principles are *presuppositions* of our methods of investigation.

What follows from this discovery? Kantians see a route to a demonstration of the *truth* of the proposition, one that can be bolstered by showing that such presuppositions are constitutive of empirical reality: 'the truth of them can be explicitly laid down on critical grounds' (*CP* 5.521). Appeal to common sense, by contrast, can 'prevent our pretending to doubt' them. As I have argued elsewhere, Peirce rejected the suggestion that showing

---

[18] As several commentators have pointed out, Peirce's 'Neglected Argument for the Reality of God' provides a very clear illustration of critical common-sensism in action. Not only is the concept of God extremely vague, but the 'Humble Argument' suggests that religious belief is a natural, common-sense belief; and the 'Neglected Argument' supplements this by a rigorous attempt to doubt it. See Murphey (1961: 365) and Anderson (1995: 137, 151, 181). This topic is discussed more fully in Chapter 11.

that something was a 'presupposition' of inquiry demonstrated its truth; at best, it warrants us in hoping that it is true, in critically accepting it as a regulative principle.[19] In the paper under discussion he adds:

[N]othing is so unerring as instinct within its proper field, while reason goes wrong as often as right—perhaps oftener. Now those vague beliefs that appear to be indubitable have the same sort of basis as scientific results have. That is to say, they rest on experience—on the total everyday experience of many generations of multitudinous populations. Such experience is worthless for distinctively scientific purposes, because it does not make the minute distinctions with which science is chiefly concerned; not does it relate to the recondite subjects of science, although all science, without being aware of it, virtually supposes the truth of the vague results of uncontrolled thought upon such experiences, and would have to shut up shop if she should manage to escape accepting them. No wisdom could ever have discovered argon; yet within its proper sphere, which embraces objects of universal concern, the instinctive weight of human experience ought to have so vastly more weight than any scientific result, that to make scientific experiments to ascertain, for example, whether there be any uniformity in nature or no, would vie with adding a teaspoonful of saccharine to the ocean in order to sweeten it. (*CP* 5.522)

Instinctive beliefs (whether products of nature or nurture) represent an evolutionary heritage which supports our taking them seriously. Although we cannot point to the particular experiences that ground them, we can claim airily with other common-sense philosophers: 'everything counts for them, and nothing counts against them'. Although this guarantees the truth of no individual proposition, it warrants us in mistrusting our tendency to demand a philosophical answer to our apparent doubts about each. Inquiry rests upon a store of empirically based practical wisdom.[20]

Both Cartesians and Kantians complain that there are normative issues, questions of justification, which the common-sense philosophy wrongly ignores. We are to accept propositions simply because they have not been criticized; but the fact that a belief has not been criticized does not entitle us to hold it. In an interesting passage, Peirce responds that this objection equivocates on 'because'. If the claim is a causal one, then it is true that belief in the proposition is causally sustained by our failure to criticize it: the common-sensist 'does not doubt certain propositions that he would have doubted if he had criticized them' (*CP* 5.232). But the burden of the objection is that the belief is accepted '*on the ground* that it has not been

---

[19] See Chapter 7.
[20] This discussion thus reinforces themes developed in Chapter 1 and discussed further in Chapters 10 and 11.

criticized' (ibid.); and Peirce rejects this because 'such beliefs are not "accepted" '. Philosophical reflection enables one 'to recognize that one has had the belief-habit as long as one can remember, and to say that no doubt of it has ever arisen is only another way of saying the same thing'. I am never in the position of wondering whether I should acquire it. I need no further reasons for it. It forms the background of firm belief against which my doubts and inquiries arise. If I do not doubt a proposition, then I take it to be true, and I have no need to ask why I should believe it. As Peirce suggests, launching into an inquiry into the latter question 'virtually falls into the Cartesian error of supposing that one can doubt at will'. At best, we can seek an explanation of our holding these beliefs; and we can see how some explanations may then lead us to doubt them. But unless we come up with such a reason, we have no need to look for reasons in support of common-sense propositions. We have always believed them, and we have no reason to suppose this belief illegitimate.

The distinctions being exploited here are important for Peirce's position and they may still be unclear. As an example of a common-sense belief consider the claim that there is order in nature. Now, Peirce denies that I need any reason to accept this proposition. This is because I do not 'accept' it, since it is something that I have always believed. The way to understand this, I suggest, is that Peirce is denying that we are ever in a state of being agnostic about whether there is order in nature, looking for evidence or arguments that will enable us to decide one way or the other. We do not need the sort of support that would be required to enable us to replace agnosticism by firm belief, to acquire the belief through an act of conscious acceptance. The process of criticism is an attempt to force ourselves into just that position: if criticism succeeds, then doubt or agnosticism would be appropriate and a search for reasons to accept either this proposition or its negation would have to begin. When we terminate this process of criticism, then we have a new piece of information: it has proved impossible to doubt the proposition that there is order in nature. Although this information cannot serve as a positive reason for *accepting* it, it is hard to deny that it has a role in supporting or securing my belief. I can be more confident of its legitimacy than I was before. I now have a reason to accept that this is not one of those beliefs which I ought to doubt. In that case, the fact that I have failed to criticize the belief that there is order in nature provides rational support for continuing to believe it, even if it does not provide a reason for accepting it. Peirce must attach great weight to this distinction between 'providing rational support for continued belief' and 'providing reasons for acceptance'. It is not yet fully clear why.

Two considerations may be relevant here, and they will be examined further in the following section. First, reasons required to establish that there is no positive reason to doubt a proposition can be weaker than reasons which justify a move from agnosticism to acceptance of it. Indeed, such reasons need not exhaust the rational support or sustenance that the belief in question possesses. Second, the two cases place different restrictions on the resources that can be used in seeking these reasons. If I am currently agnostic about whether there is order in nature, it would be question-begging to try to settle the matter by means of an inquiry which presupposed that nature displayed order. If I currently hold that belief, and I am wondering whether I can be given reason to doubt it, then it is not at all obvious that a similar restriction applies. It is easy to see how an empirical investigation could have the self-refuting result that our abilities to carry out effective empirical investigations were much more limited than we had supposed. Even if we would not thereby be justified in accepting the conclusion of this inquiry, we would be rational to suspend judgement about our cognitive capacities. And if our inquiry did *not* have this result, we would not be reasoning in circles to judge that our initial confidence in empirical methods of inquiry had received further support.[21]

If his own account of the matter is to be believed. Peirce's use of the term 'critical' is massively over-determined. As well as emphasizing the importance of trying to *criticize* indubitable propositions and the *critical* character of our acceptance of them, it signals the fact that he is a *critic* of the orthodox common-sense tradition. Yet more, the doctrine is 'but a modification of Kantism' or the critical philosophy: indeed it is the form that the *critical* philosophy should have taken according to this sympathetic *critic*.[22] In a famous passage, Peirce continues that 'The Kantist has only to abjure from the bottom of his heart the proposition that a thing-in-itself can, however indirectly, be conceived; and then correct the details of Kant's doctrine accordingly, and he will find himself to have become a Critical Common-sensist.'[23] We acknowledge that these first principles cannot be defended through empirical inquiry; we acknowledge that they

---

[21] These fine dialectical distinctions are reminiscent of debates about how far naturalized epistemology can meet our philosophical needs. I return to this issue at the end of the following section.

[22] Evidence for this over-determination can be found in *CP* 5.452, the section of 'Issues of Pragmaticism' from which the quotations in this paragraph are taken. Peirce's rejection of the transcendental philosophy is explored in more detail in Chapters 7 and 12.

[23] Compare 'The kind of Common-sensism which . . . criticizes the Critical Philosophy and recognizes its own affiliation to Kant has surely a certain claim to call itself Critical Common-sensism' (*CP* 5.525).

cannot be criticized. But we reject the demand that we still have an obligation to vindicate our reliance upon them though an a priori proof of their legitimacy or of their constitutive status.

5. Common Sense, Self-control and Pragmaticism

Two questions remain to be addressed. Why did Peirce think that critical common-sensism was a consequence of his pragmaticism? And why did he start to place weight on this in 1905? When he tried to formulate and defend his pragmatism in lectures at Harvard in 1903, he emphasized the phenomenological defence of his categories and wrote very little about common sense. Three years later, writing in *The Monist*, there is little phenomenology and much common sense. What explains the change? It may just be a tactical shift. Abstract speculations about Firstness, Secondness, and Thirdness were unlikely to win converts to Peirce's pragmatism. And there can be no doubt that he continued to believe that his categories provided the best tool for analysing experience and (indeed) common sense itself. So our fundamental question concerns why Peirce thought that his version of pragmatism committed him to the existence of these vague common-sense certainties. Why does the practice of scientific inquiry require as background this body of vague beliefs whose content is not specifically scientific? How is pragmatism implicated in the answer to this question?

Before examining some passages in which this is discussed, we should make an initial conjecture.[24] Once we notice that it would be circular to use induction to defend induction, indeed to try to use the method of science to assess the truth value of any proposition which is virtually presupposed by the idea of scientific inquiry, the status of these fundamental commitments is apt to become problematic. We avoid circularity and scepticism, it seems, only by giving them a distinctive epistemic status: they are a priori principles of rationality, to be defended through logical or philosophical investigations whose methods do not involve reliance upon experience and experiment. A philosopher who thinks that the method of science (in a broad sense) is the only respectable method of inquiry will be embarrassed by this; as will a pragmatist who believes that the meanings

---

[24] Some of the points discussed here are taken further in Hookway (1993) and in Chapter 9. C. F. Delaney also emphasizes that critical common-sensism combines themes characteristic of contemporary foundationalist and coherentist approaches to epistemology (1993: 169, 115–18)

of significant propositions can be clarified by tracing their consequences for possible experience. There is thus a problem of reconciling two views:

1. Rationality requires a body of beliefs, principles, and inferences whose acceptance is not conditional upon the upshot of future scientific inquiries and the future run of experience.
2. There is no 'non-scientific knowledge' (where 'scientific' is understood broadly): propositions are only significant if their truth would make a difference to future experience.

The conjecture is that critical common-sensism was embraced as the only way of achieving this reconciliation.

Confirmation is found in a passage from 'Issues of Pragmaticism'. Having recalled that pragmatism was originally defended as a rule for rational self-control of beliefs and assertions, Peirce observed:

Now control may itself be controlled, criticism itself subjected to criticism; and ideally there is no obvious definite limit to the sequence. But if one seriously inquires whether it is possible that a completed series of actual efforts should have been endless or beginningless . . . , I think he can only conclude that . . . this must be regarded as impossible. It will be found to follow that there are, besides percep-tual judgements, original (i.e., indubitable because uncriticized) beliefs of a general and recurrent kind, as well as indubitable acritical inferences. (*CP* 5.442)[25]

Undermining the sceptical impact of a regress of reflection, self-criticism, and justification is the root of critical common-sensism.

In a manuscript entitled 'The Basis of Pragmaticism' (1903, *CP* 5.497–501), another reason is offered why 'pragmaticism will be sure to carry critical common-sensism in its arms' (*CP* 5.499). This rests again on the idea that pragmatists place emphasis upon the analogies between thinking and 'endeavour': inquiry and reasoning are forms of problem-solving *activity*; and there are similarities between the control of action and the control of reasoning. 'Action in general is largely a matter of instinct', so the pragmatist will expect the same to hold for the psychology of belief formation. Since 'irresistible instinctive desires are such familiar

---

[25] In a review of Wundt's *Principles of Physiological Psychology*, published in 1902, Peirce claimed that pragmatism was 'only an endeavour to give the philosophy of common sense a more exact development, especially by emphasizing the point that there is no intel-lectual value in mere feeling *per se* but that the whole function of thinking lies in the regu-lation of conduct' (*CP* 8.199).

and such almost unvarying phenomena', it is to be expected that there will be unvarying instinctive habits of belief and inference as well. In other words: we would expect the philosophical psychology of belief and inference to be analogous to that of desire and action; and critical common-sensism is the result of taking these analogies seriously. Where the first argument suggested that critical common-sensism solved problems that might otherwise embarrass pragmatism, this one claims, more modestly, that pragmatists are likely to be predisposed to find common-sensism extremely plausible.

This argument had been obscurely prefigured in 'Issues of Pragmaticism' (*CP* 5.440), once again in the context of a discussion of self-control. Having remarked that 'the machinery of logical self-control works on the same plan as moral self-control, in multiform detail', Peirce turns to 'certain obvious features of the phenomena of self-control'. He observes that they 'can be expressed compactly and without any hypothetical addition . . . by saying that we have an occult nature of which and its contents we can only judge by the conduct that it determines and by phenomena of that conduct.' His point seems to be that it is an error to assume that all that is relevant to the process of conscious reasoning is present in consciousness and is open to view. There is a constant interplay between conscious reflection and processes, tendencies, and mechanisms which are not open to view. Our philosophical account of self-controlled reasoning will depend upon an inference to the best explanation of the relevant phenomena. At this point, the considerations from 'The Basis of Pragmaticism' can be introduced as a way of emphasizing the great plausibility of the claim that we are guided by a body of relatively universal and stable instinctive habits of belief and inference.

We can put these points together with the remarks about how to block the regress of justification and reflection as follows. One of the phenomena of logical reflection is that we do not embark on such a regress: we rest upon a body of propositions that we find indubitable, even if we cannot say what our reasons are for accepting them. One way to try to criticize or doubt these fundamental beliefs would be to seek an explanation of them: where do they come from? Some answers to that question would lead us to lose confidence in them—if, perhaps, they were placed in us by an evil demon or resulted from indoctrination from our teachers. Our best explanation of our having those beliefs and habits—if we are pragmatists—is that they are instinctive states with the properties that Peirce describes. Kantians and Cartesians offer different explanations which do not appeal to pragmatists. This does not provide us with a reason to accept or trust these beliefs and habits: since we do not yet doubt them, we do not need a reason to accept them. Rather, it leads us to see that our attempt to criticize or doubt them has failed; our best understanding of where they come from simply reinforces our instinctive trust in them. They are uncriticized, and, it is reasonable to think, they are uncriticizable. This accords with the pattern of support described at the end of the last section. Critical common-sensism recommends that we treat our cognitive instincts with caution, we should question them and beware of applying them too widely. But so long as we have been careful and questioned them, they can be trusted; by and large our instincts are vehicles for progress. Indeed, we respond to evidence and reasons that we are not *consciously* aware of: we cannot take control of how our common sense develops or how perceptual beliefs (for example) are shaped by our experience and our battery of conceptual capacities. The common-sensist insists that this need not prevent our trusting our cognitive capacities. I will often trust the testimony of other people when I know little about the sort of evidence that they possess for their claims; I should similarly trust myself, even if much of my cognitive activity is hidden from conscious reflection.

9

Sentiment and Self-Control

1. Rationality and Sentiment

How far does the search for justified opinions, reasonable habits of deliberation, and satisfactory methods of inquiry depend upon the possession of attitudes and aptitudes which essentially involve the sentiments or passions? When Hume claims that reason can only be a slave of the passions, we naturally take this to signal the limits of human rationality; he is interpreted as insisting that our ends are simply given and are not susceptible to rational evaluation. Reason is thereby alleged to depend upon something extraneous to itself. My aim in this chapter is to explore some ways in which sentiments, feelings, and passions can serve reason and deliberation. They are not extraneous or antagonistic to rational self-control but are, rather, integral to it. The themes that we shall examine suggest that an adequate understanding of epistemic rationality must include an account of the rational sentiments.

Peirce makes apparently conflicting remarks about the relations of reason and sentiment. Sometimes they are quite sharply contrasted. When discussing the a priori method of settling opinions in 'The Fixation of Belief', he comments that it makes opinion a matter of taste or fashion. His argument for the view that this introduces a capricious or accidental element into the fixation of belief rests on the observation that 'sentiments in their development will be very greatly determined by accidental causes', and he suggests that someone who notices that a belief has been caused by something 'extraneous to the facts . . . will experience a real doubt of it so that it ceases to be a belief' (W3: 253).[1] It thus appears that reflective inquiry could not survive the discovery that 'sentiment' has a role in how it is carried out. So in this fairly early paper, Peirce appears to see

---

[1] There are also passages, to be discussed below, in which Peirce attacks the view, associated with certain 'German logicians' that logical soundness be explained by appeal to a 'sentiment of logicality', or *'logisches Gefühl'*; see MS 448.

sentiment as the enemy of reason. And this is because, in many such cases, there is no reason to suppose that 'sentimental' preferences are a guide to the truth.

A slightly different view emerges when Peirce discusses the demands of practical life and the sources of religious belief. In the Cambridge Conferences lectures of 1898 (*RLT*; see also Chapter 1), and elsewhere, he argues that reflective self-controlled inquiry employing the method of science cannot produce the sort of 'living belief' required for action, producing instead a kind of tentative detached assent which is fully aware of its own fallibility. Living belief depends upon instinct, common sense, and 'sentiment'. His position, which he describes as 'conservatism' and 'sentimentalism', acknowledges the role of sentiment in the formation of (real) belief: but the consequence of this recognition is not the living doubt that he predicted in 'The Fixation of Belief' or any kind of sceptical gloom. The consequence is, rather, a deep mistrust of reason and reflection in connection with any matters of vital importance.

But there are other passages in which Peirce claims that sentiment has an ineliminable role even in reflective deliberation and scientific inquiry.[2] In 'The Doctrine of Chances', we learn that induction rests upon the altruistic 'logical' sentiments of faith, hope, and charity: and it is noteworthy that this paper is a sequel to 'The Fixation of Belief', where he had claimed that an origin in sentiment was fatal to a belief's stability. And in 1868, he wrote that an altruistic 'sentiment' which is 'entirely unsupported by reasons' is 'rigidly demanded by logic' (W2: 272). A number of passages from towards the end of his life similarly emphasize the sentimental basis of all reasoning.

Peirce's discussion of these topics is related to his later concern with *self-control*. Rationality involves self-control: an agent is rational to the extent that he or she is able to monitor actions and deliberations, taking responsibility for how well they are conducted and for their successes and failures. Anything limiting such self-control in carrying out an activity prevents our carrying it out in a fully rational manner, and limits the degree to which we can be held responsible for its upshot. Pragmatist logicians typically study logic and methodology by applying this truism about rationality to the forms of conduct which are the primary concern of logic: inquiry and deliberation. A rational agent is better equipped to regulate

---

[2] One further example is provided by Peirce's assertion that 'reasoning and the science of reasoning strenuously proclaim the subordination of reasoning to sentiment' (*CP* 1.673), taken from an alternate draft of the first lecture of the Cambridge Conferences (MS 435).

those 'activities', having the ability to distinguish good deliberations from bad and being motivated to repudiate those inferences and methods of inquiry which do not come up to scratch.

One might see Peirce's late insistence that logic depends on ethics and aesthetics as a recognition of this. The attempt to ground logic in the other 'normative sciences' is part of a search for an understanding of norms which could provide a unified model of self-control, and hence of rationality; and it was central to his attempt to defend pragmatism in the Harvard lectures of 1903. Later developments in his thought display a growing sense of the demands and complexities of self-control. For example, one might naturally judge that if some of our beliefs and responses are instinctive, or if our reasoning is influenced by our sentiments or emotions, this limits our self-control and rationality. But Peirce increasingly insisted that instinct and sentiment were *required* for rational self-control rather than being in conflict with it. Thus, in 1898, he affirmed that 'reasoning and the science of reasoning strenuously proclaim the subordination of reasoning [evidently including scientific reasoning] to sentiment' (*CP* 1.673). This is connected with the claim from the 1870s that not only does 'logic' require 'altruism', but it calls for a trio of logical *sentiments*: rational self-control depends upon emotion and affect.

This chapter examines some of Peirce's mature views about the requirements of rational self-control: it investigates why he thinks that sentiments or emotions are required for self-control and why he denies that this should lead us to feel alienated from our deliberations. The topic is a large one, and the chapter cannot deal with all the issues it raises. Section 2 examines the issues raised in 'The Doctrine of Chances', especially the claim that rationality depends upon altruism. After considering Hilary Putnam's critical response to Peirce's position in section 3, we raise the possibility that Peirce's appeal to sentiments represents a move towards the position that Putnam himself favours. This idea is developed in section 4: the role Peirce assigns to emotions and sentiments is part of an attempt to simulate epistemological foundationalism: rational norms have a phenomenological immediacy even if they reflect a range of cognitive commitments. The closing three sections look more closely at the cognitive role of feeling and emotion in Peirce's philosophy, drawing on David Savan's 'Peirce's Semiotic Theory of Emotion' (1981), one of the few papers to have taken this work seriously. The final section of the chapter (section 7) returns to the claims about altruism and rationality from 'The Doctrine of Chances'.

2. Rationality and Altruism

In 'The Doctrine of Chances', Peirce makes use of three related but distinct theses. The first is that the scientific method can only be used to settle doubts and answer questions by someone who is a member of a community of inquirers; since all reflective reasoning employs the 'method of science', it follows that a sense that one belongs to such a community is a precondition of rationality. The second is that science and rationality require a distinctive ethical outlook. Reliance upon induction, probabilities, and statistical reasoning in ordering our opinions demands altruism: 'to be logical men should not be selfish' (W3: 284). This requires a high degree of unselfishness: 'he who would not sacrifice his own soul to save the whole world is, as it seems to me, illogical in all his inferences, collectively' (ibid.).[3] Moreover, and thirdly, this altruism should be manifested in *sentiment*: logic and scientific rationality call for three benevolent 'dispositions of the heart' (W3: 285).

Peirce's argument for these views depends upon his understanding of probability. Very roughly, a probability statement is a 'guiding principle' which determines a genus of arguments. If the chance of a coin coming up heads when tossed is .47, then 'it is a real fact' that 'a given mode of inference sometimes proves successful and sometimes not, and that in a ratio ultimately fixed'. Consider the inference: the coin was tossed, so it will have come up heads: 'As we go on drawing inference after inference of the given kind, during the first ten or hundred cases the ratio of successes may be expected to show considerable fluctuations; but when we come into the thousands and millions, these fluctuations become less and less; and if we continue for long enough, the ratio will approximate toward a fixed limit' (W3: 280–1). He proposes to define the probability of a mode of argument as 'the proportion of cases in which it carries truth with it'. This analysis explains the rationality of relying upon probabilities when the inference form in question is one which will be 'repeated indefinitely'. But, he worries:

An individual inference must be either true or false, and can show no effect of probability; and therefore, in reference to a single case considered in itself, probability can have no meaning. Yet if a man had to choose between drawing a card from a pack containing twenty-five red cards and a black one, or from a pack

---

[3] An almost identical passage appears in writings from ten years earlier (CP 5.354).

containing twenty-five black cards and a red one, and if the drawing of a red card were destined to transport him to eternal felicity, and that of a black one to consign him to everlasting woe, it would be folly to deny that he ought to prefer the pack containing the larger proportion of red cards, although, from the nature of the risk, it could not be repeated. It is not easy to reconcile this with our analysis of the conception of chance. (W3: 281–2)

If reliance upon 'probable deductions' is defended by arguing that, *in the long run*, the policy of drawing such inferences will serve us well, then it is hard to see how employing this policy *on a single occasion* can be defended. We might add (and note for further reference) that if reliance on such deductions receives this sort of 'practical' vindication, it is hard to see how, on any particular occasion, it can warrant belief in its conclusion. At best we ought to have the reflective thought that 'going by' such inferences will, in the long run, pay off; but that thought has no relevance to the present case where no such 'long run' is relevant to our decision.

Peirce appears to argue as follows: although *I* can carry out only one inference of the sort described, *we* can carry out lots; and so, by relying on probabilities I adopt a policy which, although it may not benefit *me* ought, if consistently carried though, to benefit *us*. The conclusion then drawn is that if I care about how well the community at large will do, the inferential policy which may condemn me to everlasting woe can be rationally endorsed.

The problems stem from an account of probability judgements which encourages us to understand the rationality of using probabilities as a guide to life in terms of the consequences of adopting a general policy of doing so but which makes it hard to explain the wisdom of drawing just one such inference. And I noted, as Peirce does not on this occasion, that it is then hard to see how someone drawing such inferences in a reflective manner can adopt the conclusion as a *belief*. But Peirce's suggestion, that my sense that it would be rational for me to choose the red pack in the case described provides evidence of how profoundly I am imbued with love of mankind, is, on the face of it, crazy. Suppose choosing a red card brought me eternal bliss at the expense of everlasting woe for all the rest of mankind.[4] We can see how altruism and a capacity for self-sacrifice could lead someone to choose the black card in such circumstances. But we can also see how, if they are rational and guided by self-interest, the

---

[4] In Hookway (1985) a similar worry was raised by considering the absurdity of the response 'I have no interest in the welfare of my fellow human beings, so I may as well choose the predominantly black pack' (p. 215).

probabilities require them to choose the red one. It is hard to see how Peirce can explain this.

We need to distinguish the use of probabilistic reasoning in science from its role, in everyday life, in settling what Peirce was later to call 'vital questions'. I assume that a choice which determines whether I obtain eternal bliss or everlasting woe concerns a 'vital question'. As we noted in the first section, Peirce often insisted that when we confront matters of vital practical or moral importance, we should trust to what he variously called instinct, sentiment, and common sense rather than to deliberate self-controlled reasoning to solve our problems. Insisting that 'all sensible talk about vitally important topics must be commonplace, all reasoning about them unsound, and all study of them narrow and sordid' (*CP* 1.677), he claimed that, concerning such matters 'reasoning is at once an impertinence towards its subject-matter and a treason against itself' (*CP* 1.671). His defence of a form of 'sentimentalism' or 'conservatism' stressed that wisdom requires us to trust our instinctive or sentimental responses to vital issues rather than the rationalizations of reflective deliberation.[5] Sentiment, he supposed, reflects the wisdom of the centuries; it guides our desires and actions without being subject to critical self-control.

The matter is otherwise in science where we try to subject our reasoning to rigorous control, reflecting on the rules we use and on their legitimacy: 'I would not allow sentiment or instinct any weight whatsoever in theoretical matters, not the slightest.' So, during the 1890s at least, Peirce drew a sharp distinction between theory and practice: theory belongs with reason, self-control, and mistrust of 'sentiment or instinct'; but in connection with practical or 'vital' issues, reasoning and reflection are false gods, and wisdom requires sentiment and instinct to rule. If the example of the black and red cards presents a vital question, and if Peirce can show that we rely upon instinct or sentiment in coping with it, it is unclear that anything follows about the role of sentiment and instinct in reasoning (including probabilistic reasoning) which employs the method of science. Peirce's example is irrelevant to the philosophical point he wishes to make.

---

[5] Note that Peirce's desire to ground our everyday moral responses in sentiment does not make him an ally of ethical emotivism. He is not an ethical anti-realist and would, I am sure, have no objection to describing everyday ethical judgements as knowledge claims. Sentiments can be the vehicles of our most secure knowledge. He is not sceptical about everyday moral knowledge but about trusting theory and reflective reasoning in order to solve pressing moral and prudential questions. Sentimental judgements are generally ones that it does not occur to us to doubt, and thus ones that we do not need to makes objects of inquiry. Such views reflect his affinities with philosophers of the Scottish common-sense school.

However, this distinction between scientific issues and vital questions probably exaggerated Peirce's considered opinion even at the time. We have already noted some passages in which he stresses the role of sentiment in reasoning, but we should now add another component of his position: his view of science takes very seriously the idea that we carry out scientific investigations as members of a community. From the 1860s, he claimed that the concept of reality 'essentially involves the notion of a COMMUNITY, without definite limits, and capable of a definite increase of knowledge' (W2: 239). This is because it is defined in terms of a consensus that is 'fated' or 'destined' to occur among members of such a community. We value our own contributions to scientific inquiry not for the truths we uncover in the short run, but for the contribution they make to the eventual progress of the larger scientific community towards the truth. And this is reflected in a highly social conception of the self: in 1898 he affirmed that 'we' are 'mere cells of the social organism' (*CP* 1.647, 1.773; *RLT*: 121). The concept of the self only becomes necessary as conflict of testimony obliges us to find somewhere to locate error; and to be a self is to be a possible member of some community. It is not controversial that seeing oneself as a member of a community involves an ethical commitment: one's own good is more closely tied to the good of other members of the community than it is to outsiders.[6] And the organic metaphors that Peirce favoured are inconsistent with an attempt to ground these moral commitments in an individualistic contractarian manner: if my link to other members of my community is more immediate than such an individualistic picture would allow, it is plausible that it is manifested in sentiment.

To return, now, to our problem of probabilities: why should we allow probabilities to guide our conclusions about particular cases? The question has two forms: one about the role of such reasoning in practical matters; the other about the role of such reasoning in science. And the comments I have just made suggest that they will have different answers.[7] In connection with practical matters, we have an instinctive habit of going by probabilities, and many generations of experience have confirmed us in this practice. The uncertainties that arise when we ask what legitimates it simply confirm the folly of expecting much help from reason in

---

[6] Except for Peirce, there are no outsiders: 'This community must not be limited, but must extend to all races of beings with whom we can come into immediate or mediate intellectual relation. It must reach, however vaguely, beyond the geological epoch, beyond all bounds' (*CP* 2.654).

[7] These remarks develop an interpretation suggested in Hookway (1985: 215–16.)

connection with vital questions. In science, where rational reflection is in place, the 'altruistic' solution may not be absurd: in science, according to Peirce, the value we attach to our own efforts is inseparable from an awareness that we are contributing to the eventual success of the community to which we belong. Peirce's example was unfortunate (due, I suspect, to the unsettled state of his thought in the 1870s): he considered a vital or practical question; and he responded to it as if it raised a scientific question dependent on rational self-control. He *ought* to have insisted that in science—where, alone, rational self-control is possible—our practice of reasoning depends upon our membership of a community of inquirers bound together by these fundamental altruistic 'logical sentiments'. And in that case, his cited claim that instinct has no sway over theoretical matters is itself a misstatement of the view that we should not trust our instincts about the *truth* of particular claims and hypotheses. Sentiment and instinct still ground our inferential policies by holding together the scientific community.

This diagnosis helps to make sense of a puzzling passage immediately following the announcement that those unprepared for self-sacrifice are illogical in all [their] inferences collectively.[8] As Isaac Levi reports, Peirce 'removes all the teeth from the demand for altruism' (1980: 133).

Now it is not necessary for logicality that a man should himself be capable of the heroism of self-sacrifice. It is sufficient that he should recognize the possibility of it, should perceive that only that man's inferences who has it are really logical, and should consequently regard his own as being so only so far as they should be accepted by the hero. So far as he thus refers his inferences to that standard, he becomes identified with such a mind. (W3: 284)

Applied to the case of the pack of cards (and indeed to any vital question) this seems plain crazy: why should thoughts about such heroes have any influence upon the practical decision one makes at all. But if we think of someone relying upon probability judgements in the course of carrying out scientific investigations, it articulates a more familiar and respectable thought. We need think only of someone whose investigations are wholly motivated by thoughts of tenure, prestige, or financial gain, but who acknowledges that these benefits will be secured only if his inquiries meet standards that would recommend themselves to someone possessed of the

---

[8] This form of words is curious. It is unclear what the force is of saying that the illogicality is a property of 'all of his inferences collectively'; does this contrast with the suggestion that certain specific inferences (the one under discussion, for example) are irrational?

true scientific spirit—and thus, according to Peirce, capable of true hero-ism. The idea of a scientific community is integral to scientific activity even if one is not wholly motivated by a sense of one's identity within such a community; although Peirce would, of course, deny that the person just described is possessed of the true scientific spirit.

3. Putnam's Response: A Primitive Obligation to be Rational

Hilary Putnam has credited Peirce with identifying a fundamental prob-lem about rationality (1987: 80 ff): we all agree that it is rational to rely upon probabilities on particular occasions—let us express this fact by saying that probabilities are motivating. The problem is to say why; and Peirce's example of the pack of cards appears to show that it is not enough to say that a general policy of acting on probabilities will have the result that one acts on a reliable basis on the majority of occasions. Rather than talking of motivation, we might also talk of *consolation*: if I choose the predominantly red pack but then pick the black card, then I am unlucky but my exposure to everlasting woe is not my fault; if I choose the predom-inantly black pack and pick a black card, then I should hold myself respon-sible for my demise. Why?

As I understand him, Putnam dislikes Peirce's solution to his 'puzzle': he sees the appeal to 'altruism' and the 'community' as a desperate device for rescuing the strategy of justifying relying upon probabilities by pointing to the long-term results of doing so. This is analogous to rule utilitarianism in ethics. One justifies relying upon the probability by reasoning: 'Maybe I am not going to benefit by adopting this rule of action, but I am contribut-ing to a policy that will benefit the community as a whole, so my action will have good consequences.' The rule utilitarian answer is that I have chosen according to a rule, the general adoption of which would lead to the best overall consequences. And the problem is to explain why I should be motivated or consoled by that.

Putnam's favoured answer to the problem about probabilities would appeal to 'an *underived*, a *primitive* obligation of some kind to be reason-able ... which—contrary to Peirce—is *not* reducible to my expectations about the long run or my interest in the welfare of others or my own welfare at other times' (1987: 84–5); and he makes a Wittgensteinian appeal to the bedrock where his spade is turned. But—contrary to Putnam—it is not obvious that Peirce makes this strong reductive claim. The references to altruism and the long run support the interpretation, but the importance attached to instinct and sentiment might give us pause. When Peirce discusses the role of instinct and sentiment in settling vital questions, it seems clear that they make the rightness of acting in one way rather than another *immediately* evident: there is no place for rational justification or calculation, which are both inappropriate where instinct and sentiment hold sway. That leaves it very puzzling what role altruism has in this immediate, sentimental response, but we shall only understand Peirce's position when we see how our instinctive sentimental attachment to an inference or course of action can itself be a form of 'altruism'. Applying this to the case of probabilities, Peirce seems to want a position which combines two features. First, the rightness of going by probabilities is phenomenologically immediate: we find it instinctively or sentimentally correct. But second, these immediate sentimental responses stand in some intimate relation to 'altruism'. There may yet be ingredients in the Peircean position which Putnam would dislike, but I suggest that it avoids the crude reductionism he finds in it. However, addressing this issue must wait until we have cleared some more of the ground: we shall return to it in section 7.

It is interesting to ask how far Peirce's solution to his problem is a form of nominalism (see Hacking, 1980: 157). Even if we understand probabilities as propensities, as determining what would happen in various possible trials rather than what does happen in actual trials, it still attempts to explain the rationality of acting on the basis of a probability by reference to a wider class of (actual or possible) applications of the probability judgement in question: we are to consider what *would* occur if we *were* to act on this probability in an indefinite range of possible cases. The problem is to understand how that can be motivating—or how it can provide consolation as we pick the black card from the predominantly red pack. Possibly we avoid this problem only if (with Putnam) we acknowledge that rationality is an irreducible element of our experience; the reasonableness of going by probabilities is not to be understood in means–end terms at all—it is not enough simply to talk about possible means–end relations, or about 'would-be's. If this is correct, it again places Peirce's focus on sentiment in an interesting perspective. If rationality requires us to perceive the appropriateness or reasonableness of conclusions, inferences, or procedures *immediately* (if we require immediate awareness of these forms of thirdness), must this awareness be suffused with *sentiment*? In the remainder of this chapter, I want to sketch some reasons for favouring an affirmative answer to these questions. If I am successful in this, then Peirce's view may be close to the one that Putnam presents as an alternative and preferable stance.

4. Rational Demands as Immediate: Mimicking Foundationalism

All this talk of *immediacy* may suggest a kind of foundationalism which, we all know, is foreign to Peirce's epistemology. In this section I shall argue briefly that the project of mimicking (without endorsing) foundationalism is fundamental to much of Peirce's later philosophy.[9] The claim that scientific activity rests upon altruism is connected to his insistence that one should hold a detached uncommitted attitude towards current opinions, whether they be conclusions of probabilistic inferences or the current deliverences of induction and the scientific method. Belief, we noticed, 'has no place in science': this appears to suggest that we should take this uncommitted detached attitude towards *any* opinion obtained through the scientific method. Now this raises a question about the epistemological status of a host of beliefs that we rely upon in doing science. For example, a Peircean 'scientist' must be committed to the existence of other inquirers who make up the scientific community and a host of commonsense and perceptual beliefs about the world; she must accept that scientific progress is possible and believe that by working hard and well she can contribute to it; she must be confident of the items of background knowledge used in constructing experiments and making observations; she must be confident that her sense of plausibility (her abductive sense) will serve the cause of progress and believe that attempting to contribute to scientific progress is a worthwhile and sustainable life even if she makes no permanent discoveries, and so on. And since self-control requires reflection on the methods and inference patterns involved and the ability to satisfy oneself that employing such inferences will contribute to achieving one's aims, materials must be available for carrying out these monitoring reflections.

Peirce appears, then, to confront a dilemma: if respectable scientific inquiry yields opinions which are detached and fallible, what is the source of our firm confidence in our ability to do science well? We might suppose that our confidence in the methods of science or in the possibility of making progress is grounded in distinctively philosophical reasoning: the philosophers Peirce denigrates as 'transcendental apothecaries' (*CP* 2.113) would defend a kind of epistemological or methodological dualism—we have a priori knowledge of the possibility of progress or of the adequacy

---

[9] This topic is discussed in more detail, and its philosophical importance defended, in Hookway (1993).

of induction, or we defend it by claiming that it is presupposed by rational reflection and self-control. But Peirce is anxious to avoid any suggestion of there being nonscientific knowledge of reality; and the point about presupposition may give grounds for hoping that progress is possible but gives no grounds for believing that it is (see Chapter 7).

But the alternative suggestion that such knowledge is grounded scientifically appears equally unattractive if belief has no place in science. For if we are to take an uncommitted attitude towards the knowledge which grounds our participation in scientific activity, affirming only that it is useful to accept such things at this stage of scientific activity, then problems of (at least) two kinds arise. One might think that a regress or circle was in the offing: if my 'assurance' that I can contribute to scientific progress is viewed as the result of a practical policy—having such an assurance is defended as a means of contributing to scientific progress—then it presupposes some sort of assurance that progress can be secured. And even if that problem can be overcome, so that it is 'tentative and uncommitted' all the way down, it is hard to understand how anyone could be motivated to carry out scientific activity: unless I can be confident that I am making a contribution, the rationality of scientific activity is hard to understand. There is a danger that a living confidence in the value and possibility of science is required to engage with the will, in order to motivate someone to undertake scientific discoveries; but that having such living confidence indicates that one lacks a true scientific sensibility.

What this leads to is a first description of the strategy involved in Peirce's later work. In effect, he wants to *mimic* an epistemological dualism without fully endorsing one. Without claiming that we have a special nonempirical nonscientific source of knowledge, he wants to explain how we have a basis of confidence and certainty which serves as a starting point for controlling and evaluating scientific inquiries. And this confident basis must not be merely subjective: we must be aware of the value of scientific activity and we must be confident of the value of our contribution. If we were certain of fundamental commitments, inferences, and perceptual judgements, while reflectively aware that no opinion deserves more than detached assent, then we might reasonably feel alienated from our cognitive ventures. My conjecture is that an appeal to sentiment is required in order to avoid such sceptical alienation: we require a kind of acceptance of fundamental commitments which is neither grounded in non-scientific inquiry, nor detached and tentative, nor undeserved. This is possible only if these commitments enjoy a sort of secure immediacy, and my claim is that, in Peirce's view, an appeal to logical sentiments is intended to provide this.

Before elaborating upon this, it will be useful to list some themes involved in this attempt to simulate epistemic dualism. We shall mention three, all of which are relevant to understanding the role of sentiments in rationality. First, Peirce displays his Kantian allegiance by appealing to regulative ideas or hopes, claiming at one point that all the laws of logic are hopes. We have no grounds for belief, concerning any question we propose inquiring into, that it has a definite answer which inquiry would eventually settle on. But inquiry would falter unless, when considering such a question, we hoped that it would; so it is a sound practical policy to rely upon such 'hopes'. Inquiry and deliberation rest upon a framework of assumptions and standards which function as hopes; and inquirers incur the obligation eventually to explain why those hopes were, in fact, warranted. One task of (properly scientific) metaphysics is to provide an account of reality which explains why those hopes were in fact correct.[10] Although these themes became prominent in Peirce's thought only after the mid-1890s, they were implicit in the early discussions of probabilistic reasoning: one of the logical sentiments was *hope* that the scientific community would endure for long enough to benefit from the policy of drawing inferences on the basis of probabilities.

A tension may be suggested by these remarks which will be important, a kind of ambiguity in the idea of a 'hope'. If it corresponds to the Kantian notion of a 'regulative idea', then hopes are likely to be tentative and uncommitted. We are conscious that we have no basis for accepting the truth of what we hope for; but we resolve to behave as if it were true, since that provides our best chance of success in our endeavours. 'Sentiment' suggests something less detached, less subject to rational assessment, something that Peirce elsewhere called 'a living hope' (*CP* 7.506). The question to bear in mind is: what force is there in this additional claim that this hope be a 'sentiment'? And part of the answer is: it is hard to see how the mere hope that scientific progress is possible—defended on the grounds that if it is not possible, full rational self-control is impossible—could *motivate* someone to scientific activity and to valuing rational self-control. We need to understand how hope engages with the will, and we shall find that linking hopes with sentiments suggests a way of accounting for this.

The second component in Peirce's attempt to mimic epistemological

---

[10] This theme in Peirce's work is discussed in greater detail in Chapter 7 and in Hookway (1985: ch. 9).

dualism exploits his claim that there are 'pre-logical sciences'. Although they use the scientific method (induction, deduction, and the rest), they are not subject to logical self-control and yield 'practically infallible' knowledge. One of these sciences, in fact, needs no foundations at all: mathematics. Although we can make mistakes in carrying out proofs, and there is thus a limited fallibility, mathematics is not answerable to an independent reality: we cannot raise normative issues about whether or not our mathematical techniques may conceal from us the true nature of an independent world of mathematical objects; and this is supposedly connected with the claim that mathematics is concerned with the full range of possibilities and not just with the real world. I do not want to say anything more about mathematics here (but see Hookway 1985: ch. 6). We should note that another pre-logical science, fundamental to Peirce's account of epistemic norms, is ethics: logic is to draw on the results ethics (and aesthetics) in grounding our inferential practice.

Third, Peirce appeals to a range of *acritical judgements*; two sorts are relevant. Perceptual judgements, like 'That book is red', although fallible, are certain and not normally subject to critical self-control. This means that it is impossible to take a detached attitude towards them: their acceptance is not grounded in a practical policy, since it results from no policy at all. And, second, we possess many 'common-sense certainties' which are equally acritical and certain: these are mostly vague, but present a general view of ourselves, our surroundings, and the relations between them, and offer a sort of 'folk psychology' and an evolving 'folk physics' which ground our scientific endeavours.[11] Since they are not subject to rational self-control, they are certain; but they are also 'empirical', resulting from an inchoate mass of experience collected over many generations. Any attempt to *state* what justifies them will distort and underestimate the mass of experience upon which they have depended. Once again, they contribute to Peirce's attempt to mimic an epistemological dualism within a perspective which claims that only the 'scientific method' provides knowledge of reality; he says, indeed, that recognition of such common-sense certainties is what 'Kantism' comes to when we abandon the horrors of the transcendental perspective. These too link with our theme. Peirce's describes such common-sense certainties as 'instincts' and links them with sentiments; we have to understand why it was important for him to do so.

---

[11] For examples and further discussions of such judgements, see Chapter 8 and Hookway (1990).

5. Sentiments and Rational Control over Action

Peirce's most detailed explanation of the role of sentiments and emotional responses in reasoning is found in a lecture delivered to the Lowell Institute in Cambridge in 1903 (*CP* 1.91ff). Peirce's target is the German logicians who attempt to ground logic psychologically by appeal to a feeling of logicality. Noting the parallels between such views and those who ground ethics in a feeling of approval, and recognizing that such views lead to subjectivism and relativism, Peirce undertakes to 'describe the phenomena of controlled action' and to make sense of the role of feeling in deliberation and action. Those he criticizes are rightly sensitive to the role of feeling and pleasure in these phenomena, but they misinterpret this role by insisting that only pleasure or the thought of it can motivate people to act. We do not treat inferences or ends as good because they give us pleasure; rather, they give us pleasure because we find them good. We take pleasure in doing what we find to be good, but we do not do it for the sake of this resulting pleasure. The cases Peirce considers involve practical deliberation, but the points he makes apply to theoretical inquiry as well. Moreover, although pleasure is not an emotion, it is plausible that our sentiments and emotions are primarily manifested in feelings such as pleasure and displeasure.

Employing his categories, Peirce contrasts three ways in which we reflect on our 'ideals of conduct': certain kinds of conduct have 'an esthetic quality'—we judge them 'fine', taking pleasure in their firstness; our ideals can conflict, and we find such inconsistencies 'odious' and strive to eliminate them—we consider them in their secondness; and, third, we explore what living by such an ideal would be like, assessing in detail the aesthetic qualities and potential conflicts of the consequences of accepting such an ideal. Deliberation about the acceptability of such ideals can lead us to form a general intention to adopt them; we propose rules and strategies designed to enable us to carry out these general intentions. The use of expressions like 'esthetic quality' and 'odious' shows that the endorsement of ideals and repudiation of inconsistencies does not take the form of propositional assent: our judgement is manifested in feeling.[12] Indeed, our conscious formulation of an ideal and our decision to adopt it depend upon evaluations which are primarily sentimental, primarily a matter of

---

[12] A similar claim is found in William James's essay 'The Sentiment of Rationality', in *The Will to Believe*. It is discussed, and used to provide some background to Peirce's view, in Hookway (1993).

feeling. It is only by trusting such aesthetic responses that we can formulate plans and direct our lives.

The same holds when we reflect upon our attempts to achieve our ideals and goals. Recognition that we acted as we decided and that this accorded with our general intentions and ultimate ideals takes the form of 'a judgment and a feeling accompanying it, and directly afterward a recognition that feeling was pleasurable or painful'. Notice that the pleasure *follows* the judgement: we do not notice the pleasure and conclude that we acted well; we judge that we acted well and thus feel pleasure. Our actions are not carried out for the sake of the pleasure we derive from reflecting on their success. The pleasure is a kind of nondiscursive acknowledgement of the goodness of our ends and the successes of our actions. As David Savan (1981) argued, Peirce defends a cognitivist account of the emotions and sentiments: our feeling of pleasure is a cognitive state. Our pleasure in our action is the form taken by our knowledge that we acted reasonably and appropriately. Ideals inform our conduct and can be interpreted in our feelings even if they are not precisely articulated or formulated.

Philosophical aesthetics and ethics (both pre-logical sciences) do not offer help in resolving practical issues: they attempt to describe and explain our capacities for aesthetic pleasure and self-controlled action by investigating what it is possible to admire unconditionally and what it is possible to adopt as an ultimate end for conduct; ethics considers 'as a matter of curiosity, what the fitness of an ideal of conduct consists in, and to deduce from such definition of fitness what conduct ought to do' (*CP* 1.600). Peirce comments that many people doubt the 'wholesomeness' of such study: his own view appears to be that so long as we recall that it is a purely theoretical study and (I suppose) don't allow it to alter our habits of living, no serious harm is likely to be done. Skipping many obscurities and complexities, Peirce's view is that what can be admired without reservation, and what can be sought as an ultimate aim, is reason and its growth. Our sense of pleasure in our deliberations responds to their rationality and to the reasonableness of our ideals. Our conscience constrains us to 'make our lives more reasonable', and Peirce concludes: 'What other distinct idea than that, I should be glad to know, can be attached to the word liberty? We take pleasure in acting and reasoning freely and reasonably' (*CP* 1.602).

The last quotation confirms that Peirce holds that the role of sentiment and feeling in reasoning and inquiry does not reveal the limits of rational self-control. That we trust our logical sentiments can be a sign of our wisdom and rationality; our instinctive sense of which actions and reasonings are to be trusted can reflect our grasp of what is required of a reasonable agent. This, according to Peirce, is why turning our back on reflective self-control in connection with vital questions diminishes neither our rationality nor our freedom. Our sentimental attunement to the demands of reason exceeds our intellectual understanding of what rationality involves.

If a habit or attitude of mine is not subject to self-control, then it becomes possible for me to feel alienated from it, seeing it is an obstacle to my living freely and rationally. The role of the sentiment of pleasure in the operation of such a habit or attitude disarms such alienation; it is the self's acritical acknowledgement of its mental functioning. Second, and connectedly, it is one of Peirce's theses about emotions and sentiments that they are interpreted in other emotional attitudes: they spread (*CP* 5.223, 7.936). The pleasure I take in an inference spreads into approval of larger inferences which draw on this one and into sentiments of approval toward actions which depend upon the inference. Our sentimental reactions form a coherent and intelligible system which contributes to the unity of the self.

Peirce's view of the emotions receives a clear expression in the 1860s in the *Journal of Speculative Philosophy*. Emotions, he tells us, are 'predicates'; they arise when our attention is drawn to 'complex and inconceivable circumstances', as when we are guided by instinct or common sense: 'If a man is angry, he is saying to himself that this is or that is vile or outrageous . . . passions only come to consciousness through tinging the objects of thought' (W2: 229). Recognizing the state as one of anger is a reflective judgement about it, once that indicates, normally, that the anger is beginning to subside.[13] Thus the logical sentiments are manifested in my making certain inferences with no sense of alienation, in my instinctively judging an inference 'fine' or a proposal 'promising', and in this sense of the soundness of an inference or judgement 'spreading' to other inferences and hypotheses which depend upon it. The sentiment is a knowing or thinking, but one that is not embedded in a conscious framework of deliberation and reasons; it is not subject to self-control, but its integration with our other aptitudes and practices ensures that its instinctive character does not lead us to repudiate it as an external imposition upon our rationality.

---

[13] I am indebted to the discussion of this topic in Savan's 'Peirce's Semiotic Theory of Emotion' (1981: 321 ff).

6. Peirce's Cognitive Theory of Sentiments

As David Savan has taught us, sentiments and emotions are distinguished from other 'cognitive states' by a number of features. They are not subject to rational self-control: in this, they resemble perceptual judgements and differ from scientific hypotheses. They are interpreted in 'affect': they engage with the will, providing imperatives that will motivate us to action. And they 'are not value neutral' (Savan 1981: 328): as we saw above, when we are angry with someone, we disapprove of them; our love of someone or something is a form of approval. When Peirce argues that reasoning must rest upon sentiment, he claims that some of our epistemic and logical evaluations must be realized in states which share the other features of emotions: they are not subject to rational self-control and they are interpreted in affect. In earlier sections of this chapter, we explored some of Peirce's reasons for thinking that this must be so. The aim of this section is to use some of Savan's ideas to understand how sentiments serve this role before concluding by returning to the claims from 'The Doctrine of Chances' about the bearing of logical sentiments in the use of probability judgements.

Savan mentions two specific areas where views about the emotions are relevant to Peirce's work. When, in 'The Fixation of Belief', Peirce speaks of doubt being an unsettled state which motivates us to carry out inquiries, he has in mind the way in which conflict in our beliefs disturbs our normal easy satisfaction with our opinions, and evokes an emotional response which is interpreted in affect, in a determination of the will. Savan refers to this as 'an affective theory of doubt and belief' (1981: 327; see also Chapter 10). In the light of the remarks of the previous section, this encourages us to view the cognitive agent as someone who has confidence in his or her cognitive emotions. They are trusted to provide guidance about when to question assumptions and when to follow the argument where it leads. And the agent is confident that this trust in her emotional reactions will lead her to make the epistemic evaluations which rationality demands.

In the last section of his paper, Savan wrote:

Our twentieth century has almost lost the sense of a distinction between the emotions and the sentiments. The sentiments are enduring and ordered systems of emotions, attached either to a person, an institution, or, in Peirce's case, a method. Love is the prime example of a sentiment. One who loves will be joyful but also sad, angry, and jealous, and also fearful and careless. But the joy and sadness, jealousy and carelessness, anger and fear are all bound together within one sentiment of love. Just as Peirce spoke of methods of fixing belief, the logical sentiments are ways of fixing emotions. (1981: 331)

The inquiring self is commanded by a stable system of emotional attitudes, by fundamental values which govern the instinctive responses which guide his or her reasoning and inquiries. Without such a sentimental grounding, the method of science could not be sustained: confidence in our premises has to produce confidence in our conclusions; surprising conclusions must provoke pressing questions about our premises.

We need this cognitive confidence which only sentiments and their attendant emotions can sustain.[14] It seems to me that David Savan was exactly right when he argued that, for Peirce, the 'aim' of these logical sentiments is 'true stability in our beliefs and in our lives', asserting that they 'convert the goal of stability into a norm for criticizing, rationalizing and controlling our emotions' (1981: 331). Moreover, altruism and the other logical sentiments alluded to above are aspects of love or *agape*, the fundamental logical sentiment: unless we possess this kind of identification of our own good with that of the community (and indeed with that of the Universe) we cannot possess the required confidence in our ability to control our emotional responses to beliefs, inferences, and inquiries.

From the late 1890s, Peirce insisted that logic was the third of a trio of normative sciences and that it depended upon ethics and aesthetics. He suggests that, unless we carry out investigations in ethics and aesthetics, our claim to be able to subject our inquiries to rational self-control is in doubt. For logic explains the possibility of rational self-control. There is no space to explain in detail why he takes this view, but it will be useful to make a comment about it.

We might wonder whether our logical sentiments do in fact serve our cognitive needs, whether trusting them will enable us to arrive at stable answers to our questions and to make progress towards the truth. In fact, Peirce insists that there is no guarantee of such cognitive progress: at best we are rational to *hope* that our inquiries will succeed and to hope that our logical sentiments will serve our purposes. Moreover, reflecting upon my own responses to arguments and methods, I might wonder whether these

---

[14] I have emphasized the need for this kind of confidence in order to sustain our inquiries in 'Belief, Confidence and the Method of Science' (Chapter 1), and in 'On Reading God's Great Poem' (Chapter 11). The latter chapter makes use of David Savan's ideas to argue that Peirce (at some stages in his career) saw scientific observation as a form of religious experience.

habits of sentimental response might not be idiosyncratic and irrational: am I right to trust my instincts and sentiments? Confidence in inquiry requires both that these hopes are genuinely motivating and that my puta- tive logical sentiments are experienced as expressions of defensible logical and epistemic norms. I have already argued that these hopes can be moti- vating only if they are manifested in sentiments, in something that engages with the will. But the second worry remains, that the evaluations expressed by my sentiments may not be in accord with the demands of rationality. And Peirce's anxieties about the a priori method making opinion a matter of taste or fashion (W3: 253) suggest that he was alert to this problem. Since 'sentiments in their development will be very greatly determined by accidental causes', we need an understanding of why our logical senti- ments can be trusted. Ethics and aesthetics are intended to meet this anxi- ety: phenomenological reflection upon what I can admire and dislike, upon what can engage with the will and what can disturb it, upon which methods can be sustained and which must be abandoned, enables us to arrive at a description of the values which our sentiments express. By investigating our sentimental responses, inquiries in the normative sciences enable us to understand them and to satisfy ourselves that logical self-control is indeed possible. Once we recognize the role of sentiments in self-control, the need for a systematic account of our right to rely upon our sentiments emerges. Research in the normative sciences then becomes necessary (see Hookway 1985: ch. 2).

Our values and ideals, ethical and logical, are revealed in sentimental judgements; the normative sciences attempt to describe the ultimate ideals by reference to which these sentimental reactions are understood to oper- ate, and by reference to which they interact with our practice of self- control. They are 'theoretical investigations', which help us to understand why our being guided by sentiment, our dependence on intellectual processes which we do not understand or control, does not diminish our freedom or sense that we can control our lives and inquiries. And we have seen Peirce suggest that so long as we are constrained to act or deliberate in accord with reason, our intellectual freedom is not put into question by the fact of our being constrained. So, it seems, ethics and logic must explain how our acritical practices put us into harmony with reason rather than compromising our freedom.

Ethics is concerned with appropriate ultimate ends for the control of conduct; and Peirce's view appears to be that any ultimate end is ethically acceptable which enables the self to function as a rational integrated unity. At one point he says that the only evil is not to possess an ultimate end; but he appears to hold that reflection on the consequences of living by some ends in various possible circumstances will show that they are not capable of achieving the kind of rational unification required for the continued existence of a person. We may question whether such unification has to have the hierarchical structure Peirce describes, that we have to be rationally ordered by reference to a single 'ultimate ideal'; and we may be disturbed by the perfunctory and cavalier fashion in which he carries out his 'ethical' investigation: but it seems clear that this is what he has in mind. We seek a specification of our ultimate goal which gives us a theoretical understanding of the nature of our ethical sentiments, which gives us confidence in our right to guide our lives with the illumination they provide.

As well as guiding our conduct in the light of ethical norms, we guide our reasonings in the light of logical norms. Peirce is insistent, first, that it is not obvious that the obligation to subject our deliberations to full logical self-control is traceable to the ultimate ideals of conduct described by ethics; and, second, that we are aware of norms, and undergo sentiments, which are answerable to the needs for carrying out inquiries and deliberations properly. Hence one task for logic is to formulate the 'ultimate ideal' by reference to which the norms employed in reasoning are defended. And, very quickly, Peirce takes it that the ultimate ideal to which our logical sentiments respond is something like the indefinite *growth* in knowledge and understanding. And this, he thinks, moves beyond the individual: desiring full self-control over one's reasonings requires the kind of wider perspective he has described as altruistic.

7. Altruism and Induction

In conclusion, we must return to our attempts to understand the discussion of the red and black cards in 'The Doctrine of Chances', and make a suggestion concerning how it should be understood. Our problem concerns how altruism is involved in our sense that it would be rational for someone to prefer the pack made up predominantly of red cards. Recall that one interpretation treats the passage as flawed: since Peirce was then confused about the different demands of rationality in theory and practice, he took an example of someone attempting to solve a vital question and used it to illustrate a point about our reliance upon probabilities when carrying out scientific investigations as members of a scientific community.[15] If we attend to cases where rational self-control has a role, the claims about altruism are less crazy than they appear. We are misled into finding them more peculiar than they are because we forget that Peirce is talking about logical *sentiments*, so that he does not deny that (phenomenologically) we find these inferences and predictive strategies immediately rational. Reflection about the good of the community has no role in our use of probabilities.

This solution leaves unexplained our sense that it *is* rational to prefer the predominantly red pack. Hence we can advance to a more complex or sophisticated picture. We draw the black card from the predominantly red pack, and with everlasting woe beckoning, we feel the consolation that at least we made our choice rationally. This is the product of the habits of inference (habits of sentimentally finding inferences 'fine') that make up our *logica utens*. These habits would not take the form they did unless we also participated in inquiries of a non-vital kind, where rational self-control has a role, and a deference to the interests of the wider community of inquirers is (according to Peirce) appropriate. Thus we only receive the consolation of having acted rationally as we advance to meet our fate because we possess a body of rational habits which genuinely involve 'altruism' in Peirce's sense. Although reflections of an altruistic kind have no application *in this case*, we respond to it as we do only because the relevance of altruistic considerations to other cases is something which engages with (and has influenced the development of) our sense of rationality.

While I see no reason for Peirce to deny this, I suspect that (from his point of view) it is not the whole story. For if this is all that is to be said, then provided I have time to think, I am likely to find my consolation rather shallow: it is the by-product of the operation of a system of cognitive aptitudes whose application to the present case is questionable. The appeal of Putnam's notion of a primitive conception of rationality is clear; and the importance for Peirce of repudiating any reliance upon reasoning and self-control in connection with vital matters seems relevant here too. His conservatism and sentimentalism ought to lead him to pour scorn upon any attempt to interrogate or understand the basis of the consolation we receive when we respond 'reasonably' to vital questions. Perhaps he would agree that we have here a primitive conception of rationality—one that does not need any rational or logical defence. And he could defend this by saying that *in such cases*, common sense insists that we should go

---

[15] This interpretation appears to be defended in Hookway (1985: 215–16).

by probabilities; the sentimental responses which guide practical conduct and those that guide scientific reasoning are in harmony.

As I have emphasized elsewhere, Peirce employs two conceptions of belief or acceptance whose relations are a complex matter (see Chapter 1). 'Practical belief' is that on which we act: we trust our beliefs in planning our actions and responding to vital questions. A 'scientific belief' is something which it is reasonable to regard as 'settled' at the current stage of inquiry: it is compatible with such 'belief' that we expect that it will eventually be revised or repudiated as inquiry proceeds. It is quite possible that a theoretical proposition might be looked on as 'established' in the second of these senses, while anyone who used it as a basis for action or as relevant to settling vital questions would be deemed unwise. Our strategies for regarding propositions as 'settled' are judged by how well they contribute to furthering the growth of knowledge, whereas our strategies for forming practical beliefs are influenced by how well they enable us to put our lives in order. If 'reasoning' is to have a role in settling vital questions, there must be a substantial degree of harmony between these strategies: 'common sense' (our primitive conception of practical rationality) guides us when our 'logical sentiments' can be trusted in connection with practical matters.

In fact, in Peirce's own thought, there is more to be said about the integration of these different elements of our practices. Peirce's later writings employ a religious outlook which leads him to assert that 'The very first command that is laid upon you, your quite highest business and duty, becomes, as everyone knows, to recognize a higher business than your business ... a generalized conception of duty which completes your personality by melting it into the neighbouring parts of the universal cosmos' (*CP* 1.673). Insisting that 'the very supreme commandment of sentiment is that man . . . should become welded into the universal continuum', he emphasizes that this should occur not only with respect to his 'cognitions, which are but a superficial film of his being, but objectively in the deepest emotional springs of life' (ibid.). However, even if we do not share Peirce's anticipation of this 'joyful Nirvana in which the discontinuities of [one's] will shall have all but disappeared' (ibid.), his emphasis on the role of sentiments in rationality cannot be ignored. Although this religious outlook may allow a role for 'altruism' even when choosing between eternal felicity and everlasting woe, it is important that appeal to the logical sentiments is separable from these religious views and has a fundamental role in Peirce's account of rationality.

10

Doubt: Affective States and the Regulation of Inquiry

Pragmatists challenge a sharp separation of issues of theoretical and practical rationality. This can encourage a sort of anti-realism: our classifications and theories are shaped by our interests and practical concerns. However, it need not do this. A more fundamental theme is that cognition is itself an activity, the attempt to solve problems and discover truths effectively and responsibly. Evidence has to be collected, experiments have to be devised and carried out, dialogues must be engaged in with fellow inquirers, decisions must be made about when we have scrutinized our opinions enough to trust our results. Even if our goals are 'purely cognitive', the attempt to achieve them through inquiry and deliberation is an activity. The normative standards that guide inquiry, like those governing any activity, will include standards of practical rationality. Indeed we might suggest that a belief is *justified* so long as it is the product of responsible, well-executed inquiry.

It is uncontroversial that our affective states have a role in practical rationality. We assess the rationality of desires and goals, and we can examine the role of emotions and attitudes in planning our conduct and carrying out our plans. Emotion can serve both as an aid to practical rationality and as an impediment to it. The classical pragmatists claimed that it also has a role in theoretical or cognitive rationality. For Peirce, one of the defining features of scientific inquiry is the fact that it is guided by a distinctive desire. And, as I have argued elsewhere, both Peirce and James insisted that distinctive sentiments were required for us to be able to reason well and trust our inductive strategies (see Chapter 9 and Hookway 1993). I believe that contemporary epistemology has suffered through its failure to take seriously the role of affective factors in cognition, and this chapter forms part of an attempt to remedy this lack.[1]

[1] For an interesting exception to this, see Catherine Elgin's book *Considered Judgment* (Elgin 1996).

My concern is with the role of states of *doubt*, of finding things puzzling or problematic. After introducing the issue and explaining its importance (section 1), I take note of some puzzling and influential claims on this topic made by Peirce in some of his most famous writings (section 2). After discussing what is puzzling about his claims, the remainder of the paper pursues three topics. First, I argue that theoretical rationality requires a distinctive kind of self-trust, which must include trust in our affective responses to propositions, inferences, and inquiries. Second, I argue that this can be used to explain why our instinctive feelings of doubt (or lack of doubt) possess a defeasible authority over philosophical challenges and arguments. Finally, I raise some issues about how we should think about the cognitive dimension of emotions. If the claims made here are correct, then the Peircean views alluded to are much less puzzling than initially appears.

1. Doubt

To *doubt* a proposition is to take an evaluative stance towards it. In ordinary English, this may involve thinking that it is probably false: if I doubt that the mechanic has finished servicing my car, then I tentatively anticipate that he has not. But, especially in philosophy, it also covers cases where we find that the available evidence is insufficient to warrant either acceptance or rejection of a proposition—or hold that it is unclear whether the evidence is sufficient for that purpose. Of course, evaluations using this concept have been central to epistemology for two thousand years: standard sceptical arguments suggest a mismatch between our practice of doubting propositions and the evaluative standards which, we accept, we should employ. Reflection upon the structure of our system of beliefs is supposed to suggest that there are many things that we do not naturally doubt, or that we find it impossible to doubt, that in fact merit the evaluative stance which doubt involves. Much post-Cartesian epistemology has agreed that deep sceptical doubts should be used to raise the fundamental philosophical problems about knowledge. If I cannot rule out the possibility that my disembodied brain is suspended in a vat of chemicals, and stimulated by powerful scientists to experience a wholly illusory external world, then I ought to abandon my everyday beliefs about my surroundings, and initiate inquiries into just how reliable my senses are.

As a matter of fact, of course, we do not *feel* such doubts. While acknowledging them as philosophical 'ought's, we retain our everyday confidence in our beliefs about the world. Like some other philosophers influenced by the common-sense tradition, Peirce and the other pragmatists tend to dismiss these philosophical anxieties as 'unreal', 'unnatural', 'paper doubts'; We should not doubt in philosophy what we do not doubt in our hearts. An issue is thus raised about whether the fact that we do not *feel* any doubt about our everyday beliefs should be assigned any philosophical weight. Does the fact that I feel certain of the existence of the external world have any legitimate authority over the considered philosophical judgement that this is a matter that intellectual responsibility *requires* me to doubt? Is there any way of sustaining the view that our natural dispositions to doubt and certainty possess any sort of intellectual authority?

These cases are superficially similar to many others where we (reasonably) judge that we ought to doubt propositions which our actions and motivations show that we rely upon in practice, and which we have no inclination to make objects of serious inquiry. Our failure to doubt *these* things is taken as a sign of irrationality. Examples might include the trust one continues to give to a close friend when presented with evidence that seems to establish that she has been unfaithful, or the readiness with which one hangs on to pet theories in the face of evidence that (one acknowledges) ought to be disturbing. If someone were to point out that our behaviour shows that we do not really doubt these things as grounds for denying that there is anything wrong with our refusal to take the counterevidence seriously in practice, we would respond that our failure to doubt these propositions is an epistemic failing. It does not show that we *ought* not to doubt them. Our failure to doubt these propositions 'in our hearts' may reveal the weakness of our epistemic characters rather than the superior epistemological authority of our 'hearts'. If weight is to be attached to the fact that we do not take sceptical doubts seriously, then it is necessary to explain how they differ from the irrational failure to adjust one's beliefs to the evidence that we have just described. Why isn't our refusal to take sceptical 'doubts' seriously similarly a mark of irrationality?

Sometimes Peirce defends his strategy by pointing out that doubts normally require 'a reason': we need grounds for doubting propositions that we currently accept. He appears to think that the Cartesian method of doubt calls for ungrounded unreasoned doubts: we are to doubt things simply by deciding to do so. However, this cannot be quite right. The first *Meditation* is full of reasons for questioning the legitimacy of currently held opinions. One might argue that the reasons offered by sceptical challenges are of the wrong kind: doubts are improperly entered or raised (See

Cavell 1979; Williams 1991). However, there is little sign of Peirce arguing in this fashion in the passages under discussion. While it is incumbent upon someone who rejects the significance of these familiar sceptical challenges to try to *explain* what is wrong with them, the prima facie authority of our instinctive refusal to doubt need not be based upon the details of such an explanation.

We need not rule out the possibility that it will turn out that this *is* 'irrationality', or perhaps a way of coping with our desperate epistemological position. No adequate explanation of what is wrong with the challenges may be forthcoming. Any authority claimed for our instinctive dispositions to doubt and inquire may thus be defeasible. The question we have to consider concerns how it can possess even a defeasible authority. The position to be sketched below allows for the possibility that we are rational to trust our instinctive feelings of doubts and rationality. Such trust is defeasible; we can envisage circumstances in which we would be forced to give it up. But, in general, we have more reason to trust our instinctive judgements of rationality than we do the products of distinctively philosophical reasoning. This, I shall suggest, is a pervasive theme in pragmatist epistemology, and represents an important epistemological insight.

2. Doubt and Belief

In 'The Fixation of Belief', Peirce adopted a simple picture of 'inquiry': our stable corpus of settled beliefs is shaken by a 'surprising experience' which gives rise to doubt about some of the propositions that were previously believed (W3: 247 ff). These doubts motivate us to the activity of inquiry which is an attempt to eliminate the doubt, to replace it by a new settled belief concerning the propositions in question. I believe that my car has been serviced, but on reaching the garage, the doors are locked and there is no sign of the car awaiting collection outside. Had the service been completed, I would have expected it to be there, so a question is raised: perhaps they did not finish it after all. The unexpected experience presents me with a *problem*: the experience does not cohere with previously settled beliefs. Inquiry is an attempt to solve that problem, to remove the incoherence in my beliefs and expectations. Whether 'surprising experience' is the only thing that can present me with a problem may be questioned. But let us grant that it provides one possible source of problems which inquiries can try to solve.

Peirce's positive account of doubt exploited the view that propositional attitudes such as doubt and belief are to be distinguished by reference to their causal roles in shaping behaviour and cognition. There are two important differences between belief and doubt. Beliefs guide our desires and shape our actions: 'The feeling of belief is a more or less sure indication of there being established in our nature some habit which will determine our actions' (W3: 247). If I believe that the mechanic has completed the service, I shall head for the garage to collect my car. When I am in a state of doubt concerning a proposition, I will lack this sort of guidance in how to act. Doubt, in contrast, has a different positive effect: it is 'an uneasy and unsettled state from which we struggle to free ourselves and pass into a state of belief' (ibid.). Thus both belief and doubt produce actions, but where beliefs prompt actions which would promote our goals if the belief were true, doubt prompts inquiry designed to eliminate the doubt.[2]

The second difference is that the effect of belief upon action is conditional. I shall only act upon my belief if I already possess a *desire* whose satisfaction requires use of my car as well as a body of appropriate background beliefs about my distance from the garage, the route to be taken to get there, and so on. Rather than make us act immediately, a belief 'puts us into such a condition that we shall behave in such a way when the occasion arises' (ibid.). The motivational force of doubt, we learn, is not conditional: it immediately stimulates us to action until it has been destroyed. So while the motivational force of a belief depends upon the presence of a desire, doubt is apparently intrinsically motivating. No independent desire to eliminate the doubt is required for us to be motivated to carry out the appropriate inquiry.

At first sight, this is extremely implausible, and it will be useful to work out exactly why this is. Peirce's account of doubt gives it two apparently distinct roles. First, it is an epistemic notion, an acknowledgement that the evidence available, or the results of our deliberations, require us to suspend judgement on the matter in hand. A reason for doubt suggests that we should abandon a settled belief or continue to suspend judgement on the matter. But, second, it essentially involves possession of reasons for action; a reason for doubting some proposition is a reason for inquiring into its truth value. The availability of this 'reason to inquire' does not, appears, require the co-operation of a desire to have a settled opinion concerning this truth value. Peirce treats doubt as a unified psychological

---

[2] Characterizing the kind of role in shaping actions which beliefs possess and doubts lack is not easy. If my doubt that the car is ready for collection leads me to take the bus or train when I head for town, then that state can shape actions other than inquiries into the proposition doubted. I shall not pursue this issue here.

state which embodies an epistemic evaluation and provides a reason for action. Well-entrenched Humean prejudices about reasons for action encourage the suspicion that Peirce has misidentified a complex hybrid state as a unitary one, and that this is the source of his claim that doubts motivate actions unconditionally. The state of doubt that he describes, the state of finding something doubtful or problematic, is composed of the epistemic state of finding that the evidence warrants suspension of judgement concerning the truth value of the proposition together with the *desire* not to be agnostic about it.

Another observation supports the same view. We can partially characterize someone's cognitive position at a particular time by listing their differing attitudes towards different propositions. Ignoring complexities introduced when we allow that beliefs may differ in strength, we might divide propositions into four classes:

1. those that the agents accepts or believes;
2. those that the agent rejects or disbelieves;
3. those about which the agent is (calmly) agnostic;
4. those concerning which the agent is in a state of *doubt*: whether to believe or disbelieve them presents the agent with a problem.

Calm agnosticism and active doubt both involve suspension of judgement concerning the truth of the proposition in question. But the agent is motivated to resolve this indeterminacy in the case of doubts, while agnosticism can be calm and undisturbing. Agnosticism need provide no immediate reason for carrying out an inquiry, while, according to Peirce and other pragmatists, doubt does provide such a reason. It seems plausible that suspension of judgement on the proposition is a component of each. In the fourth class, this suspension of judgement is accompanied by a desire which is absent in the third. Once again, the idea of a unified state which is both an epistemic evaluation and the source of a reason for action seems problematic. Doubt appears to be a hybrid state composed of a state of agnosticism and a desire:

A is in a state of doubt concerning whether p if, and only if,
i) A is agnostic concerning whether p
ii) A desires to have a firm opinion concerning whether p

Peirce's original suggestion that doubt was a distinctive kind of mental state with a characteristic functional role in motivating inquiry is weakened.

Suspension of belief and the desire to inquire appear to be distinct existences.

It is not yet clear whether the failure of Peirce's claims about doubt would undermine the uses made of the notion of 'real doubt' in the discussions alluded to above. The following section will begin to look at the role that 'real doubts' may have in our practice of inquiry and epistemic evaluation. We shall begin by looking at some claims of Peirce's and then move on to a defence of a view which is related to his. On this basis, in later sections of the chapter, reasons will be given for rejecting the arguments just offered for the view that doubt should be seen as a hybrid or compound state which is composed of distinct states of suspension of judgement and desire.

3. Doubt and the Regulation of Inquiry.

What then is the role of states of doubt in carrying out inquiries? Our earlier discussion suggested that they are required for us to be motivated to carry out inquiries, providing the initial *push* required to ensure that we take problems seriously and try to solve them. However, this claim can be questioned.

Suppose that my philosophical reflections persuade me that I ought to doubt the existence of the external world. I judge that I have a reason to begin an inquiry which tries to answer the question: Is there an external world? Although I feel no doubt that the external world exists, I may judge that this should be given no weight. Natural selection may have provided us with drives that prevent our efforts to reproduce being obstructed by the effects of reading too much philosophy. If I judge that I ought to investigate whether there is an external world and find it difficult to take such an inquiry seriously, it is not at all obvious that my reflective judgement should defer to my unreflective habits of doubt and investigation. Furthermore, it seems that we *can* inquire into the matter, even if no motivation is provided by a real doubt. I can ask the question: Is there an external world? And I can reflect upon the strategies I might follow in order to answer it. It would be hard to deny that a sequence of actions designed to find the correct answer to a question that I have formulated counts as an inquiry. So the claim that without real doubt there is no inquiry seems to be straightforwardly false.

In 'The Fixation of Belief', Peirce considers those philosophers who 'have imagined that to start an inquiry it was only necessary to utter a question whether orally or by setting it down on paper':

But the mere putting of a proposition into the interrogative form does not stimulate the mind to any struggle after belief. There must be a real and living doubt, and without this all discussion is idle ... When doubt ceases, mental action on the subject comes to an end; and, if it did go on, it would be without a purpose. Except that of self-criticism. [3] (W3: 248)

Two different complaints are suggested by this passage. The first, considered above, is that without 'living doubt', there is no deliberation or inquiry. Unless there is real doubt, 'mental action on the subject comes to an end'. The passage then appears to retreat from this bold claim: any apparent inquiry that did occur would be idle or without purpose. Perhaps idle or purposeless cognitive activity is not inquiry properly so-called. The philosopher described in the previous paragraph may believe he is carrying out an inquiry when he is not, in fact, doing so.

Here is one way to set the issue up. Having enunciated the question 'Is it the case that *p*?', someone can engage in an activity which they understand as an attempt to inquire into whether *p*. It is hard to see how the lack of a 'real doubt' prevents this being the case. For the lack of a real doubt to render this attempt 'idle', we need an explanation of how the lack of a doubt has implications for the way in which the activity is conducted. Since inquiry is an activity that can be subject to rational self-control, can be subject to norms, we would need to tell a story about how the real doubt can have a role in the normative regulation of the inquiry. In the absence of a 'real doubt', the activity will not be controlled in the way that an inquiry should be. Doubt is not necessary only as a *stimulus* to real inquiry; it has a continuing role in monitoring the inquiry, in taking responsibility for how successful it is.

There is support for the claim that this idea is present in Peirce's discussion, although that is not essential to the claims I want to make here. In 'Some Consequences of Four Incapacities' (1868) Peirce objects to the method of doubt:

We cannot begin with complete doubt. We must begin with all the prejudices which we actually have when we enter upon the study of philosophy. These prejudices are not to be dispelled by a maxim, for they are things that it does not occur to us can be questioned. Hence this initial scepticism will be mere self-deception, and not real doubt; and no one who follows the Cartesian method will ever be satisfied until he has formally recovered all those beliefs which in form he has given up. (W2: 212)

---

[3] The final sentence was added to this 1877 passage in 1903 (*CP* 5.376).

The suggestion here appears to be that unless we *really doubt* a proposition, our residual attachment to it will interfere with our deliberations. Part of the point is that we are not open to the truth: we will only accept one upshot to our inquiry, so we are not entering into it in the true scientific spirit. Also present is the suggestion that the belief will shape our inquiries in ways that we are unlikely to notice and unable to control. Unless real doubt is present, the inquiry will not be properly sensitive to norms of epistemic rationality. Can we make sense of this possibility?

The position to be sketched in the remaining sections of this chapter explores how doubt may have an ineliminable role in the regulation and organization of responsible rational inquiry. Unless we are guided *inter alia* by our doubts, we will not be able to solve problems and answer questions effectively.

4. Habits and Evaluations

A pragmatist approach to mind, action, and cognition attaches importance to the fact that we possess batteries of habits which contribute to the shape of our character and whose action helps to determine the will. As well as habits that contribute to posture and gait, and as well as those which comprise practical skills such as the ability to ride a bicycle or dance a waltz, we possess cognitive habits. These include what Peirce called our *logica utens*, habits of inference, inquiry, and argument. My habits of inductive reasoning, my standards of plausibility and implausibility, my judgements of what stands in need of defence and what goes without saying, reflect and determine patterns in my systems of beliefs and my cognitive practice. Although we might be able to describe these patterns by formulating general principles or rules which they reflect, it is an important part of the phenomenology of deliberation and inquiry that we need not be reflectively aware of any such principles when we are guided by these habits. Their operation is not mediated through reflection upon the standards that they embody, and, in many cases, we are incapable of such reflection. The importance of this point for understanding practical rationality has long been acknowledged. It is part of the contribution of pragmatist logicians to emphasize that the same is true of theoretical or epistemic rationality.

This observation has immediate relevance to the matter we have been discussing. First, these are largely habits of *evaluation*: they guide us in recognizing when an inference is a good one, when evidence is sufficient for belief in some proposition, when hypotheses are so implausible that we need not take steps to eliminate them before accepting a rival, and so on. We are guided by habits of evaluation, and often we cannot explain or sometimes even describe the standards which guide our evaluations. Our sense that we are inquiring responsibly and effectively calls for confidence in our instinctive and habitual cognitive skills; it calls for a distinctive kind of 'self-trust'. We must be confident that trusting our *logica utens*, our habits of reasoning and evaluation, will guide us towards the truth. Our judgements track values that have positive logical (or practical) merit. We can have confidence in our judgements, taking responsibility for how well our inquiries are conducted, only if we assign a presumptive authority to these habitual evaluations, even if we cannot reflectively explain what this authority consists in. On pain of a crippling form of scepticism, we cannot reasonably hope to replace all such habitual evaluation by explicit acknowledgement of rules and formal standards. This is evident from the fact that (habitual) judgement is always involved in the application of explicit formal rules to complex real cases. In general, confidence in our ability to inquire responsibly requires a degree of trust in our habits of cognitive evaluation.

Of course, it is compatible with this that such habits of evaluation are flawed. Much irrationality depends upon flaws in our epistemic character: we are naturally and habitually disposed to accept attractive conclusions on the basis of inadequate evidence or to be unreasonably cautious. Our standards of reasoning (including habitual ones) guide us in identifying circumstances in which we would be irresponsible to trust our intuitive standards of reasoning. It is compatible with this that rationality is possible only if we assign our intuitive or instinctive standards a prima facie or presumptive plausibility. Responsible reasoning requires confidence or self-trust.[4]

Included among these cognitive habits and instincts is our capacity to find beliefs or propositions *doubtful*. When evidence conflicts with an established belief, our habitual *logica utens* leads us to judge whether it is sufficient to unsettle that belief. When inquiry into a matter calls for information where we are currently agnostic, habits of inquiry can contribute to making that matter problematic: the question emerges as one which we are motivated to answer. Hence if cognitive rationality and epistemic responsibility require a presumptive, but defeasible trust in our cognitive

---

[4] The epistemic importance of the idea of self-trust has been emphasized by Keith Lehrer (1997).

habits, then it requires such a confidence in our capacity to judge when something is open to doubt.

We should emphasize one consequence of these observations. An important distinction can be drawn between:

1. those norms and patterns of evaluation which guide us in the conduct of activities including those of inquiry and investigations; and
2. those norms and standards of evaluation which we believe are guiding us in these activities.

Cartesian epistemology requires that reflection and introspection can ensure that these coincide. If we are responsible, we are guided only by norms that we can reflectively formulate and endorse. The style of pragmatist epistemology that we are concerned with here rejects this Cartesian view. If our practice conflicts with those abstract normative standards which, we believe, we *ought* to be guided by, there is a defeasible presumption in favour of the norms implicit in our practice. We question our habitual standards only if we have evidence that they have led us into error or we can explain what is wrong with them. If we abandon this presumption, then responsible, confident reasoning and inquiry are not possible. Although this does not establish that the presumption is *true*, it does establish that it would be irrational and self-defeating to reject it while continuing to hold that we can participate in responsible ratiocination. Self-trust is a necessary condition for responsible rationality.[5]

5. Doubts and Anxieties

How could states such as doubt have a role in organizing and regulating inquiries? When I judge that something ought to be done—for example, that I ought to check whether it rained in New York yesterday—my judgement has two features that call for philosophical explanation. First, it has a *normative* character: we need to understand how the judgement is

---

[5] I shall not discuss in detail exactly why the sort of self-trust described here is rational. At least two strategies suggest themselves, both familiar from pragmatist writings. First, it could be defended as a regulative presumption. If it is not warranted, then responsible rationality would be impossible, so it is rational to proceed on the *hope* that it is warranted. Second, appeal could be made to the fact that it is 'natural' and, indeed, unavoidable much of the time. If my behaviour shows that I endorse it, then, in the absence of a positive reason for doubting it, I am warranted in relying upon it.

related to, or grounded in, defensible epistemic ideals. Irrationality often involves being guided by such judgements when their normative status is questionable. The sort of self-trust we considered in the previous section involves trusting that our habitual and unreflective judgements about how we ought to conduct our inquiries reflect adequate epistemic norms. Second, it has the power to guide or motivate inquiries and deliberations. We have a tendency to act as our 'ought' judgements decree. Such questions arise whether the norms concern how we should act or whether they govern our cognitive activities and functions.

What form does this 'motivation' take when the evaluations we make take the form of doubting some proposition? One answer to this question is familiar and straightforward: having judged that its status is problematic, we are motivated to the sorts of actions and activities that serve as components of inquiries. Since inquiry is an activity, epistemic norms produce actions just as practical norms do. But there is another answer too. Our evaluations 'spread' to other propositions, beliefs, and inferences that are suitably related to the object of our initial evaluation. When I believe a proposition, I am defeasibly committed to approving of any proposition which follows from it; when I approve of a form of inference, I am committed to accepting the results of its employment; when I doubt a proposition, I am committed to reassessing my endorsement of beliefs and inferences which depend upon it. Epistemic evaluations bring with them a network of commitments; we are committed to related evaluations of other beliefs, inferences, doubts, and inquiries. We can carry out inquiries guided by the habits of epistemic evaluation described in the last section only if we can be confident that our evaluations will spread through our beliefs and regulate our inquiries in accordance with this network of normative commitments. One way in which we might argue that inquiry in the absence of real doubt will be idle, or will be improperly regulated, would involve suggesting that our normative commitments would not then be reflected in the ways in which our epistemic evaluations spread through our whole corpus of beliefs and inferences. There will be no basis for a crucial kind of self-trust or confidence; we can no longer trust our habits of doubt, belief, and inference.

Once we reject the Cartesian ideal that we have reliable access to the normative standards that guide our inquiries and deliberations, we will best understand our ability to keep track of our epistemic commitments by acknowledging that we trust our cognitive habits to ensure that our evaluations spread through our system of beliefs in an appropriate way. If our evaluations do not engage with these habits, then we may begin to doubt that we can track appropriate epistemic norms as we deliberate and conduct our inquiries. And, the suggestion will be, inquiries that are focused on 'unreal doubts' will be guided by evaluations which do not engage with our habits of evaluation in the right way.

An illustration of some of these points may be helpful. Suppose that I intend to carry out a task co-operatively with a friend. Information emerges which may cast doubt upon the friend's reliability or trustworthiness. But this new evidence is not decisive: it points towards the unreliability of the friend, but whether it should be sufficient to sway my opinion is a matter for judgement. Now compare two cases. I may genuinely come to doubt my friend's reliability: I take the evidence to be sufficient to raise a genuine doubt. Alternatively, I may judge that the evidence *ought* to shake my confidence, that it warrants a doubt which I do not, as a matter of fact, feel. In the latter case, my view about the friend's unreliability will affect my plans and other opinions only if I explicitly recall my judgement about how I ought to have responded. In the former case, the active real doubt will ensure that I am doubtful about beliefs and proposals which depend upon the friend's reliability without my needing to recall the judgement that I earlier made. I can trust my habits of cognitive evaluation, confident that (in most cases and in normal circumstances) new doubts will emerge when required by the initial doubt. Real doubts can regulate inquiries in ways that formally acknowledged but 'unreal' or 'unfelt' doubts do not.

In the last paragraph I spoke of unreal doubts as 'unfelt'. This introduces a further important theme in pragmatist epistemology. If habitual assessments are going to provide evaluations of our cognitive position which spread through our beliefs and inferences, helping us to honour our evaluative commitments, then it is important that evaluative states such as doubt have a strong affective flavour. Our doubts evaluate our cognitive situation rather as our emotions evaluate ourselves and our surroundings. The idea that sentiments and emotions have an ineliminable role in epistemic rationality was defended by both Peirce and William James, and I shall not discuss their views on the matter here.[6] Instead I shall simply try to make the idea plausible.

We can do so by considering an analogy. We might suppose that when I come to *doubt* a proposition, I become *anxious* about any tendency to accept it that I still possess; I shall also become anxious about any other beliefs I hold which may depend upon it. Suppose then that we think of

---

[6] I have done so in Chapter 9, as well as in Hookway (1993 and 1994*b*).

doubt as a particular kind of anxiety. We can then understand doubt better by looking at more familiar cases of anxiety. It is an emotional response which normally involves the belief that I am in a position that involves a danger or risk of some harmful outcome. It also involves dispositions or inclinations to behave in distinctive ways, to focus on distinctive features of my situation to the exclusion of others, and to have thoughts and questions of particular kinds occur to me. We are familiar with how excessive anxiety can be incapacitating, undermining our ability to make sound judgements about how we should act. But it is also plausible that someone who never felt anxiety would be likely to fail to take necessary precautions and, in consequence, to embark on foolhardy projects. The successful regulation of actions may require, or at least be promoted by, the possession of an appropriate tendency to feel anxiety when one's situation presents a sufficient degree of risk or danger. By making me sensitive to risks and dangers, unreflectively alert to possible hazards, it may enable me to act spontaneously and effectively and prevent me carelessly exposing myself to unnecessary risks. The emotional state provides a tool for collecting relevant information and planning actions in the light of it: we might even say that it is the form taken by my cognitive awareness of the riskiness of my position. It embodies my evaluative stance towards my situation. While we can explain my actions only by alluding to my desire to avoid the dangers in question, it would be a mistake sharply to distinguish my cognitive search for information about risks and dangers from my motivating anxieties.

Think of an experienced hiker, someone with a deep understanding of the local terrain, of the chances and effects of changes in the weather, of her own strengths and weaknesses, and so on. This knowledge can be manifested in judgements about, for example, when weather conditions make a particular route too risky. It is natural to think of this as involving more than just a body of propositional knowledge. It involves a complex kind of skill which may be manifested in the walker's ability to feel anxiety or feel secure in different circumstances: she will listen to the judgements of her heart, trusting her habits of judgement and her ability instinctively to *read* the weather and the terrain. When she trusts her judgements on such matters, she is, in a sense, using her own cognitive habits as a reliable instrument for judging the riskiness of the situation, she accepts the testimony of her own affective nature. When she feels alarmed or anxious, she is likely to seek an alternative route; when she feels secure in her position, she will not investigate the possibility of an alternative.

The way this case has been described might be misleading. It can appear to contrast an excessively intellectualist picture of deliberation with the suggestion that we should proceed in a somewhat zomboid manner, trusting our instincts and totally dispensing with reflection and careful thought about the position. My intention is, rather, to *emphasize* that inquiry and deliberation involve a complex interplay of intellectual reflection and trusting acquiescence in habitual judgements and sentimental responses. Finding a situation to be risky or dangerous is an assessment or evaluation of it. The situation has features which are likely to threaten my security or the success of my actions. Second, once I am anxious about my situation, I will be motivated to avoid risks, to find alternative actions if possible, to take care not to expose myself unnecessarily to danger. This motivation is immediate or unconditional: my evaluation does not merely inform me that *if* I wish to avoid danger or risk, I should avoid acting in these circumstances. Through sensing the danger in my circumstances, I am *already* motivated to take precautions and avoid acting if possible. I can decide that I should act in spite of feeling the anxiety: the reasons I possess are defeasible. And I can *recognize* that my evaluations should be ignored because they are irrational; they reflect a character that is *too* timid, too ready to be incapacitated by slight dangers. In spite of this, in general, my anxiety will be an assessment of the situation which does not need to be supplemented by the desire to avoid danger to affect my dispositions to action and to colour my deliberations.

The third point, relevant to the assessment of the hybrid view, is that these habitual and sentimental evaluations of our position can have a *content* which is not simply the content of some *belief* that the person has. Consider someone who is irrationally afraid of frogs (see Elgin 1996: ch. 5, especially 146–6). He can simultaneously judge intellectually that frogs present us with no danger at all and affectively represent them as alarming or threatening. The affective representation tends to influence his behaviour, which he must fight against; he should not listen to the testimony of the heart; his self-trust should be qualified. Such examples illustrate that we should not view the cognitive aspect of anxiety as a simple combination of a belief and an attitude towards it. Our agent does not really possess the belief in question and the content only influences his planning and deliberation through its emotional representation. In that case, it is plausible that even where belief and emotion are not in conflict, so that we trust the latter to guide our deliberations and our actions, the primary representation can be the emotional one. We believe the path to be dangerous *because* we trust our affective representation of it as risky, *because* we find ourselves motivated to avoid it or to take special care. I don't form a calm assessment of the degree of danger that I face, and then feel anxiety or not according to how desires and emotions interfere with this calm assessment. I normally *trust* my immediate emotional responses to arrive at a sensitive and reliable assessment of the degree of danger. My assessment of the situation is most directly expressed in the ways in which I am motivated to respond to it.

As we saw, feelings of anxiety and judgements about degree of risk can fail to be in harmony. I can judge that there is no danger, while anxieties shape my deliberations causing me to expend much effort on considering possible dangers. And the calm confidence with which I deal with a situation can undermine my judgement that it is risky or alarming. We may explain away such cases: my feelings are neurotic and should be ignored. But there is a genuine possibility that, in some cases at least, affective responses are more trustworthy than reflective considered ones. This is because they can reveal an habitual sensitivity to subtle features of the situation which are not formally acknowledged by calm reflection. Habitual evaluative practices can reflect extensive experience and an acute sensitivity to the fine details of our environment. In such cases we do better to trust the ways in which our affective natures shape our deliberations, taking seriously the questions that are pressed upon us.

As we noted above, Peirce's remark about doubt suggest that it involves a kind of anxiety about any inquiry that relies upon a doubted proposition. Just as anxiety immediately motivates us to avoid danger or mitigate its effects, so doubt motivates us to remove the uncertainty that attaches to the proposition. And just as anxiety reflects the operation of 'standards' of evaluation which are not explicitly formulated or reflectively applied, so are our doubts informed by our habitual and unreflective standards for assessing evidence. Once we take account of the fact that decisions about whether to accept or reject propositions must be made in the light of the totality of other information we possess, it is easy to see that they involve the manifestation of judgement, and not just the mechanical application of rules in the light of limited bodies of relevant evidence. Just as we can trust our affective responses to the dangers of the hillside, so we can trust our habitual or instinctive judgements about the acceptability of propositions. Such judgements can guide both our decision that some proposition should be made an object of investigation and our subsequent reflection that it has passed sufficient tests and can now be firmly accepted. And just as our awareness of danger may receive its primary manifestation in an affective representation, in an immediate motivation to avoid the danger or eliminate it, so our awareness that a proposition is poorly supported may receive its primary manifestation in a state of doubt or of epistemic anxiety. Possessing such affective presentations may be as essential to the successful pursuit of truth as a well-attuned sense of danger is to survival in the hills.

A plausible account of cognitive evaluation will thus incorporate both conscious application of principles and habitual evaluations. It must allow for the fact that we often criticize or lose trust in our evaluative habits: critical self-trust or confidence is the attitude towards our cognitive habits that seems appropriate. The conclusion of this section is that we can make sense of some of the distinctive features of pragmatist ideas about doubt through acknowledging that many of our evaluative standards are habitual and manifested through our affective responses to our beliefs and inquiries.

6. Conclusion: Doubt and Agnosticism

At the end of section 2, we considered the suggestion that *doubt* is a sort of hybrid state compromised of a state of suspension of judgement and a desire: I am in a state of doubt concerning whether *p* if, and only if, I am agnostic about whether *p* and I desire to have an opinion on the matter. Agnosticism or suspension of belief provides a common core to states of real doubt and calm agnosticism; these states differ solely in that the former also contains a desire for information. This view appeared to be plausible, yet it was at odds with Peirce's claim that doubt was a distinct kind of psychological state characterized by the fact that it provided an immediate, unconditional motivation to inquiry. Although it is possible that we could combine the claim that states of real doubt have an important role in the regulation of belief and inquiry with the hybrid view of doubt, I shall now suggest that this is not the best strategy to adopt. 'Agnosticism' is not a unitary psychological state constituting the common core to complex states such as doubt and calm agnosticism.

A common view of how information is stored in our minds employs a distinction between different kinds of belief. Some beliefs are explicitly psychologically real: I believe that my computer is black because I have explicitly registered that piece of information. There are other propositions which I believe only because the information they express is readily available to me: when asked whether I have a prime number of siblings, I can answer immediately, although this involves an inference from more fundamental beliefs. In another case, I may believe that I am in a dangerous situation where this consists in my trusting a largely affective response to my position. In each case, I possess a piece of information, and it can guide my actions and deliberations in analogous and intelligible ways. The 'psychological reality' of the beliefs is quite different.

Consider two cases where I rapidly descend into the valley because the weather is becoming dangerous. In each case, it is true that I believe that the situation is becoming dangerous; and in each case I desire to avoid danger. The first case is one in which the belief and desire are 'distinct existences'. Perhaps I have accepted the testimony of a radio weatherman that it will soon become foggy; and I have formed a general policy of avoiding exposure to fog on high ground. The second is a case in which I trust my judgement of the changing conditions, listening to my heart's reasons. My belief that the weather is dangerous reflects trust in my anxious reaction, in my urge to leave the hilltops as soon as I can. In that case, although I possess both belief and desire, they are not distinct existences; were the desire absent, I would lack the belief.

A related point was made by Thomas Nagel (1970). That someone is in pain itself provides a reason for helping them; it does not need to be accompanied by an *independent* desire to contribute to the alleviation of suffering. Perhaps we could not recognize something as a *person* who was *in pain* unless we possessed dispositions to sympathize, feel concern, and offer help when we could. Possession of the concept of pain commits us (defeasibly) to a sympathetic concern for those we identify as subjects of pain. It does not follow from this that we do *not* desire to help those whose pain we acknowledge. It is sufficient that the recognition of the pain and the desire are not independent: we have a defeasible inclination to help this person in virtue of having *recognized* that she is in pain. I would have reason to help them if and only if I believed they were in pain and I desired to alleviate the suffering of people in pain. But it would be wrong to suppose that this reason could be factored into the recognition that the person is in pain and a separate and contingent sympathetic desire.

A related distinction may be drawn among propositions that we are agnostic about. There are at least three possibilities. Some propositions may be consciously acknowledged to be unsettled: I *may* have a file of propositions concerning which, I am aware, I suspend judgement. In other cases, the vast majority, my agnosticism may consist in the fact that the proposition is 'stored' nowhere at all. In such cases, it may be difficult to tell whether I am agnostic about the matter, or whether I possess information which, in the circumstances, I cannot recall. There may be no effective way of establishing whether I am agnostic about it. A third possibility

is relevant here. I may have a relatively stable belief which is rarely manifested in action. When evidence comes in that challenges it, then the question whether that is sufficient to warrant agnosticism may not be settled
until the belief becomes relevant to a further inquiry. I am agnostic if, were
I to need to rely on this information, I would enter a state of active doubt.
It is only in this situation that the habitual criteria of evidential assessment
become operative and can make a judgement on the sufficiency of the
disturbing evidence. It is not settled whether I am agnostic about the
proposition until it is fixed whether we should be motivated to inquire
into the matter. We trust our affective dispositions to doubt to determine
whether we are agnostic about the proposition or not. In such cases, we are
agnostic about the proposition *in virtue of the fact that we are disposed to
doubt it*. If that is right, then we cannot view the state of agnosticism as a
psychological constituent of the doubt.

   If this is right, then the hybrid view becomes implausible. We can agree
that 'calm agnosticism' and 'real doubt' both involve suspension of judgement. The hybrid view goes beyond this in claiming that this suspension
of judgement is a unitary kind of psychological state which forms a
psychological constituent of each. This further view now seems implausible. In some cases, I suspend judgement in a proposition *in virtue of*
doubting it; in other cases, I suspend judgement in virtue of the fact that
neither it, nor its negation, is stored accessibly in my mind. There may be
other kinds of suspension of judgement too. But the idea of real doubt as
a distinctive cognitive state, with a fundamental role in regulating
inquiries, can be retained.

   It does not follow from this that Cartesian worries are of no philosophical significance. I am not arguing that these observations refute scepticism. It is conceivable that the habitual patterns of evaluation we have
been discussing are impediments rather than aids to the responsible search
for the truth. A weaker conclusion does follow, however: rationality
requires a defeasible confidence or trust in our habits of inquiry and evaluation.[7] When philosophical models of rationality cast doubt upon our
habits of reasoning and inquiry, our confidence in our habits can warrant
us in (at least) hoping that this is to be explained through inadequacies in
our philosophical models.

---

   [7] This then gives rise to the philosophical task of arriving at an explanation of our
cognitive habits and goals that vindicates this presumption of their adequacy. If we fail in
this task, then scepticism may be unavoidable. Much of Peirce's work can be read as an
attempt to carry out this task.

11

On Reading God's Great Poem

1. Introduction

As Michael Raposa has noted, it is often assumed that Peirce's writings on religion have 'rather tenuous connections with the rest of the system', being of 'biographical' rather than 'fundamental systematic interest' (Raposa 1989: 3).[1] Raposa himself is one of a number of scholars who have disputed this, arguing that not only were Peirce's religious views a reflection of 'his commitments and ideas in other areas', but they also 'had a shaping influence' on all areas of his work (1989: 13). The contrary view is not surprising, especially among those trained to read Peirce as anticipating a set of logical and semantic views close to those of the Vienna Circle. Although such misreadings are now rare, the relations of Peirce's religious writings to the rest of his work remain puzzling. At least two sets of issues are involved. First, are his views on religious matters consistent with the rest of his philosophical outlook? Can religious concepts be elucidated using the pragmatic principle? Does it make any experiential difference whether propositions about God are true? Does Peirce's evolutionary cosmology encourage a metaphysical outlook incompatible with faith in a personal God? A second issue concerns whether Peirce's views on science, logic, and language require this religious framework. Does Peirce believe that serious scientific activity would be impossible for a non-believer? Could someone adopt Peirce's views about science, logic, and mathematics while rejecting his religious outlook? If his religious outlook was consistent with his other views but was not required by his logical doctrines, then it would still represent a separable and interesting component of his philosophical achievement. But its importance for the assessment of his overall philosophical position would be much greater if he claimed that science and logic require religious belief.

Peirce's most important religious writings mostly date from his last two

---

[1] The quotation is taken from an editorial note by Hartshorne and Weiss (*CP* 6. v).

decades: his famous 'Neglected Argument' for the reality of God was published in 1908, just five years before his death. Few constructive contributions to the philosophy of religion were published earlier than 'The Marriage of Science and Religion' and 'What is Christian Faith?', which originally appeared in *The Open Court* in 1893, soon after his first extended treatment of metaphysical issues. I shall discuss below whether philosophical significance attaches to this growing interest in such matters towards the end of Peirce's philosophical career. Much recent scholarship on his philosophy of religion has examined the relations between his religious views and his metaphysics, exploring his conception of God and of our relation to God. Important too has been the attempt to understand the structure of Peirce's 'Neglected Argument'. Although later sections of this chapter will attempt to understand the role and structure of Peirce's argument, I shall begin by addressing a rather different issue. What is the role of religious belief in scientific activity? I shall argue that Peirce's view of science involved regarding scientific observation as a form of religious experience and that he held that only a believer could engage in inquiry in the true scientific spirit.

2. Religion and Science

Peirce inherited from his father a view of science as a kind of religious duty. Where Benjamin Peirce insisted that 'the universe is a book written for man's reading', his son stressed that the purpose of 'theoretical' science was 'simply and solely the knowledge of God's truth' (*CP* 1.239), the Universe as a whole being 'a symbol of God's purpose', and 'God's great poem' (*CP* 5.119). Moreover, since he reached philosophical maturity as the debate over the conflict between Darwinism and religion was at its peak, reconciling the claims of science and religion was always present among Peirce's concerns.

Many passages from after 1890 illustrate this religious outlook. Raposa cites a letter to Lady Welby in which Peirce identified 'a man of science' as one who truly has 'Faith in God' (*SS*: 75). And in *The Open Court*, religion is described as 'a sort of sentiment, or obscure perception, a deep recognition of something in the circumambient All', and as 'essentially a social, a public affair': 'It is the idea of a whole Church, welding all its members together in one organic, systemic perception of the Glory of the Highest— an idea having growth from generation to generation and claiming a supremacy in the determination of all conduct, private and public' (*CP*

6.429). The true religious outlook requires an attitude describable as the 'religion of science':

It is a religion, so true to itself, that it becomes animated by the scientific spirit, confident that all the conquests of science will be triumphs of its own, and accepting all the results of science as scientific men themselves accept them, as steps toward the truth, which may for a time appear to be in conflict with other truths, but which in such cases merely await adjustments which time is sure to effect. (*CP* 6.433)

Although Peirce's most constructive writings on religious matters are relatively late, it will be easier to understand his growing concern with religious matters in his final decades if we register some of the religious ideas that were present in his writings before 1880. The remainder of this section will identify some important themes from three of these earlier works. The first of these, from 'Some Consequences of Four Incapacities', published in 1868 in the *Journal of Speculative Philosophy*, contributes to making it surprising that Peirce should subsequently find a place for God in his philosophical system. He was contemptuous of the Cartesian use of God to provide ultimate explanations of natural phenomena: 'Scholasticism had its mysteries of faith, but undertook to explain all created things. But there are many facts which Cartesianism not only does not explain, but renders absolutely inexplicable, unless to say that "God makes them so" is to be regarded as an explanation' (W2: 212). Unless he turned his back on this objection to Cartesianism, the role of religious belief in Peircean science must avoid this charge. If belief in God is required to sustain our confidence in the possibility of science, it must not do so by providing ultimate explanations of phenomena.

An unpublished paper from the same period, 'Critique of Positivism' (W2: 122–30), addresses the 'weak point' in positivism, its claims about religion:

If, therefore, I am asked as a theist what I have to reply to the arguments of the positivists, I reply in the first place, that positivism is only a particular species of metaphysics open to all the uncertainty of metaphysics, and its conclusions are for that reason of not enough weight to disturb any practical belief. We awake to reflection and find ourselves theists. Now those beliefs which come before reflection to all men alike are generally true, and the reason is that the causes which produce fallacies—depend upon a conscious process of reasoning. But apart from the weight of common-sense which must be presumed to attach to theism, the fact that it is my belief throws the burden of proof upon its opponents. And metaphysical conclusions ought not in the present state of the science to weigh in practical affairs. (W2: 127–8)

Religious belief is characterized as *practical*; it belongs to *common sense*; and, it is argued, metaphysical inquiry (indeed any inquiry involving reflection) has no authority to assess its legitimacy.

In the same paper Peirce contends that although it is wrong to defend a belief by pointing to the pleasant consequences of holding it, 'a man fights the battle of life better under the stimulus of hope; and we ought not to complain, therefore, that men lean toward the hopeful belief' (W2: 123). In order to demonstrate that 'scepticism is not so comfortable or inspiriting a state as theistic belief', he introduces the 'undoubted fact' that 'all men and all animals love life'. Our love of life has for its object, in decreasing degree of strength, ourselves, our families, our country, our race; 'and finally it is still a deep and lively emotion even in its reference to intellect in general' (W2: 124). Now, 'the love of life is more than a love of sensuous life: it is also a love of the rational life.' Moreover, personality is something that is shared, something we have in common with other people. Thus: 'the love of the life of others is still a passion which centres in ourselves because we love them as having something in common with ourselves, that is, because a part of them is identical with a part of ourselves' (W2: 124–5). This, he thinks, encourages a life which contributes to the growth of reason and culture. I shall not discuss his reasons for doubting whether a positivist can sustain these hopes and aspirations, but we should ask why he thinks that theism reinforces optimism:

The capital principle [of theism] is this, that nature is absolutely conformed to an end; or in other words, that there is reason in the nature of things. Now . . . so far as we attain true culture so far will the sum of all our impulses come to the love of reason as it necessarily is, and therefore so far as we are as we ought to be so far are we perfectly gratified by what according to the nature of things, takes place, which is another way of saying that whatever is is best. Now this is not only a consolation; it is the very sum, quintessence and acme of all consolation. (W2: 126)

As well as stressing the legitimacy of beliefs whose source lies in hope, he presents a view of the aims of life and of the kind of 'consolation' provided by religious belief which informed his philosophy until his death.

The third of these early passages, 'The Order of Nature', published in

Popular Science Monthly in 1878, challenges arguments which ground religious belief in design, the order of nature, or in 'evidences'. But Peirce denies that religion itself is thereby threatened. Both the Buddhist who denies that there could be an actual existing Deity, and those who employ the ontological argument to argue that existence is an essential character of the perfect being, adopt a religious outlook preferable to those that rely upon 'evidences'. For as soon as a Deity presents himself:

and manifests his glorious attributes, whether it be in a vision of the night or day, either of them recognizes his adorable God and sinks upon his knees at once; whereas the theologian of evidences will first demand that the divine apparition shall identify himself, and only after having scrutinized his credentials and weighed the probabilities of his being found among the totality of existences, will he finally render his circumspect homage, thinking that no characters can be adorable but those which belong to a real thing. (W3: 307)

And in this paper too: 'it would be folly to suppose that any metaphysical theory in regard to the mode of being of the perfect is to destroy that aspiration toward the perfect which constitutes the essence of religion' (W3: 322).

So metaphysical reflection offers little support for, and poses no threat to, religious belief. The reality of God is not viewed as a matter for scientific investigation; common sense and sentiment are to rule in connection with such 'practical' or 'vital' matters; and the Cartesian use of religious ideas to ground our confidence in science is flawed. If the role of reflection in religious matters is so restricted, why did Peirce devote so much energy to 'religious' questions in his later work?; and why did he think it necessary to provide an *argument* for God's reality? It is to these questions that we now turn (cf. Raposa 1989: ch. 4).

3. Instinctive Beliefs and Normative Science

We have noted Peirce's claim that belief in God is part of common sense. After 1900, Peirce placed more explicit stress upon doctrines which he drew from the common-sense tradition, claiming to be a critical commonsensist (*CP* 5.438–52; see also Chapter 8). Describing common-sense beliefs as instincts, he emphasized that such beliefs can guide conduct without receiving explicit formulation or assent. Many deep common-sense certainties function as unacknowledged habits of inference or expectation; a proposition which is consciously denied may yet form part of our instinctive view of the world. It is important to distinguish several different ways in which these developments affect Peirce's religious views.[2]

First, according to his later writings, instinctive beliefs are certain largely because they are vague: when we attempt to replace vague opinions by precise formulations, they become dubitable hypotheses:

I further opine that pretty nearly everybody more or less believes that God is real, including many of the scientific men who are accustomed to think the belief is entirely unfounded. The reason they fall into this extraordinary error about their own belief is that they precide (or render precise) the conception, and, in doing so, inevitably change it; and such precise conception is easily shown not to be warranted. (*CP* 6.496)

Moreover, our instinctive beliefs are unquestionably reliable only in contexts appropriate to a 'primitive mode of life': their relevance in situations remote from these familiar ones is always questionable; and as science grows, common-sense certainties may change. Thus, even if religious belief is instinctive, it may be appropriate only at an unsophisticated stage of culture: perhaps we have grown beyond religious belief; perhaps we should now question it. Moreover, since we naturally try to replace vague hypotheses by precise ones, the common-sense source of belief in a Deity will not make us content with our vague beliefs about His nature. Appeal to common sense cannot settle the logical and epistemological issues as Peirce may once have supposed that it did.

Second, if common-sense beliefs are manifested in habits of inference, expectation, and interpretation, as well as in conscious assent to propositions, we can be wrong about what our cognitive instincts require. We may confidently deny some proposition while our cognitive habits show that we really accept it; or we may declare that something has the backing of common sense when our certainty reflects the operations of cognitive elaboration. Thus not only may common sense itself be transcended as inquiry proceeds, but we cannot trust our initial judgements of what common sense requires. At best there is a cognitive presumption in favour of beliefs that appear to form part of common sense after severe criticism. This means that even if Peirce continues to ground belief in God in common sense, he must assure himself both that this belief is genuinely part of common sense and that it retains its relevance to our concerns in the new world revealed by the theoretical sciences. His later common-sensism is 'critical'.

---

[2] These issues about the nature and role of common sense are discussed more fully in Chapters 8 and 9.

Third, the first two considerations were directly concerned with the nature of specifically religious belief. However, Peirce insisted that a wide range of instinctive beliefs was fundamental to scientific activity. Our abductive instincts have a role in determining which hypotheses are worth taking seriously, and 'instinct . . . must be the ultimate cause of belief in all cases' (CP 5.383). This means that we can only carry out inquiries in a self-controlled manner if we are confident of our instincts. Unless we are optimistic that relying upon our instinctive sense of plausibility will take us to the truth, it is hard to see how it can be rational to participate in scientific investigation. Why should we trust our instinctive sense of plausibility in accounting for the strange worlds revealed by the theoretical sciences? How can we be confident that if they do prove unreliable, the resulting errors will be corrected? I suspect that such optimism or confidence is part of the solace provided by religious belief: it illustrates how belief is necessary for self-controlled participation in science.

From the 1890s, Peirce became more self-conscious about the character of logical self-control. An example of this was the claim, new after 1900, that logic was to be grounded in ethics and aesthetics. Peirce had previously been dismissive of the need to address ethical and aesthetic matters as part of his philosophical project; they belonged with the practical, to be left to common sense, sentiment, and instinct. Once we start reasoning about the sorts of end that can be endorsed as objectively correct, and see this reflection as necessary in order to determine how logical principles and methods can rationally be employed, then questions about the nature of objective values become important. If we find value in our lives by contributing to 'the growth of concrete reasonableness', or by 'participating in the process of creation', then, it seems, we can contribute to science, confident in the value of our activity, only if we adopt a religious attitude. We must distinguish two themes. First, once the nature of objective values becomes philosophically important, new interest attaches to what makes such values possible. Given Peirce's religious outlook, this was bound to provoke closer attention to the nature of religious belief. But second, if logic is grounded in ethics and aesthetics, so that recognition of ethical and aesthetic values supports self-controlled participation in scientific inquiry, then the claim that science itself rests upon religious belief takes on a more concrete form. Discussion of the grounds for belief in God forms part of an explanation of how science is possible.

Michael Raposa has documented how the claim that scientific activity requires a religious attitude becomes steadily more prominent in Peirce's writings (1989 passim). We have noticed that Peirce links such an attitude to an optimistic faith that one's actions will succeed or contribute to a growing reasonableness in the world. Without such a faith in relying upon one's instincts and relying upon our sense of what is objectively worthwhile, joining the church of scientific investigators would be hard to justify: it could not be reconciled with the belief that we are capable of logical self-control. If this is correct, it raises a problem which can serve as a test for an adequate exegesis of Peirce's argument for God's reality. We noticed above that Peirce was scornful of Descartes's use of God in his epistemological and metaphysical investigations: to explain something by saying that God made it so is tantamount to treating it as inexplicable. Hence we should hope for an understanding of Peirce's religious views which acquits him of the charge that, in his later writings, he succumbed to the errors that he criticized in the Cartesians. Reference to Descartes alerts us to another problem: if belief in God is required to vindicate our trust in our cognitive instincts, and belief in God is vindicated by showing that it is instinctive, Peirce would be arguing in a circle. It would be equally circular to ground religious belief in investigations which themselves employed the scientific method. Does Peirce's philosophy of religion exhibit such circularity?

Making progress with these issues requires us to explore several matters. First, we must examine the structure of Peirce's argument for God's reality, his 'Neglected Argument'. A second task is to make sense of the importance of the claim, noted in the previous section, that religious belief is something practical and a matter of 'sentiment'. The third of these issues grows out of Peirce's occasional claim that God was 'directly perceived'. Progress with understanding the structure of Peirce's thought about God will require us to consider his account of religious experience and its relations both to scientific observation and to sentiment.

4. The 'Neglected Argument'

Any treatment of Peirce's religious ideas will ultimately be judged by the sense it makes of Peirce's 'neglected' argument for the reality of God. First, some background. As we saw in Chapter 1, Peirce distinguished inquiry into practical or 'vital' matters from serious scientific inquiry. The latter calls for careful logical self-control but it can produce no 'living' belief: we look on current results as provisional and are unwilling to use them as the basis of vital decisions on which much turns. It is irrational to rely upon reason to settle practical matters: we trust to instinct or sentiment in settling everyday moral issues; common sense is to be trusted more than the scientific method. We saw how in his earlier writings Peirce described religious belief as a 'practical' matter: he thought it was a matter for sentiment; common-sense certainty was enough to ground our living certainty in God's reality. Someone who holds that, while the evidence strongly suggests that God is real, we should suspend judgement until inquiry has progressed further would not display a proper religious attitude: we require living belief in God's reality.

In that case, an 'argument' for God's reality should not mirror the kind of defence hypotheses received in the sciences. But Peirce offers mixed signals concerning whether this is the case. In *CP* 6.468–77, he describes the three stages involved in any scientific inquiry and explains what grounds their validity. All inquiry begins from a surprising observation and arrives at an abductive or retroductive suggestion, an hypothesis which would explain those surprising observations and is considered worthy of further test. The second deductive stage involves careful examination of this hypothesis in order to derive testable consequences from it. The third stage, induction, carries out observations and experiments in order to establish whether these testable consequences in fact obtain. We need not consider Peirce's explanation of why induction and deduction can be trusted, but it is important that he thought that science rests on *il lume naturale*: its successes depend upon assuming that hypotheses which seem 'facile and natural' are worth taking seriously (*CP* 6.477). The mark of scientific intelligence, he stresses, is to insist that this retroductive endorsement is only the first step in the evaluation of an hypothesis. As with any other hypothesis, the claim that God is real must pass through the two further stages. This seems to treat this claim as a scientific hypothesis to be tested by appeal to evidence. Does this represent a change of mind on Peirce's part? In order to answer this, we must examine some of the details of the argument.

There is evidence that Peirce was unhappy with applying the scientific model to this argument. In the original paper he asserted that his argument consists in three nested arguments. The simplest is the humble argument. The second extends the humble argument in a way available to theologians who have not been trained in logic: roughly, they can describe the humble argument, suggest that it ought to convince any normal man, and claim that there is a presumption in favour of whatever convinces any normal man. The third argument embodies the three-stage pattern and Peirce backs away from his obligation to present it: 'it would require the establishment of several principles of logic that the logicians have hardly dreamed of' *(CP* 6.485). A fuller discussion is provided in an additament dating from around 1910 *(CP* 6.486–91; MS 844): we shall examine the argument presented there.[3]

The first retroductive stage is the most important part of the argument. Peirce invites us to the 'refreshing' intellectual activity of 'pure play' or 'musement', claiming that 'religious meditation [can] grow up sponta-neously out of Pure Play without any breach of continuity' *(CP* 6.458). He predicts that anyone who reflects in a spontaneous manner upon all that appears to them in any way will soon pass from noticing the variety of phenomena to being struck by the degree of homogeneity or regularity; and in time, 'second-order' homogeneities will become evident, such as the pervasiveness of *growth* and the beauty of the world. Such reflection 'will inevitably suggest the hypothesis of God's reality':

In the Pure Play of Musement the idea of God's Reality will be sure sooner or later to be found an attractive fancy, which the Muser will develop in various ways. The more he ponders it, the more it will find response in every part of his mind, for its beauty, for its supplying an ideal of life, and for its thoroughly satisfactory explanations of his whole threefold environment. *(CP* 6.465)

The appeal to musement rather than controlled scientific observation is required in order to reveal that belief in God is 'natural' or 'instinctive': it does not result from particular cosmological assumptions of scientific prejudices but, rather, reflects the free flow of the human mind. Only prej-udice could inhibit this natural development: Peirce may be rather naive in assuming that prejudice can be so easily avoided and in claiming that the products of *his* musings may be taken as an indication of where those of other people would end up. Still, it is important that he is recommend-ing a procedure to people (a thought experiment) which would bring them to recognize God's reality.

The tension between practical certainty and theoretical inquiry emerges immediately in an interesting way. On occasion, Peirce treats the process of musement as if it were *itself* an argument for God's reality ('the humble argument'). But if it corresponds merely to the retroductive stage of scien-tific inquiry, it should not be an argument for that conclusion at all: at most it would establish that this was an hypothesis sufficiently plausible to

---

[3] Peirce's claim that he presents an 'argument' rather than an 'argumentation', 'a process of thought reasonably tending to produce a definite belief' rather than something proceeding on 'definitely formulated premises' *(CP* 6.456), may also express unease about how far his argument fits more familiar patterns.

be worthy of further testing. So is it an argument or an abductive suggestion? In one respect, this can be a false opposition. The process of retroduction leads the inquirer 'to regard his conjecture, or hypothesis, with favour':

As I phrase it, he provisionally holds it to be 'Plausible'; this acceptance ranges in different cases—and reasonably so—from a mere expression of it in the interrogative mood, as a question meriting attention and reply, up through all appraisals of Plausibility, to uncontrollable inclination to believe. (*CP* 6.469)

Assuming that the case we are concerned with is of the last mentioned kind, we can conclude that the humble argument rests content with this 'uncontrollable inclination to believe'. Those who are trained in science and logic have learned suspicion of such 'uncontrollable inclinations': the second and third stages of the investigation respond to such suspicion and assess the legitimacy of the inclination—'retroduction does not afford security' (*CP* 6.470). In the spirit of critical common-sensism (see Chapter 8), Peirce tries to bring the belief under control.

This is relevant to a suggestion of Michael Raposa's. Responding to some puzzles about what inductive testing could amount to in the case of God's reality, he conjectures that the operation of musement itself serves as a kind of inductive testing of the hypothesis. As a claim about the humble argument, this is correct; moreover, it is unquestionable that experience prompts retroductive suggestions in a way that resembles inductive testing. But if we are to reproduce the three stages of scientific inquiry, exercising logical self-control in our reasoning about the Deity, musement should result only in the proposal that an hypothesis is worthy of further testing. Whatever corresponds to induction in the full argument must be distinguishable from the process of musement. Somebody who feels that musement provides the entire logic of belief in God might point to Peirce's earlier insistence that sentiment and common sense should carry the day on practical matters, and his claim that the question of God's reality is a practical matter. But that is to question whether the further stages Peirce invokes are necessary at all.

A sense that the three-stage model of inquiry is being stretched to fit the neglected argument becomes stronger as we progress through Peirce's discussion. A retroductive suggestion is recognized to provide a promising explanation of a range of familiar or puzzling phenomena: in some cases (like the present one) it is so promising as to be irresistible. But in the case of belief of God (and 'in most instances where conjecture mounts the high peaks of Plausibility'), 'the inquirer is unable definitely to formulate just what the unexplained wonder is; or can only do so in the light of the hypothesis' (*CP* 6.469). The hypothesis is plausible because it provides the best explanation of phenomena which are only discernible if one accepts that very hypothesis: the hypothesis brings pattern and relationship to our attention which it then offers to explain. In such cases, 'argument' is possible—we can be brought to see the truth in question—but argumentation (proof) is not: we cannot establish a set of premises that would be acceptable to the sceptic and show that the hypothesis is supported by them.

If the hypothesis of God's reality does have this character, it becomes difficult to see how the second and third stages of the scientific method are to be applied: what empirical consequences can be derived from the hypothesis? And how can we establish whether they obtain if they consist in patterns that only a believer can discern?[4] Peirce acknowledges some of these difficulties:

The hypothesis can only be apprehended so very obscurely that in exceptional cases alone can any definite and direct deduction from its ordinary abstract interpretation be made. How, for example, can we ever expect to be able to predict what the conduct would be of an omniscient being, governing no more than one solar system for only a million years or so? How much less if, being also omnipotent, he be thereby freed from all experience, all desire, all intention! (CP 6.489)

How should we understand this puzzling passage? Our understanding of vague hypotheses relates them to empirical testing as follows: a vague hypothesis is true if at least one precisification of it can survive severe empirical testing. But such is the vagueness and abstractness of the hypothesis of God's reality that we can entertain no serious possibility of our ever possessing a precisification of it that stands a chance of being adequate; and our failure to construct such a precisification could never be a sign that none was to be found. Refuting vague hypotheses is always problematic because it involves establishing the truth of a negative existential claim—there is not a precisification of this hypothesis which is empirically acceptable. But in that case, how can the scientific method have a role in the argument for God's reality?

---

[4] The problems raised here resemble those facing any vague common-sense claim. We cannot point to specific experiences that would conflict with 'Fire burns'. It is empirically grounded in 'the traditional experience of mankind' (*CP* 1.654). There may be little to say in its favour but 'everything counts for it and nothing counts against it'. Yet it can still be looked upon as an hypothesis. These issues are also addressed in Chapters 5 and 8.

Peirce's response to this difficulty is very puzzling. He points to the 'commanding influence' which the hypothesis has 'over the whole conduct of its believers' (*CP* 6.490). It is not clear what this means. Peirce develops the suggestion by referring to his pragmaticism and by gesturing toward his evolutionary cosmology. Raposa suggests that 'it is the ongoing task of philosophy to attempt to explicate the God-hypothesis and it is the goal of a truly scientific cosmology to gather evidence that can be brought to bear on that notion' (1989: 133). But it is hard to see how this is related to the remark quoted at the beginning of this paragraph; and we have seen that Peirce is generally sceptical of using metaphysics to defend religious belief. Moreover, it fits poorly with the remarks of the previous paragraph that it is implausible that we can derive definite predictions from the God hypothesis.

It is useful now to introduce another claim that Peirce has made about the structure of his philosophy. In order to carry out scientific investigations, we have to rely upon intellectual hopes, propositions functioning as regulative ideas. Unless they are true, our inquiries will never succeed, but we can provide no non-circular demonstrations of their truth. An inquirer should proceed 'as if' no proposition is inexplicable, but he has no respectable reason to believe this assumption to be true. Rather, he should act on the hope that it is true—if he does not do this, he may assume that certain explicable phenomena have no explanation and thus miss out on important truths. One role of a metaphysical theory is to explain what the world must be like if those hopes are to succeed: it shows how the world is if these regulative ideas are actually true. If it is correct that scientific activity requires belief in God, then we might expect that subsequent metaphysical investigation is required to construct a cosmological account of reality which finds room for that assurance. We should argue in a circle if this cosmology entered in our grounds for accepting the God hypothesis. But if acceptance is grounded in a rational hope or in common sense, we expect metaphysics to vindicate it.

In that case, Peirce's philosophical system requires an argument that will vindicate acceptance of the reality of God without appealing to his metaphysical system. But he also needs a metaphysical explanation of what the reality of God consists in. It is very unclear whether the neglected argument is supposed to incorporate both of these, or whether it occupies just the former role. Does it form part of Peirce's metaphysics, or does it have a role within his logic, within his vindication of the method of science? He may not be very clear about this himself, but it is useful to distinguish some different elements in his thought on the matter. If he is to remain true to his earlier claim that the reality of God should be more certain than any metaphysical theory, it would be useful to find an interpretation of the argument which does not depend upon his cosmology.

One possibility is suggested in Raposa's book:

Since the meaning of the idea of God is revealed in human conduct, a test of the reality of that being might consist in a long-range assessment of the fruitfulness, the success of behaviour that conforms to this hypothesis as ideal. If God is real then behaving as if God were real ought to be efficacious. But this is an obscure enough proposal and, ultimately, the test that Peirce would be proposing here would involve the gathering of data ranging over the entire scope of human history. (1989: 134)

In other words, if God is indeed real, then certain ideals of conduct would be vindicated: the attempt to contribute to the growth of concrete reasonableness would succeed; patterns would be found in our experience and activities which could not be discerned by a non-believer. That adopting the ideals of conduct that come with belief in God proves fulfilling—we have the sense that we are succeeding in our endeavours—ought to confirm that belief. If the belief were not true, we would expect our projects to appear hollow and run into the ground. The hypothesis is confirmed by the fact that the ideals that it prescribes can be sustained.

If the test of religious belief is made to rest on the sustainability of the ideals which result from religious belief rather than more vaguely upon 'the fruitfulness, the success of behaviour that conforms to this hypothesis as an ideal', Raposa's charge of obscurity is a little unfair. Moreover, the strategy resembles one employed by Peirce around 1903 in his work on ethics and aesthetics: he proposed that we find out what would be a possible end for conduct or what could be an object of unconditional admiration by investigating what end can be sustained (or phenomenon admired) come what may. And the charge that testing the hypothesis in this manner 'would involve gathering data ranging over the entire scope of human history' is also confused. As Peirce himself stressed, we do not test an hypothesis concerning the properties of gold by trying to examine as many instances as possible. So long as we have no doubts about the purity of our sample, we shall treat a small quantity of the metal as a representative of all others. Experiments are repeated to guard against experimental error or impure samples. To repeat them endlessly in order to examine as many samples as possible is obsession rather than science. While the study of human beings may not exactly parallel that of a metal, it does not contravene the rules of scientific method to experiment on a few people (or even just on myself). That belief in God's reality proves fulfilling provides strong (but fallible) evidence that the ideals it provides us with are indeed good ones.[5]

A more revealing objection to this proposal for testing the hypothesis of God's reality is that it misuses Peirce's pragmatism. A proposition is true if the experiential predictions which can be derived from it are all satisfied. This proposal is that a proposition is to be taken as true if believing it has good consequences. Only the believer can see God's presence in the world. The non-believer may object that the apparent comfort or solace resulting from belief is false since it creates the phenomena which appear to the believer to confirm it. The scientific spirit is to test an hypothesis before adopting it as a scientific belief. In this case, the humble argument produces a kind of living certainty before the second and third stages of testing. Peirce seems to be moving towards the kind of pragmatism more commonly associated with William James. This too may be unfair. For it must be part of the content of the vague hypothesis that God is real that if someone believes in His reality they will have a fulfilling life, finding the world to be rational and able to see their own lives as contributing to the growth of concrete reasonableness. Belief in God should provide me with a fulfilling life only if God is indeed real.

As I mentioned above, Raposa suggests that the hypothesis could be tested through a sort of thought experiment: 'Musement itself constitutes a kind of experiment' (1989: 134). This seems importantly correct, but we need to distinguish two kinds of experiment that can be involved: first, in musement, the God hypothesis is thrown up by playful reflection on all that appears, and Peirce proposes that each individual should try that for himself, expecting each to reach the same result; but, second, the hypothesis is also tested (experimentally?) in an analogous way but without musement being involved. It is put to work in our lives, and it is tested by the transforming influence it has on those lives: it makes possible a meaningful life in pursuit of ultimate ends whose value can be endorsed.

I conclude this section with two related comments. We noticed above that Peirce drew a sharp distinction between theory and practice: the former required a detached attitude towards current opinions, while the latter required living belief; the former was subject to rational self-control, while the latter was the domain of instinct, common sense, and sentiment. The God hypothesis has a curiously ambiguous relation to this opposition.

---

[5] Just as a chemist studies a structure which is present in all samples of gold, so I can take it that 'personality in general' is present as part of me (W2: 124–5).

As Peirce wrote in the 1870s, it is a practical matter: only living belief will serve. But his search for an argument, and his insistence that the method of science be employed in constructing the argument, shows that it has links with the theoretical: most important, I suggest, religious belief is required for the *practice of theoretical science*.

Second, recall that in 1867 Peirce wrote that 'a man fights the battle of life better under the stimulus of hope; and we ought not to complain, therefore, that men lean toward the hopeful belief' (W2: 123). We have noted that for the mature Peirce, the presuppositions of logic had the status of *hopes*. But in making this claim, Peirce was distinguishing hopes from beliefs properly so-called. If belief in God is required to sustain one's commitment to the aims of science, and if the believer experiences phenomena unavailable to the non-believer, then mere hope will not do. The scientist will require a living belief in God's reality. Once again, belief in the reality of God bridges the divide between theory and practice: it is not merely a practical matter because it does not relate to a restricted context; but we are not to take the attitude towards it which is appropriate to a theoretical conjecture. We might say: we need a living belief in God while reflectively aware that all that is logically legitimate is a hope.

While admitting that the argument escapes the charge of circularity, I have to report that my own attempts to carry out Peirce's thought experiment do not have the effect he describes. It is just not obvious that a period of playful reflection upon one's experience does render the hypothesis of God's reality either plausible or compelling. And the observation that my difficulties result from being brought up in a twentieth-century secular culture only invites the response that Peirce's 'success' can receive a corresponding sociological explanation. Another response to my report is possible, however, and it introduces some difficult issues in Peirce's theory of signs: perhaps my exercise in musement did produce belief in God's reality but I failed to notice that it did. I doubt that this response is promising either, but it leads us to consider: what is involved in believing in the reality of God?

5. Signs and Sentiments: Religious Experience

The neglected argument is an exercise in sign-interpretation together with a commentary upon that interpretation. Musement issues in an abductive suggestion which finds pattern in the variety of experiences we have during the musing 'experiment': 'The musing intellect is gently drawn to the truth about nature by the beauty of God's purposes, themselves embodied in natural facts. Such facts are to be perceived, barring any blindness to their real character, as the representation of those divine intentions' (Raposa 1989: 144). We saw that Peirce envisaged the possibility of believing a proposition whose truth one sincerely denied: the belief shapes one's life and experience but lack of self-knowledge prevents one from recognizing this. Two roles for the musement thought experiment can then be envisaged: it forces us to recognize that we have believed in God's reality all along; or it produces belief in God's reality. If it only serves the latter function, it may not produce conscious assent. In that case, the second and third stages of the argument might be required to force us to recognize that we possess a living belief in God's reality; or a developed cosmology might be required to force us to recognize the nature of our religious response. Progress with the issues here raised requires attention to Peirce's account of religious experience.

Pre-theoretically we distinguish religious experience from ordinary external scientific experience. Raposa's comment suggests, surely correctly, that, within Peirce's philosophical perspective, ordinary scientific experience might be understood as a species of religious experience. The point is well put by Vincent Potter:

the phrase 'religious experience' is an ellipsis for 'experiencing the world religiously'. What makes experience religious is not some special content but rather the realization that it has another aspect or dimension, namely as disclosing or revealing God. In a word it is a question of understanding the significance of human experience. (1996: 151)

I am interested in how far the materials from Peirce's theory of signs help us to understand this possibility. This connects with another of the comments from Peirce's early writings about God, his claim that religious belief was intimately related to sentiment. If religious experience is, in some manner, suffused with sentiment, is it possible to construe scientific experience as a species of religious experience? Can emotionally coloured experience be experience of a world suffused with God?

Raposa points out that 'what Peirce most often meant by "experience" ... is that entire, complex semiotic event ('semiosis'), the linking of an object and meaning via the mediation of a sign' (1989: 140). Experience, so understood, involves interpretation: it is the product of an instinctive or acritical abductive insight; there is no brute uninterpreted experience. Hence there is no contradiction between Peirce's insistence that God must be directly perceived and the claim that doing so involves understanding what is experienced or grasping its significance. Thirdness or mediation is present in all experience. But something must be distinctive about the thirdness involved when the world is experienced 'religiously'. Normally the thirdness involved in perceptual experience is manifested in its continuity, and in the degree of anticipation which it always involves: consider the perceptual jolt of surprise involved when we realize that the wheels of the train we 'see' moving on the other side of the platform are not turning. If the excessive vagueness of the God hypothesis means that no anticipation of the future run of experience is involved, if nothing would produce this jolt of perceptual surprise, what form of thirdness is involved in religious experience?

If we are to look for an answer, we must return to Peirce's earlier insistence that the reality of God is a practical matter which is to be settled by sentiment. Raposa expresses Peirce's response clearly: 'The meaning of "God" is comprehended in feeling, "interpreted in our religious adoration and the consequent effects upon conduct" (*CP* 8.262). For Peirce, in fact, emotion is vague, incomprehensible thought. . . . That . . . is why the highest truths can only be felt (MS 891)' (1989: 58). From 1868, Peirce insisted that an emotion was attached to an object as 'a predicate', it embodies an hypothesis: being angry about something is a way of finding it bad, being afraid of it is a way of finding it dangerous. Thus, it seems, accepting God's reality involves experiencing things in an emotionally coloured way (W2: 229–30; Savan 1981: passim).

So how do emotions differ from other vague thoughts? In particular, what is distinctive in the way that emotions are interpreted? Savan argues that the 'dynamical' interpretant is *affect*: my emotional response to one phenomenon tends to spread in an unreflective manner, determining my emotional response to other phenomena and practical projects (1981: 327–8). And 'emotions are not value neutral. If I am angry at something, that is because I appraise it—usually uncritically—as bad' (p. 328). Emotions embody values that determine actions: the actions are felt uncritically to be required of us; and a process of reflection upon the emotion, searching for a final interpretant, will lead to a formulation of the values or norms that it contains. Reflection can lead me to recognize that I am (or have been) in an emotional state which I would not have recognized when its grip on me was strongest (W2: 206).

What then can we say about the emotional content of religious experience? Primarily it involves love (*agape*), and Savan has noted the importance of this sentiment in making science and rationality possible: 'the genius of a man's logical method should be loved and reverenced as a bride' (W3: 287). Love 'presides over generation and birth, bringing order out of disorder' and it involves 'a willingness to sacrifice our own limited interests, to sacrifice ourselves, for the sake of the object of our love' (Savan 1981: 333). As Peirce put it in 1868, 'Logic rigidly requires, before all else, that no determinate fact, nothing which can happen to a man's self, should be of more consequence to him than everything else. He who would not sacrifice his own soul to save the whole world is illogical in all his inferences, collectively.' (W2: 270–1) Someone whose scientific experience has a religious character finds it inviting him to contribute to the search for reason and pattern, and to subordinate himself to a community of inquirers which sees itself as continuous with the world which it investigates. Accepting such invitations is one element in experiencing the world religiously, and, presumably, *agape* is manifested in other areas of our lives too. One might, reasonably, question whether this attitude is actually required if we are to avoid illogicality. And even if it is so required we can ask whether such experience is properly described as 'religious'. However, we are now in a better position to understand the role of musement.

It is implausible that musement should create the possibility of *agape* in someone previously incapable of it. However, recall Peirce's claim that someone's 'anger consists in his saying to himself "this thing is vile, abominable, etc." ', it being 'a mark of returning reason to say, "I am angry" ' (W2: 206). Interpretation of an emotion involves recognizing the range of its manifestations, identifying the kind of emotion that it is, and formulating the norms and values which it expresses. So reflection or meditation could achieve the following: I recognize a large range of experiences and responses as belonging to the same emotional syndrome. I recognize all the manifestations of the same *agape*; and I seek a final interpretant of this *agape*, a formulation of the ideal or value which it expresses. It is like coolly recognizing many facets of my behaviour as manifesting a common resentment or envy and acknowledging the valuations which are the source of the attitude.

If this is correct, it connects with our claims about the structure of the 'Neglected Argument'. The content of the hypothesis of God's reality engages the will and emotions rather than the understanding: it presents a vague imperative rather than rules for predicting the consequences of our actions. And it would also explain the strained character of Peirce's attempts to apply the scientific method to the hypothesis. The special character of its vagueness means that it can only be tested by determining whether the kinds of action we are invited to carry out can in fact provide an ideal which sustains a whole life. They are presented in perception as appropriate or required, but experience contains no reason for accepting them: it is 'infinitely incomprehensible'. Moreover, we can see how only living belief can serve: unless we believe in God's reality we shall not have the appropriate feelings and we shall not know what we are being invited to do. Mere hope is inadequate. But the sort of testing described in the 'Neglected Argument' must assure us that the invitation is not the product of a particular context or occasion: having no reason to accept the invitation, we need to assure ourselves that accepting it is a possibility.

In that case, scepticism about Peirce's view of the degree of self-sacrifice required for science may be accompanied by another doubt. The humble argument expects any muser to connect the framework of emotional responses we have described to acceptance of the reality of the God of the Christian tradition. It is surely unlikely that anyone who did not possess a very distinctive kind of intellectual sophistication would do that.

12

Avoiding Circularity and Proving Pragmatism

1. Introduction

In the years following William James's public commitment to pragmatism in 1898, Peirce made a number of attempts to prove his own version of the doctrine. Dissatisfied with the arguments he had employed in 'How to Make our Ideas Clear', his first defence of the doctrine, he tried again in his Harvard lectures of 1903 and yet again in a series of papers in *The Monist* in 1906.[1] Careful examination of Peirce's manuscripts points to several others. It is unclear whether Peirce ever constructed a proof that fully satisfied him: he noted in 1911 that his proof was still unfinished since he lacked a conclusive demonstration that there were just three forms of reasoning. Although it was the 1903 version which persuaded him of the truth of the doctrine, he subsequently admitted that it 'left too many difficulties' (MS 279).[2]

Interpreting this material presents considerable difficulties. The 1903 argument relies heavily upon Peirce's phenomenological defence of his categories and upon the claim that, like other norms of reasoning and inquiry, the pragmatist principle must be established within a discipline of logic which relies upon more abstract analyses of aesthetic and ethical norms. These themes are not present in the articles towards a proof published in *The Monist* in 1906; the stress there upon Peirce's 'critical common-sensism' is not anticipated in 1903. Some of the later work made essential use of Peirce's new system of formal logic, the existential graphs. Are there several different strategies of proof? Or does Peirce have a single strategy, employing different tactical means of carrying it out or communicating his results on different occasions?

My aim in this chapter is limited. Rather than offering an analysis of the

---

[1] The best current source for these texts is *EP2*. The Harvard lectures are at pp. 133–241, and the material written for *The Monist* is at pp. 331–433.

[2] A useful survey of some of Peirce's different attempts to prove pragmatism is to be found in Max Fisch's paper 'The "Proof" of Pragmatism', in Fisch (1986).

1903 argument or comparing it with those sketched in later papers and manuscripts, we are concerned with a preliminary issue. I want to say something about how Peirce conceived the task of looking for the proof: What intellectual needs prompted his search? What conditions must be met before such a proof could succeed? These points are important for understanding the structure of Peirce's later thought, particularly the character of what he described as his architectonic. The particular emphasis I will use here grows out of an attempt to understand some differences between the pragmatisms of Peirce and James.[3]

On several occasions, Peirce compared his pragmatism or 'pragmaticism' with the views expressed by other self-styled pragmatists. Especially when comparing himself with James, Peirce emphasized that his pragmatism formed part of his logic—he pointed out that he had accepted it during the 1870s as a kind of 'logical gospel'. In the work of the author of *Pragmatism*, he alleged, this 'logical principle' became 'transmogrified' into a doctrine of philosophy. This identification of the pragmatist maxim as part of logic has important consequences for issues about the need for a proof and about the kind of proof is needed. This may have been in his mind when Peirce wrote, in one of his articles for *The Monist*, that:

From this original form [of pragmatism] every truth that follows from any of the other forms can be deduced, while some errors can be avoided into which other pragmatists have fallen. The original view appears, too, to be a more compact and unitary conception than the others. But its capital merit, in the writer's eyes, is that it more readily connects itself with a critical proof of its truth. (*CP* 5.415)

If this is correct, we can only understood the search for a proof if we are clear about what is involved in treating pragmatism as a thesis to be established within logic.

2. The Pragmatist Principle: Logic and Methodology

Peirce's pragmatist principle was presented in 'How to Make our Ideas Clear', the second of the *Illustrations of the Logic of Science*. Before considering its importance for the 'logic of science', we should be clear about its content. It is presented as a tool for clarifying the contents of concepts, ideas, and hypotheses, for being reflectively aware of the content of these

---

[3] Another attempt at such a comparison can be found in Hookway (1997).

representations. Rather than present one of Peirce's definitions, I shall offer my own paraphrase. Suppose I want to be clear about the content of the hypothesis that *salt is soluble in water*. Part of such a clarification could consist in listing the experiential consequences I would expect experiments and other actions to have if the hypothesis were true: If salt is, indeed, soluble, then if I were to stir a sample of salt in unsaturated water at a normal temperature and pressure, then the salt would dissolve. The antecedent of this conditional statement specified an action that could be carried out, and the consequence describes an experiential consequence that the action would have if the hypothesis were true. This clarification yields information that would help me to test the hypothesis: if it does not dissolve when added to such water then, *ceteris paribus*, it is not soluble. Peirce's pragmatism holds that a full listing of the conditionals of this kind that can be derived from an hypothesis provides a *complete* clarification of the content of the hypothesis: no component in its cognitive meaning has been left unclarified. If no such conditionals can be derived from the hypothesis, then it is empty and lacks cognitive meaning.

As is clear from 'How to Make our Ideas Clear', this principle is valuable in two different ways: it yields information about propositions and hypotheses that will help us to test them efficiently using the scientific method; and it alerts us to propositions that appear to be meaningful but which are, in fact, cognitively empty. We can ignore for the present issues about whether the conditional propositions which elucidate the meaning of some proposition must be analytic or whether they can be synthetic, about whether the list of conditionals must be short or whether it can, in principle, be of indefinite length. We shall also ignore the question of what background knowledge can be appealed to when establishing whether a conditional claim belongs to the list. For the record, I see no reason why Peirce should not grant that the conditionals can be synthetic and that the list can be long. He could also adopt a holistic view of how they are derived from our scientific views. What is important is that the principle is a tool for clarifying ideas and propositions, that the clarifications are of a broadly verificationist character, and they both help us to see how to test hypotheses efficiently and to avoid wasting time over meaningless pseudo-propositions. A proof of pragmatism must demonstrate that this is the form to be taken by a complete clarification of an hypothesis. The most famous application of the principle is Peirce's elucidation of our concept of truth or reality. Suppose that a proposition expresses a definite question (it is not vague): if it is true, then anyone who inquired into it long enough and well enough (using the method of science) would eventually arrive at the stable verdict that it was true.[4]

As Max Fisch insisted, Peirce's pragmatism falls within the third branch of logic, 'methodeutic' (1986: 374). The first branch, 'Speculative Grammar', yields a general account of representation, of signs and meaning. Critical logic analyses and classifies the different forms of arguments used within scientific inquiry. Methodology, or 'methodeutic', attempts to formulate rules and strategies for carrying out inquiries that will enable us to eliminate falsehood and arrive at truth as efficiently and effectively as possible. It will enable us to avoid wasting time by taking seriously the empty garbage which makes up 'ontological metaphysics', and it will help us to achieve the kind of perspicuous representation of the contents of our hypotheses which will enable us to carry out experimental inquiries into them efficiently and economically. The first of these virtues was evident from the anti-metaphysical use to which the doctrine was put in 'How to Make our Ideas Clear', and the importance of the latter is evident from the claim, in the Harvard lectures, that pragmatism provides 'the whole logic of abduction'.[5]

The fact that the pragmatist principle is a rule of *method* yields an important moral concerning the structure of the proof: it must have a two-stage character. Since pragmatism is a methodological principle, it is something which should be vindicated in terms of means and ends. We have an aim (or set of aims) which are characterized by the goals specified by the method of science: we want to contribute to the advance of our knowledge of real things whose characters are entirely independent of our opinions about them but which interact with our senses in systematic ways. And the method (the pragmatist principle), is to be justified by showing that adopting it as our *only* technique for clarifying the meanings of concepts and hypotheses provides the best way of achieving our purpose.[6]

But, second, it will not suffice simply to show that adopting the pragmatist principle provides the best means available for pursuing efficiently some aim that we happen to have. In Kantian terminology, that would

---

[4] For a fuller discussion of this account of truth, see Chapters 2 and 3.

[5] This connection between pragmatism and scientific method is also evident from a letter to the Italian pragmatist Calderoni which identifies the doctrine with the claim that the inductive method is 'the only essential' to clarifying the meanings of hypotheses (*CP* 8.213).

[6] One key to the difference between the versions of pragmatism defended by Peirce and James lies in the different 'ends' to which the methodological rule is put by each.

defend pragmatism as a distinctive kind of hypothetical imperative, as a rule of skill: if you want to use the method of science, you ought to use the pragmatist principle for clarifying hypotheses. A proof that we ought to adopt the pragmatist principle in our inquiries, rejecting opinions that cannot be clarified through its use and incurring no fear that it may lead us to overlook crucial elements of the meanings of our hypotheses, requires a demonstration that we *ought* to adopt the aim in question. If it is the best means towards the achievement of a goal that we *ought* to adopt, then we should make use of it in all of our reflective inquiries. Let us assume that the aim in question relates to the desire to make progress in the sciences and to settle our doubts by arriving at answers which meet Peirce's characterization of truth. Then an argument will have to show, first, that it is possible and desirable to adopt this aim and, second, that adopting the pragmatist principle is an effective means towards achieving it.

The famous 1877 paper, 'The Fixation of Belief', is concerned with the first stage in this argument, with establishing what our aim in inquiry should be. Of the four methods considered in that paper, only the method of science can be consistently employed, and this fixes a definite goal which is to guide us in our inquiries. It employs the 'fundamental hypothesis' that

There are real things, whose characters are entirely independent of our opinions about them; those realities affect our senses according to regular laws, and, though our sensations are as different as our relations to the objects, yet, by taking advantage of the laws of perception, we can ascertain by reasoning how things really are; and any man, if he have sufficient experience and reason enough about it, will be led to the one true conclusion. (W3: 254)

'The Fixation of Belief' argues that we *ought* to carry out our inquiries in order to contribute to the discovery of this 'one true conclusion'. It claims to establish the correctness of adopting this goal. All that then remains for the proof of pragmatism is to establish the means–ends claim: employing the pragmatist principle provides our best chance of contributing to the achievement of that goal. In the argument structure of the *Illustrations of the Logic of Science*, there is one small twist. Once it has been defended, the first use of the pragmatist principle is to clarify the aim, to work out exactly what we mean by the true and the real (see Chapters 1 and 2 for further discussion of these arguments).

So our first conclusion is: a proof of pragmatism must establish that it yields all the clarification that our concepts and hypotheses need receive if we are efficiently and effectively to pursue defensible cognitive ends.

3. Explanation and Persuasion: Defending Logical Norms

Any attempt to argue for a set of logical norms or standards of cognitive rationality faces a structural problem. Which norms or standards can we appeal to in defending a contested norm or standard? It is common to worry that if we *use* some form of argument in the course of trying to justify that very form, then our defence involves a culpable kind of circularity. There is something wrong, we suppose, with justifications of induction that rely upon induction. In that case, it seems, there should also be something wrong with justifications of deductive reasoning which themselves employ deductive reasoning. It is easy to see that if these worries about circularity are genuine, it will be difficult to avoid scepticism about our rational capacities. However, we cannot simply dismiss them, for sometimes avoiding such circularity is important. If we appeal to those very norms whose defence we are engaged in, then our argument will not persuade anybody who is initially doubtful of our conclusion. This initial doubt will prevent their taking our argument seriously. In this section, we shall discuss how these worries about circularity affect the attempt to proof pragmatism.

The phrase 'justifying a logical rule' is ambiguous; it can apply to different kinds of undertaking. Michael Dummett has made use of a distinction between two kinds of justification that 'logical principles' can receive and this will help us to understand these issues. He called them 'suasive' and 'explanatory' justifications (1978: ch. 17). A suasive justification, as the name suggests, must be able to persuade someone who is initially doubtful of whether the principle ought to be adopted: the justification or proof responds to a *real* doubt. In that case, the kind of circularity that I have mentioned must be avoided: otherwise the proof will persuade only those who are already convinced. But a logician can also inquire into the justification of logical principles which are not, in fact, controversial. Nobody doubts that *modus ponens* is a valid logical principle, but we may still ask for its justification. Such a justification will enable us to *understand* why the principle is a good one, but it needs to be sufficient to persuade a doubter. Dummett calls this an explanatory justification, and it is not subject to the same strictures on circularity. The fact that I use arguments whose form is that of *modus ponens* in the course of explaining why *modus ponens* is a good form of inference need disturb no one's logical scruples. It accords with this that Peirce claimed that deductive logic can yield theoretical understanding of aspects of our mathematical reasoning which themselves need no (suasive) justification. Although we have no doubt of the validity of *modus ponens*, we can come to understand why such arguments are compelling by tracing their validity to the transitivity of the sign relation.[7]

The principle of pragmatism is controversial so it requires a suasive justification. A defence of pragmatism which presupposes the correctness of the pragmatist principle would be viciously circular. Peirce's proof will avoid circularity only if the standards and principles relied upon when he constructs his proof do not require a suasive justification; they must be standards for which only an explanatory justification is required. The remainder of the chapter will defend these two claims and explore ways in which Peirce's logic escapes sceptical attacks based on charges of circularity.

First, why does pragmatism require a suasive vindication? The proof he offers is addressed at doubters, for example at people who think that scientific hypotheses can possess a core of meaning which escapes elucidation through use of the pragmatist principle or who are certain that propositions of 'ontic metaphysics' are plainly meaningful in spite of the verdict of pragmatism.[8] It has to be proved 'in the teeth of Messrs. Bradley, Taylor, and other high metaphysicians, on the one hand, and of the entire nominalistic nation, with its Wundts, its Haekels, its Karl Pearsons, and many other regiments, in their divers uniforms, on the other' (*CP* 5.468). If Peirce's proof is to be good enough, then, although it need not actually convince these various opponents, Peirce must be able to show that they *ought* to have been convinced, given standards of proof and rationality which they already accept. Only self-deception, irresponsibility, or lack of understanding could prevent their accepting the proof. We may wonder at this ambition, but, given that many people show by their practice that they rely upon hypotheses which are not licensed by pragmatism, we can see that a suasive justification of pragmatism is required. And this accords with the observation that the pragmatist principle is to be defended as a methodological principle, as providing the best means to some cognitive end.

As the quotation from *CP* 5.468 shows, Peirce's suasive justification for pragmatism addresses two sets of doubters: 'high metaphysicians' and

---

[7] This is explained in more detail in Hookway (1985: 195–7).

[8] Indeed, as Fisch emphasizes, 'proof' is only required or appropriate where there are doubts to be addressed. He cites *CP* 3.342: 'proof does not consist in giving superfluous and superpossible certainty to that which nobody ever did or ever will doubt, but in removing doubts which do, or at least might at some time, arise' (Fisch 1986: 362–3).

nominalists. Since it is reasonable to expect that their doubts will be of very different kinds, it is important to identify just what these challenges to pragmatism are. The high metaphysicians believe that there are concepts which are important for science and for philosophy whose content would not be revealed through a pragmatist clarification. At least two versions of this view are addressed by Peirce: a Kantian claim that even science makes use of such concepts; and a more radical metaphysical position that insists upon the importance of non-scientific knowledge. In his *Critique of Pure Reason*, Kant argued that the ideas of practical reason have a regulative role in fixing how we combine empirical laws into a unified system of explanatory knowledge.[9] We exploit these ideals by thinking of how the world would be if it were created in order to be knowable by us. When Peirce distinguished pragmatism from 'practicalism', he explicitly rejected this Kantian claim: the concepts we use for structuring our knowledge into a unified whole (not least, the concept of continuity) are no more resistant to pragmatic clarification than ordinary empirical concepts (*CP* 5.412). The second sort of high metaphysician might follow Royce in accepting the possibility of a priori non-scientific metaphysics: the method of science is not the only respectable method for settling belief. The latter differ from Peirce in their account of the proper ends to use in evaluating methods for clarifying ideas; the former disagree about the means that are available and necessary for pursuing ends which they share with him. If the proof is to be effective, it must be able to persuade these thinkers to abandon the use of concepts and hypotheses which they currently find attractive. It must be sufficiently powerful that they are unable to treat its conclusion as a *reductio ad absurdum* of some of Peirce's premises. Thus Peirce looks to phenomenology, semiotic (speculative grammar), and critic to show that self-controlled inquiry can only be sustained through the use of concepts whose conceptual roles ensure that the pragmatist technique can clarify them.

What sort of challenge does Peirce anticipate from the nation of nominalists? Peirce's pragmatist principle is basically rather rich. Like his fellow pragmatist William James, he thinks that experience is a good deal richer than many philosophers allow: we experience external things as external, we experience interactions between those things and we are aware of their sensory impacts upon us, and we experience law-governed interactions— mediated transitions—between things we experience, and real continuity in the ways that processes develop. The nominalist complains that the

---

[9] This concern is explicit in the letter to Calderoni (*CP* 8.212).

pragmatist conception of experience is is too rich since it uses conceptual resources which should not be available to a responsible exponent of the method of science. These resources include direct realism about our knowledge of external things and the objectivity of subjunctive or modal notions. The conditional predictions uncovered when the principle is applied concern what *would* happen when, for example, salt is stirred in unsaturated water: they concern 'would be's, and they describe experience in terms that implicate the external world. Many philosophers sympathetic to empiricism and nominalism would deny that Peirce was entitled to take these things for granted. He had no sympathy for the view that the objects of immediate experience are private sense data; and he was no friend of Humean views of laws and causation. Hence he needed to show that these resources are available in defence of pragmatism.[10] This leads to his phenomenological defence of his categories, which tries to show that experience is a good deal richer than many philosophers have supposed.

Peirce's proof must thus be able to convince both sets of rivals of their errors, using materials that stand in no need of a suasive justification. The most important part of the proof is likely to consist in an explanation of just what these materials are. The nominalist will anticipate that the resources are insufficient to establish that even the clarifications that Peirce offers are intellectually respectable, and the high metaphysicians will insist that the available resources enable us to see how concepts are intelligible and perhaps necessary for science, which Peirce's pragmatist principle would lead him to reject. Much will depend upon Peirce's view of what materials are available to construct his proof.

4. Naturalism and the Transcendental Philosophy

Peirce had argued for his pragmatist principle in the 1870s, both in the manuscripts recording his uncompleted attempt to write a logic text and in the second paper of the *Illustrations of the Logic of Science*, 'How to Make our Ideas Clear'. He was subsequently dissatisfied with these attempts, his main complaint being that his argument depended upon 'a psychological principle' (*CP* 5.28). Before and after the 1870s, he rejected any attempt to ground logic and epistemology in psychology. This dissatisfaction is

---

[10] This demand for a rich conception of experience is connected to Peirce's insistence that his pragmatism is close in content to James's radical empiricism. This is discussed further in Hookway (1997).

expressed in the first of the 1903 lectures on pragmatism delivered at Harvard. Having pointed out that he depended in 1878 upon the claim that 'belief consists mainly in being deliberately prepared to adopt the formula believed in as a guide to action', he asked how we know that this was true:

My original article carried this back to a psychological principle. The conception of truth, according to me, was developed out of an original impulse to act consistently, to have a definite intention. But in the first place this was not very clearly made out, and in the second place, I do not think it satisfactory to reduce such fundamental things to facts of psychology. For man could alter his nature, or his environment would alter it if he did not voluntarily do so, if the impulse were not what was advantageous or fitting. Why has evolution made man's mind to be so constructed? (*CP* 5.28)

The point made here is itself 'not very clearly made out', and runs together several themes from the first two papers of the *Illustrations of the Logic of Science*. One of these is the claim that a belief is a habit of action which leads to the conclusion that the pragmatist principle can be defended by showing that it provides a criterion of identity for habits of action. No high metaphysician would concede that very readily. Of more immediate concern is the claim that his conception of truth can be traced to 'an original impulse to act consistently, to have a definite intention'. Peirce here refers to the arguments in 'The Fixation of Belief' which attempt to show the inadequacy as methods of settling belief of the methods of tenacity and authority and the a priori method. In each case, he points out that use of the method would require us to tolerate 'inconsistent' beliefs of a sort which we cannot tolerate. Once we notice that others have tenaciously adopted different beliefs or have accepted a different authority, the results of using these methods cannot be sustained: 'the social impulse is against [them]'.

We can fill out Peirce's objection as follows. An argument of this sort shows that, as a matter of psychological fact, we seek consistency and cannot tolerate inconsistencies. If this leads to the conclusion that the method of science is the only one which can be reflectively adopted, the 'can' employed is a psychological one. But we have seen that a successful proof of pragmatism requires a demonstration that this method is the one we *ought* to adopt, that it is a good or rational standard to use in our inquiries. A claim about our psychological impulses cannot establish this: not least because, as Peirce points out, our psychology is malleable. If Peirce is to defend the method of science by showing that it is the only one that can be reflectively employed, the 'can' employed in this formulation must not be a purely psychological one. Peirce questions his earlier work on the grounds that it was psychologistic or naturalistic[11] and he endorses the objection (still widely accepted) that a naturalistic approach to logic and epistemology eliminates the normative dimension which is essential to epistemological reflection. If Peirce is to employ the strategy I have described, he must create room for a non-psychological 'can' in these formulations.

The writings of the 1870s also suggest a different argumentative strategy, one which avoids this objection. We might describe this strategy as 'transcendental'. Whatever his attitude towards it in the 1870s, Peirce later rejected this kind of argument too. Early in 'The Fixation of Belief', Peirce suggests that some logical norms are 'absolutely essential as guiding principles.' These are 'necessarily taken for granted in asking whether a certain conclusion follows from certain premises' and they are 'already assumed when the logical question is first asked' (CP 5.369). Various facts and principles are presuppositions of logical reflection. This seems to have two consequences. First, the fact that we are capable of rational reflection shows that (either consciously or tacitly) we accept these facts and principles. Second, unless these facts and principles are correct, the whole process of reflection and inquiry would be a sham. As suggested above, Peirce seems to think that the fundamental hypotheses of the method of science are either included among these fundamental presuppositions or they can be derived from them. We value the kinds of consistency alluded to above because they are either included in, or implied by these assumptions.

Two questions can be raised about this strategy. First, how do we identify what these presuppositions are? 'The Fixation of Belief' contains no explicit discussion of this. The arguments it employs seem to be naturalistic: if we do not tolerate results obtained by using methods that conflict with some principle P, then this provides evidence that P is among the presuppositions of the logical question. The methods of tenacity and authority and the a priori method all collapse because they tolerate various kinds of inconsistency, so it is plausible that those kinds

---

[11] The rejected approach is 'naturalistic' in the sense in which that word is used by Quine and others who defend 'naturalized epistemology'. It is compatible with this that there are other uses of 'naturalism' according to which Peirce belongs within that tradition. Thus, although he denies the relevance to logic of information drawn from the psychology and the natural sciences, Peirce repudiates the supernatural and insists that philosophy must be scientific.

of inconsistency are required by these presuppositions. Such arguments are clearly not adequate to their purpose.

Second, showing that something is a presupposition of the logical question does not establish that it is *true*. I may base activities upon assumptions which are, in fact, mistaken, in which case the activity does not possess the value I took it to have. Subsequently, Peirce was extremely rude about those who employed this transcendental strategy:

> I am not one of those transcendental apothecaries, as I call them—they are so skilful in making up a bill—who call for a quantity of big admissions, as indispensable Voraussetzungen of logic ... I do not admit that indispensability is any ground of belief. It may be indispensable that I should have $500 in the bank—because I have given checks to that amount. But I have never found that the indispensability directly affected my balance, in the least ... A transcendentalist would claim that it is an indispensable 'presupposition' that there is an ascertainable true answer to every intelligible question. I used to talk like that, myself; for when I was a babe in philosophy my bottle was filled from the udders of Kant. But by this time I have come to want something more substantial. (*CP* 2.113)

Showing that something is presupposed by logical reflection may give us grounds for *hoping* that it is true. It gives us no grounds for *believing* that it is true.

So we are now in a position to understand some of the demands upon Peirce's proof of pragmatism. It is not enough for him to show that the more fundamental logical norms are ones which are psychologically irresistible: the question will still arise of whether we *ought* to allow ourselves to be guided by them. Nor is it enough to show that our practices 'presuppose' the correctness of these norms: for, again, this is insufficient to establish that they are, in fact, correct. However, as we have seen, Peirce does seem to be committed to showing that the 'suasive' question of their correctness does not arise: there is no alternative to relying upon them. In some fashion, their irresistibility must bear testimony to their correctness.

Peirce retains the idea that we rely upon a large body of 'knowledge' which is 'pre-logical' or 'antecedent to logic'.[12] In a loose sense of the word, it represents 'presuppositions' of the logical question: we take this 'knowledge' for granted in formulating our goals in inquiry and in defending

---

[12] The explosion of scare quotes in this paragraph is an acknowledgement that describing mathematics, phenomenology, and the normative sciences as 'sciences' and as providing 'knowledge' can be misleading. It can suggest that all those kinds of logical reflection which are essential to inquiries in the special sciences of physics, chemistry, etc. have a role in these pre-logical disciplines too. It is important for Peirce's strategy that this is not so.

logical norms and principles. But our acceptance of this 'knowledge' is not grounded in the observation that it is presupposed by logic. On the contrary, as well as pre-logical 'knowledge' there are pre-logical 'sciences'.[13] Before we start discussing how best to investigate the truth about reality—how, for example, we should monitor our inductive strategies—we can carry out investigations into a system of phenomenological categories and into the fundamental aesthetic, ethical, and logical norms. Rather than vindicating his categories by showing that they are adequate for the description of reality, Peirce tries to show that they are adequate for describing all *possible* objects of thought and experience. And rather than vindicating ethical norms by showing that they will guide us to act well in the world as it actually is, he tries to defend them by showing that they could be sustained in any *possible* world. The logical norms which guide inquiry into the nature of *reality* need have no application in these investigations into the structures of possibilities. They represent conditions of intelligible thought and action: we identify fundamental norms and basic categories by noticing how it is possible to think or act. 'Thought' or 'reflective action' which fail to conform to these standards are, simply, not possible: it is not thought or reflective action at all.

It is not my aim to explore or evaluate Peirce's conception of the pre-logical sciences here. The important point is that his later attempts to vindicate his pragmatism exploit the claim that there is a substantial body of material which is presupposed by logic and which thus does not depend upon any principle which receives or requires a suasive defence within logic. Moreover, this material's special status is not defended naturalistically: it is not claimed merely that we do not doubt these things. Nor is it defended transcendentally: Peirce does not argue that these things must be true because they are presupposed by logic. His proof depends upon there being a further possibility which is realized by his work in phenomenology and the normative sciences.

This non-transcendental alternative to psychologism shares with the transcendental approach the claim that there is a body of information which can be assumed when we begin our logical investigations. This may lead us to re-open the question of whether the transcendental strategy is actually used in 'The Fixation of Belief' at all. Perhaps the passages we referred to are, instead, an anticipation of the views developed in detail

---

[13] Peirce's work on the classification of the sciences is an attempt to identify these 'pre-logical sciences'. A selection of this work is published in *CP* 1.180–283. The 'pre-logical sciences' are mathematics, phenomenology, aesthetics, and ethics.

twenty years later. This is supported by the fact that Peirce's criticisms of the earlier article focus on its psychologism rather than on any supposed transcendentalism and by the fact that Peirce had already expressed misgivings about transcendental approaches to philosophy in the 1860s. It is a reasonable conjecture that when he wrote 'The Fixation of Belief' Peirce did not have a very clear understanding of the form of argument he was employing. He did not self-consciously claim that various statements were true simply on the grounds that they were presupposed by the logical question, but nor did he have a conception of a distinctive kind of pre-logical investigation which could bring these truths to light. The question of which form of argument he was employing may have no clear answer.

5. Pre-logical Inquiries

Peirce seeks a suasive proof of pragmatism that rests on materials that are uncontroversial, which his rivals could only reject through inadvertance of self-deception. Unless this is the case, high metaphysicians and nominalists will be able to reject his conclusion by questioning some of the assumptions of the argument. Many will think it unlikely that we can find proofs that meet this condition and, indeed, that a 'contrite fallibilist' should share their doubts. But it seems evident that Peirce *sought* such a proof and that aspects of the structure of his late thought could encourage the hope that it was possible. This section describes some of the varieties of uncontroversial knowledge which he thought were available. All are forms of pre-logical knowledge: they are not subject to some of the sources of error that we find in the special sciences and thus there is no substantial role for criticism in the light of controversial logical norms when we seek them.

As we saw above, Peirce thought that the practice of a priori reasoning which secures our mathematical knowledge requires no foundation, although we can try to *explain* how it works (Hookway 1985: ch. 6). In that case, no suasive defence is required of the validity of a simple deductive argument such as 'All swans are birds, and no birds are mammals, so no swans are mammals'.[14] A view similar to Peirce's is suggested by Hilary

---

[14] It is compatible with this that it may be controversial how logicians should represent the form or structure of such an argument, and opinions may differ concerning what explains its validity. But these debates would not induce any doubts about the validity of particular arguments such as this one. Hence, although a defence of a particular system of formal logic should not rely upon premises which presuppose the correctness of that

Putnam, who applauds the Kantian insight that 'illogical thought is not, properly speaking, thought at all':

It is this that brought home to me the deep difference between an *ontological* conception of logic, a conception of logic as descriptive of some domain of actual and possible entities, and Kant's (and I believe Frege's) conception. Logic is not a description of what holds true in 'metaphysically possible worlds' . . . It is a doctrine of *the form of coherent thought*. Even if I think of what turns out to be a 'metaphysically impossible world', my thought would not be a thought at all unless it conforms to logic. (1994: 247)

On this view, Putnam argues, 'logical truths do not have negations that we (presently) understand'. On any of the variety of views which might claim to fit this pattern, it would be inappropriate to ask for a *suasive* defence of a fundamental logical norm because a doubt of it could not be coherently formulated. The role of mathematics ('the practice of necessary reasoning') in Peirce's system of knowledge suggests a similar view, and it would encourage the idea that this practice is the common possession of pragmatists, metaphysicians, and nominalists. No one doubts *modus ponens.*

Much philosophical knowledge depends upon observation. But this too should be utterly controversial—although philosophers often go wrong through failing to notice what should be plain to view. There are two aspects to this claim. In a passage prescient of Wittgenstein's *Philosophical Investigations*, Peirce borrows a term from Jeremy Bentham and describes philosophical observation as 'coenoscopic'. Philosophy 'contents itself with observations such as come within the range of every man's normal experience, and for the most part of every waking hour of his life. . . . These observations escape the untrained eye precisely because they permeate our whole lives' (*CP* 1.241). Phenomenological observation is presumably a species of this. One strategy for defeating the nominalist is to reflect on all that can be experienced or thought in any way at all and to use simple mathematical techniques to notice the categorical structure of all that appears. Only prejudice can then prevent someone noticing that experience is a good deal richer than nominalists claim. The reality of thirdness is missed simply because it is such a pervasive feature of our lives. The Harvard lectures use phenomenological techniques to establish the truth of realism, a necessary premise in the argument for pragmatism.

particular formalization, there is no objection to its using arguments of the kind which it is trying to formalize. Theoretical debates internal to *logica docens* need not threaten those aspects of our *logica utens* which they are trying to make sense of.

Common-sense views provide another pervasive and easily missed feature of our experience. As we saw in Chapter 8, such beliefs are often present as habits and instincts and hence easily ignored in reflective thought. Moreover, they grow out of experience even if their vagueness ensures that they cannot be empirically tested or given a suasive justification. Thus they are easily mistaken for items of substantial a priori knowledge. Once again, the nominalist can be reminded that this shared common-sense view of things is suffused in realist commitments: inattention to the evident features of everyday experience is a source of philosophical error. We now see how Peirce hoped that coenoscopic uncontroversial observation should disarm nominalist anxieties and thus contribute to the proof of pragmatism. We can also see where he might run into difficulties. The phenomenological strategy required him to establish that experience did display mediation and continuity and to show that this sufficed for vindicating realism. And these results had to be uncontroversial, able to persuade convinced nominalists.[15]

What demands did the challenge of the high metaphysicians make on the structure of Peirce's 'proof'? Two related themes are relevant here. First, there were philosophers who were committed to the project of a priori speculative metaphysics, believing that we could obtain knowledge of absolute mind, the nature of God, or the structure of value in ways of which Peirce would disapprove. They used ideas which would not survive the pragmatist test. The claims that Peirce made for his test would be true only if anyone who examined its credentials responsibly and with a due concern for the truth would be fated to agree with them. Hence Peirce must show how those we have just described could be included in the destined consensus or explain why they are disqualified from participation in serious inquiry. More troublesome were those who argued that science itself depended upon such 'metaphysical' ideas. As we saw, Kant believed that science employed regulative ideas of explanatory unity and completeness which had a non-empirical character. In Chapter 4 we discussed Josiah Royce's argument that the concepts of truth and belief depended upon the idea of an absolute mind of which finite human minds formed parts. Others might worry that mathematics dealt with a realm of non-empirical objects: it was essential to science yet its concepts would resist pragmatic clarification. And yet others may argue that objective values—including

---

[15] Hookway (1997) explores the relations between pragmatism and nominalism from another perspective. James's pragmatism, in contrast to Peirce's, was supposed to be compatible with nominalism; and Peirce's realism explains why he saw a more initimate connection between pragmatism and radical empiricism than James.

ideals of truth and understanding which set the goals for science—could only be discovered through an a priori investigation. So what reason is there to suppose that someone who uses the pragmatic principle as her only tool for clarifying ideas would be fated to share in the consensus on the truth?

Peirce's work on scientific metaphysics contributes to his attempt to deal with these issues: see Chapters 6 and 7. His common-sensism is important too: some explanatory ideals which seem to be untestable are in fact vague common-sense certainties (see Chapter 8). The phenomeno-logical defence of his categories suggests ways in which Peirce can argue that experience is richer than his critics would suppose. He tried to show (how successfully is unclear) that the crucial concept of continuity—the lynchpin of the 'synechistic' strain in his philosophy—could receive a pragmatic clarification. His work in the normative sciences would, presumably, enable us to see how reflection on experience could ground consensus about what can be accepted as an end for action or for thought and inquiry (Hookway 1985: 58–66; Potter 1967). And Peirce's philosophy of mathematics is an attempt to make objectivity compatible with a denial that mathematical knowledge is a priori in a way that would render it 'metaphysical' in a pejorative sense (Hookway 1985: ch. 6). So there are themes in his later philosophy which are designed to meet different aspects of this challenge.

More important, because more systematic, is the work on the theory of signs which preoccupied Peirce through much of his last decade (see, for example, his correspondence with Lady Welby, *SS*). Reflective clarity about the meaning of a thought, word, or concept involves reflective clarity about the cognitive role of a sign. Hence the high metaphysicians must hold that there are meaningful signs whose cognitive roles cannot be fully described through application of the pragmatist principle. If Peirce could provide a complete classification of the different kinds of possible sign, and if the adequacy of this classification was uncontroversial, then this would contribute to constructing the required proof. Each kind of sign in the classification—each kind of concept, proposition, or inference—could be surveyed in order to see whether it would provide a counterexample to Peirce's claim. Grounding the classification in the application of the cate-gories to the different aspects of the relation of signification offered the hope that an uncontroversial classification could be found. It is unclear whether Peirce believed he had succeeded in this enterprise, but it is certain that he saw this as a fundamental step in the construction of a proof of pragmatism.

6. Conclusion

Peirce requires a suasive defence of pragmatism. Providing this commits him to a non-suasive vindication of more fundamental (non-method-ological) logical norms. These are to be defended by showing that (in a sense) there is no reflexive, responsible, self-controlled inquiry without them: if reflection is to be taken to the utmost, we can only employ the method of science. My aim has been to emphasize this two-stage structure in order to clarify the sources of Peirce's architectonic conception of philosophy and the structure of his later work.

The following characterization of pragmatism helps us to see how this is reflected in Peirce's envisaged proof.

According to . . . Pragmatism, the true meaning of any product of the intellect lies in whatever unitary determination it would impart to practical conduct under any and every conceivable circumstance, supposing such conduct to be guided by *reflexion carried to an ultimate limit*. (*CP* 6.490, my emphasis)

The reference to 'reflexion carried to an ultimate limit' expresses a picture of cognitive responsibility which is, I believe, exceedingly important in shaping Peirce's mature thought. The two elements of the defence of prag-matism can be presented as stages in an account of 'reflexion carried to an ultimate limit'. If we attempt to obtain the kind of self-knowledge and self-control which is represented by this ideal, then our inquiries can only be guided by these aims. Any other goal in inquiry will inevitably be unset-tled by such reflective self-criticism. If our inquiries are to be guided by reflection carried to an ultimate limit, then they will be (not *ought* to be, but *can only be*) carried out in the light of the standards and norms char-acterizing the method of science. We can avoid the method of science only by imposing limits on the scope of reflection. And in that case, Peirce thinks, the pragmatist principle provides all the clarification required for us to carry out such inquiries responsibly and effectively.

This description of the task of constructing a proof of pragmatism receives support from Peirce's remarks upon the 'architectonic' structure of his venture.

Pragmatism was not a theory which special circumstances had led its authors to entertain. It had been designed and constructed, to use the expression of Kant, architectonically. Just as a civil engineer, before erecting a bridge, a ship, or a house, will think of the different properties of all materials, and will use no iron, stone, or cement, that has not been subjected to tests; and will put them together in ways minutely considered, so, in constructing the doctrine of pragmatism the properties of all indecomposable concepts were examined and the ways in which they could be compounded. Then the purpose of the proposed doctrine having been analyzed, it was constructed out of the appropriate concepts so as to fulfil that purpose. In this way, the truth of it was proved. (*CP* 5.2)

This shows that Peirce saw his defence of pragmatism explicitly in means–ends terms. The principle is to be shown to achieve a certain purpose: we are to analyse the appropriate purpose, carefully evaluate the concepts to be used in constructing our means to its achievement, and then develop the principle which best serves our purpose.

REFERENCES

Almeder, Robert (1980). *The Philosophy of Charles S. Peirce*. Oxford: Basil Blackwell.

Anderson, Douglas R. (1995). *Strands of System: The Philosophy of Charles Peirce*. West Lafayette, Indiana: Purdue University Press.

Apel, Karl-Otto (1980). *Towards a Transformation of Philosophy*. London: Routledge and Kegan Paul.

—— (1981). *Charles S. Peirce: From Pragmatism to Pragmaticism*, trans. John Michael Krois. Amherst: University of Massachusetts Press.

—— (1995). 'Transcendental Semeiotic and Hypothetical Metaphysics of Evolution: A Peircean or Quasi-Peircean Answer to a Recurrent Problem of Post-Kantian Philosophy', in Kenneth L. Ketner (ed.), *Peirce and Contemporary Thought: Philosophical Inquiries*. New York: Fordham University Press, 366–97.

Ayim, Maryann (1981). 'Theory, Practice and Peircean Pragmatism', in Kenneth L. Ketner *et al.* (eds), *Proceedings of the C. S. Peirce Bicentennial International Congress*. Lubbock: Texas Tech Press, 45–53.

Blackburn, Simon (1984). *Spreading the Word*. Oxford: Oxford University Press.

Brandom, Robert B. (1994). *Making it Explicit*. Cambridge Mass.: Harvard University Press.

Brent, Joseph (1993). *Charles Sanders Peirce: A Life*. Bloomington: Indiana University Press.

Brock, Jarrett (1975). 'Peirce's Conception of Semiotic', *Semiotica* 14: 124–41.

—— (1979). 'Principal Themes in Peirce's Logic of Vagueness', *Peirce Studies* 1: 41–9.

—— (1980). 'Peirce's Anticipation of Game-theoretic Logic and Semantics', in M. Herzfield and M. D. Lenhart (eds), *Semiotics*. New York: Plenum Press.

—— (1997). 'The Development of Peirce's Theories of Proper Names', in Nathan Houser, Don D. Roberts and James Van Evra (eds), *Studies in the Logic of Charles Sanders Peirce*. Bloomington: Indiana University Press, 560–73.

Cavell, Stanley (1979). *The Claim of Reason*. Oxford: Oxford University Press.

Coates, John (1996). *The Claims of Common Sense: Moore, Wittgenstein, Keynes and the Social Sciences*. Cambridge: Cambridge University Press.

Colapietro, Vincent M. (1989). *Peirce's Approach to the Self: A Semiotic Perspective on Human Subjectivity*. Albany NY: SUNY Press.

Craig, E. J. (1987). *The Mind of God and the Works of Man*. Oxford: Oxford University Press.

Davenport, H. William (1981). 'Peirce's Evolutionism and his Logic: Two Connections', in Kenneth L. Ketner *et al.* (eds), *Proceedings of the C. S. Peirce Bicentennial International Congress*. Lubbock: Texas Tech Press, 307–12.

Delaney, C. F. (1993). *Science, Knowledge and Mind: A Study in the Philosophy of C. S. Peirce*. Notre Dame: University of Notre Dame Press.

de Tienne, André (1988). 'Peirce's Search for a Method of Finding the Categories', *Versus* 49: 103–12.

Dewey, John (1938). *Logic: The Theory of Inquiry*. Boston: Holt, Rinehart, and Winston.

Dileo, Jeffrey R. (1997). 'Charles Peirce's Theory of Proper Names', in Nathan Houser, Don D. Roberts and James Van Evra (eds) *Studies in the Logic of Charles Sanders Peirce*. Bloomington: Indiana University Press, 574–94.

Donnellan, Keith (1966). 'Reference and Definite Descriptions', *Philosophical Review* 77: 281–304.

Duggan, T. (1984). 'Thomas Reid on Memory, Prescience and Freedom', in Vincent Hope (ed.), *Philosophy of the Scottish Enlightenment*. Edinburgh: Edinburgh University Press, 32–46.

Dummett, Michael (1959). 'Truth', *Proceedings of the Aristotelian Society* 59: 141–62.

—— (1978). *Truth and Other Enigmas*. London: Duckworth.

—— (1981). *The Interpretation of Frege's Philosophy*. London: Duckworth.

Elgin, Catherine Z. (1996). *Considered Judgment*. Princeton NJ: Princeton University Press.

Engel-Tiercelin, Claudine (1986). 'Le Vague est-il réel? sur le réalisme de Peirce', *Philosophie* 10: 69–96.

Fine, Kit (1975). 'Vagueness, Truth and Logic', *Synthese* 30: 265–300.

Fisch, Max (1986). *Peirce, Semeiotic and Pragmatism*. Bloomington: Indiana University Press.

Forster, Paul D. (1996). 'The Unity of Peirce's Theories of Truth', *British Journal of the History of Philosophy* 4: 119–47.

Frege, Gottlob (1970). *Translations from the Philosophical Writings of Gottlob Frege*. Oxford: Basil Blackwell.

—— (1972). *Conceptual Notation and Related Articles*. Oxford: Oxford University Press.

—— (1979). *Posthumous Writings*. Oxford: Basil Blackwell.

—— (1980). *Philosophical and Mathematical Correspondence*. Oxford: Basil Blackwell.

—— (1984). *Collected Papers on Mathematics, Logic and Philosophy*. Oxford: Basil Blackwell.

Fumagalli, Armando (1995). *Il Reale nel Linguaggio*. Milan: Vita e Pensiero.

—— (1996). 'El Indice en la Filosofia de Peirce', *Annuario Filosofico* 29: 1291–312.

Goodman, Nelson (1954). *Fact, Fiction and Forecast*. Cambridge Mass.: Harvard University Press.

Grice, Paul (1989). *Studies in the Way of Words*. Cambridge Mass.: Harvard University Press.

Hacking, Ian (1980). 'The Theory of Probable Inference', in D. H. Mellor (ed.),

Science, Belief and Behaviour: Essays in Honour of R. B. Braithwaite. Cambridge: Cambridge University Press, 141–60.

Hausman, Carl (1993). *The Evolutionary Philosophy of Charles S. Peirce.* Cambridge: Cambridge University Press.

Hilpinen, Risto (1982). 'On C. S. Peirce's Theory of the Proposition: Peirce as a Precursor of Game-theoretical Semantics', *The Monist* 65: 182–8.

Hookway, Christopher (1985). *Peirce.* London: Routledge and Kegan Paul.

—— (1988a). 'Reference, Causation and Reality', *Semiotica* 69: 331–48.

—— (1988b). 'Pragmaticism and "Kantian Realism" ', *Versus* 49: 103–12.

—— (1990). 'Critical Common-sensism and Rational Self-control', *Nous* X: 397–411.

—— (1992). 'The Idea of Causation: Some Peircean Themes', *Transactions of the Charles S. Peirce Society* XXVIII: 261–88.

—— (1993). 'Mimicking Foundationalism: on Sentiment and Self-control', *European Journal of Philosophy* 1: 156–74.

—— (1994a). 'Iconicity and Logical Form', *Histoire Epistemologie Langage* 16: 53–64.

—— (1994b). 'Cognitive Virtues and Epistemic Evaluations', *International Journal of Philosophical Studies* 2: 211–27.

—— (1994c). 'Review of Murray G. Murphey *The Development of Peirce's Philosophy*', *Transactions of the Charles S. Peirce Society* XXX: 667–85.

—— (1997). 'Logical Principles and Philosophical Attitudes: Peirce's Response to James's Pragmatism', in Ruth Anna Putnam (ed.), *The Cambridge Companion to William James.* New York: Cambridge University Press, 145–65.

—— (1998). 'Peirce, Charles Sanders', in Edward Craig (ed.), *The Routledge Encyclopedia of Philosophy.* London: Routledge, vol. VII, 269–84.

—— (2000). 'Pragmatism: Common-Sense and the Limits of Science', in M. Stone and J. Wolff (eds), *The Proper Ambition of Science.* London: Routledge.

Horwich, Paul (1990). *Truth.* Oxford: Basil Blackwell.

Houser, Nathan, Don D. Roberts, and James Van Evra (eds) (1997). *Studies in the Logic of Charles Sanders Peirce.* Indianapolis: University of Indiana Press.

James, William (1907). *Pragmatism: A New Name for some Old Ways of Thinking.* Cambridge Mass.: Harvard University Press (1975).

—— (1909). *The Meaning of Truth: A Sequel to 'Pragmatism'.* Cambridge Mass.: Harvard University Press (1975).

—— (1912). *Essays in Radical Empiricism.* Cambridge Mass.: Harvard University Press (1976).

—— (1920). *Collected Essays and Reviews.* London: Longmans, Green and Company.

Johnston, Mark (1993). 'Objectivity Refigured: Pragmatism without Verificationism', in J. Haldane and C. Wright (eds), *Reality, Representation and Projection.* Oxford: Oxford University Press, 85–130.

Kant, Immanuel (1783). *Prolegomena to any Future Metaphysic.* Indianapolis: Bobbs-Merrill (1950).

Lehrer, Keith (1997). *Self Trust: A Study of Reason, Knowledge and Autonomy.* Oxford: Oxford University Press.

Levi, Isaac (1980). 'Induction as Self-Correcting According to Peirce', in D. H. Mellor (ed.), *Science, Belief and Behaviour: Essays in Honour of R. B. Braithwaite.* Cambridge: Cambridge University Press, 127–40.

Lipton, Peter (1991). *Inference to the Best Explanation.* London: Routledge.

Liszka, James (1996). *A General Introduction to the Semeiotic of Charles Sanders Peirce.* Bloomington: Indiana University Press.

Locke, John (1690) *An Essay Concerning Human Understanding*, ed. P. Nidditch. Oxford: Oxford University Press, 1975.

Miller, Dickinson (1893) 'The Meaning of Truth and Error', *Philosophical Review* 2: 408–25.

Misak, Cheryl (1991). *Truth and the End of Inquiry.* Oxford: Oxford University Press.

—— (1998). 'Deflating Truth: Pragmatism *vs.* Minimalism', *The Monist* 81: 407–25.

Murphey, Murray G. (1961). *The Development of Peirce's Philosophy.* 1st edn, Cambridge Mass.: Harvard University Press; 2nd edn, Indianapolis: Hackett, 1993.

Nadin, M. (1980). 'The Logic of Vagueness and the Category of Synechism', *The Monist* 63: 351–63.

Nagel, Thomas (1970). *The Possibility of Altruism.* Oxford: Oxford University Press.

Niklas, Ursula (1988). 'On the Practical and the Theoretical in Charles S. Peirce', *Versus* 49: 31–8.

Nozick, Robert (1981). *Philosophical Explanations.* Cambridge Mass.: Harvard University Press.

Oehler, Klaus (1987). 'Is a Transcendental Foundation of Semiotics Possible?: A Peircean Consideration', *Transactions of the Charles S. Peirce Society* XXIII: 45–62.

Ogden, C. K. and I. A. Richards (1923). *The Meaning of Meaning.* London: Kegan Paul, Treach, Trubner and Co.

Pape, Helmut (1984). 'Laws of Nature, Rules of Conduct and their Analogy in Peirce's Semiotics', *Transactions of the Charles S. Peirce Society* XX: 209–39.

Peirce, Charles (ed.) (1883). *Studies in Logic, by Members of the Johns Hopkins University.* Boston: Little Brown.

Popper, Karl (1972). *Objective Knowledge.* Oxford: Clarendon Press.

Potter, Vincent (1967). *Charles Peirce on Norms and Ideals.* Amherst: University of Massachusetts Press.

—— (1996). *Peirce's Philosophical Perspectives*, ed. V. M. Colapietro. New York: Fordham University Press.

Price, Huw (1988). *Facts and the Function of Truth.* Oxford: Basil Blackwell.

Putnam, Hilary (1981). *Reason, Truth and History.* Cambridge: Cambridge University Press.

—— (1987). *The Many Faces of Realism*. LaSalle Ill.: Open Court.

—— (1990). *Realism with a Human Face*. Cambridge Mass.: Harvard University Press.

—— (1994). *Words and Life*. Cambridge Mass.: Harvard University Press.

Ramsey, F. P. (1931). *The Foundations of Mathematics*. London: Routledge and Kegan Paul.

—— (1978). *Foundations*. London: Routledge and Kegan Paul.

Raposa, Michael (1989). *Peirce's Philosophy of Religion*. Bloomington: Indiana University Press.

Reid, Thomas (1975). *Thomas Reid's Inquiry and Essays*, eds Keith Lehrer and R. E. Beanblossom. Indianapolis: Hackett.

Royce, Josiah (1885). *The Religious Aspect of Philosophy*. Gloucester, Mass.: Peter Smith, (1965).

—— (1900). *The World and the Individual*. London: Macmillan.

—— (1913). *The Problem of Christianity*. New York: Macmillan.

Savan, David (1981). 'Peirce's Semiotic Theory of Emotion', in Kenneth L. Ketner *et al.* (eds), *Proceedings of the Charles S. Peirce Bicentiennial International Congress*. Lubbock: Texas Tech Press, 319–33.

Sellars, Wilfrid (1963). *Science, Perception and Reality*. London: Routledge and Kegan Paul.

—— (1968). *Science and Metaphysics*. London: Routledge and Kegan Paul.

Shope, Robert K. (1978). 'The Conditional Fallacy in Contemporary Philosophy', *The Journal of Philosophy* 75: 397–413.

Skagestad, Peter (1981). *The Road of Inquiry*. New York: Columbia University Press.

Sluga, Hans (1980). *Gottlob Frege*. London: Routledge and Kegan Paul.

Sprigge, T. L S. (1993). *American Truth and British Reality*. LaSalle: Open Court.

—— (1997) 'James, Aboutness and his British Critics', in Ruth Anna Putnam (ed.), *Cambridge Companion to William James*. Cambridge: Cambridge University Press, 125–44.

Thompson, Manley (1953). *The Pragmatic Philosophy of C. S. Peirce*. Chicago: Chicago University Press.

van Fraassen, Bas C. (1980). *The Scientific Image*. Oxford: Oxford University Press.

Wiggins, David (1987). *Needs, Values, Truth*. Oxford: Basil Blackwell.

Williams, Michael (1991). *Unnatural Doubts*. Oxford: Basil Blackwell.

Wittgenstein, Ludwig (1953). *Philosophical Investigations*. New York: Macmillan.

—— (1967). *Remarks on the Foundations of Mathematics*. Oxford: Basil Blackwell.

—— (1969). *On Certainty*. Oxford: Basil Blackwell.

Wright, Crispin (1992). *Truth and Objectivity*. Cambridge Mass.: Harvard University Press.

INDEX